Sport for Development and Peace

Sport for Development and Peace

Foundations and Applications

Edited by
Robert E. Baker
Craig Esherick
Pamela Hudson Baker

ROWMAN & LITTLEFIELD
Lanham • Boulder • New York • London

Published by Rowman & Littlefield
An imprint of The Rowman & Littlefield Publishing Group, Inc.
4501 Forbes Boulevard, Suite 200, Lanham, Maryland 20706
www.rowman.com

86-90 Paul Street, London EC2A 4NE

Copyright © 2022 by The Rowman & Littlefield Publishing Group, Inc.

All rights reserved. No part of this book may be reproduced in any form or by any electronic or mechanical means, including information storage and retrieval systems, without written permission from the publisher, except by a reviewer who may quote passages in a review.

British Library Cataloguing in Publication Information Available

Library of Congress Cataloging-in-Publication Data

Names: Baker, Robert E., 1957– editor. | Esherick, Craig, editor. | Baker, Pamela Hudson, 1961– editor.
Title: Sport for development and peace : foundations and applications / edited by Robert E. Baker, Craig Esherick, Pamela Hudson Baker.
Description: Lanham, Maryland : Rowman & Littlefield, 2022. | Includes bibliographical references and index. | Summary: "This comprehensive, practical text examines both the overarching foundations and functional applications of Sport for Development and Peace (SDP), using managerial, sociological, historical, political, and other multidisciplinary frameworks"—Provided by publisher.
Identifiers: LCCN 2021026084 (print) | LCCN 2021026085 (ebook) | ISBN 9781538163320 (cloth) | ISBN 9781538124864 (paperback) | ISBN 9781538124871 (epub)
Subjects: LCSH: Sports—Sociological aspects. | Sports and globalization. | Peace-building. | Economic development.
Classification: LCC GV706.5 .S732524 2022 (print) | LCC GV706.5 (ebook) | DDC 306.4/83—dc23
LC record available at https://lccn.loc.gov/2021026084
LC ebook record available at https://lccn.loc.gov/2021026085

Contents

List of Figures and Tables   vii

Introduction   ix

Part I: Foundations of Sport for Development and Peace

1   History and Foundations of Sport for Development and Peace   3
Robert E. Baker, George Mason University, USA

2   Sociological Perspectives on Sport for Development and Peace   25
Scott R. Jedlicka, Washington State University, USA

3   Sport Development: A Sheep in Wolf's Clothing?   39
*B. Christine Green, George Mason University, USA, and
Edward Horne, University of New Mexico, USA*

4   Inclusion and Diversity in Sport for Development and Peace   61
*Pamela Hudson Baker, George Mason University, USA, and Morgan Strimel,
George Mason University, USA*

5   Sport, Conflict Resolution, and Diplomacy   81
*Stuart Murray, Bond University, Australia, and Shinae Haidley,
Bond University, Australia*

6   Sport's Economic Utility: The Essential Place of Economic
Development in Sport-for-Development Programs   105
Laurence Chalip, George Mason University, USA

7 Corporate Social Responsibility and Sport for Development and Peace: New Media, Communication, and Engagement for Greater Impact   121
   Kathy Babiak, University of Michigan, USA, and Javier Abuín-Penas, University of Vigo, Spain

8 Linking Sport Events with Sport Participation and Development   141
   Marijke Taks, University of Ottawa, Canada, and Georgia Teare, University of Ottawa, Canada

9 Evaluation and Analytics in Sport for Development and Peace   159
   Bill Gerrard, University of Leeds, UK, and Robert E. Baker, George Mason University, USA

Part II: Applications of Sport for Development and Peace

10 Governments and Sport for Development   181
    Carrie LeCrom, Virginia Commonwealth University, USA, and Per G. Svensson, Louisiana State University, USA

11 Discoveries from an Intimate View into Sport Programs as a Catalyst for Change   201
    Soolmaz Abooali, George Mason University, USA

12 For-profit Involvement in Sport for Development and Peace   217
    Craig Esherick, George Mason University, USA

13 Current Trends and Future Directions in Sport for Development and Peace   229
    Jon Welty Peachey, University of Illinois, USA, and Nico Schulenkorf, University of Technology Sydney, Australia

Selected Bibliography   247

Index   253

About the Editors   257

About the Contributors   259

Figures and Tables

Figure 1.1: Sport for development and peace in action when this Israeli sport administrator attends a Sports Visitor Program event. 4

Figure 1.2: Inclusive sport brings people together as this athlete from Iraq embraces the opportunity to join a wheelchair basketball game. 13

Figure 2.1: Young women participate in the Soweto Academy volleyball team practice in the informal settlement of Kibra in Nairobi, Kenya. The volleyball team "The Mighty Minnows" has become a rallying point for the school and surrounding community. 26

Figure 3.1: Pyramid model of sport development pathways. 40

Figure 3.2: Dimensions of development. 55

Figure 4.1: Sport can be a universal language for all people, which is apparent in this encounter between a deaf athlete from the Pacific islands and a child with Down syndrome. 63

Figure 4.2: Intersectionality in sport for development. 65

Figure 5.1: Sport brings people together as reflected in this sign created by secondary school students in Moscow during a Russia–America youth ice hockey exchange. 83

Figure 5.2: Teamwork provides the building blocks of change. 91

Figure 6.1: Facets and potential outcomes of sport as an economic engine. 107

Figure 6.2: Shared experiences, such as this Special Olympics event attended by a group of Sports Visitors from Egypt, can unify participants around common goals. 113

Figure 7.1: Corporate programs, such as this NBA Cares initiative in Tanzania, can impact communities in a variety of meaningful ways. 124

Table 7.1: Followers and following data. 128

Figure 7.2: Call-to-action presence on tweets. 132

Table 8.1: Examples of tangible and intangible impacts of sport events. 143

Figure 8.1: Elements to be managed when leveraging sport events to build sport participation. 150

Figure 8.2: Event leverage framework. 152

Figure 9.1: The logic model of evaluation and systems thinking in SDP programs. 160

Figure 9.2: Education is the foundation for development as shown with this group of participants in India. 163

Figure 10.1: US Ambassador Tim Roemer speaking to a group at a basketball clinic in New Delhi, India. 188

Figure 10.2: Partnership among local and government leaders can fuel community engagement in SDP. 191

Figure 11.1: Celebrating new friendships among basketball players from the Democratic Republic of the Congo and the United States. 203

Figure 11.2: Representation of Designers' and Implementers' key areas of knowledge about how and why sport is used to address conflict and create positive change. 210

Figure 12.1: Former Secretary of State John Kerry looks on as a young girl in Algiers scores a goal at a Nike facility. 223

Figure 12.2: Collaboration among key players supports effective implementation of SDP initiatives. 224

Figure 13.1: SDP can be a vehicle for attaining and sustaining goals. 230

Figure 13.2: This group in Mauritania shows us that every voice matters when building SDP programs. 235

Introduction

This book is a collection of thirteen coordinated chapters focused on specific aspects of sport for development and peace (SDP), with contributions from internationally recognized experts in the field. It is organized into two parts, the first focused on the foundations of SDP and the second on specific applications of SDP. While distinct voices are evident in the writing style and perspectives presented, they collectively offer a comprehensive look at many substantive and interconnected SDP topics. The goal of this book is to inform current and future SDP managers about these crucial topics in order to impact best practices in the field. Professional development and advanced education initiatives in areas such as international relations, foreign service, administration of non-profits, crisis management, conflict resolution, and sport management also may benefit from this content. Further, we hope to disseminate important underlying knowledge and examples that can inform and influence the future investigation of SDP.

    The foundational section of this book begins with an introduction to SDP, addressing its history and the frames through which it has previously been viewed. The sociological aspects of SDP are subsequently addressed, providing yet another framework through which SDP can be understood. Specific goals of SDP—such as development, inclusion, and sport participation—are examined in detail, followed by SDP's diplomatic, peacebuilding, and conflict resolution goals. The policy and economic implications of SDP are also explained, as is the relationship between SDP and corporate social responsibility. Finally, the evaluation and assessment of SDP programs is discussed, including the prospect for analytical applications. Following this foundational content, the application section of this book begins by providing examples and insights into governmental involvement in SDP. Additionally, not-for-profit applications are examined, as are corporate and for-profit SDP enterprises.

The book concludes with a discussion of the current trends and future implications of SDP.

Each chapter begins with intended student learning objectives and concludes with relevant learning activities, such as discussion questions or case studies. These activities are tailored for each chapter's individual content, including strategies for success and success stories. These activities are meant to be thought-provoking and engaging and to serve as vehicles for discussion. Additionally, they provide an immediate opportunity for readers to apply and make connections to the concepts and best practices from their corresponding chapters to enhance learning and growth.

I
FOUNDATIONS OF SPORT FOR DEVELOPMENT AND PEACE

1

History and Foundations of Sport for Development and Peace

Robert E. Baker

OBJECTIVES

Upon completing this chapter, students will:

- Describe the value of sport as a vehicle to achieve nonsport objectives.
- Define sport for development and peace (SDP).
- Distinguish between development *of* sport and development *through* sport.
- Identify the breadth and depth of SDP program objectives.
- Explain the key theoretical underpinnings of SDP.
- Describe practical applications of SDP.

WHY SPORTS?

The proliferation of sport for development and peace is rooted in sport's unique attributes that enable it to contribute to nonsport-related development and peace endeavors. These attributes include the universal popularity of sport that transcends national, cultural, socioeconomic, and political boundaries. When properly conducted, sport engages both participants and spectators alike. Its presence is felt in virtually all communities. Sport is an omnipresent global communication platform, reaching the masses with the capacity to invoke public education and social mobilization. Sport has the capacity to bring people together, including players, teams, coaches, volunteers, and spectators. It cuts across social and economic boundaries. Sports can empower, motivate, and inspire people, often highlighting the best of individual efforts and achievements.[1]

Sport is a social institution with structural power that allows it to influence society on a large scale while fostering individual interaction on a local level.[2] Nelson Mandela famously acknowledged, "Sport has the power to change the world." He went on to note, "It has the power to inspire, it has the power to unite people in a way that little else does. It speaks to youth in a language they understand. Sport can create hope, where once there was only despair. It is more powerful than governments in breaking down . . . barriers. It laughs in the face of all types of discrimination."[3]

As a universal language, "sport is a gigantic and powerful medium for the international spread of information, reputations and relationships" that possesses interest levels that "exceed those of any other subject matter, including political news and the movies."[4] The global interest in sport results in its massive economic and social impacts and its capacity to function as a broad cultural change agent.[5]

Figure 1.1. Sport for development and peace in action when this Israeli sport administrator attends a Sports-Visitor Program event. *Credit*: Ashi Fachler

HISTORICAL DEVELOPMENT OF SPORT FOR DEVELOPMENT AND PEACE

SDP has been referenced as a "new" social movement or multitrack diplomatic strategy emerging in the last thirty years to support broader conflict resolution and developmental objectives. However, while growing in prominence, SDP is not a recent phenomenon. Sport has historically been employed to prop up the social order. The antecedents of today's SDP rest in the premise of sport being used for broader purposes. While sometimes referenced as "sport for good," sport was also utilized in supporting colonialism and imperialism in the eighteenth and nineteenth centuries.[6]

In 1894, Pierre de Coubertin, founder of the modern Olympics, noted, "I remained convinced that sport is one of the most forceful elements of peace and I am confident in its future action."[7] Sport was emerging as a viable mechanism to advance developmental and diplomatic objectives. Through the twentieth century, the emergence of progressive social movements, the spread of nongovernmental organizations (NGOs), and the acknowledgement of the United Nations that sport can be an avenue to "experience equality, freedom, and a dignified means for empowerment" further contributed to the prominence of sport in developmental and peacebuilding realms.[8]

Sport had been regularly used in an ad hoc way to pursue nonsport objectives since the 1920s.[9] Several notable incidents reflecting the value of sport in development, peace, and diplomatic efforts are evident in the twentieth century. "Ping-pong diplomacy" employed by the United States and China in the early 1970s, wherein competitors in table tennis served as unofficial emissaries in breaking down borders, resulted in the opening of diplomatic relations. Mandela used sport during the 1995 Rugby World Cup to fight apartheid in South Africa and unite the South African people.

TIMELINE

SDP continues to evolve because of ongoing international interests impacting policy. The following is a chronology of some key events in the international diplomatic and developmental agenda. In 1978, the United Nations Educational, Scientific and Cultural Organization (UNESCO) General Conference adopted the International Charter of Physical Education and Sport. In 1997, the Government of the European Commission focused special attention on sport during the Amsterdam treaty negotiations, during which it was stated that "the Conference emphasizes the social significance of sport, in particular its role in forging identity and bringing people together."[10] In 2001, the UN Secretary-General Kofi Annan appointed Adolf Ogi (former president of the Swiss Confederation) as the first Special Adviser on Sport for Development and Peace to enhance the network of relations between UN organizations and the sports sector. In 2002, the UN Secretary-General convened the UN

Inter-Agency Task Force on Sport for Development and Peace to review activities that involve sport within the UN system. In 2003, the first International Conference on Sport and Development was held in Magglingen, Switzerland. The conference was the first international, high-level event on sport and development, involving participants and athletes from sports federations, governments, UN agencies, the media, business, and civil society. Also in 2003, the first Next Step conference, "International Expert Meeting on Development in and through Sport," was held in Amsterdam, the Netherlands. The Next Step conference was established to target practitioners, mostly at the grassroots level, to share experiences and best practices in SDP.[11]

In 2004, "Harnessing the Power of Sport for Development and Peace," a forum in Athens, Greece, was hosted during the Olympic Games and brought together political leaders and experts in development to discuss the potential of sport in achieving development goals. This forum laid the foundation for the Sport for Development and Peace International Working Group (SDPIWG), creating a new policy framework for the use of SDP. In 2005, the International Year of Sport and Physical Education was proclaimed by the General Assembly of the United Nations, and the SDPIWG was formed with representatives from ministries of sport, youth, and development from fifteen countries; directors of UN agencies; and NGOs in the SDP space. Also in 2005, the second Magglingen Conference on Sport and Development was held in Switzerland. The year 2005 also saw the second Next Step conference in Livingstone, Zambia, and the establishment of the Commonwealth Advisory Body on Sport. In 2007, the third Next Step conference was held in Windhoek, Namibia. This marked the inaugural meeting of the SportandDev.org Steering Board. Also in 2007, the European Commission published a white paper on sport, stating it would promote the use of sport as a tool in international development policy.[12]

In 2008, the International Olympic Committee (IOC) and the UN agreed on an expanded action plan using sport to reach the goals of the UN. Also in 2008, the UN Secretary-General Ban Ki-moon appointed Wilfried Lemke as the Special Adviser on SDP. And in July 2008, the UN Secretary-General established a trust fund for SDP. In 2009, the first UN-IOC Forum on SDP was held in Lausanne, Switzerland. In 2010, SDP was highlighted at the 2010 FIFA World Cup. In 2011, the second UN-IOC Forum on SDP was held in Geneva, Switzerland. Also in 2011, the fourth Next Step conference was held in Trinidad and Tobago. In 2012, a meeting of SDP experts was held at the Commonwealth Secretariat to develop Commonwealth SDP guidelines. In 2013, the third UN-IOC Forum on SDP was held in New York. The forum closed with a call for a United Nations International Day of Sport and Physical Activity, which was subsequently proclaimed to be on April 6 by the sixty-seventh United Nations General Assembly.[13]

In 2014, the fifth Next Step conference was held in New Delhi, India. On April 6, 2014, the UN observed the inaugural International Day of Sport for Development and Peace globally. Also in 2014, an SDPIWG meeting was held in Geneva, Switzerland, to address gender-based violence in and through sport. In 2015, sport was recognized as an important enabler in Sustainable Development Goals (SDGs). Also in 2015, the Beyond Sport Summit launched child safeguards to make sport safer for children. In 2017, the UN Secretary-General António Guterres announced that the United Nations Office on Sport for Development and Peace (UNOSDP) was closed. Also in 2017, the sixth International Conference of Ministers Responsible for Physical Education and Sport adopted the Kazan Action Plan. In 2018, the International Working Group of the World Conference on Women and Sport was held in Gaborone, Botswana.[14]

The UN formally recognized the power of sport as a vehicle for development and peacebuilding when it established the International Year of Sport and Physical Education in 2005, highlighting "the significant role that sport can play in accelerating progress towards the achievement of the Millennium Development Goals (MDGs) . . . and to better integrate sport into the developmental agenda as well as into efforts to achieve lasting peace."[15] Sport's attributes make it a valued element in more holistic tactics directed toward the eight MDG benchmarks aimed at (1) eradicating extreme poverty and hunger; (2) achieving universal primary education; (3) promoting gender equality and empowering women; (4) reducing child mortality; (5) improving maternal health; (6) combating HIV and AIDS, malaria, and other diseases; (7) ensuring environmental sustainability; and (8) developing a global partnership for development.[16]

Acknowledging that "[s]port as a universal language has been found to bridge social, religious, racial, and gender divides, hence contributing to lasting peace," the UN established a short-lived United Nations Office on Sport for Development and Peace.[17] This office was to promote dialogue, facilitate collaborations, and provide supports for SDP endeavors. The UN further noted that it "has proved it has the ability to help Governments and communities harness the positive aspects of sport in international development programmes and projects."[18] The International Day of Sport for Development and Peace emerged as "an annual celebration of the power of sport to drive social change, community development and to foster peace and understanding."[19] Using sport as a vehicle to serve development, peace, and diplomatic interests has gained prominence both as a strategic tool and as the subject of academic investigation.

WHAT IS SPORT FOR DEVELOPMENT AND PEACE?

Sport continues to play a strategic role in augmenting developmental, diplomatic, and peacebuilding efforts.[20] SDP initiatives and programs are concerned with using sport as a mechanism to affect positive change. Right to Play International defined SDP as "the international use of sport, physical activity, and play to attain specific development and peace objectives," while also acknowledging "the right of all members of society to participate in sport and leisure activities."[21] Successful SDP programs honor the rights of all members of society to participate in sport and leisure activities. These programs intentionally prioritize development, peace, and inclusivity;

embody positive sport values; and safeguard the integrity of the sport experience. Robust SDP programs combine sport and play with other nonsport elements to enhance their effectiveness.

Sport is a visible and viable means to enrich peacemaking, conflict resolution, intercultural understanding, and both personal and community development.[22] The relationship among varied objectives pursued through SDP endeavors reveals the complex intersections among international SDP concepts and programming that reflect subtle distinctions in emphases and terminologies. While related terms exist, such as *sport for development* (SFD), *sport for change, sport diplomacy,* and *sport for good*, all are interrelated and fall within the broad SDP agenda.[23] SDP has many such component parts, including corporate social responsibility (CSR), which are each addressed in more depth in forthcoming chapters.

SDP includes "the intentional use of sport, physical activity and play to achieve specific development objectives in low- and middle-income countries and disadvantaged communities in high-income areas."[24] SDP initiatives vary in the use of "all forms of physical activity that contribute to physical fitness, mental well-being and social interaction, such as play, recreation, organized or competitive sport, indigenous sports and games."[25] In the context of SDP, sport includes an array of activities adapted to all ages and abilities and emphasizes the positive outcomes of sport.[26] Sport can be targeted toward those in greatest need, as SDP efforts often address refugees, child soldiers, the impoverished, victims of conflict and natural disasters, victims of discrimination, and people with disabilities.[27] SDP is therefore often focused on mass participation sport and not elite sport.[28]

SDP initiatives leverage sport to achieve developmental or peacemaking goals. For example, sport has benefits such as individual development, health promotion, disease prevention, gender equity, social assimilation, peacebuilding, conflict resolution, and disaster and trauma assistance.[29] Sport can espouse positive health benefits while also serving to prevent violence, increase awareness of health risks, and promote intercultural respect.[30] The transference of the many intersecting aims of SDP to life beyond sport is also sought after.[31] The UNOSDP[32] enumerates sport's influence for development and peace: (1) sport has a unique power to attract, mobilize, and inspire; (2) sport embodies participation, inclusion, and citizenship; (3) sport reflects values such as respect, acceptance, collaboration, and equity; and (4) sport is relevant to an array of circumstances, both in the short and long term.[33]

While its roots go back much further, SDP is a rapidly expanding phenomenon in the twenty-first century. The UN acknowledges the noteworthy role sport plays in development and peace efforts and encourages the use of sport in broadly defined development agendas.[34] The application of the concept of development is often associated with growth, progress, evolution, and constructive transformation.[35] SDP initiatives engage in four key areas of development: (1) promoting human rights and combatting discrimination; (2) ensuring equal access to the benefits of sport and physical activity; (3) safeguarding participants; and (4) ensuring integrity in sport.[36]

SDP includes initiatives resulting in the development *of* sport, but often, the underlying purposes of such programs are centered on development *through* sport. In the context of SDP, development of and through sport is a means to an end. Those ends include the enrichment of participants' lives and communities and extends to the betterment of the broader society.[37] The distinction between *sport development* and *sport for development* is examined much more thoroughly in chapter 3 (Green and Horne), but one core understanding is that SFD involves the process of changing and growing sport, conceivably for the benefit of individual participants or a specific sport itself. On the other hand, the recognition that SDP is focused on using sport as a vehicle to foster nonsport developmental outcomes provides the foundation of many SDP programs. Sport has tremendous potential to accelerate development and peace efforts worldwide.

SPORT FOR DEVELOPMENT AND PEACE: A GLOCAL PERSPECTIVE

Developmental and diplomatic interests manifest at both the global and local level. The universality of sport affords SDP initiatives a means to pursue these diverse global and local interests. In the pursuit of joint global and local interests, the concept of glocalization has emerged. The term *glocalization* itself suggests a seemingly dichotomous concept involving homogeneity and heterogeneity. The balance between sameness and difference among stakeholders in an SDP initiative yields glocalization, or local applications reflected in global agendas and global interests reflected in local programs.[38] For example, in business, differentiating global brands for a specific market reflects glocalization, and in diplomacy, accomplishing global diplomatic agendas through local actions reflects glocalization. SDP initiatives often involve an international agenda pursued through local programming. Glocal SDP programs connect global with local interests and activities.[39] The use of sport as a change agent requires an awareness of local interests and intercultural sensitivity among stakeholders.[40] Local interactions are, therefore, the foundation for broader developmental, cultural, and diplomatic change. In that sense, glocal SDP programs reflect the importance of local actions in global interests and vice versa.[41]

SDP occurs at the local level through people-to-people programs such as intercultural exchanges, while some globally significant sport-related ventures, such as the Olympic Games, function at both the global and local levels. On a broad international level, the Olympic Movement aims to "contribute to building a peaceful and better world by educating youth through sport practiced in accordance with Olympism and its values."[42] Yet, on a local level, this is achieved through the interaction of individual athletes, administrators, and spectators involved with the Olympics, reflecting the glocal nature of the Olympics.

Supporting a glocal frame, global liberalism supported by local populism yields a framework within which sport can be a valuable mechanism in fostering peace and social justice.[43] Judy Kuriansky[44] contends that interpersonal interactions and intergroup interventions are essential in fostering peace and resolving differences. While top-down SDP initiatives commonly attract resources, the grassroots initiatives humanize stakeholders and enhance mutual understanding.[45] Within SDP, goals represent numerous agendas, including peacebuilding and conflict resolution, the enhancement of cross-cultural understanding, and community development.[46] The influence of glocalized, sport-based developmental and diplomatic efforts can yield improved cross-cultural relationships among diverse stakeholders or advance an inclusive social justice agenda at a local level.

THEORETICAL FOUNDATIONS AND PRACTICAL APPLICATIONS

Evidence indicates that development and peacebuilding interests can be supported via sport-based initiatives, which have become not only more prevalent over the past decade, but more widely studied as well.[47] Global agendas pursued at the grassroots level are framed by Michael Beer and Nitin Nohria's[48] Theory E and Theory O. Theory E characterizes top-down change; this is often economically efficient and yields quicker change, yet the results may not be sustainable over time. Theory O, or bottom-up change, often takes longer and costs more to effect large-scale change than Theory E but yields more lasting results. Regardless of the direction of the SDP initiative, change is a long-term process.[49]

Beer and Nohria[50] offered this theoretical framework of Theory E and Theory O that can be applied to the SDP landscape. Top-down initiatives are more commonplace and often receive desirable attention because of the support of governments and NGOs. While top-down diplomatic initiatives more regularly attract resources, bottom-up initiatives are essential in personalizing the engaged stakeholders and facilitating reciprocal understanding.[51] Bottom-up approaches also enhance the accuracy of perceptions on the ground, thereby reducing misconceptions. They can even be a unifying force among stakeholders.[52] Efficacy in achieving many SDP goals is enhanced through bottom-up, grassroots initiatives, which can induce lasting changes. It could be concluded that the combination of Theory E for efficiency and resources allocation and Theory O for effectual change is most likely to yield desired, sustainable results. Gennady Chufrin and Harold Saunders determined that "while governments negotiate around interests and issues, citizens play a crucial role in changing behavior and relationships, for it is in the public political arena . . . that issues are reframed, comparable interests recognised, perceptions changed, fears allayed."[53]

The use of sport as a change agent necessitates cultural sensitivity and acknowledgement of diversity in local populations.[54] Gordon Allport's[55] contact hypothesis suggests that enabling contact among diverse stakeholders can lessen hostility, diminish stereotypes, and stimulate more tolerant attitudes. Interactive contact with dissimilar individuals or groups cultivates new knowledge and reduces the associated trepidation. The nature of sport itself often yields proximity and interaction among participants. In alignment with Allport's contentions, any forced interaction through sport must be meaningful to the stakeholders to optimize its effectiveness. Superficial contact cannot enable grassroots development or cultural change. Sport emulates contact hypothesis mechanisms wherein collaborative interaction can change mindsets. Diverse stakeholder's recognition of common sport interests can effectively influence their acceptance of disparities.

Cross-cultural SDP experiences often necessitate cooperation that can yield understanding and camaraderie. Meaningful, interdependent exchanges contribute to acceptance. Allport specifically notes that "the effect is greatly enhanced if this contact is sanctioned by institutional supports (i.e., by law, custom or local atmosphere), and provided it is of a sort that leads to the perception of common interests and common humanity between members."[56] This points to the utility of sport as a mechanism to enhance individual and collective awareness. Allport's contact hypothesis promotes interactive contact among diverse stakeholders as a means to facilitate awareness and acceptance. Sport requires interaction among participants, making it the type of direct interaction that can lessen animosity and stimulate tolerance. Engagement in sport experiences commonly reflects Allport's hypothesis wherein collaborative interaction can yield empathy and acceptance in transforming stakeholder attitudes.

Grassroots SDP initiatives grounded in the principles of Allport[57] and Beer and Nohria[58] can effect change. These local interactions are the foundation for broader developmental and cross-cultural change. Broad changes evolve from individuals within a culture. The universality of sport provides an opportunity to achieve symbiotic global and local goals. While sport provides a mechanism, sport for development theory suggests that combining sport with cultural and educational elements is essential for SDP initiatives to achieve their developmental, diplomatic, and cultural aims.[59]

Theoretical frameworks offer guiding principles and theoretical constructs that help determine if, when, and how SDP programs are meeting their objectives.[60] One of the most comprehensive of these is presented by Alexis Lyras and Jon Welty Peachey[61] who provided a theoretical framework for the examination of SFD programming. While SDP may exhibit distinctions related to diplomatic and conflict resolution frameworks, the overall SFD framework broadly encompasses initiatives with more specific aims toward SDP.[62] This SFD model frames the study of (1) foundational philosophies; (2) impacts assessment; and (3) organizational, sport, educational, and cultural elements of SFD programs that create change in the participants.

Lyras and Welty Peachey[63] concluded that the foundation of an SDP program should be grounded in the appropriate philosophy. Since there is consternation over what is considered an *appropriate philosophy* in SDP, this has led to an increasing call for attention to the philosophical underpinnings of SDP programs. Previous work in SDP assumed that sport was a panacea of glocal development and diplomatic problems while purporting to know the desires of program recipients regardless of where they were situated geographically, politically, socially, or economically.[64] As a result, the shift to examine the underlying philosophies of SDP initiatives has framed a particular focus on "decolonising" SDP programs[65] and ensuring local input and local sustainability of such programs.[66]

As a philosophical starting point, Lyras and Welty Peachey,[67] along with Robert Baker and Craig Esherick,[68] argued that SDP programs that seek goals of promoting cultural understanding need to be grounded in principles of Theory O and of Allport's[69] contact hypothesis, which has provided guidance for how meaningful change between dissimilar groups or individuals can occur. Again, Theory O posits that bottom-up change, although it takes longer and costs more to generate an impact, creates more sustainable long-term results in that engagement and interaction change participants' perceptions toward other stakeholders.[70] Contact hypothesis argues that meaningful, interactive contact between dissimilar individuals can change perceptions that people have of each other. According to the contact hypothesis, prerequisite conditions for the interaction to bring about the desired change exist. The SDP program must foster these conditions that facilitate interaction and decrease negative perceptions.[71] These conditions are that (1) contact must be between groups or people of equal status; (2) there should be common goals for the framework and purpose of the contact; (3) the individuals or groups should be working together toward a mutually beneficial goal; and (4) positive change will most likely occur when the contact is supported by societal authorities, structures, or institutions.

If there is a ranking perceived in the group, it will be difficult for participants to actively engage and perceive the value of their individual contributions. Efforts should be made to equalize status such as, for example, educational background, wealth, or skill. In SDP programs, diverse stakeholder interests are not always well defined or agreed upon, which can hinder program efficacy[72]; yet common goals must be evident. SDP programs should be designed to allow intergroup collaboration through cooperative activities to achieve common goals. SDP programs should ensure that the interaction occurs within a socially sanctioned activity such as school, sports, or governmental exchanges to facilitate change. Additionally, a fifth recommendation is that contact should increase "friendship potential" wherein individuals and groups mingle together informally, interacting to potentially form friendships.[73] The contact hypothesis contends that SDP programs with active engagement and cooperation between people of similar status are more effective at fostering change over ones where participants passively observe or where contact is imposed by higher-status stakeholders.[74] Research supports the theory that well-designed interaction between groups can decrease prejudices and stereotypes and also lead to increased knowledge about others, enhanced empathy, trust and forgiveness, and strengthened social relationships.[75] Therefore, it is important to philosophically align SDP programs with these theoretical principles.

Lyras and Welty Peachey[76] contend that effective SDP initiatives include well-designed sport, educational, and cultural components. Further, they note that "it is not just sport that achieves positive outcomes, for according to the sport-plus model, sport is one pillar in an intervention and should be supplemented with other resources and social supports."[77] A central element of SDP programs that is both attractive and effective is sport itself. Involvement in sport experiences engages participants in ways that nonphysical activities cannot. SDP programs generally include sport participation that can range from sport clinics to games and contests to large-scale tournaments. Regardless of the sport or type of activity, the way that sport programming is designed and implemented is critical to the outcomes it produces.[78] Lyras and Welty Peachey[79] offer the following principles to "undergird the sport and physical activity components: (a) an inspiring moral philosophy, (b) educationally oriented engagement of the sport experience, (c) inclusive teams, (d) quality experiences, and (e) linking sport with cultural enrichment activities and active citizenship." These recommendations enable programs to align with principles of contact hypothesis and engender the foundations for realistic experiences that enhance the likelihood of transfer.

The use of sport-based developmental and diplomatic efforts can advance either an inclusive social justice agenda or a conflict resolution agenda. Sport can be a valuable mechanism in pursuing such agendas aimed at fostering peace and social justice by increasing popular support of global liberalism—a dominant political ideology.[80] Yet the varied interests driving the rapidly evolving SDP sector reflect

Figure 1.2. Inclusive sport brings people together as this athlete from Iraq embraces the opportunity to join a wheelchair basketball game. *Credit*: Center for Sport Management at George Mason University

its "diverse political actors and ideologies."[81] Richard Giulianotti further classified four policy areas and related SDP stakeholder segments: (1) neoliberal social policies embodied by private commercial interests engaged in CSR; (2) developmental interventionist policies affiliated with NGOs and community-based programs; (3) strategic developmentalist policies associated with governments and sport federations; and (4) social justice policies associated with social movements and related NGOs. For example, the NBA has generated developmental opportunities through programs such as Basketball without Borders.[82] Involvement in CSR has grown[83] as many companies, such as Nike, have CSR goals, and many companies, such as Coca-Cola, reap CSR rewards.[84] Additionally, both governmental and NGO engagement in SDP has increased as sports have demonstrated their value in developmental and diplomatic outcomes.[85]

The *Journal of Sport for Development* identified the following SDP research themes: *Sport and disability* focuses on research related to sport as a vehicle for the development, access, inclusion, and human rights of people with disabilities. This section encourages critical thinking and diversity of perspectives, welcoming research at the intersection of theory and practice. *Sport and education* presents research and case studies related to interventions that use sport to advance education, youth development, and life skills. Rather than focusing on sport education, this section discusses the role of sport in achieving the academic and social outcomes of youth. The theme of *sport and gender* presents research and case studies related to interventions using sport to promote gender equality, challenge gender norms, and empower girls and women in disadvantaged environments.

Sport and health presents a wide range of outcomes associated with physical, mental, and social well-being. This is the effect of SDP programs on the risk factors for communicable and noncommunicable diseases, including the direct effect of sports programs on physical activity. It also examines the role that sport can play in preventive education and health promotion interventions. The theme of *sport and livelihoods* presents research and case studies on interventions using sport to improve the livelihoods of disadvantaged people, from programs focusing on vocational skills training to rehabilitation and social enterprise. *Sport and peace* focuses on projects that use sport as a vehicle for reconciliation and peacebuilding. The concept of peace is broadly defined to include connotations of personal, community, and social well-being, as well as the absence of conflict and tension between groups. In particular, this section examines the possibilities of creating peace between individuals and groups in socially, culturally, or ethnically divided societies. The *sport and social cohesion* theme includes projects in the areas of community empowerment, social inclusion and integration, and diversity management. It focuses on social impact assessments and capacity-building initiatives that can lead to social cohesion, skills enhancement, and overall community development.

Directed toward these and other thematic objectives, many SDP programs have claimed robust outcomes yet rely on largely anecdotal evidence to support these claims.[86] The perception of exaggerated claims regarding the benefits of SDP programming necessitates the need for reliable program evaluation to document purported SDP outcomes.[87] Roger Levermore noted, "The lack of convincing large-scale evaluation might contribute to the doubt that some development agencies have shown for the sport-for-development movement."[88] Moreover, stakeholders are calling for more quantifiable data to demonstrate the impact of SDP programs.[89] Fred Coalter[90] concluded that a lack of funding, resources, and expertise contribute to the lack of evaluations.

Documenting outcomes via appropriate evaluation is an essential component of SDP programming. A deeper discussion of evaluation and the use of analytics is found in chapter 9 (Gerrard and Baker). Documentation of program efficacy is increasingly necessary and has created enhanced tools for evaluation and improved measures to capture the outcomes of SDP initiatives.[91] The use of goal-based program evaluation measures will inform future programming. SDP programs should undertake in-depth analyses of various program philosophies, elements, structures, processes, and activities "for the purpose of identifying core elements relative to active or passive engagement directed toward objectives."[92] Evaluation essentially identifies how the SDP program can deliver (or not) its objectives while guiding and refining future objectives. Nico Schulenkorf[93] suggested that examining effective management based on both sport- and nonsport-related outcomes is an essential evaluation for SDP initiatives. Theoretical grounding of the managerial analysis will inform the interpretation and explanation of the outcomes.[94] SDP scholars continue to press for the need for better program design, management, and evaluation of programs such that the desired outcomes are more likely to be achieved and so that other programs can learn best practices both in design and implementation of effective SDP programs.[95]

A SUCCESS STORY

Grassroots sport diplomacy initiatives underpinned by the principles of Allport[96] and Beer and Nohria[97] can effect change. SDP organizations, for example Right to Play, Grassroots Soccer, Pour3Points, and Peace Players International, are an essential part of glocal development and peace efforts. Local interpersonal interactions are the foundation for broader intercultural change.[98] An example of a successful SDP program is the Sport Diplomacy Initiative (SDI), a cooperative agreement between the US Department of State Department of Sports Diplomacy and George Mason University's Center for Sport Management.

The SDI Sports Visitor Program served nearly 1,200 participants in eighty-one groups. Participants included athletes, coaches, administrators, and advocates from eighty-three countries. Most, but not all, groups were mixed gender. Each group visited the United States for approximately two weeks. Participants engaged in sport activities and cultural and educational experiences as well. Each program included exposure to inclusive sport experiences, leadership development, and interpersonal exchanges with local individuals.

The broadly stated goals of SDI Sports Visitor Program were to enable participants to (1) learn more about US society and culture, thereby countering negative stereotypes; (2) improve their leadership skills through activities that introduce team building, conflict resolution, inclusion, and respect for diversity; (3) apply these skills toward productive and positive change in their local communities through sports; and (4) establish partnerships to share knowledge and skills with their peers and the broader community. These broad program goals were supported by specific SDI outcome objectives in which participants would (1) learn about American culture and the American people, the American sport system, diversity and disability issues in inclusive sport, and sport-specific techniques; (2) multiply the impact of the experience upon returning home; (3) value the program experience as a measure of satisfaction; and (4) maintain contact as program alumni. The SDI evaluation system was developed to measure outcomes associated with these objectives, with each objective assessed through at least one quantitative measure and supported by qualitative and observational evidence. The complexities of a program serving participants who ranged from youth athletes to adult coaches and who spoke many different languages required an evaluation system that employed simple, culturally sensitive, direct self-reporting measures. The measurement tools included quantitative instruments such as a coordinated preprogram and postprogram survey instruments.

The SDI Sports Visitor Program evaluated specific program outcomes relevant to the aforementioned objectives. Program outcomes, such as an increased awareness of American culture, are the result of the SDI programming related to program objectives and measured by the noted instruments. The activities in which visitors were engaged were evaluated in relation to the specific outcome goals and objectives. For example, in supporting the goal for visitors to learn more about US society and culture, thereby countering negative stereotypes, SDI facilitated opportunities for the sports visitors to engage with US citizens. Additionally, SDI documented outputs such as the number of visitors served by the initiative, the number of programs in which they participated, the number of US citizens engaged, the locations of visits, the cultural and sporting events attended, and so forth. Overall, a review of the SDI Sports Visitor Program provided an analysis of the mechanisms and processes utilized for goal-driven program efficacy.[99]

Questions

1. Develop a hypothetical SDP program proposal, addressing the following:
    a. The purpose of the SDP program and its explicit goals
    b. Which stakeholders will participate in the planning and implementation
    c. Potential partnerships
    d. How the program will be funded
    e. How the program will be evaluated

2. Identify an existing SDP program. Research it and assess it in the following areas:
   a. What is the purpose of the program?
   b. What is the foundational framework?
   c. How is it funded?
   d. Who are the participants?
   e. Who are partners?

Strategies for Success

1. Understand the frameworks underpinning SDP programs.
2. Include a range of stakeholders in SDP program development.
3. Determine unique circumstances and SDP program goals.
4. Form partnerships in support of explicit SDP program purposes.
5. Develop an evaluation system tied to the program goals.

NOTES

1. Right to Play, "What Is Sport for Development and Peace? Harnessing the Power of Sport for Development and Peace: Recommendations to Governments," 2008, https://www.sportanddev.org/sites/default/files/downloads/what_is_sport_for_development_and_peace.pdf.

2. Jay Coakley, *Sports in Society: Issues and Controversies*, 12th ed. (New York: McGraw-Hill Education, 2017); Eric R. Wolf, "Distinguished Lecture: Facing Power—Old Insights, New Questions," *American Anthropologist* 92, no. 3 (1990): 586–96, https://doi.org/10.1525/aa.1990.92.3.02a00020.

3. Nelson Mandela, "Speech by Nelson Mandela at the Inaugural Laureus Lifetime Achievement Award," May 25, 2000, Inaugural Laureus Lifetime Achievement Award, Monte Carlo, Monaco.

4. Barry Sanders, "Sports as Public Diplomacy," *CPD* Blog (August 31, 2011): para. 1, https://uscpublicdiplomacy.org/blog-sport-public-diplomacy.

5. Robert E. Baker and Craig Esherick, "Sport-Based Peace Initiatives: Playing for Peace," in *Building Cultures of Peace: Transdisciplinary Voices of Hope and Action*, ed. Elavie Ndura-Ouédraogo and Randall Amster (Newcastle upon Tyne, UK: Cambridge Scholars Publishing, 2009), 102–24.

6. Tegwen Gadais, "Sport for Development and Peace: Current Perspectives of Research," in *Sports Science and Human Health: Different Approaches*, ed. Daniel Almeida Marinho et al. (London: IntechOpen, 2021), 27–40, https://doi.org/10.5772/intechopen.83154.

7. Pierre de Coubertin, "Le rétablissement des Jeux Olympiques: Revue de Paris," Olympic World Library, 1894, 15, https://library.olympic.org/Default/doc/SYRACUSE/471847/le-retablissement-des-jeux-olympiques-discours-fondateur-restoring-the-olympic-games-founding-speech.

8. "International Year of Sport and Physical Education 2005," para. 2, United Nations, accessed November 19, 2015, http://www.un.org/sport2005/a_year/ayear_for.html.

9. Sportanddev.org, accessed April 4, 2021, https://www.sportanddev.org.
10. Opinion of the Economic and Social Committee on "Voluntary Organizations and Foundations in Europe," Official Journal C 095, March 30, 1998, page 99.
11. Sportanddev.org.
12. Sportanddev.org.
13. Sportanddev.org.
14. Sportanddev.org.
15. United Nations, 2003, GA 58/6, https://www.un.org/depts/dhl/resguide/r58_resolutions_table_eng.htm.
16. Right to Play, "What Is Sport for Development and Peace?"
17. UNESCO, "Sport for Development and Peace," United Nations Educational, Scientific and Cultural Organization, accessed June 2019, http://www.unesco.org/new/en/social-and-humansciences/themes/physical-education-andsport/sport-forpeace-and-development/.
18. UNESCO, "Sport for Development and Peace."
19. The International Olympic Committee, "International Day of Sport for Development and Peace," para. 1, accessed April 4, 2021, https://www.olympic.org/idsdp.
20. Baker and Esherick, "Sport-Based Peace Initiatives: Playing for Peace"; Alexis Lyras and Jon Welty Peachey, "Integrating Sport-for-Development Theory and Praxis," *Sport Management Review* 14, no. 4 (November 2011): 311–26; Alexis Lyras, "Olympic Education in Practice: Educational Components of a Sport for Peacebuilding Intervention," in *Olympism, Olympic Education and Learning Legacies*, ed. Dikaia Chatziefstathiou and Norbert Müller (Newcastle upon Tyne, UK: Cambridge Scholars Publishing, 2014), 245–59; Nico Schulenkorf, "Managing Sport-for Development: Reflections and Outlook," *Sport Management Review* 20, no. 3 (June 2017): 243–51.
21. Right to Play, "What Is Sport for Development and Peace?"
22. Baker and Esherick, "Sport-Based Peace Initiatives: Playing for Peace."
23. Robert E. Baker, Pamela H. Baker, Anya Evmenova, and Craig Esherick, "Implementation and Evaluation of International Sport Development, Peace, and Diplomacy Programs," November 2012, symposium conducted at the meeting of the annual conference of the Sport Management Association of Australia and New Zealand, Sydney, Australia; Baker and Esherick, "Sport-Based Peace Initiatives"; Lyras and Welty Peachey, "Integrating Sport-for-Development Theory and Praxis"; Marlene A. Dixon, Arden J. Anderson, Robert E. Baker, Pamela H. Baker, and Craig Esherick, "Management in Sport for Development: Examining the Structure and Processes of a Sport Diplomacy Initiative," *International Journal of Sport Management and Marketing* 19, nos. 3–4 (2019): 268–92; Jon Welty Peachey, George B. Cunningham, Alexis Lyras, Adam Cohen, and Jennifer Bruening, "The Influence of a Sport-for-Peace Event on Prejudice and Change Agent Self-Efficacy," *Journal of Sport Management* 29, no. 3 (2015): 229–44, https://doi.org/10.1123/jsm.2013-0251.
24. United Nations Inter-Agency Task Force on Sport for Development and Peace, "Sport as a Tool for Development and Peace," 2003, https://www.sportanddev.org/sites/default/files/downloads/16__sport_for_dev_towards_millenium_goals.pdf.
25. United Nations Inter-Agency Task Force on Sport for Development and Peace, "Sport as a Tool for Development and Peace"; Justin A. Richards, Zachary A. Kaufman, Nico Schulenkorf, Eli A. Wolff, Katie Gannett, Katja Siefken, and Gaspar Rodriguez, "Advancing the Evidence Base of Sport for Development: A New Open-Access, Peer-Reviewed Journal," *Journal of Sport for Development* 1, no. 1 (2013): 1–3.

26. United Nations Office on Sport for Development and Peace, "Sport and Sustainable Development Goals," 2017.

27. Bruce Kidd, "A New Social Movement: Sport for Development and Peace," *Sport in Society* 11, no. 4 (2008): 370–80; Douglas Hartmann and Christina Kwauk, "Sport and Development: An Overview, Critique, and Reconstruction," *Journal of Sport and Social Issues* 35, no. 3 (2011): 284–305; Right to Play on behalf of the Sport for Development and Peace International Working Group, "Harnessing the Power of Sport for Development and Peace: Recommendations to Governments," September 15, 2008, https://www.sportanddev.org/en/article/publication/harnessing-power-sport-development-and-peace-recommendations-governments.

28. David R. Black, "The Ambiguities of Development: Implications for Development through Sport," *Sport in Society* 13, no. 1 (2010): 121–29; B. Kidd and P. Donnelly, eds., *Literature Reviews on Sport for Development and Peace* (Toronto, ON: International Working Group on Sport for Development and Peace, 2007).

29. Megan Chawansky and Matthew Holmes, "Sport, Social Development and Peace," *Sport in Society* 18, no. 6 (2015): 752–56; Kidd, "A New Social Movement: Sport for Development and Peace."

30. Andrew J. Webb and Andre Richelieu, "Sport for Development and Peace Snakes and Ladders," *Qualitative Market Research* 18, no. 3 (2015): 278–97; Nico Schulenkorf, Emma Sherry, and Katie Rowe, "Sport for Development: An Integrated Literature Review," *Journal of Sport Management* 30, no. 1 (2016): 22–39.

31. Roger Levermore, "Sport: A New Engine of Development?" *Progress in Development Studies* 8, no. 2 (2008): 183–90.

32. United Nations Office on Sport for Development and Peace, "Sport and Sustainable Development Goals," 2017.

33. Fred Coalter, "Sport-for-Development: Going beyond the Boundary?" *Sport in Society* 13, no. 9 (2010): 1374–91; Simon C. Darnell, "Power, Politics and 'Sport for Development and Peace': Investigating the Utility of Sport for International Development," *Sociology of Sport Journal* 27, no. 1 (2010): 54–75.

34. Baker and Esherick, "Sport-Based Peace Initiatives: Playing for Peace"; Lyras and Welty Peachey, "Integrating Sport-for-Development Theory and Praxis"; United Nations, "2005 International Year of Sport and Physical Education," accessed January 5, 2009, https://www.un.org/sport/sites/www.un.org.sport/files/documents/pdfs/IYSPE%202005/IYSPE_2005_Facts.pdf.

35. Lyras and Welty Peachey, "Integrating Sport-for-Development Theory and Praxis"; Kenneth I. Maton, "Empowering Community Settings: Agents of Individual Development, Community Betterment, and Positive Social Change," *American Journal of Community Psychology* 41, nos. 1–2 (March 2008): 4–21.

36. United Nations, "Recovering Better: Sport for Development and Peace," Department of Economic and Social Affairs, December 15, 2020, https://www.un.org/development/desa/dspd/recovering-better-sport-for-development-and-peace.html.

37. Schulenkorf, "Managing Sport-for-Development: Reflections and Outlook."

38. Roland Robertson, "Glocalization: Time-Space and Homogenity-Heterogeneity," in *Global Modernities*, ed. Mike Featherstone, Scott Lash, and Roland Robertson (London: Sage, 1995), 25–44.

39. Göran Svensson, "'Glocalization' of Business Activities: A 'Glocal Strategy' Approach," *Management Decision* 39, no. 1 (2001): 6–18, https://doi.org/10.1108/EUM0000000005403.

40. Alexis Lyras, "Organizational Change Theory: Sport for Peace and Development," *The Chronicle of Kinesiology and Physical Education in Higher Education* 2 (2008): 14–16, www.nakhe.org/ChronicleQuest.

41. Robertson, "Glocalization: Time-Space and Homogenity-Heterogeneity."

42. International Olympic Committee, "Olympic Charter," July 17, 2020, 15, www.olympic.org/Documents/olympic_charter_en.pdf.

43. Guy Ben-Porat, *Global Liberalism, Local Populism: Peace and Conflict in Israel/Palestine and Northern Ireland* (Syracuse, NY: Syracuse University Press, 2006).

44. Judy Kuriansky, *Beyond Bullets and Bombs: Grassroots Peacebuilding between Israelis and Palestinians* (Portsmouth, NH: Praeger, 2007).

45. Michael Beer and Nitin Nohria, eds., *Breaking the Code of Change* (Boston: Harvard Business School Press, 2001).

46. Baker and Esherick, "Sport-Based Peace Initiatives: Playing for Peace."

47. Baker and Esherick, "Sport-Based Peace Initiatives: Playing for Peace"; Richard Giulianotti, "The Sport, Development and Peace Sector: A Model of Four Social Policy Domains, *Journal of Social Policy* 40, no. 4 (2011): 757–76, https://doi.org/10.1017/S0047279410000930; Kidd, "A New Social Movement: Sport for Development and Peace"; Lyras and Welty Peachey, "Integrating Sport-for-Development Theory and Praxis."

48. Beer and Nohria, *Breaking the Code of Change*.

49. Graeme Simpson, Brandon Hamber, and Noel Scott, "Future Challenges to Policy-Making in Countries in Transition," paper presented at the meeting of the Comparative Experiences of Policy Making and Implementation in Countries in Transition Workshop, Derry/Londonderry, Northern Ireland, February 2011, www.csvr.org.za/docs/international/futurechallenges.pdf.

50. Beer and Nohria, *Breaking the Code of Change*.

51. Beer and Nohria, *Breaking the Code of Change*.

52. Baker and Esherick, "Sport-Based Peace Initiatives: Playing for Peace."

53. Gennady I. Chufrin and Harold H. Saunders, "A Public Peace Process," *Negotiation Journal* 9, no. 3 (1993): 158, https://doi.org/10.1111/j.1571-9979.1993.tb00698.x.

54. Lyras, "Organizational Change Theory: Sport for Peace and Development."

55. Gordon W. Allport, *The Nature of Prejudice* (Cambridge, MA: Addison-Wesley, 1954).

56. Allport, *The Nature of Prejudice*, 281.

57. Allport, *The Nature of Prejudice*.

58. Beer and Nohria, *Breaking the Code of Change*.

59. Alexis Lyras, "Characteristics and Psycho-Social Impacts of an Inter-Ethnic Educational Sport Initiative on Greek and Turkish Cypriot Youth" (PhD diss., University of Connecticut, January 2007); Lyras and Welty Peachey, "Integrating Sport-for-Development Theory and Praxis."

60. George B. Cunningham, Trevor Bopp, and Michael Sagas, "Overcoming Cultural Barriers in Sport Management Study Abroad Programs: The Influence of Extended Intergroup Contact," *International Journal of Sport Management* 11, no. 3 (2010): 347–59; Lyras and Welty Peachey, "Integrating Sport-for-Development Theory and Praxis"; Schulenkorf, "Managing Sport-for-Development: Reflections and Outlook"; Schulenkorf et al., "Sport for Development: An Integrated Literature Review"; Welty Peachey et al., "The Influence of a Sport-for-Peace Event on Prejudice and Change Agent Self-Efficacy."

61. Lyras and Welty Peachey, "Integrating Sport-for-Development Theory and Praxis."

62. Lyras and Welty Peachey, "Integrating Sport-for-Development Theory and Praxis"; Schulenkorf, "Managing Sport-for-Development: Reflections and Outlook"; Schulenkorf et al., "Sport for Development: An Integrated Literature Review."

63. Lyras and Welty Peachey, "Integrating Sport-for-Development Theory and Praxis."

64. Fred Coalter, *A Wider Social Role for Sport: Who's Keeping the Score?* (London: Routledge, 2007); Fred Coalter, *Sport for Development: What Game Are We Playing?* (London: Routledge, 2013); Nico Schulenkorf and Ramón Spaaij, "Commentary: Reflections on Theory Building in Sport for Development and Peace," *International Journal of Sport Management and Marketing* 16, nos. 1–2 (2015): 71–77.

65. Darnell, "Power, Politics and 'Sport for Development and Peace': Investigating the Utility of Sport for International Development"; Simon C. Darnell and Lyndsay Hayhurst, "Sport for Decolonization: Exploring a New Praxis of Sport for Development," *Progress in Development Studies* 11, no. 3 (2011): 183–96; Simon C. Darnell and Tarminder Kaur, "C. L. R. James and a Place for History in Theorizing 'Sport for Development and Peace,'" *International Journal of Sport Management and Marketing* 16, no. 2 (2015): 5–17; Lyndsay M. C. Hayhurst, "The Power to Shape Policy: Charting Sport for Development Policy Discourses," *International Journal of Sport Policy* 1, no. 2 (2009): 203–27; Tess Kay, "Developing through Sport: Evidencing Sport Impacts on Young People," *Sport in Society* 12, no. 9 (2009): 1177–91.

66. Coalter, *A Wider Social Role for Sport: Who's Keeping the Score?*; Matthew Holmes, Davies Banda, and Megan Chawansky, "Towards Sustainable Programme Design? An Examination of CSR Initiatives within a Zambian SfD NGO," *International Journal of Sport Management and Marketing* 16, no. 2 (2015): 36–51; William Massey, Meredith A. Whitley, Lindsey Blom, and Lawrence H. Gerstein, "Sport for Development and Peace: A Systems Theory Perspective on Promoting Sustainable Change," *International Journal of Sport Management and Marketing* 16, nos. 1–2 (2015): 18–35; Schulenkorf, "Managing Sport-for–Development: Reflections and Outlook"; Schulenkorf and Spaaij, "Commentary: Reflections on Theory Building in Sport for Development and Peace."

67. Lyras and Welty Peachey, "Integrating Sport-for-Development Theory and Praxis."

68. Baker and Esherick, "Sport-Based Peace Initiatives: Playing for Peace."

69. Allport, *The Nature of Prejudice.*

70. Beer and Nohria, *Breaking the Code of Change.*

71. George B. Cunningham, Trevor Bopp, and Michael Sagas, "Overcoming Cultural Barriers in Sport Management Study Abroad Programs: The Influence of Extended Intergroup Contact," *International Journal of Sport Management* 11, no. 3 (2010): 347–59; George B. Cunningham and Nicole Melton, "The Moderating Effects of Contact with Lesbian and Gay Friends on the Relationships among Religious Fundamentalism, Sexism, and Sexual Prejudice," *Journal of Sex Research* 50, nos. 3–4 (2012): 401–8; Thomas F. Pettigrew and Linda R. Tropp, "A Meta-analytic Test of Intergroup Contact Theory," *Journal of Personality and Social Psychology* 90, no. 5 (2006): 751–83; Thomas F. Pettigrew, Linda R. Tropp, Ulrich Wagner, and Oliver Christ, "Recent Advances in Intergroup Contact Theory," *International Journal of Intercultural Relations* 35, no. 3 (2011): 271–80.

72. Lyras and Welty Peachey, "Integrating Sport-for-Development Theory and Praxis."

73. Thomas F. Pettigrew, "Intergroup Contact Theory," *Annual Review of Psychology* 49, no. 1 (1998): 65–85; Pettigrew and Tropp, "A Meta-analytic Test of Intergroup Contact Theory."

74. See also Simon C. Darnell, "Orientalism through Sport: Toward a Said-ian Analysis of Imperialism and 'Sport for Development and Peace,'" *Sport in Society* 17, no. 8 (2014):

1004–14; Darnell and Hayhurst, "Sport for Decolonization: Exploring a New Praxis of Sport for Development."

75. Cunningham et al., "Overcoming Cultural Barriers in Sport Management Study Abroad Programs: The Influence of Extended Intergroup Contact"; Cunningham and Melton, "The Moderating Effects of Contact with Lesbian and Gay Friends on the Relationships among Religious Fundamentalism, Sexism, and Sexual Prejudice"; Miles Hewstone, Ed Cairns, Alberto Voci, Juergen Hamberger, and Ulrike Niens, "Intergroup Contact, Forgiveness, and Experience of 'The Troubles' in Northern Ireland,'" *Journal of Social Issues* 62, no. 1 (2006): 99–120; Pettigrew and Tropp, "A Meta-analytic Test of Intergroup Contact Theory"; Pettigrew et al., "Recent Advances in Intergroup Contact Theory."

76. Lyras and Welty Peachey, "Integrating Sport-for-Development Theory and Praxis."

77. Welty Peachey et al., "The Influence of a Sport-for-Peace Event on Prejudice and Change Agent Self-Efficacy."

78. Laurence Chalip, "Toward a Distinctive Sport Management Discipline," *Journal of Sport Management* 20, no. 1 (2006): 1–21; Stacy M. Warner and Marlene Dixon, "Understanding Sense of Community from an Athlete's Perspective," *Journal of Sport Management* 25, no. 3 (2011): 258–72.

79. Lyras and Welty Peachey, "Integrating Sport-for-Development Theory and Praxis," 317.

80. Ben-Porat, *Global Liberalism, Local Populism: Peace and Conflict in Israel/Palestine and Northern Ireland*; Charles Jones, "Review: Global Liberalism: Political or Comprehensive?" *The University of Toronto Law Journal* 54, no. 2 (2004): 227–48, www.utpjournals.press/loi/utlj.

81. Giulianotti, "The Sport, Development and Peace Sector: A Model of Four Social Policy Domains."

82. Jason Means and John Nauright, "Going Global: The NBA Sets Its Sights on Africa," *International Journal of Sports Marketing and Sponsorship* 9, no. 1 (2007): 40–50.

83. Kathy Babiak and Richard Wolfe, "More Than Just a Game? Corporate Social Responsibility and Super Bowl XL," *Sport Marketing Quarterly* 15, no. 4 (2006): 214; Matthew Walker and Aubrey Kent, "Do Fans Care? Assessing the Influence of Corporate Responsibility on Consumer Attitudes in the Sport Industry," *Journal of Sport Management* 23, no. 3 (2009): 743–69.

84. Ron Cregan, "CSR and Sport: Rewards of Being a Good Sport," *Brand Strategy* 223 (2008): 54–55; Paul Snell, "Nike Reveals CSR Targets for 2011," *Supply Management* 12, no. 12 (2007): 7.

85. Baker and Esherick, "Sport-Based Peace Initiatives: Playing for Peace"; Laura Misener and Daniel S. Mason, "Urban Regimes and the Sporting Events Agenda: A Cross-National Comparison of Civic Development Strategies," *Journal of Sport Management* 22, no. 5 (2008): 603; Aaron C. T. Smith and Hans M. Westerbeek, "Sport as a Vehicle for Deploying Corporate Social Responsibility," *Journal of Corporate Citizenship* 25 (2007): 43–54.

86. Coalter, "Sport-for-Development: Going beyond the Boundary?"; Lyras, "Characteristics and Psycho-Social Impacts of an Inter-Ethnic Educational Sport Initiative on Greek and Turkish Cypriot Youth"; Lyras and Welty Peachey, "Integrating Sport-for-Development Theory and Praxis."

87. Coalter, "Sport-for-Development: Going beyond the Boundary?"; Dixon et al., "Management in Sport for Development: Examining the Structure and Processes of a Sport Diplomacy Initiative"; Kidd, "A New Social Movement: Sport for Development and Peace"; Roger Levermore, "Evaluating Sport-for-Development Approaches and Critical Issues," *Progress in*

Development Studies 11, no. 4 (2011): 339–53; Meredith A. Whitley, Tanya Forneris, and Bryce Barker, "The Reality of Implementing Community-Based Sport and Physical Activity Programs to Enhance the Development of Underserved Youth: Challenges and Potential Strategies," *Quest* 66, no. 2 (2013): 218–32.

88. Levermore, "Evaluating Sport-for-Development Approaches and Critical Issues," 340.

89. Kidd, "A New Social Movement: Sport for Development and Peace"; Levermore, "Evaluating Sport-for-Development Approaches and Critical Issues"; United Nations Development Program, *Handbook on Planning, Monitoring and Evaluation for Development Results* (New York: United Nations Development Program, 2009); United States Department of State, "Bureau of Educational and Cultural Affairs (ECA) Request for Grant Proposals, (RFGP)," *Sports Youth Visitor Program* Federal Registry 75, no. 198 (2010): Federal Registry 63247–63257; accessed November 19, 2015, http://eca.state.gov/organizational-funding.

90. Coalter, "Sport-for-Development: Going beyond the Boundary?"

91. Clay Doherty, "Measuring the Impact of Sports on Youth Development," United States Agency for International Development (USAID), March 10, 2011, http://blog.usaid.gov/2011/03/measuring-the-impact-of-sports-on-youth-development/.

92. Robert E. Baker, Pamela H. Baker, Christopher Atwater, and Heather Andrews, "Sport for Development and Peace: A Program Evaluation of a Sport Diplomacy Initiative," *International Journal of Sport Management and Marketing* 16, nos. 1–2 (2015): 16, https:/doi.org/10.1504/IJSMM.2015.074932.

93. Schulenkorf, "Managing Sport-for-Development: Reflections and Outlook."

94. Lyras and Welty Peachey, "Integrating Sport-for-Development Theory and Praxis"; Schulenkorf, "Managing Sport-for-Development: Reflections and Outlook"; Schulenkorf et al., "Sport for Development: An Integrated Literature Review."

95. Baker, Atwater, and Andrews, "Sport for Development and Peace: A Program Evaluation of a Sport Diplomacy Initiative"; Baker, Baker, Evmenova, and Esherick, "Implementation and Evaluation of International Sport Development, Peace, and Diplomacy Programs"; Coalter, "Sport-for-Development: Going beyond the Boundary?"; Lyras, "Characteristics and Psycho-Social Impacts of an Inter-Ethnic Educational Sport Initiative on Greek and Turkish Cypriot Youth"; Lyras, "Olympic Education in Practice: Educational Components of a Sport for Peacebuilding Intervention;" Lyras and Welty Peachey, "Integrating Sport-for-Development Theory and Praxis"; Schulenkorf, "Managing Sport-for-Development: Reflections and Outlook"; Schulenkorf et al., "Sport for Development: An Integrated Literature Review."

96. Allport, *The Nature of Prejudice.*

97. Beer and Nohria, *Breaking the Code of Change.*

98. Baker, Baker, Atwater, and Andrews, "Sport for Development and Peace: A Program Evaluation of a Sport Diplomacy Initiative."

99. Dixon et al., "Management in Sport for Development: Examining the Structure and Processes of a Sport Diplomacy Initiative."

2

Sociological Perspectives on Sport for Development and Peace

Scott R. Jedlicka

OBJECTIVES

This chapter will:

- Describe the sociological theories upon which the efficacy of SDP programs might be evaluated.
- Discuss the goals of SDP programs in the context of critical sociological theory.
- Explain the role of policy and politics in the establishment of SDP programs.
- Address assumptions made by SDP programs.
- Examine the assumption that sport and SDP are intrinsically positive.
- Formulate some ideas for the improvement of SDP programs in the future.

Sport for development and peace (SDP) has been described as "the use of sport to exert a positive influence on public health, the socialisation of children, youths and adults, the social inclusion of the disadvantaged, the economic development of regions and states, and on fostering intercultural exchange and conflict resolution"[1]; more succinctly, SDP has been characterized as "the most recent version of the ideology of 'sport for good.'"[2] It has been called "an international movement" and "a recognised strategy of social intervention in disadvantaged communities throughout the world."[3] Given these expansive and rather glowing descriptions, one cannot help but be drawn in by SDP's intuitive practical appeal as well as its historicity: The notion that sport can have a positive, transformative impact on individuals and societies is embedded in the foundational logics of Muscular Christianity and Olympism, two nineteenth-century philosophies which have indelibly shaped modern sport. The temptation to believe in sport's power to contribute to progressive social change is difficult to resist. However, accepting this premise on blind faith ignores the

Figure 2.1. Young women participate in the Soweto Academy volleyball team practice in the informal settlement of Kibra in Nairobi, Kenya. The volleyball team "The Mighty Minnows" has become a rallying point for the school and surrounding community. *Credit*: Marlene Dixon, Texas A&M University

complexities and challenges of using sport as a development tool, an ignorance that can result not just in failure to realize sport's vast potential, but in outcomes squarely at odds with the SDP movement.[4] To avoid the pitfalls associated with an uncritical approach to sport, SDP researchers and practitioners have increasingly relied on perspectives and frameworks from the field of sociology to inform their analyses and programs. The application of sociological theory to SDP has led to more incisive critiques of sport and its capacity to produce social change, and as a consequence, to a better understanding of the ways in which sport can be used as a development tool.

"PESSIMISM OF THE INTELLECT, OPTIMISM OF THE WILL"

Readers familiar with the SDP literature may recognize this section's title from Fred Coalter's 2013 book, *Sport for Development: What Game Are We Playing?*[5] The phrase, derived from a passage in Antonio Gramsci's *Letters from Prison*, is employed to capture the essential tension between the sober intellectual obligations of the social scientist, on one hand, and the hopeful convictions that inspire SDP programs and practitioners on the other. In other words, the practitioner's earnest rectitude can often complement scientific observation, measurement, and analysis, but it is not a suitable substitute. The distinction is especially salient when empirical evidence challenges or undermines the beliefs of so-called sport-for-development evangelists because, as Coalter argues, "to view research simply as an ideological partner that proves 'success' . . . is to reduce the role of social science to confirming what we already think that we know to be the case."[6] The identification of this fundamental conflict in SDP studies implies a dual approach to the application of sociological theory and methods. The first conceptualizes sport as a tool or intervention and is concerned with measuring the effects of SDP programs on participants and targeted populations to improve sport's efficacy in achieving development outcomes. The second approach is somewhat more reflexive and critical and is concerned with evaluating SDP as a social institution in itself, particularly the ways in which the social structures and ideologies that shape the SDP movement also reinforce embedded biases and power differences. This approach, like the first, ultimately seeks to improve sport and its use as a social intervention but differs in its analytical orientation. If the first approach focuses on *how* to improve SDP projects and programs, the second interrogates the assumption that SDP is necessarily *good* and focuses on *why* (and perhaps whether or under what conditions) SDP efforts ought to be pursued.

While these two approaches to sociological inquiry in SDP are not mutually exclusive, they each call for somewhat different theoretical tools to accomplish their respective tasks. The evaluation of SDP interventions tends to rely on organizational, political, and social psychological theories to assess the efficacy of sport programming and often employs traditional methods of quantitative and qualitative measurement. Analyses of SDP as a social institution tend to adopt a broader frame, drawing connections between sport and other social institutions (race, gender, health, religion, education, etc.) while also relying on methods and (usually critical) perspectives from fields such as history, economics, and cultural studies. Again, these two ways in which researchers study SDP should not be viewed as opposed or conflicted. Rather, they reflect the notion that sport is composed of "enduring relationships, stories, meanings, and social forms that people create together but that exist independent of them."[7] Understanding sport in this way allows researchers to simultaneously treat it as a dependent variable (to study the factors that influence the nature of sport) as well as an independent variable (to examine sport's impact on society). Whether sport is considered to be a *cause* or an *effect* (or both), the ultimate objective of most sport-related intellectual activity is to generate explanations for why, in a given context, sport takes on its particular characteristics and why it produces certain results.

SPORT AS AN INTERVENTION

Discussions and descriptions of SDP invariably invoke the *uses* of sport, a term usually intended to signify the ways in which exposing people to sport (as either spectators or participants) can elicit desired effects and which is based in an understanding of sport as a cultural practice.[8] Such uses of sport can generally be categorized as either *productive* or *corrective*, labels that roughly correspond to the *development* and *peace* components of sport for development and peace. Productive uses of sport might include the promotion of education, social inclusion, and healthy lifestyle practices, while corrective uses of sport include the mitigation of deviant behaviors (crime, violence, etc.) as well as the resolution of more intractable forms of social and political conflict. In either case, the study of sport as an intervention is heavily informed by symbolic interactionism, a major sociological school of thought that "considers the subjective understandings that develop among individuals to be the primary means by which society is 'socially constructed.'"[9] This perspective focuses on "processes of social learning and development" and "how people come to know and give meaning to themselves, others, and the things and events in their lives."[10] In short, the efficacy of sport interventions is increasingly understood to be intimately connected to the ways in which the people targeted by such interventions interpret their sport experiences within the contexts of their day-to-day lives.

SPORT FOR SOCIAL DEVELOPMENT

Perhaps the most basic development goal for SDP initiatives is overcoming social exclusion, or, stated differently, promoting social inclusion.[11] Social exclusion has been defined as "a [set of] process[es] that negatively affects the rights, recognition and/or resources of targets of social exclusion and/or their opportunity to participate in key activities in different societal domains."[12] Conversely, social inclusion is often understood in reference to the development of social capital, defined by Pierre Bourdieu as

> the aggregate of the actual or potential resources that are linked to possession of a durable network of more or less institutionalized relationships of mutual acquaintance and recognition—or in other words, to membership in a group—which provides each of its members with the backing of the collectivity-owned capital, a "credential" that entitles them to credit in the various senses of the word.[13]

Because (especially team) sports are communal activities, requiring personal and group interaction as well as the shared use of space, they are often considered to be key components of social inclusion strategies. However, the relationship between sport and the development of social capital is complicated by a number of factors, not least of which is the observation that sport is a fundamentally voluntary activity: the socially included person has the *privilege* of choosing whether and how to play.[14] Though sport may be uniquely suited to building social capital, this ability is arguably diminished by the authoritative prescription of sport participation as a necessary treatment for the socially excluded. In turn, this insight informs a robust research agenda that has developed around the notion of *perceived barriers* to participation in sport and physical activity, with much of this work grounded in the assumptions of the symbolic interactionist framework. While large *n* studies examining the correlates of sport participation remain prevalent and useful, they are increasingly complemented by research designed to understand particular attitudes and beliefs about sport participation among those belonging to socially excluded groups.[15] Through identifying and eliminating perceived obstacles to sport participation, SDP programs can empower individuals to exercise autonomy in making choices about how to spend their leisure time.

An emphasis on individual perceptions and their role in social behavior is also evident in research concerning the relationship between sport and health. Perhaps unsurprisingly, despite an established link between physical activity and positive health outcomes, sport participation is often stymied by participants' injury fears, negative attitudes about competition, and self-perceptions of relative skill and ability.[16] Especially for young athletes, the influence of family members and peers is instrumental in determining the extent of sport participation.[17] Similar to the notion of using sport to create more inclusive societies, the successful use of sport for health promotion is predicated on fashioning sport experiences that are appealing to prospective participants while accounting for potentially negative perceptions of sport.

Barriers to sport participation are sometimes conceptualized in terms of potential participants' misperceptions about sport and their capacity to participate in it. However, sport itself can contribute to constructing or reinforcing these barriers. For instance, many sport programs are organized around an orthodox gender ideology that normalizes heterosexual masculinity and is, by extension, exclusive of athletes who do not conform to this norm.[18] Despite popular accounts of sport as a platform for overcoming racial and ethnic divisions, sport just as often reinforces oppressive racial ideologies.[19] An overemphasis on elite athletic development can detract from health and social outcomes and ultimately drive down participation rates.[20] In short, sport can contribute to social exclusion just as easily as it can contribute to social inclusion. The implications for SDP are clear. While SDP interventions should be promoted in ways that account for the circumstances, perceptions, and lived experiences of targeted populations, programming should also be adaptable to the needs, attitudes, and beliefs of participants.

REDUCING CRIME, VIOLENCE, AND CONFLICT THROUGH SPORT

In addition to being used to build a more inclusive society, sport is often looked to as a corrective intervention, a method for curing social ills ranging from petty crime and delinquency to longstanding international political conflict. However, the intricate relationship between sport and violence complicates the uses of sport as a method of curbing deviant behavior. Some of the complexity surrounding violence in sport stems from semantic confusion, as there exists a "bewildering constellation of terms that has been used to define the subject matter, many of which have been used interchangeably and often carelessly."[21] In some high-contact sports, violent behavior is a necessary component of game play, and the skillful use of violence is correlated with competitive success in combat sports. The essential question for many sport sociologists is whether sport offers a (relatively safe and controlled) setting for the expression of humans' inherently violent tendencies or whether sport teaches, normalizes, and celebrates violent behavior.[22] While much of the research in this area is concerned with violence among athletes, spectator violence has also received scholarly attention.[23] In both cases, social identity theories feature prominently in explanations of violent behavior, as researchers tend to link violence to "a powerful need to belong, to connect, to be respected."[24] This is particularly true for male athletes, lending further support to the argument that sport-based interventions must account for the relationship between sport participation and self-identity in order to be effective.

If violence cannot be easily divorced from sport, can sport still be an appropriate intervention for curbing deviant behavior? To some extent, questions about the possibility of achieving crime reduction through sport are subsumed under the social inclusion rubric; theoretically, reducing the social isolation and marginalization of certain groups will reduce the likelihood that members of those groups will engage in antisocial behaviors. At the same time, empirical evidence suggests that, in some instances, sport programming specifically implemented as a crime reduction intervention can be an effective tool.[25] However, these interventions rarely have "built in techniques for monitoring their impact on levels of crime or drug use; as a result, it is difficult to be sure about what impact, if any, they have on rates of crime or drug use. Moreover, the absence of any clearly articulated theoretical rationale for these schemes means that, even where success is claimed, it is unclear what specific aspects of the schemes account for that claimed success."[26] As with the use of sport for social inclusion, the application of a sociological lens suggests that sport cannot be unilaterally imposed on a population to achieve the desired end results.

A similar logic applies at the national and international levels where SDP initiatives focus on reducing conflict and building peace between belligerent factions or states. The rhetoric of international sport organizations, particularly the International Olympic Committee, is riddled with references to sport's peace-promoting effects, and this language is increasingly echoed by the United Nations.[27] Despite pervasive beliefs in sport's ability to transcend political conflict, the use of sport for such purposes has been described as "playing with fire" given the "destructive potential" of sport to exacerbate, rather than heal, existing divides.[28] As noted SDP scholar and practitioner John Sugden wrote, after being forced to abandon an SDP program when armed conflict erupted in the Middle East, "Complex political and social problems are usually unresponsive to simplistic solutions" and "culturally focused peace initiatives can work only when preceded by military and political accommodations."[29] Sugden's latter point suggests a need for contextualizing SDP research and practice within broader sociological frameworks.

The difficulties associated with developing and implementing successful sport interventions suggest that while identity-based theories can help identify obstacles to participation (and thus shape programs that are more engaging and potentially more effective than those that do not account for participants' identities and socially constructed perceptions of sport), they are nonetheless limited in the extent to which they can inform SDP as a social, political, and intellectual project. In many cases, SDP programs are implemented by an amalgam of public and private entities, each pursuing interests that are at times conflicted with the interests of others as well as the goals of the program itself. Even if interorganizational conflict is not an issue, intraorganizational (i.e., bureaucratic) complications can lead to suboptimal outcomes. In either instance, theories of power, authority, and decision making can provide a clearer picture of the impact political processes can have on SDP efforts.

THE ROLE OF POLICY AND POLITICS IN SPORT INTERVENTIONS

Like many other types of sport programming, SDP initiatives are often collaborations among private for-profit (e.g., corporate sponsors), private nonprofit (e.g., nongovernmental organizations), and public (i.e., governmental) actors. For-profit actors are likely to be concerned with the public relations aspects of SDP, while nonprofit and public agencies are apt to be more directly concerned with how development efforts serve particular constituencies (and by extension, how serving or satisfying these constituencies meets an agency's medium- and long-term objectives).[30] The reality that SDP programs are developed and delivered by organizations with disparate and often conflicted interests means that those interests inevitably influence the nature of sport interventions.[31] This is especially true for international interventions, which typically involve organizations from the Global North implementing programming in countries of the Global South.[32] Indeed, what it means to be involved in sports development is often politically contested, and SDP organizations must often compete with elite sport organizations for resources and legitimacy.[33]

While a major focus of SDP research is identifying the social conditions under which sport interventions can *work*, making sense of the extant political preconditions—essentially, the interests and balance of power among relevant stakeholders—is arguably just as relevant to understanding the potential efficacy of SDP projects. Familiarity with legislative processes, strategic planning, and competitive positioning can be beneficial to many types of sport organizations, but these capacities are especially salient for SDP organizations that may tend to rely more heavily on volunteer staff.[34] Perhaps more importantly, an incorporation of political concepts into SDP studies allows for a more general consideration of how SDP as an institution relates to, is embedded in, and affects fundamental social structures and ideologies. As noted earlier, it is tempting to treat sport as an inherently positive (or at least value-neutral) activity. However, a prominent sector of SDP research has relied on critical theory to deconstruct and challenge this view of sport, ultimately pushing the field to reevaluate the possibilities and limits of using sport to achieve development goals.

CRITICAL PERSPECTIVES ON SDP

If Coalter's "optimism of the will" describes attempts to apply sociological theory to improve SDP programs (primarily through a better understanding of participants and the contexts in which they engage with sport), the "pessimism of the intellect" refers to an emerging body of literature that takes a critical, reflexive approach to SDP. This is not to suggest that critical perspectives on SDP are wholly cynical about sport's capacity to serve development goals. Rather, critical voices provide a necessary counterbalance to ebullient but often specious claims about sport's potential uses. In theoretical terms, critical perspectives are often contrasted with structural functionalist approaches that treat sport and sport-related phenomena as relatively fixed elements of a given institutional configuration.[35] The juxtaposition may be somewhat of a false dichotomy, as all but the most radical sport sociological research acknowledges that sport serves some manner of social function. Instead, the use of structural functionalism as a foil for critical theorizing about sport might be attributed to the conflation of structural functionalism with an instrumental positivist epistemology, a resistance to the notion that social structures determine behavior, as well as structural functionalism's perceived conservative bias.[36]

Sport sociologist Jay Coakley illustrates the supposed distinction between critical sport sociology and structural functionalism using the example of youth sport participation in the United States:

> Nearly all the research on sport participation and educational achievement has been done in the United States where sport participation is institutionally linked with schools, attendance patterns, eligibility to play school sports, formal team selection processes, grades, and social status among peers and teachers. Under such conditions, it is not surprising that studies consistently show a positive sport participation–academic achievement relationship. However, this tells us more about the organization of schools than the developmental implications of playing sports, and it provides no information about developmental outcomes among young people whose participation occurs outside of school-sponsored sports.[37]

Coakley's argument does not seem to dispute the basic assumption that sport serves a social function, but rather contests the epistemological, methodological, and ideological choices that inform conventional approaches to research. His observation that "outcomes associated with sport participation are contingent and vary with contextual factors" provides the foundation for the sociologically driven sport intervention research discussed earlier.[38] However, it also creates an opportunity to consider SDP as a social institution. Whether or not there exists an actual schism between critical and structural functionalist approaches to SDP, the prevailing critical scholarship has expanded the intellectual conversation beyond the notion that sport is something to be *used*. Through locating and critiquing SDP within the confines of major contemporary social theory, these perspectives have called for a reconsideration of sport's essential elements and organizing principles.

Intellectual critiques of SDP as an institution have borrowed from any number of sociological traditions, but most commonly proceed from theories of power, conflict, and change. While much of this work is in the Marxist tradition, Bourdieu is often identified as the social theorist who has most explicitly included sport within the broader scope of his work.[39] More specifically, Simon Darnell identifies three theoretical frameworks in which critique and theory building in SDP might take place:

1. Gramscian hegemony, which "illustrates the ways in which ideas attain a notion of common sense within relations of dominance and consent" and "the processes by which relatively powerful groups secure their hegemonic position in and through social and political negotiation with subordinated classes"
2. Foucauldian bio-power, "the ability to confer positive change and encourage action deemed appropriate and civil" exercised "across the two poles of the body and the population"
3. Postcolonial theory, a perspective concerned with "the enduring regimes of power and knowledge that proceeded from the dominance of racialized persons by northern stewards through notions of prosperity, respectability and social change"[40]

Each, in its own way, deals with issues of power and ideology. Applied to SDP, these frameworks allow researchers to situate SDP within broader structures of power and to ask questions about the extent to which SDP challenges or reinforces those relationships.

One such question is whether SDP programs challenge or reproduce the causes of the problems they are intended to solve.[41] The proliferation of international SDP efforts, in particular, is intertwined with processes of neoliberal globalization, resulting in "an environment where various non-state actors congregate to promote market-oriented approaches to development."[42] This sort of environment normalizes capitalist social relations and precludes any critique of how markets might contribute to economic inequality. Because many SDP programs seek to address poverty and its related social problems, an inability to identify the basic causes of poverty in a given setting renders these efforts ineffectual. Moreover, to the extent that SDP efforts serve to reinforce the necessity of exploitative economic relations, they can, on balance, do more harm than good. Critiques grounded in conceptions of hegemony have addressed other types of power relations, such as gender and race.[43]

Questions of power can be extended beyond the realm of intergroup social relations and into the realm of bodily and population control. As Darnell writes, "A recurring theme in SDP logic is that of power in its productive sense—often termed 'empowerment'—by which SDP stakeholders often refer to the use of sport to encourage and support positive change in others."[44] This seemingly banal insight, on closer inspection, implies that power over one's body, power over the bodies of a given population, and the ability to define *positive change* are part of a greater discursive struggle, one in which SDP can simultaneously be viewed as a constructive and repressive institution.

The concentration of SDP efforts in the Global South has led many SDP scholars to apply a postcolonial theoretical lens to their research.[45] Critical work in this vein occurs at two levels. The first acknowledges the colonial histories of the locations in which SDP initiatives are often implemented and the fact that many of the ills these efforts are intended to solve are part of colonial legacies of exploitation and domination. The second recognizes that many SDP organizations—which arguably exert a great deal of control over when, where, and how sport is used for development purposes—are based in the Global North and are thus positioned to either maintain or disrupt colonial power structures.[46] This observation complicates popular SDP narratives, as it suggests that the very notion of SDP cannot be decoupled from (and in some instances, may be an extension of) historical colonial oppression.

CONCLUSION

The adoption of sociological perspectives in SDP research is largely a response to "organisations that triumphally profess to have made substantial differences to disadvantaged communities," but whose "evangelical zeal does not seem to correlate with the actual impact of trumpeted programmes."[47] While the advancement of the field has done much to dispel this myth-driven naiveté and develop a more sophisticated understanding of sport's potential for aiding in development efforts, it has also prompted deeper questions about SDP's relationship to intractable global issues, including economic, gender, and racial inequality. Sociological theories and frameworks provide the tools with which researchers can question long-held assumptions about sport's efficacy as an intervention as well as the ideological underpinnings of SDP itself.

Questions

1. Provide one example in your own life as to how sport can bring people together. Provide another example of how sport can do the opposite (drive people apart).
2. What does the author mean by the "Global North" and the "Global South"? How does this relate to a discussion of SDP programs and sociological theory?
3. Provide two counterarguments to the Coakley quote the author uses on page 32.

4. What "violent" or "high-contact" sports are the author talking about on page 30? Can these sports provide participants with positive experiences that can help make them better members of the community? If the answer is yes, provide examples.
5. Distinguish between critical and structural functionalist perspectives on SDP.

Learning Activity

1. Research an SDP program that is from the Global South.
2. Identify one SDP program in each of the major categories (for-profit, non-profit, and public). Review the websites of each of these programs.
3. Choose one of the theories the author identifies on page 33 and conduct additional research on this theory.

Strategies for Success

1. SDP programs should work in partnership with the local population, being careful not to make assumptions. Every community has unique issues that have to be addressed during the planning stages of the program.
2. SDP program goals should be clearly stated and achievable. Program leaders should guard against overly optimistic claims of success.
3. Identify obstacles that can prevent sport participation in the targeted population.
4. Identify what aspects should be present for sport to be considered a positive and effective tool in development activities.

NOTES

1. Alexis Lyras and Jon Welty Peachey, "Integrating Sport-for-Development Theory and Praxis," *Sport Management Review* 14, no. 4 (2011): 311–26, https://doi.org/10.1016/j.smr.2011.05.006.

2. Peter Donnelly, Michael Atkinson, Sarah Boyle, and Courtney Szto, "Sport for Development and Peace: A Public Sociology Perspective," *Third World Quarterly* 32, no. 3 (2011): 589–601, https://doi.org/10.1080/01436597.2011.573947.

3. Bruce Kidd, "A New Social Movement: Sport for Development and Peace," in *Sport and Foreign Policy in a Globalizing World*, ed. Steven J. Jackson and Stephen Haigh (New York: Routledge, 2009), 22–32; Bruce Kidd, "Cautions, Questions and Opportunities in Sport for Development and Peace," *Third World Quarterly* 32, no. 3 (2011): 603–9, https://doi.org/10.1080/01436597.2011.573948.

4. Fred Coalter, "Sport-for-Development: Going beyond the Boundary?" *Sport in Society: Cultures, Commerce, Media, Politics* 13, no. 9 (2010): 1374–91, https://doi.org/10.1080/17430437.2010.510675.

5. Fred Coalter, *Sport for Development: What Game Are We Playing?* (New York: Routledge, 2013), 3.

6. Coalter, *Sport for Development*, 4. The term "sport evangelists" is often attributed to Richard Giulianotti, "Human Rights, Globalization and Sentimental Education: The Case of Sport," *Sport in Society: Cultures, Commerce, Media, Politics* 7, no. 3 (2004): 355–69, https://doi.org/10.1080/1743043042000291686.

7. David Karen and Robert E. Washington, eds. *Sociological Perspectives on Sport: The Games outside the Games* (New York: Routledge, 2015).

8. John Hughson, David Inglis, and Marcus W. Free, *The Uses of Sport: A Critical Study*. (London: Routledge, 2004).

9. Karen and Washington, *Sociological Perspectives on Sport*, 10.

10. Jay Coakley, *Sports in Society: Issues and Controversies*, 11th ed. (New York: McGraw-Hill Education, 2015), 33.

11. Mike Collins and Tess Kay, *Sport and Social Exclusion*, 2nd ed. (New York: Routledge, 2014); see also Ramón Spaaij, Jonathan Magee, and Ruth Jeanes, *Sport and Social Exclusion in Global Society* (New York: Routledge, 2014).

12. Spaaij et al., *Sport and Social Exclusion in Global Society*, 33.

13. Pierre Bourdieu, "The Forms of Capital," in *Handbook of Theory and Research for the Sociology of Education*, ed. John G. Richardson (New York: Greenwood, 1986), 241–58.

14. Collins and Kay, *Sport and Social Exclusion*, xiv.

15. See, for instance, Wendy Z. Hultsman, "The Influence of Others as a Barrier to Recreation Participation among Early Adolescents," *Journal of Leisure Research* 25, no. 2 (1993): 150–64, https://doi.org/10.1080/00222216.1993.11969915; Lorraine B. Robbins, Nola J. Pender, and Anamaria S. Kazanis, "Barriers to Physical Activity Perceived by Adolescent Girls," *Journal of Midwifery and Women's Health* 48, no. 3 (2003): 206–12, https://doi.org/10.1016/S1526-9523(03)00054-0; Laurien M. Buffart, Tessa Westendor, Rita J. G. van den Berg-Emons, Henk J. Stam, and Marij E. Roebroeck, "Perceived Barriers to and Facilitators of Physical Activity in Young Adults with Childhood-Onset Physical Disabilities," *Journal of Rehabilitation Medicine* 41, no. 11 (2009): 881–85, https://doi.org/10.2340/16501977-0420.

16. Ivan Waddington, "Sport and Health: A Sociological Perspective," in *The Handbook of Sports Studies*, ed. Jay Coakley and Eric Dunning (Thousand Oaks, CA: Sage, 2000), 408–21.

17. Bente Wold and Norman Anderssen, "Health Promotion Aspects of Family and Peer Influences on Sport Participation," *International Journal of Sport Psychology* 23, no. 4 (1992): 343–59; Sharon Wheeler, "The Significance of Family Culture for Sports Participation," *International Review for the Sociology of Sport* 47, no. 2 (2012): 235–52, https://doi.org/10.1177/1012690211403196.

18. Coakley, *Sports in Society*, 181–83.

19. C. Richard King, David J. Leonard, and Kyle W. Kusz, "White Power and Sport: An Introduction," *Journal of Sport and Social Issues* 31, no. 1 (2007): 3–10, https://doi.org/10.1177/0193723506296821.

20. Tom Farrey, *Game On: The All-American Race to Make Champions of Our Children* (New York: ESPN Books, 2008).

21. Kevin Young, *Sport, Violence and Society*, 2nd ed. (New York: Routledge, 2019).

22. Michael A. Messner, "When Bodies Are Weapons: Masculinity and Violence in Sport," *International Review for the Sociology of Sport* 25, no. 3 (1990): 203–20, https://doi.org/10.1177%2F101269029002500303.

23. Richard Giulianotti, Norman Bonney, and Mike Hepworth, eds., *Football, Violence and Social Identity* (New York: Routledge, 1994).

24. Michael A. Messner, "Male Athletes, Injuries, and Violence," in *Sociological Perspectives on Sport: The Games outside the Games*, ed. David Karen and Robert E. Washington (New York: Routledge, 2015), 446–55.

25. Douglas Hartmann and Brooks Depro, "Rethinking Sports-Based Community Crime Prevention: A Preliminary Analysis of the Relationship between Midnight Basketball and Urban Crime Rates," *Journal of Sport and Social Issues* 30, no. 2 (2006): 180–96.

26. Andy Smith and Ivan Waddington, "Using 'Sport in the Community Schemes' to Tackle Crime and Drug Use among Young People: Some Policy Issues and Problems," *European Physical Education Review* 10, no. 3 (2004): 279–98.

27. Ingrid Beutler, "Sport Serving Development and Peace: Achieving the Goals of the United Nations through Sport," *Sport in Society: Cultures, Commerce, Media, Politics* 11, no. 4 (2008): 359–69, https://doi.org/10.1080/17430430802019227; see also Richard Giulianotti, "Sport, Peacemaking and Conflict Resolution: A Contextual Analysis and Modelling of the Sport, Development and Peace Sector," *Ethnic and Racial Studies* 34, no. 2 (2011): 207–28, https://doi.org/10.1080/01419870.2010.522245.

28. Peter Donnelly, "From War without Weapons to Sport for Development and Peace: The Janus-face of Sport," *SAIS Review of International Affairs* 31, no. 1 (2011): 65–76, https://doi.org/10.1353/sais.2011.0015.

29. John Sugden, "Anyone for Football for Peace? The Challenges of Using Sport in the Service of Co-existence in Israel," *Soccer and Society* 9, no. 3 (2008): 405–15, https://doi.org/10.1080/14660970802009023.

30. Richard Giulianotti, "The Sport, Development and Peace Sector: A Model of Four Social Policy Domains," *Journal of Social Policy* 40, no. 4 (2011): 757–76, https://doi.org/10.1017/S0047279410000930.

31. Simon C. Darnell, "Power, Politics and 'Sport for Development and Peace': Investigating the Utility of Sport for International Development," *Sociology of Sport Journal* 27, no. 1 (2010): 54–75, https://doi.org/10.1123/ssj.27.1.54.

32. Roger Levermore, "Sport in International Development: Time to Treat It Seriously?" *The Brown Journal of World Affairs* 14, no. 2 (2008): 55–66.

33. Barrie Houlihan and Anita White, *The Politics of Sports Development: Development of Sport or Development through Sport?* (New York: Routledge, 2002).

34. Patti Millar and Alison Doherty, "Capacity Building in Nonprofit Sport Organizations: Development of a Process Model," *Sport Management Review* 19, no. 4 (2016): 365–77, https://doi.org/10.1016/j.smr.2016.01.002; Lucie Thibault, Trevor Slack, and Bob Hinings, "A Framework for the Analysis of Strategy in Nonprofit Sport Organizations," *Journal of Sport Management* 7, no. 1 (1993): 25–53, https://doi.org/10.1123/jsm.7.1.25; Laurence Chalip, "Policy Analysis in Sport Management," *Journal of Sport Management* 9, no. 1 (1995): 1–13, https://doi.org/10.1123/jsm.9.1.1.

35. Cora Burnett, "Assessing the Sociology of Sport: On Sport for Development and Peace," *International Review for the Sociology of Sport* 50, nos. 4–5 (2015): 385–90, https://doi.org/10.1177/1012690214539695.

36. John W. Loy and Douglas Booth, "Functionalism, Sport and Society," in *The Handbook of Sports Studies*, ed. Jay Coakley and Eric Dunning (Thousand Oaks, CA: Sage, 2000), 8–27.

37. Jay Coakley, "Youth Sports: What Counts as 'Positive Development'?" *Journal of Sport and Social Issues* 35, no. 3 (2011): 306–24.

38. Coakley, "Youth Sports," 318.

39. Pierre Bourdieu, "Sport and Social Class," *Social Science Information* 17, no. 6 (1978): 819–40, https://doi.org/10.1177/053901847801700603; Pierre Bourdieu, "Program for a Sociology of Sport," *Sociology of Sport Journal* 5, no. 2 (1988): 153–61. Bourdieu's concept of social capital, in particular, has been deployed to study how sport contributes to social development.

40. Simon C. Darnell, *Sport for Development and Peace: A Critical Sociology* (New York: Bloomsbury Academic, 2012).

41. Fred Coalter, "The Politics of Sport-for-Development: Limited Focus Programmes and Broad Gauge Problems?" *International Review for the Sociology of Sport* 45, no. 3 (2010): 295–314, https://doi.org/10.1177/1012690210366791.

42. Lyndsay M. C. Hayhurst, Brian Wilson, and Wendy Frisby, "Navigating Neoliberal Networks: Transnational Internet Platforms in Sport for Development and Peace," *International Review for the Sociology of Sport* 46, no. 3 (2011): 315–29, https://doi.org/10.1177/1012690210380575.

43. Simon C. Darnell, "Sport, Race, and Bio-politics: Encounters with Difference in 'Sport for Development and Peace' Internships," *Journal of Sport and Social Issues* 34, no. 4 (2010): 396–417, https://doi.org/10.1177/0193723510383141; Lyndsay M. C. Hayhurst, Tess Kay, and Megan Chawansky, eds., *Beyond Sport for Development and Peace: Transnational Perspectives on Theory, Policy and Practice* (New York: Routledge, 2016).

44. Darnell, *Sport for Development and Peace*, 29.

45. The *Global South* refers generally to the countries of Asia (excluding Japan, South Korea, Taiwan, Singapore, and the regions of Hong Kong and Macau), Africa, Oceania (excluding Australia and New Zealand), Central America, and South America.

46. Simon C. Darnell and Lyndsay M. C. Hayhurst, "Sport for Decolonization: Exploring a New Praxis of Sport for Development," *Progress in Development Studies* 11, no. 3 (2011): 183–96.

47. Nico Schulenkorf and Daryl Adair, "Sport-for-Development: The Emergence and Growth of a New Genre," in *Global Sport-for-Development: Critical Perspectives*, ed. Nico Schulenkorf and Daryl Adair (London: Palgrave Macmillan, 2013), 3–14.

3

Sport Development: A Sheep in Wolf's Clothing?

B. Christine Green and Edward Horne

OBJECTIVES

This chapter will:

- Distinguish between sport development and sport for development.
- Describe the effects of the sport development pyramid.
- Discuss the key tasks associated with sport development, such as recruitment, retention, and transition.
- Contrast the *up-or-out* versus *cradle-to-grave* sport systems.
- Describe the potential benefits and concerns of competition in sports.
- Discuss how the implementation of sport impacts both sport and nonsport developmental objectives.

The term *development* has been defined as "the act, process, or result of developing."[1] Not a very helpful definition. The lack of precision is a particular problem when studying development in the context of sport because the word *development* is used in many different ways. To alleviate the confusion, it is useful to be clear about what is meant by *sport development*.

In practice, development is often equated with growth, progression, expansion, and other versions of positive change.[2] This is particularly true in the field of sport and development, in which development is portrayed as a means by which to enhance the lives of participants, their communities, and the broader society.[3] It is important to note that exactly *what* is being developed and how one chooses to develop it are open to interpretation. Consider the term *sport development*. There are a number of ways to unpack the meaning of this phrase. Are we developing sport? A particular sport? Sport participants? Sport organizations? Although these differ in the object of development and the potential process of development, they share the fundamental assumption that the goal is improving sport. Alternatively, sport can be considered the tool or process used to develop something else. Over time, terminology has evolved to differentiate the two. Sport development has come to be associated with processes designed to develop sport itself. *Sport for development* (and a host of similar terms) is now understood to describe the use of sport to facilitate the development of other (nonsport) outcomes. But is this separation useful or does it undermine programs' capacity to deliver a full range of benefits to participants? Let's look first at the core elements of sport development.

Sport development is driven by two overarching goals: (1) to increase participation in sport; and (2) to enhance the quality of athletic performance. In theory, these goals are intertwined. A large participant base ostensibly creates a more extensive pool of athletes from which elite performers can be identified and trained. Thus elite sport programs have a stake in the recruitment and retention of participants in other programs from which they might draw athletes. Programs serving athletes at lesser skill levels train their participants to transition to more elite programs. They can then use the prestige of producing athletes for the "next level" to recruit more, and potentially more highly skilled, athletes to their own program. In this way, programs that differentiate themselves based on skill and competitive level of their athletes enjoy a symbiotic relationship with programs from which they recruit participants as well as those recruiting their athletes. The often-used analogy to represent this system is the sport development pyramid (figure 3.1). The pyramid is a simplified representation of the pathway athletes take to go from beginner to elite performer.[4]

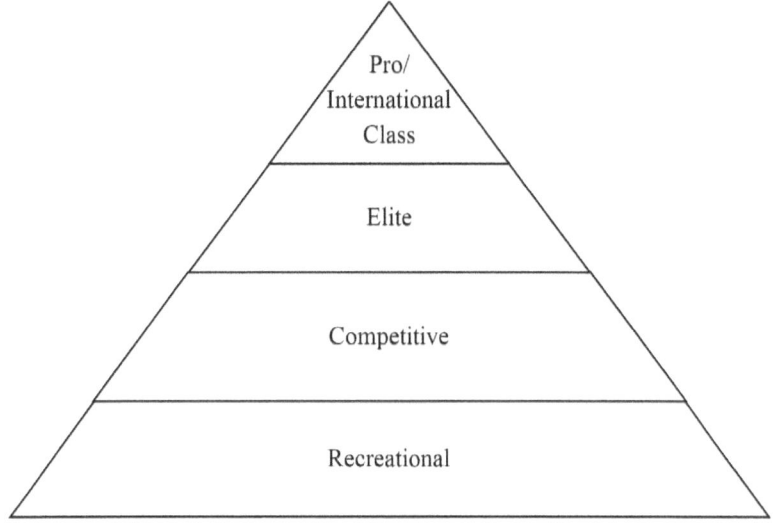

Figure 3.1. Pyramid model of sport development pathways.

Entry into a sport occurs at the base of the pyramid. There are few, if any, skill requirements as this is considered the place for beginners. Thus the base of any particular sport would be expected to have the largest number of participants. In theory, participants can enter a sport at any age. In practice, the base of the pyramid tends to be served by youth sport organizations. Each layer of the pyramid represents increasingly skilled athletes served by fewer, more competitive-focused programs. In this way, participation opportunities narrow as one moves up the levels of the pyramid. It makes sense that as the competitive levels increase, the pool of athletes with the requisite skill level needed to be successful will decrease. And yet one could argue that the structure of most sport programs, particularly those in the United States, artificially limits the number of athletes that move to the next level of the pyramid through try-outs and limits on the number of teams at each level (at least within programs). For example, according to the Sports and Fitness Industry Association, 4.2 million youth ages six through twelve participated in basketball in 2018.[5] Of those 4.2 million youth players, fewer than 1 million played at the high school level (540,769 boys and 399,067 girls).[6] The number of participants declines alarmingly as the competitive level increases, with just 35,325 NCAA college basketball players (18,816 males and 16,509 females),[7] 450 professional NBA players,[8] and only 144 professional WNBA players.[9] A key assumption underlying pyramid-based sport development systems is that the cream will rise to the top. Therefore, each program within a sport system must consider three key tasks to sustain their organization: recruitment, retention, and transition of athletes. But is this all that different from the key tasks of sport for development?

Sport-for-development programs must also attract participants and retain them in the program long enough to obtain the development outcomes of interest. Although less explicit than in the case of sport development, there would seem to be an underlying goal of helping participants transition to more advanced settings. Note that *advanced* in this case is not sport-related. Rather, it is related to the development outcomes and skills core to the organization's mission. Sport-for-development programs focused on individual development often operate on a deficit model,[10] whereby participants are identified and selected based on a perceived lack—lack of access, opportunity, voice, power, and so on. For example, Skateistan is dedicated to "empowering children through skateboarding and education."[11] They describe their focus this way:

> We are an award-winning international non-profit organization which empowers children through skateboarding and education in Afghanistan, Cambodia and South Africa. By combining skateboarding with creative, arts-based education, we give children the opportunity to become leaders for a better world. Our focus is on groups who are often excluded from sports and educational opportunities, especially girls, children living with disabilities and those from low-income backgrounds.

Their program in Afghanistan serves children who are not in school. It provides them with the education needed to transition back into the public school system. Thus their transition is critical to their ongoing education.

KEY TASKS OF SPORT DEVELOPMENT

Let's examine each of these tasks and compare the objectives, experiences, and outcomes with those of sport-for-development programs (i.e., programs whose main goal is not sport performance but some other development outcome).

Recruitment

The first and most critical task of any sport program is to obtain participants. Although we rarely discuss it in these terms, the recruitment task is essentially a marketing exercise. A marketing perspective suggests that sport programs should be designed to meet the needs of the market (i.e., potential customers). It is then a matter of effectively identifying and communicating the benefits of the sport program (i.e., the product/service) to potential customers. This is complicated by the fact that initial recruitment into sport generally occurs at a young age (four to seven years old). Although some programs recruit children as young as age two or three, the American Academy of Pediatrics suggests six as a more appropriate age to begin participation in team sports.[12] Although the sport participant is the consumer, the parent is the one purchasing the sport experience for the child. Therefore, the marketing messages must be two-pronged: (1) they should present the sport experience in a way that appeals to kids; and (2) they should present the benefits of the experience to appeal to parents' desires for their children. We know that children are attracted to sport by its potential for fun.[13] They want to be involved in the action, to develop skills, and to play with their friends. This holds true for children and young people of all ages.[14] Parents have deeper expectations for their child's sport participation. Parents see sport as a venue for achievement, competitiveness, discipline, and teamwork.[15]

The key recruitment tasks for sport organizations are to generate interest in the sport and to stimulate purchase. In other words, sport organizations need to make the sport (and their sport programs) attractive to potential participants and their parents. They must be interested enough to take action and register to participate. This sounds straightforward, but remember that kids and parents often seek different experiences and outcomes from youth sport experiences.[16] So sport organizations need to position themselves to be attractive to both participants (kids) and purchasers (parents). This can be difficult, with sport organizations often relying on shibboleths to convince parents that participation will provide a host of development outcomes that go beyond the sport setting—for example, self-discipline, getting along with others, and competing successfully. Notice that these life skills are expected to happen automatically, just by playing sport. Few sport organizations do anything to explicitly include programming to provide development outcomes beyond the development of sport skills. In fact, implementation matters! Sport participation can just as easily teach children to behave unethically, to put individual success over team success, and to value winning above all else. It is not the sport, per se, that makes the difference. It is the way in which the sport is implemented and the intentionality of the program design that ensures positive outcomes for children (or doesn't). These are the very kinds of outcomes that are explicit in sport-for-development programs. Yet sport-for-development programs have their own issues when it comes to recruitment.

Sport-for-development programs are designed to deliver benefits beyond the sport itself. Their focus may be on health, education, empowerment, conflict resolution, inclusion, or a host of other development outcomes.[17] None of these benefits require sport participation. And yet the field of sport for development is built upon the association of sport and development outcomes. Consequently, programs often use sport as a hook to attract participants to programs seeking to develop nonsport outcomes.[18] Since youth programs seek to appeal to both participants and their parents, it would seem to be a reasonable marketing strategy: sell the sport and the fun it engenders to participants, and sell the development and the nonsport benefits to parents. However, when participants enter a sport program, they expect to gain sport skills.[19] When programs use the promise of sport to attract participants, they have an obligation to provide quality sport or they risk losing their participant base. This obligation includes developing participants' sport skills. And yet many of these programs fail to see the sport element as core to their development mission. Consequently, the focus and resources are there to support the nonsport elements of the program, and the sport elements are peripheral. This may be necessary to attract parents and funding bodies, but it can be insufficient to maintain participation long enough to deliver the intended benefits.[20] Other sport-for-development programs are built on the belief that sport, in and of itself, provides positive benefits to participants.[21] If that is the case, then one can merely provide some kind of sport experience to deliver the intended benefits. Again, programs must be designed and implemented to deliver the intended benefits or they will fail to attract or keep participants. As Douglas Hartmann and Christina Kwauk argue, "[I]f sport is to have a productive effect in development (and it can and often does), it is typically when sport programs are organized and structured in purposive, systematic ways to achieve them."[22]

In summary, both types of programs use sport to attract participants. Each, at least for children, must target the needs and desires of participants as well as purchasers. And, although the two program types may appeal to distinctive sets of motives and target markets, the key task is to design and implement a program that can deliver the intended benefits. Not only does this attract participants, but it also goes far in maintaining their participation.

Retention

Retention strategies are the linchpin in any sport development system. The retention process links the two processes of sport development. Recruitment in and of itself is insufficient to create elite performance. Participants must stay in the sport long enough to develop the skills necessary for elite performance. This requires attention to the socialization of participants into the subculture of the sport, program, and team.[23] It is important to note that the reasons people begin to participate in a sport are not the same as their motives to remain in the sport or with a program.[24] Rather, there is a process of discovery in which participants are exposed to elements of the sport that were unexpected. For example, rugby participants have reported joining the sport to be with friends or because family members participated. Yet when asked why they continue to play, the same participants note valuing the physicality of the sport or the sense of mastery engendered by their participation. Thus the reasons driving initial attraction to a sport or sport setting are not necessarily the reasons driving commitment to the sport, program, or team. The key task facing managers and program personnel is to help participants learn to value a range of experiences and outcomes beyond the ones that drew them to the sport in the first place and to facilitate their commitment to the sport.

Socialization processes are critical to shaping the ways in which participants interpret their experiences and the elements they learn to value.[25] When entering a sport setting, it takes time to understand the subculture of the setting, including the way things are done (e.g., what is acceptable and unacceptable behavior), the meanings attached to behaviors and rituals, and the ways in which participants value elements of the setting and the sport.[26] The socialization process occurs via interactions with other members of the subculture and affects participants' identity and commitment to the sport and the team or club. For example, skateboarders quickly learn to dress like other skateboarders, talk like them, and even mimic the moves and other behaviors of other members of the skateboard community. These elements mark them as a skateboarder to others and can become part of their self- and social identity. These actions constrain their future behavior within the subculture and reinforce their identity as a skateboarder. In this way, early behaviors are seen as *side bets* that are either reinforced or extinguished by other members of the subculture.[27] When reinforced, they also enhance and reinforce athletes' commitment to and retention in the sport. Alas, side bets are only one element of athletes' commitment and can occur without any conscious decision to commit.

Christopher Stevenson identified two key considerations in athletes' decisions to commit to a sport: (1) their potential for success; and (2) the people associated with the sport.[28] These considerations have implications for developing athletes' commitment to and thus retention in the sport. First, athletes must both see a pathway to the next level of the sport and feel that they are developing the skills to be successful at that level. Notice this is not about winning; rather, it is about mastery. Second, athletes need to feel that they belong and that the people involved in the sport, especially coaches and other athletes, are like them and support them. In short, they want to feel that they are part of a community of people who share their values and experiences.[29] When these two elements combine, participants are more likely to commit to a sport.

Commitment is often confused with specialization in sport. Yet one can commit to more than one sport. In fact, multisport athletes develop skills that enhance their capabilities across sport settings.[30] Jean Côté and his colleagues consistently show sport sampling to be associated with long-term involvement in sport and future success in elite sport settings.[31] And yet sport clubs, coaches, and administrators work to convince players (and parents of young players) that commitment requires them to drop all other sports to specialize in one (theirs, of course). This is often self-serving as it is used to retain athletes (and their fees) in a program; to keep the "best" athletes out of the hands of other coaches, programs, and sports; and to create or maintain the competitive success of the program. Too often, there is pressure to specialize too early.

This pressure is not entirely unwarranted, even when it is not in the developmental interests of the participants. Increasingly, it is necessary to specialize early to have the opportunity to make it to the next level, and therefore continue to participate. When there are multiple participation opportunities across a wide range of skill and developmental levels for all age groups, then early specialization is not necessary. However, our sport systems increasingly limit the number of opportunities to participate by imposing artificial restrictions on participation through tryouts, cuts, and fewer teams (and therefore participation opportunities) available. Opportunities are further limited when one considers the trend toward specialization and year-round participation in a single sport. The same athletes now take up more of the participation opportunities in a sport rather than moving on to another sport, and they do so at younger and younger ages. In this way, fewer athletes have a viable pathway to success in a sport.

Sport-for-development programs are avowedly less about the sport than about development. However, that does not excuse these organizations from their responsibility to develop sport skills and abilities in conjunction with the nonsport outcomes they seek. After all, that is what they promise, whether that promise is explicit or implicit. When sport is part of the program, it should also be part of the development agenda.

Like sport development programs, retention is important for sport-for-development programs. Each must retain participants long enough for them to obtain the benefits the program seeks to provide. For sport development, the benefits tend to be outcomes related to the sport itself: physical skills, mental skills, strategic knowledge, teamwork, and so on. Sport-for-development organizations, on the other hand, seek to provide benefits beyond the sport. These can be related to health, education, social inclusion, community building, empowerment, conflict resolution, or any number of nonsport outcomes. Each takes time and effort to achieve; thus organizations must retain participants to achieve their aims. When based on a deficit model, like the educational objectives of the Skateistan program discussed at the start of the chapter, success is defined as no longer needing the program (e.g., in the case of Skateistan, success is defined as integrating back into the school system). So what keeps participants engaged in these programs long enough to reap the benefits?

Much like sport development programs, participants are more likely to remain in a program when they feel competent in the activity and feel connected with others.[32] In other words, two elements are critical to retention: the capacity for success and a connection to the people involved. With sport-for-development programs, it is not clear what competence means to participants. Is it competence in the sport or the nonsport activities that matters? Can one compensate for the other? Does it vary by participant? These are important questions that need to be answered. The answers may lie in lessons from sport development. Think back to the discussion of the socialization processes that nurture participants' commitment to their sport and program. Participants learn to value their experiences in new ways through the interactions they have with other participants, coaches, and other members of the sport community. This process likely also occurs in sport-for-development programs, albeit unintentionally. And yet these programs can and should be designed intentionally to shape the value participants place on their own development, whatever the outcome of interest may be. This is particularly important for participants attracted by the sport rather than the nonsport elements of a program. Once again, implementation matters. It's less about what the program provides than how the program can shift the attitudes of its participants to more highly value their own development, both in terms of the sport (the initial attractor) and the nonsport objectives of the program.

Both sport and sport-for-development program participants stay, in large part, because of the people involved. These include the other participants, as well as program leaders. We saw in sport programs that coaches make a difference not just for their ability to enhance players' skills but also in the enthusiasm and passion they have for the sport and their ability to make participants feel that they matter. Sport-for-development programs have multiple adults involved in a mentoring capacity. Some have sport coaches deliver all program elements, some have elements (including sport) delivered by those with expertise in the nonsport foci, and still others have both sport and development experts deliver the program. Although no research has explored the roles and impact of the various human resource structures in sport-for-development programs, we do have evidence of the importance of mentors to ongoing participation.[33] Participants suggest that adult mentors must walk a fine line between sharing relevant knowledge and expertise and avoiding behaviors associated with authority figures.[34] As B. Christine Green notes, "[T]he most powerful adult-participant relationships are those in which the adult is able to empower the participant to take ownership of the programme, embracing the intended goals and processes of the programme."[35] Ownership requires that participants have a voice in the program. While this is an important element in the success of sport-for-development programs, and youth development programs more generally,[36] this aspect is surprisingly absent from expectations in traditional sport programs.

Transition

The third task of sport development speaks to the relationships among sport programs and the task of enhancing the quality of athletic performance and competitive success. Sometimes called *advancement*, the charge is to develop athletes to compete at a higher level than their current program. On the surface, this task seems straightforward. As athletes improve, they should move to a more advanced setting for training and competition. Individual sport athletes can advance fairly easily and can often remain in one setting as they advance. For example, track and field athletes may train with a large club with multiple coaches. As athletes improve, they may only have to move to a different training group within the club. This may necessitate a change in training times or even a change in the primary coach, but it is simple to do within one's home club. Tennis players advance in their rating or ranking, which then qualifies them for more competitive tournament opportunities. They may need to shift coaches as their skill improves and they achieve higher levels of competitive success. It is more complex for team sport athletes as they are committed to a team. Most leagues have policies that regulate player movement, thereby keeping players with one team at least for a season and sometimes longer. For example, the NCAA regulates athletes' eligibility and capacity to transfer to another institution.[37]

One way to ease athletes' transitions between levels is to have multiple levels within the same organization. In the United States, we see this in many of our youth sport organizations. The same club will often have intramural house (sometimes called *recreational*) leagues for beginners. These teams are mainly age-based and compete at the same site with other teams within the club. House teams do not cut participants; all are placed on a team. Some clubs use a draft-based system to create teams with an eye toward competitive parity. Others attempt to keep social groups together. As athletes improve, they can try out for transition teams within their club, sometimes called *academy teams*. These teams are a stepping stone toward the select travel teams hosted by a club. For example, the Northern Virginia Soccer Club calls its transition program the NVSC Future Stars program.[38] Its goal is "to further prepare our younger players for more competitive soccer environments and training." The Future Stars program is intended to supplement, not replace, recreational soccer participation and adds four additional matches against other local transition teams. It requires players to try out for the team and limits the number of opportunities to participate. The purpose of the program is to introduce more competition and higher levels of training to prepare athletes for more select travel teams. For many players, this is the first step toward specialization and year-round play in a single sport.

Travel teams are the next step for players seeking to advance in the sport. Travel teams require significant investment in time and money on the part of the athletes and their families[39] and nearly always require athletes to curtail other sport participation. In this way, travel teams limit player opportunities in several ways. The most obvious limitation is on the number of teams and athletes that can compete on each team. Travel teams are marketed as *select* or *elite* participation opportunities and require athletes to try out for a place on the team, thus limiting the number of roster spots available. And yet the sheer number of travel teams in a community suggests that they are not as *elite* as they claim. The other limitation is less obvious and is directly related to the resources needed to participate. Travel teams are typically coached by professional coaches, practice more often than recreational teams, and require families to commit more family time to the sport. Consequently, travel teams can be expensive and may not be feasible for families in which parents cannot afford to take time off work to shuttle their children to practices or to travel with them on weekends. Athletes from low-income families are thus disadvantaged by the emergent importance of travel teams in the American sport development system. On a positive note, some programs provide scholarships, and movement between programs within a single club can ease players' transitions by providing consistency in coaching, philosophy, and administration. But where do athletes go next to continue their development in the sport?

Many countries depend on club-based sport development systems that provide so-called *cradle-to-grave* participation within a single club. These clubs field teams at all ages and skill levels, providing opportunities to move from team to team across the lifespan.[40] Importantly, fielding multiple teams at different age and skill levels allows athletes to move up to higher levels of competition but also to stay within level, or even move from a highly competitive context to one that is more recreational in nature. Horizontal and downward transitions are rare in the US system as organizations providing sport are usually age- or skill-based and lack formal linkages among them.[41] Instead, the American system tends to provide *up or out* player movement, in which athletes transition to a more advanced competitive context via tryout or talent identification programs.[42] Athletes who fail to make the next level have few opportunities to continue their participation and instead discontinue their participation, shift to another sport, or shift their involvement from active participation to passive spectation or other leisure pursuits.[43] Thus sport development pathways that require athletes to move from program to program have great difficulty retaining athletes.[44] Some fail to make the cut and are left with few alternatives to continue their participation, others have difficulty adjusting to the new context, and a few go on to succeed at the new level. The question becomes, how can we reduce the number of athletes lost in the transition process?

Two foci can enhance the transition process for athletes: (1) organizational linkages that facilitate athlete movement; and (2) sociocultural facilitation into the setting. First, organizations from all along the sport development pathway can develop linkages to facilitate the movement of athletes from program to program. These linkages should not require athletes to move up to another team or drop out as they age out of a program. Instead, there should be clear linkages to other programs, and perhaps even to other sports, that allow athletes to continue their sport participation at the same level. Ideally, relationships among organizations would also allow athletes to move back a level during times of injury, when other aspects of their lives take precedence over their sport, or just because they enjoy a different type of setting. These changes could be temporary or more long lasting, providing athletes with the ability to transition to more competitive environments at a later date or continue participation at a level of their choice and capacity.

Second, athletes need assistance in making the transition to a new setting. When athletes transition to more advanced settings, the physical demands of training and competing increase. Coaches and trainers are aware of this and consider how best to work incrementally to assist athletes to transition effectively. However, the change is not merely about the physical demands of the new setting. Athletes are placed in a new setting in which they must adapt to a new culture, new expectations, new people and relationships, and often a change in status.[45] These are not easy adaptations, particularly when the athlete may be leaving his or her support system as part of the transition. Consequently, sport managers need to consider how best to assist athletes to adapt to the new setting both socially and psychologically. In many ways, the transition process is similar to that of *culture shock* as defined by Wikipedia:[46]

> an experience a person may have when one moves to a cultural environment which is different from one's own; it is also the personal disorientation a person may feel when experiencing an unfamiliar way of life, . . . a move between social environments, or simply a transition to another type of life.[47]

Culture shock is a process whereby individuals cycle through four phases: the honeymoon phase, crisis or culture shock, adjustment and reorientation, and adaptation.[48] Consider the example of a star high school volleyballer making the transition to college volleyball. At first, the athlete is excited and sees the differences in a positive way. As the athlete becomes more immersed in the new culture, perhaps participating in the first preseason practices prior to the start of classes, things start to go wrong. They finish last in sprints, they don't understand the offensive system, the team uses terms they are unfamiliar with and seems to have inside jokes. In other words, the differences are no longer exciting or positive; they now lead to disappointment and frustration. The athlete may long for home or for their old team, teammates, and routines. It is important that athletes understand that they will go through some culture shock, that it is normal, and that the team and the support structures are there to help them get through it. Then the support system needs to work with athletes to support them emotionally and assist them to adjust to the new setting. Once they are able to make adaptations on their own, they have entered the adaptation or acculturation stage. Each of the stages is accompanied by stress, cognitive fatigue, and threats to one's identity. For athletes, the psychological stress is accompanied by the physical stress of training and competing, and they require a new social network to affirm their belonging.[49]

Sport-for-development organizations are less likely than sport development organizations to depend on or to be part of an overall system of development with pathways to excellence. Yet they too can benefit from coordination with other development-focused organizations. Consider the A Ganar program of Partners of the Americas. The focus of the A Ganar program is described this way: "Through the power of sport, we help youth in some of the toughest communities in Latin America and the Caribbean find employment or return to school." They go on to explain their focus:

> With an innovated series of field and classroom sport-based activities, we help youth transfer lessons from sport, including teamwork, communication and leadership, into market-driven skills and attitudes. We connect our youth with mentors, and provide market-driven vocational training, internships and opportunities for community service.

Over just seven to nine months, youth emerge with the practical skills necessary to return to the classroom or launch a career.[50]

Clearly this program uses sport to attract participants and to retain them long enough to enhance their employability. And yet the targeted participants are neither in school nor in the workforce. This organization faces the same two challenges faced by sport organizations: the need to develop and formalize pathways to success and the need to assist participants in their acculturation. The end points are different, but the processes are the same. A Ganar programs require linkages with schools, vocational training centers, and businesses in the community. Without a pathway to employability, the program is not sustainable and will not achieve its goals. The second challenge is perhaps more difficult to overcome. The lives and the culture in which the youth targeted by A Ganar programs bear little resemblance to the cultures of school or work. Thus the potential for culture shock is great. In this case, the sport-based activities may be the first point of familiarity for participants. Program coordinators would do well to incorporate program graduates to assist participants in their adjustment into the structured environment of the program and its end goal: employment. In any case, the suggestions for creating a welcoming environment and stimulating participants' sense of belonging are relevant to both sport development and sport-for-development organizations and should be modified to appeal to the participant groups and the cultures in which they are embedded.

DISTINCTIVENESS

When one considers the critical tasks of sport development and those of sport for development, one begins to wonder just how distinctive they are. Both have development goals; each must recruit and retain participants and create pathways toward that development. Both have the capacity, depending on their structure and implementation, to facilitate development of sport and nonsport outcomes, although their relative focus on one or the other is unique to the organizational context. So why is sport seen as intrinsically beneficial when used in sport-for-development programs, but as potentially problematic when implemented for its own purpose? No one would argue that physical activity and skill development are not important. In fact, the health benefits of physical activity are often the focus of sport-for-development programs. Many of the obesity-oriented programs focus on physical activity, often exercise, rather than on the development of physical literacy and mastery of sport skills that would enable lifelong participation in sport. Ironically, many health-based sport-for-development programs fail to take advantage of the enjoyment that can be engendered in sport settings. Instead, they focus on exercise, an activity that often lacks the hedonic value and social connections of sport[51] all while using sport as a hook to attract participants.

Programs with the objective of developing sport, on the other hand, are quick to make claims about the positive outcomes of sport participation. Common social and psychological benefits claimed include enhanced self-esteem, goal setting, health, social relationships and friendships, learning to work together, self-discipline, and a host of other benefits.[52] Each of these can also be developed in nonsport settings or via sport-for-development programs. Studies of parents often identify the importance they place on their child learning to compete and to deal with winning and losing,[53] elements more fundamentally linked to competitive sport environments. In fact, the outsized emphasis on competition and, more specifically, on winning at all costs can negate most of the other benefits claimed for sport. Sport as we know it is inherently competitive. As this is a critical distinction between sport development and sport for development, let's examine the role of competition more closely.

The Role of Competition

Competition is a critical component of sport. Sport devoid of competition is little more than exercise. Competition can take many forms but is often equated only with winning and losing. Although imperfect, competitive outcome remains our most recognized measure of sport performance and its replacement is neither likely nor feasible. However, it is possible to consider the role of competition as distinct from the outcome of any particular competition. Timed sports such as track, triathlon, and swimming provide ready ways to compete against one's self via personal best times. Most sports do not provide such ready measures of personal growth or mastery. Alas, competition has become so fused with winning and losing as to become indistinguishable in much of our discourse. Our media overwhelm us with images and interpretations that equate winning with positive emotions, rewards, and character traits. Losing, then, is associated with negative emotions and traits such as laziness, lack of passion, and a weak character. In this way, losing is equated with failure.[54] Understanding how to learn from failure is an admirable and potentially transferable skill. Yet few programs, either sport development or sport for development, spend time teaching athletes to recognize potential positive outcomes in a loss. Instead, athletes are admired for their desire to win and their hatred of losing. In a paean to New England Patriots quarterback Tom Brady, *Business Insider* extolled the virtues of his "extraordinary competitiveness," telling stories of the temper tantrums he throws when he loses, as if that were something to which one should aspire.[55]

Concerns with Competition

Competition produces two possible outcomes: winning or losing. At least half the participants in a competition are destined to lose and therefore are considered to have failed. This is especially problematic in sport-for-development programs, the purpose of which is to provide a positive influence on participants as well as social inclusion opportunities for the disadvantaged.[56] Exposing marginalized and vulnerable populations to further failure is therefore antithetical to the very mission of sport-for-development programs. Concerns regarding the impact of competition and the social comparison processes it engenders have been evident across sport-for-development contexts.[57] In their evaluation of the Homeless World Cup, Jonathan Magee and Ruth Jeanes found that participants struggled with the intensity of the tournament environment, which they felt was overly pressurized.[58] Participants reported suffering panic attacks and were subject to goading and humiliation while competing against superior teams. The authors questioned the value of competition in this instance, instead suggesting that alternative structures would likely be more effective in eliciting desired outcomes.

Concerns with competition are not limited to sport-for-development programs. In fact, sport development contexts extend the impact of winning and losing beyond the sport participants themselves. The hypercompetitive nature that pervades most modern-day sporting environments also impacts parents, coaches, referees, sport providers, national governing bodies (NGBs), and international federations. We hear endless stories of negative actions and behaviors among parents and coaches stirred by the competitive environment in which they found themselves,[59] instances where referees have been subjected to egregious abuses, sport providers competing among one another for talented youth to the detriment of the athlete, NGBs employing initiatives that reward excellence in athletes as young as six,[60] and federations accepting bribes from nations competing for the right to host a mega-event.[61] But let's focus on the impacts on athletes throughout the system, not just on youth.

The outcome focus of competitors is a function of the win-at-all-costs mentality that competition has come to embrace. Evidence of the strong desire to win and the detrimental impact of competitive systems have even been found in adult recreational contexts. Edward Horne and Matthew Brown found that adult tennis players were willing to go to extreme lengths to gain a competitive edge.[62] Players played down their abilities and deliberately falsified their assigned ratings in order to compete at a level not reflective of their true ability to improve their chances of winning. This when nothing of significance was at stake. A competitive focus on winning above all else has been found to be even more pervasive in youth sport development contexts, largely driven by the adults involved. An emphasis on winning in this environment promotes short-term success over long-term development.[63] Consider the young basketball player who experiences a growth spurt earlier than his or her peers. This may lead to the player being positioned as a center based on superior size and strength. They spend the next few years developing a skillset specific to the position of center. However, the athlete's peers eventually experience their own growth spurts, soon reaching equitable size and strength. But that player has only learned to play center. The athlete is not equipped with the quick hands or shooting range of a point guard. While he or she may have experienced a competitive advantage in the short term, the overemphasis on short-term success has limited long-term development.

Youth sport participation is commonly believed to build characteristics and traits that are important for future success.[64] While this can be true, character development, like any other outcome, depends heavily on the environment in which participation occurs.[65] Competition, can, and often does, detract attention from activities that could develop positive characteristics and skills. Instead, the drive to win can impede both character development and athlete development. In short, competition itself does not impede development; rather, an overemphasis on winning at the expense of other outcomes takes time and energy away from activities designed to develop sport skills, personal qualities, and life skills. Once again, implementation matters; programs should be designed to ensure the outcomes that matter, both sport and nonsport.

Finding Balance

Clearly the role of competition in sport is under no existential threat. We know that competition itself does not lead to negative outcomes. In fact, social comparison processes can shape goals and thereby drive higher levels of achievement.[66] It is the overemphasis on winning at all costs that is problematic. In fact, competition can have positive effects on participants. Competition can spur athletes to train harder, to cooperate with teammates, to exercise emotional control, and to persevere in the face of challenge.[67] Other forms of competition, for positions on the team for example, can be minimized via modifications to traditional team structures. In their study examining subless soccer in which teams were allocated only the number of players that competed on the field, Brad Hill and Green found that eradicating intrateam competition provided many tangible benefits.[68] All participants experienced equal playing time and were able to play without fear of being substituted for poor play. Consequently, the less skilled soccer players (who were most in need of playing time) were not left out and received more helpful attention from the coach and the other players. Team size was sometimes uneven, as were scores when teams played short-handed. Players compensated with more creative play and increased on-field communication. Players were able to celebrate effort, improvement, and individual plays even in the face of a blowout loss. In fact, the loss was expected and was not received as a failure by players. Other sport settings have attempted, with mixed results, to eliminate keeping score as a way to deemphasize winning and losing. Removing score-keeping is largely symbolic, as it is not difficult to keep score individually. With buy-in from players, their family, and other spectators, it is possible to at least deemphasize the importance of the score. However, this must be balanced with an emphasis on other outcomes, whatever they may be. For example, in their study evaluating the Street Soccer USA Cup (a sport-for-homeless intervention), Jon Welty Peachey, Adam Cohen, John Borland, and Alexis Lyras found the promotion of sportsmanship and rewards based on good sportsmanship helped exemplify the tournament's mission and ideals and minimized the emphasis on winning.[69]

In summary, competition itself provides neither positive nor negative impacts. It is merely part of the game. It is the symbolic value of competitive outcomes that is powerful. A win-at-all costs mentality can interfere with potential positive impacts of striving to win. At the same time, artificially removing competition from sport also removes its capacity to motivate athletes' investment in the behaviors that can provide positive outcomes and life skills. As Stacy Warner and Marlene Dixon note,

> Competition within sport systems should not be viewed or studied in a simple one-dimensional manner, but rather [with the understanding] that competition is multi-dimensional and complex. . . . Internal and external competitions have very different meanings and associated outcomes.[70]

Balance seems to be the key to optimizing the potential of competitive settings to provide skills that enhance participants' lives in the long run.

IMPLEMENTATION MATTERS

The goals of sport development and sport for development are often more aligned than one would expect. Although both types of programs have existed for centuries, the distinction between the two terms has only emerged in the early twenty-first century.[71] Each strives to improve lives through sport. Sport development focuses its efforts on improving the sport, often expecting the mere fact of participation will engender a range of nonsport benefits. Not surprisingly, their structures and processes focus on providing quality sport to attract participants and ultimately create higher performing athletes. Sport-for-development organizations are much more explicit in their nonsport objectives, with the actual sport elements included to attract and retain participants. Consequently, these organizations create structures and processes focused on nonsport outcomes.

Authors have typically differentiated sport development from sport for development by treating the two as if they were antithetical ends of a single continuum.[72] It is therefore assumed that an increased focus on one (e.g., sport) takes away from the focus on the other (e.g., nonsport). We suggest that the two (sport and nonsport development) are, in fact, independent dimensions. Thus it is quite possible and even desirable to have a significant focus on *both* types of development outcomes, what we might call *purposeful sport* (Quadrant B in figure 3.2). This quadrant does not fit neatly into our current typology. Traditional sport development is clearly represented by Quadrant A: significant focus on sport, little focus on nonsport outcomes. Quadrant D represents traditional sport-for-development programs. Quadrant C programs have no explicit focus on outcomes, instead representing more casual forms of sport and physical activity. Quadrant B would seem to be the most powerful programs, at least in their potential capacity to do good or to improve lives through an explicit focus on a wide range of outcomes, both sport and nonsport related. To be successful in any quadrant, organizations must design and implement programs to intentionally and explicitly deliver target outcomes.

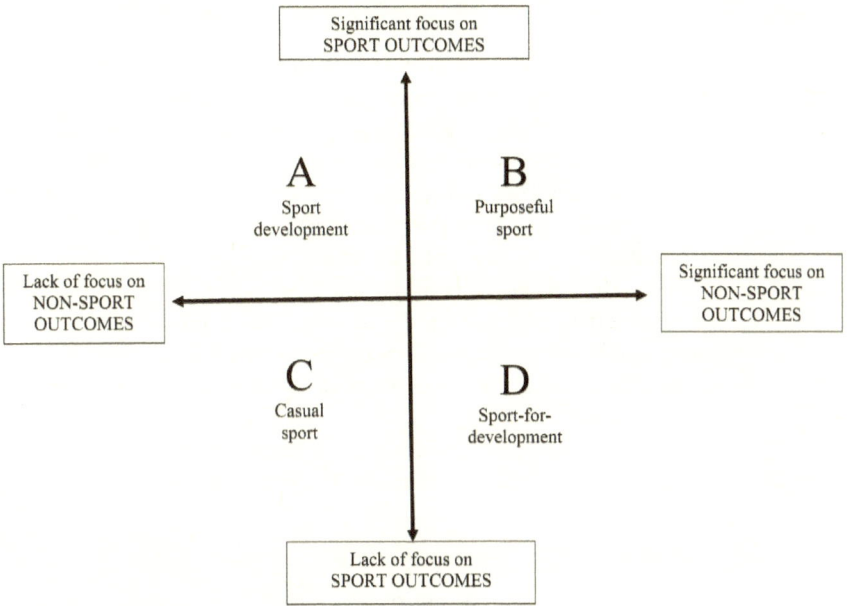

Figure 3.2. Dimensions of development.

The negligible focus of research and practice on Quadrant B reinforces the separation of sport development from sport for development. By focusing specifically on Quadrant A and Quadrant D, research and practice reinforce the notion that there is a choice to be made between the two. However, recent research suggests that the goals of sport development and sport for development are best served when the two are treated as synergistic. Program design and coaching that take seriously the psychosocial development needs of athletes can simultaneously be conducive to athlete development.[73] There are several reasons. In particular, a broader array of participants are thereby attracted into sport,[74] which enhances the pool of athletes, and they are more likely to remain and improve because of the personal value that is enabled.[75]

The pivotal challenge for integration of sport development with sport-for-development goals has not been whether it is possible; rather, the problem has been one of vision. Too often, sport programs intended to develop athletes are designed and implemented around models deriving from popular perceptions of sport training intended for elite professionals, which have disempowered preferable alternatives.[76] This is particularly problematic because popular perceptions of elite sport training misrepresent the personal development concerns around which the best coaches of elite professionals build their systems.[77] The challenge for design, implementation, and management of sport in the twenty-first century is to reenvision our systems, programs, and coaching so that development of sport and the psychosocial development of athletes are made fully symbiotic.

Questions

1. What distinguishes sport development from sport for development?
2. Identify how various sport development systems can be impacted by the sport development pyramid. Describe the effects on a specific sport program.
3. Identify a specific sport development system and describe issues surrounding participant recruitment in that system.
4. How is athlete transition addressed in various sport systems? How does the *up-or-out* versus the *cradle-to-grave* structure impact transition? How can coaches assist athletes in the culture shock of transition?
5. What are some of the problems with the current trend of sport specialization at a very young age? What are the problems for the athlete? For the youth coaches experiencing this trend in their communities? For the sports administrators? Devise some solutions.
6. Describe the potential benefits and concerns of competition in sports.
7. Develop objectives for a sport development program, a sport-for-development program, or both.

NOTES

1. "Development," *Merriam-Webster Dictionary*, accessed March 19, 2020, https://www.merriamwebster.com/dictionary/development.

2. Alexis Lyras and Jon Welty Peachey, "Integrating Sport-for-Development Theory and Praxis," *Sport Management Review* 14, no. 4 (November 2011): 311–26; Kenneth I. Maton, "Empowering Community Settings: Agents of Individual Development, Community Betterment, and Positive Social Change," *American Journal of Community Psychology* 41, nos. 1–2 (March 2008): 4–21.

3. Nico Schulenkorf, "Managing Sport-for-Development: Reflections and Outlook," *Sport Management Review* 20, no. 3 (June 2017): 243–51.

4. B. Christine Green, "Building Sport Programs to Optimize Athlete Recruitment, Retention, and Transition: Toward a Normative Theory of Sport Development," *Journal of Sport Management* 19, no. 3 (2005): 233–53.

5. Jon Solomon, "Staying in the Game: Progress and Challenges in Youth Sports," September 4, 2019, https://www.aspeninstitute.org/blog-posts/staying-in-the-game-progress-and-challenges-in-youth-sports/.

6. Christina Gough, "Number of Participants in US High School Basketball 2018/19, by Gender," September 4, 2019, Statista, https://www.statista.com/statistics/267942/participation-in-us-high-school-basketball/#statisticContainer.

7. NCAA, "NCAA Sports Sponsorship and Participation Rates Database," November 2019, http://www.ncaa.org/about/resources/research/ncaa-sports-sponsorship-and-participation-rates-database.

8. Luke Adams, "2019/20 NBA Roster Counts," August 2, 2019, https://www.hoopsrumors.com/2019/08/201920-nba-roster-counts.html.

9. NBA Media Ventures, "Players," accessed March 19, 2020, https://www.wnba.com/players/.

10. Cora Burnett, "A Critical Reflection on Sport-for-Development Discourses: A Review," *South African Journal for Research in Sport, Physical Education and Recreation* 36, no. 3 (2014): 11–24.

11. Skateistan, "Skateistan," accessed March 19, 2020, https://www.skateistan.org.

12. American Academy of Pediatrics, "Is Your Child Ready for Sports?" 2020, https://www.healthychildren.org/English/healthy-living/sports/Pages/Is-Your-Child-Ready-for-Sports.aspx.

13. Linda M. Petlichkoff, "Youth Sport Participation and Withdrawal: Is It Simply a Matter of Fun?" *Pediatric Exercise Science* 4, no. 2 (1992): 105–10; Amanda J. Visek et al. "The Fun Integration Theory: Towards Sustaining Children and Adolescents Sport Participation," *Journal of Physical Activity and Health* 12, no. 3 (March 2015): 424–33.

14. Bevan C. Grant, "'You're Never Too Old': Beliefs about Physical Activity and Playing Sport in Later Life," *Ageing and Society* 21, no. 6 (2001): 777–98.

15. Lucas Gottezén and Tamar Kremer-Sadlik, "Fatherhood and Youth Sports: A Balancing Act between Care and Expectations," *Gender & Society* 26, no. 4 (2012): 639–64; Tamar Kremer-Sadlik, Carolina Izquierdo, and Marilena Fatigante, "Making Meaning of Everyday Practices: Parents' Attitudes toward Children's Extracurricular Activities in the United States and in Italy," *Anthropology & Education Quarterly* 41, no. 1 (2010): 35–54.

16. B. Christine Green, "Action Research in Youth Soccer: Assessing the Acceptability of an Alternative Program," *Journal of Sport Management* 11, no. 1 (1997): 29–44; Keri A. Schwab, Mary Sara Wells, and Skye Arthur-Banning, "Experiences in Youth Sports: A Comparison between Players' and Parents' Perspectives," *Journal of Administration and Supervision* 2, no. 1 (April 2010): 41–54.

17. Lyras and Welty Peachey, "Integrating Sport-for-Development Theory and Praxis."

18. B. Christine Green, "Sport as an Agent for Social and Personal Change," in *Management of Sport Development*, ed. Vassil Girginov (Oxford: Elsevier, 2008), 129–46.

19. Chris Stone, "Utopian Community Football? Sport, Hope and Belongingness in the Lives of Refugees and Asylum Seekers," *Leisure Studies* 37, no. 2 (2018): 171–83.

20. Fred Coalter, "Sport-in-Development: Accountability or Development?" in *Sport and International Development*, ed. Roger Levermore and Aaron Beacom (London: Palgrave Macmillan, 2009), 55–75.

21. Douglas Hartmann and Christina Kwauk, "Sport and Development: An Overview, Critique, and Reconstruction," *Journal of Sport and Social Issues* 35, no. 3 (2011): 284–305.

22. Hartmann and Kwauk, "Sport and Development," 289.

23. Natalie L. Smith and B. Christine Green, "Positive Socialization in Sport," in *Understanding the Value of Sport Management: An Introduction to the Field*, ed. Matthew Bowers and Marlene A. Dixon (Champaign, IL: Sagamore, 2015), 39–60.

24. Green, "Building Sport Programs to Optimize Athlete Recruitment, Retention, and Transition: Toward a Normative Theory of Sport Development"; Rudolf Jakhel and Willy Pieter, "Changes in Participation Motives in Karate between 1970–1999," *Ido Movement for Culture: Journal of Martial Arts Anthropology* 13, no. 1 (January 2013): 48–57.

25. Peter Donnelly and Kevin Young, "The Construction and Confirmation of Identity in Sport Subcultures," *Sociology of Sport Journal* 5, no. 3 (1988): 223–240; Paul E. Dubois, "Competition in Youth Sports: Process or Product?" *Physical Educator* 37, no. 3 (1980): 151–54.

26. Donnelly and Young, "The Construction and Confirmation of Identity in Sport Subcultures."

27. Wilbert M. Leonard and Raymond L. Schmitt, "Sport-Identity as Side Bet: Towards Explaining Commitment from an Interactionist Perspective," *International Review for the Sociology of Sport* 22, no. 4 (December 1987): 249–62.

28. Christopher L. Stevenson, "The Athletic Career: Some Contingencies of Sport Specialization," *Journal of Sport Behavior* 13, no. 2 (June 1990): 103–13.

29. B. Christine Green and Laurence Chalip, "Sport Tourism as the Celebration of Subculture," *Annals of Tourism Research* 25, no. 2 (April 1998): 275–91.

30. Gregory D. Myer et al., "Sports Specialization, Part II: Alternative Solutions to Early Sport Specialization in Youth Athletes," *Sports Health* 8, no. 1 (2016): 65–73.

31. Jean Côté, Ronnie Lidor, and Dieter Hackfort, "ISSP Position Stand: To Sample or to Specialize? Seven Postulates about Youth Sport Activities That Lead to Continued Participation and Elite Performance," *International Journal of Sport and Exercise Psychology* 7, no. 1 (2009): 7–17; Jean Côté and Matthew Vierimaa, "The Developmental Model of Sport Participation: 15 Years after Its First Conceptualization," *Science and Sports* 29, supplement (October 2014): S63–S69; Michael Wall and Jean Côté, "Developmental Activities That Lead to Dropout and Investment in Sport," *Physical Education and Sport Pedagogy* 12, no. 1 (2007): 77–87.

32. Dawn Anderson-Butcher, "Recruitment and Retention in Youth Development Programming," *Prevention Researcher* 12, no. 2 (2005): 3–6.

33. Green, "Sport as an Agent for Social and Personal Change"; Albert J. Petitpas, Judy L. Van Raalte, Allen E. Cornelius, and Jim Presbrey, "A Life Skills Development Program for High School Student-Athletes," *Journal of Primary Prevention* 24 (2004): 325–34.

34. Andy Smith and Ivan Waddington, "Using 'Sport in the Community Schemes' to Tackle Crime and Drug Use among Young People: Some Policy Issues and Problems," *European Physical Education Review* 10, no. 3 (2004): 279–98.

35. Green, "Sport as an Agent for Social and Personal Change," 139.

36. Ann Gillard and Peter Witt, "Recruitment and Retention in Youth Programs," *Journal of Park and Recreation Administration* 26, no. 2 (2008): 177–88.

37. NCAA, "Want to Transfer?" accessed February 29, 2020, http://www.ncaa.org/student-athletes/current/want-transfer.

38. Northern Virginia Soccer Club, "NVSC Future Stars," accessed March 19, 2020, http://www.novasc.org/programs/competitive-programs/future-stars.

39. B. Christine Green and Laurence Chalip, "The Influence of Club/Travel Teams on Youth Sport," in *Youth Sports in America: The Most Important Issues in Youth Sports Today*, ed. Skye G. Arthur-Banning, Mary Sara Wells, and P. Brian Greenwood (Santa Barbara, CA: ABC-CLIO/Greenwood, 2018).

40. Barrie Houlihan and Mick Green, eds., *Comparative Elite Sport Development* (Oxford: Butterworth-Heinemann, 2008); Matthew Nicholson, Russell Hoye, and Barrie Houlihan, eds., *Participation in Sport: International Policy Perspectives* (London: Routledge, 2010).

41. Matthew Bowers, Laurence Chalip, and B. Christine Green, "Beyond the Façade: Youth Sport Development in the United States and the Illusion of Synergy," in *Routledge Handbook of Sports Development*, ed. Barrie Houlihan and Mick Green (London: Routledge, 2011), 173–83; Green, "Building Sport Programs to Optimize Athlete Recruitment, Retention, and Transition."

42. Emily Sparvero, Laurence Chalip, and B. Christine Green, "Laissez Faire Sport Development: Building Elite Athletes in the United States," in *Comparative Elite Sport Development*, ed. Barrie Houlihan and Mick Green (Oxford: Butterworth-Heinemann, 2008), 242–70.

43. Damon Burton and Rainer Martens, "Pinned by Their Own Goals: An Exploratory Investigation into Why Kids Drop Out of Wrestling," *Journal of Sport and Exercise Psychology* 8, no. 3 (1986): 183–97; Douglas E. Martin, "Interscholastic Sport Participation: Reasons for Maintaining or Terminating Participation," *Journal of Sport Behavior* 20, no. 1 (1997): 94–104.

44. K. David McCann, B. Christine Green, and Laurence Chalip, "Recruit and Retain Study," *Report to USA Rugby and World Rugby* (Boulder, CO: Sport Development Concepts, 2015).

45. Green, "Building Sport Programs to Optimize Athlete Recruitment, Retention, and Transition."

46. Wikipedia, "Culture Shock," accessed March 19, 2020, https://en.wikipedia.org/wiki/Culture_shock#cite_note-1.

47. John Macionis and Linda Gerber, "Culture," in *Sociology*, 7th ed. (Toronto, ON: Pearson Canada, 2010), 54.

48. Kalervo Oberg, "Cultural Shock: Adjustment to New Cultural Environments," *Practical Anthropology* 7, no. 4 (July 1960): 177–82.

49. Sheldon Cohen and S. Leonard Syme, *Social Support and Health* (New York: Academic Press, 1985); Adrian Furnham and Stephen Bochner, *Culture Shock* (London: Methuen, 1986); Green, "Building Sport Programs to Optimize Athlete Recruitment, Retention, and Transition."

50. Partners of the Americas, "A Ganar," 2018, https://www.partners.net/aganar.

51. Laurence Chalip, Keri Schwab, and Daniel Dustin, "Bridging the Sport and Recreation Divide," *Schole* 25, no. 1 (2010): 1–10.

52. Theresa Beesley and Jessica Fraser-Thomas, "Claims of Positive Youth Development: A Content Analysis of Mixed Martial Arts Gyms' Websites," *Leisure/Loisir* 43, no. 1 (2019): 1–25; Martin Camiré, Penny Werthner, and Pierre Trudel, "Mission Statements in Sport and Their Ethical Messages: Are They Being Communicated to Practitioners?" *Athletic Insight* 11, no. 1 (2009): 75–85; Kacey C. Neely and Nicholas L. Holt, "Parents' Perspectives on the Benefits of Sport Participation for Young Children," *The Sport Psychologist* 28, no. 3 (September 2014): 255–68.

53. Lenny D. Wiersma and Angela M. Fifer, "'The Schedule Has Been Tough but We Think It's Worth It': The Joys, Challenges, and Recommendations of Youth Sport Parents," *Journal of Leisure Research* 40, no. 4 (2008): 505–30.

54. Leah R. Vande Berg and Nick Trujillo, "The Rhetoric of Winning and Losing: The American Dream and America's Team," in *Media, Sports, and Society*, ed. Lawrence A. Wenner (Newbury Park, CA: Sage, 1989), 204–24.

55. Scott Davis, "41 Examples of Tom Brady's Extraordinary Competitiveness," August 6, 2019, https://www.businessinsider.com/tom-bradys-insane-competitiveness-examples-2017-8.

56. Lyras and Welty Peachey, "Integrating Sport-for-Development Theory and Praxis."

57. Jonathan Magee and Ruth Jeanes, "Football's Coming Home: A Critical Evaluation of the Homeless World Cup as an Intervention to Combat Social Exclusion," *International Review for the Sociology of Sport* 48, no. 1 (2013): 3–19; Joel Rookwood and Clive Palmer, "Invasion Games in War-Torn Nations: Can Football Help to Build Peace?" *Soccer and Society* 12, no. 2 (March 2011): 184–200; John Sugden and Andrew Yiannakis, "Sport and Juvenile Delinquency: A Theoretical Base," *Journal of Sport and Social Issues* 6, no. 1 (1982): 22–30.

58. Magee and Jeanes, "Football's Coming Home."

59. Chris Harwood and Camilla Knight, "Stress in Youth Sport: A Developmental Investigation of Tennis Parents," *Psychology of Sport and Exercise* 10, no. 4 (July 2009): 447–56.

60. Anne Pankhurst and Dave Collins, "Talent Identification and Development: The Need for Coherence between Research, System, and Process," *Quest* 65, no. 1 (2013): 83–97.

61. Jamil Chade, "Stadium Deals, Corruption and Bribery: The Questions at the Heart of Brazil's Olympic and World Cup 'Miracle,'" April 2017, https://www.theguardian.com/sport/2017/apr/23/brazil-olympic-world-cup-corruption-bribery.

62. Edward Horne and Matthew Brown, "The Retention of Adult Sport Participants: The Challenge of Player Ratings," *Journal of Applied Sport Management* 11, no. 1 (2019): 24–35.

63. Neeru Jayanthi, Courtney Pinkham, Lara Dugas, Brittany Patrick, and Cynthia Labella, "Sports Specialization in Young Athletes: Evidence-Based Recommendations," *Sports Health* 5, no. 3 (2013): 251–57.

64. Jean Côté and Jessica L. Fraser-Thomas, "Youth Involvement in Sport," in *Introduction to Sport Psychology: A Canadian Perspective*, ed. Peter R. E. Crocker (Toronto, ON: Pearson Prentice Hall, 2007), 266–94.

65. Dominic Erdozain, "Does Sport Build Character? A Progress Report on a Victorian Idea," *Studies in Christian Ethics* 25, no. 1 (February 2012): 35–48.

66. Joan L. Duda, "Goal Perspectives, Participation and Persistence in Sport," *International Journal of Sport Psychology* 20, no. 1 (1989): 42–56.

67. Martin Camiré, "Reconciling Competition and Positive Youth Development in Sport," *Staps* 109, no. 3 (2015): 25–39; Scott Wilkes and Jean Côté, "The Developmental Experiences of Adolescent Females in Structured Basketball Programs," *PHENex* 2 (2010): 1–21.

68. Brad Hill and B. Christine Green, "Give the Bench the Boot! Using Manning Theory to Design Youth-Sport Programs," *Journal of Sport Management* 22, no. 2 (2008): 184–204.

69. Jon Welty Peachey, Adam Cohen, John Borland, and Alexis Lyras, "Building Social Capital: Examining the Impact of Street Soccer USA on Its Volunteers," *International Review for the Sociology of Sport* 48, no. 1 (February 2013): 20–37.

70. Stacy Warner and Marlene A. Dixon, "Competition, Gender and the Sport Experience: An Exploration among College Athletes," *Sport, Education and Society* 20, no. 4 (2015): 541.

71. Simon C. Darnell, Russell Field, and Bruce Kidd, "Introduction: Theorizing the History of Sport-for-Development," in *The History and Politics of Sport-for-Development* (London: Palgrave Macmillan, 2019), 3–23.

72. Daniel Bloyce and Andy Smith, *Sport Policy Development: An Introduction* (London: Routledge, 2010); Barrie Houlihan and Anita White, *The Politics of Sport Development: Development of Sport or Development through Sport?* (London: Routledge, 2002).

73. Jessica Fraser-Thomas and Jean Côté, "Youth Sports: Implementing Findings and Moving Forward with Research," *Athletic Insight* 8, no. 3 (2006): 12–27.

74. Green, "Action Research in Youth Soccer."

75. Eleanor Quested et al., "Intentions to Drop-Out of Youth Soccer: A Test of the Basic Needs Theory among European Youth from Five Countries," *International Journal of Sport and Exercise Psychology* 11, no. 4 (2013): 395–407.

76. Laurence Chalip and B. Christine Green, "Establishing and Maintaining a Modified Youth Sport Program: Lessons from Hotelling's Location Game," *Sociology of Sport Journal* 15, no. 4 (1998): 326–42.

77. Pamm Kellett, "Organisational Leadership: Lessons from Professional Coaches," *Sport Management Review* 2, no. 2 (November 1999): 150–71.

4

Inclusion and Diversity in Sport for Development and Peace

Pamela Hudson Baker and Morgan Strimel

OBJECTIVES

This chapter will:

- Highlight the importance of inclusive sport in sport for development and peace.
- Establish what inclusive sport encompasses.
- Discuss the influence of individual diversity in sport.
- Provide strategies to promote inclusion in sport for development and peace programs.

Meet Noora. She is a young, female, Brazilian softball player. Noora is packing her bags and traveling to the United States for a two-week Sports Visitor Program during which she will explore ways to use sport for development and peace (SDP) initiatives in her home community. She will join a multinational softball delegation for which she was selected as an active player of the sport in her hometown and for showing promise as an emerging community leader. During the program, Noora will be joined by fifteen other young women who possess these same qualities, all having been selected for this opportunity to develop their leadership skills through sport. As a result of embassy-based criteria used for participation, when envisioning their intended audience, designers of the program see this young, female softball player and base programmatic decisions related to specific activities within the established curriculum on these characteristics. Upon closer examination, however, there is more to each program participant than an initial review of demographic data may show.

Consider Noora. We have established that she is a young woman in her early twenties. She is representing Brazil as an actively competitive athlete. These characteristics, which undoubtedly serve as major components of her identity, scarcely compose all of who Noora is and may neglect important aspects of her identity that may profoundly influence her interactions. For example, Noora is an individual with not just one but two disabilities; she has a diagnosis of autism spectrum disorder and an emerging mild hearing loss. She is multilingual (Portuguese, English, and Arabic) and comes from a middle-class family from São Paulo. Finally, Noora's family emigrated to Brazil from Lebanon in the 1970s and deeply values their Islamic culture. As such, Noora consistently engages in practice of the Islamic faith.

Noora, as just one of sixteen total participants, sheds light on the importance of looking beyond "young, female, Brazilian softball player" as the designated audience for whom this SDP program will be customized. Additional identity characteristics, such as her abilities and cultural background, are critical to take into consideration in the context of designing a program as interactive as that of an SDP initiative. Developing any program with only a single image of the intended audience in mind can inhibit the achievement of long-term program goals focused on community development. What is needed, then, in both design and implementation of SDP programs and inclusive sport, is a holistic perspective of participants and how their cumulative identities are likely to influence their experiences and their potential for carrying change initiatives home with them. Using Noora as our guide, let's take a closer look.

THE IMPORTANCE OF INCLUSIVE SPORT IN SDP PROGRAMS

Intentional opportunities to engage in inclusive sport are critical components of SDP programs given the immense potential to affect individual, local, and global change through its practice.[1] Within the context of SDP, inclusive sport works as a mechanism to create space for diverse individuals to have meaningful engagements with one another and in turn, meet a myriad of social, cultural, and developmental objectives.[2] These objectives, particularly those related to fostering values of diversity and inclusion, are interdependent and require careful planning efforts within SDP program teams to be achieved. Before defining inclusive sport and providing strategies for implementation, it is important to highlight the potential that inclusive sport holds for impact, beginning with the participants themselves.

At the individual level, participating in an activity where one feels valued and accepted has been shown to increase an individual's feelings of self-empowerment as well as heighten self-perceptions of efficacy and competence.[3] Individuals with disabilities, for example, have attributed positive developments in their self-confidence and overall feelings of empowerment to participating in inclusive sport.[4] Furthermore, participating in inclusive sport has the potential to instill core values related to diversity and inclusion within participants and increase their overall knowledge of inclusive practices.[5] These values can then be carefully nurtured and grown into social practices, transforming individual participants into drivers of positive, global change once they return to their communities and carry these core values into their interactions.[6]

Figure 4.1. Sport can be a universal language for all people, which is apparent in this encounter between a deaf athlete from the Pacific islands and a child with Down syndrome. *Credit*: **Center for Sport Management at George Mason University**

At the local level, inclusive sport can be used as a tool to build a cohesive culture and serve as a bridge to make critical connections between people, both in and outside of communities. Internally, sport can work as a mechanism for resocializing individuals into their own communities from which they feel they have been disconnected. War-torn countries, for example, often harness the power of sport to create a wraparound approach for reintegrating wounded warriors into their communities after they return from areas of conflict. In this postwar scenario, inclusive sport can also be utilized to heal associated collective trauma and reestablish norms in a society after having been drastically impacted by conflict.[7]

To connect communities and cultures to one another, sport can also work as a tool for engaging in conflict resolution between those who would otherwise be in opposition to one another.[8] In this instance, inclusive sport can form cross-cultural relationships by providing the space and time for individuals to recognize their common interests, build mutual understanding, and humanize one another.[9] To illustrate this, Bosnia uses sport to bring together people from conflicting Muslim cultures in a common meeting space, with sport acting as the mediator, in an effort to establish new perceptions of the imagined enemy and create the basis for future, peaceful interactions.[10] Coming together in this way and pursuing a common goal can lead to destigmatization of the other and aid in reducing the often negative cultural stereotypes brought about by conflict.[11]

In sum, the potential of inclusive sport to act as a vehicle for positive change spans from within individual participants, then to their communities, and ultimately to a global level of impact. To this end, planning efforts related to inclusive sport in SDP initiatives should be intentional to achieve optimal results for affecting change. Defining inclusive sport and providing a framework for interpreting the meaning of inclusion lays the foundation for strategies for implementing inclusive sport and designing inclusive SDP programs.

DEFINING INCLUSIVE SPORT

While the term *inclusive sport* is often selected to describe the integration of individuals with disabilities into sport, the use of the word *inclusive* suggests that the many different facets of diversity can be encompassed in the paradigm. The reach of inclusion, both as a practice and an outcome, calls for a recognition that all humans are composed of multiple, complex, intertwined identities that influence the ways in which individuals perceive and interact with the world, including the realm of sport. As a result, inclusive sport is an intricate process that, when implemented effectively and appropriately, casts a far-reaching net that ensures appropriate participation of diverse groups, cultures, and populations in its implementation. Inclusion is not meant to be the act of bringing outsiders into a setting, but rather is the development of a cohesive culture of richly diverse individuals.[12]

It is, therefore, imperative that when incorporating inclusive sport into SDP initiatives, program designers take action to carefully avoid the unintentional reinforcement of cultural or identity-based exclusion. This process begins by first understanding the multifaceted nature of individual diversity that creates the foundation of inclusion. As such, viewing each individual through the lens of intersectionality can be helpful. This approach emphasizes that an individual's identity is multidimensional, composed of many subidentities that are intertwined and interdependent on one another to collectively form who they are.[13] Think back to Noora. Based on what we know from her brief biographical statement provided by the embassy, we can predict that her identities include (at the very least) young, female, athlete, Brazilian, an individual with disabilities, multilingual, and Muslim. With knowledge of just these few aspects of Noora's identity, SDP program designers can begin to understand how those aspects might work together to influence her experiences and help her to facilitate change in her home community. However, it is also important to be open to additional identities that are not transparent in the initial framing of each participant.

Using intersectionality as a framework (see figure 4.2) for achieving inclusion fosters a critical awareness of the ways in which certain hierarchies and social dynamics can develop based on the interlocking pieces of who we are and where we come from.[14] Several aspects of diversity and identity will be identified and expanded upon in this section for consideration in SDP program design—particularly, the ways in

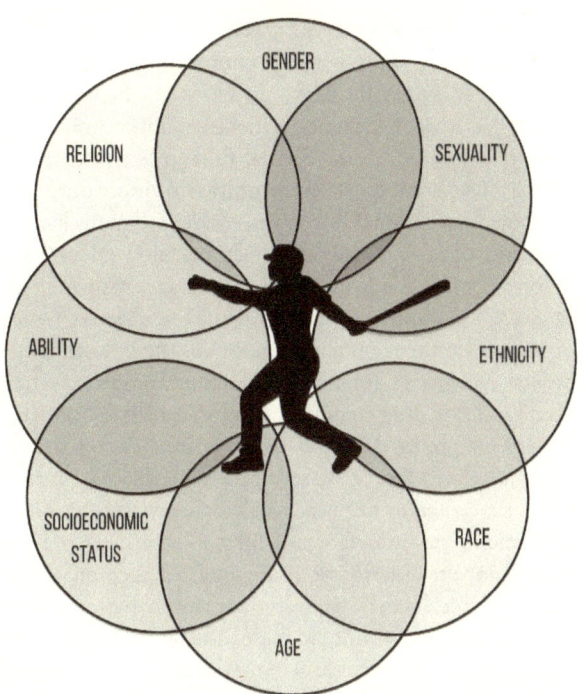

Figure 4.2. Intersectionality in sport for development.

which they have historically had the ability to influence an individual's participation in sport. While this is by no means exhaustive of the many aspects of diversity, it is meant to provide a broad overview and begin the process of painting inclusive sport outcomes with the brush of intersectionality. This same lens of intersectionality can be applied when considering the staffing of SDP programs. Representation of diversity and inclusion in all aspects of program design can provide systemic support addressing these concepts.

Ability and Disability

Inclusive sport is often grounded in efforts to intentionally integrate individuals with disabilities into recreation and physical activities. This is because individuals with disabilities have historically experienced exclusion from sport on the basis of structural barriers to participation and a broad lack of understanding on how to accommodate their needs, resulting in limited early life experiences with sport.[15] Appropriate inclusive practices have been an area of debate, however, regarding what is considered an effective approach to including a population with such diverse characteristics, resulting in many separate sport leagues and organizations exclusively for individuals with disabilities. While organizations such as these have been controversial because they practice a certain degree of segregation, they aim to offer individuals with disabilities access to sport without conforming to mainstream structures where elitism is valued and their needs would likely not be met.[16] This sheds light on the systemic complexities of facilitating inclusive opportunities on the pathway to cultivating ability in specific sports. Special Olympics and Paralympics are well-established examples of separate sport opportunities for individuals with disabilities.

In addition to these foundational initiatives, model programs have emerged offering integrated opportunities where accommodations allow a leveling of the playing field. Consider, for example, the Ironman competitions, which are challenging triathlon races that have risen in popularity as one of the ultimate tests of human endurance.[17] Not only has Ironman gained attention for the intense nature of the sport, but it has also been recognized for its creative accommodations and inclusion of individuals with disabilities. Participants with physical disabilities (e.g., paraplegic, double above-the-knee amputations), for instance, are able to participate in cycling events by using a hand-cranked cycle instead of a standard bike. Ironman also allows for what they call *special teams* to form for participants with other physical, visual, or neurological impairments, composed of one fully abled athlete and one athlete with a disability. These teams are able to use individualized accommodations, such as a tandem bike, a tether (typically for swimming), or simply have one member act as an elbow-lead guide for the other, to fully include athletes with disabilities in Ironman events.[18] Ironman's inclusive efforts have set an example for other sport organizations as they notably take both visible and invisible disabilities into consideration. Such an integrated approach also has not been without controversy as accommodations are sometimes viewed as changing the rules.

Initial thoughts of disability can too often be confined to those seen on the surface, when the term actually encompasses a wide range of abilities and limitations. The Centers for Disease Control and Prevention reports that one in four adults in the United States has a disability and that 10.8 percent of those disabilities are related to cognition, which impacts how one acquires and processes information.[19] Zooming out further, the World Health Organization suggests that more than one billion individuals globally—15 percent of the total population—live with some form of disability, and that even if one does not have a disability right now, one likely will at some point in one's lifetime.[20] This is because disability can be "visible or invisible; temporary or long term; static, episodic, or degenerating; painful or inconsequential."[21] The impacts of visible disabilities as a barrier to sport are relatively obvious; as such, alternative sport opportunities have emerged making use of different rules, equipment, and technologies. For example, wheelchair basketball, sled hockey, or sitting volleyball are just a few ways to include individuals with disabilities in competitive events. It is also important to consider the more hidden aspects of disability relative to how individuals may experience barriers to sport on the basis of invisible disabilities, such as autism, learning disabilities, anxiety disorders, or specific medical conditions (e.g., diabetes, asthma, concussion), which may be less transparent to program designers.

Think again of Noora. Without disclosing on her own, SDP program designers would be unlikely to know that part of her identity includes being on the autism spectrum. Autism is a developmental disability that can impact the way a person interacts, communicates, and processes information. It is often not a stand alone diagnosis as individuals on the spectrum typically have other comorbid diagnoses (e.g., anxiety, epilepsy, depression).[22] Even her mild hearing impairment may be hard to detect until engaging with her in person, especially if she has learned to compensate on her own. It is important not only to recognize the ability differences a participant brings to the program but to expand each participant's capacity to embrace differing abilities. Providing access to alternative sport experiences within SDP programs provides an intentional expansion of awareness for participants. Participants in sport for development initiatives, such as the Sports Visitor Program sponsored by the US Department of State, have shown significant growth in their familiarity with including people with disabilities in sport.[23] When asking participants to create an action plan for catalyzing and sustaining change, creating inclusive experiences for individuals with a wide range of abilities and disabilities can be a profoundly impactful area of focus. This concept of visible versus invisible aspects of one's ability-based identity extends into many remaining facets of intersectionality, shedding light on the possibility that Noora has several other identities for consideration—some of which are apparent and others of which are not.

Gender

Gender is an aspect of identity that has been evolving in recent years and is beginning to be examined and understood on a deeper level. Here, we address the general experiences in sport of those who identify as either male or female, while acknowledging that this is only part of gender-based experiences in sport. The historical relationship between gender and sport has been one entangled with an ongoing battle to deconstruct gender norms perpetuated by hegemonic masculinity both on and off the field. Women are, as an example, often excluded from competitive sports as a result of hegemonic masculine practices that stigmatize females as being fragile or delicate, subtly reinforcing a strong association between masculinity and athleticism.[24] Even in communities where women are, at least on the surface, included in sport, they are still often marginalized by the media as television coverage focuses on male leagues and positions females as being less interesting to watch.[25]

Conversely, the inclusion of men in female-dominant sports, such as those considered to be noncontact and less competitive, is an area equally in need of attention by further challenging gender norms and heteronormative practices in sport. Male perceptions of sport that influence their choices in participation have been shown to be irrefutably connected to sexuality.[26] Specifically, in an effort to avoid being perceived as weak or feminine by their peers, men may avoid sports in which they would be required to embody stereotypically feminine characteristics. Both male and female participants, therefore, can find themselves in situations in sport where they are faced with the choice of whether or not to conform to the perceived expectations of themselves related to their gender and ultimately surrender pieces of themselves and their identities.[27]

Sexuality

Examining the relationship between sexuality and sport can take many different directions, but typically, overarching themes at their crossroads include perpetuated heterosexism, prevailing homophobia, and intentional efforts by members of the LGBTQ+ community to deconstruct gender norms as they relate to sexuality through sport. Any discussion of sexuality as it relates to sport would be remiss to not include the immense influence of intersectionality, specifically related to gender. Speaking generally, individuals who are of a sexual minority may avoid spaces of sport because of a fear of retaliation based on their perceptions of heteronormative cultural practices.[28] The word *fear* is selected intentionally here because in some cultures, individuals in the LGBTQ+ community still experience high rates of abuse, exclusion, and violence based on homophobic attitudes.

Furthermore, homophobia in sport can manifest itself in ways more covert than violence, such as through subtle expressions through humor or the perpetual performances of norms that reinforce hegemonic heterosexuality.[29] Young males, in particular, have openly expressed rejection toward participating in sport that they view as being female dominant, claiming that they would make them "gay."[30] Statements such as these insinuate a negative connotation with homosexuality and further contribute to the marginalization of individuals of sexual minorities in sport. Tying sexuality to sport creates environments that may not be welcoming to the LGBTQ+ community, and further disseminates the message that athleticism is directly related to masculinity.

Race and Ethnicity

Sport's hegemonic complexities arise not only from being produced within a framework of perpetuated masculinity but in an often-interrelated way also within the context of racial and ethnic power relations. To illustrate this relationship and further demonstrate the impact of intersectionality, Agnes Elling and Annelies Knoppers emphasized that women who are ethnic minorities participate in sport at overwhelmingly lower rates than those of ethnic majority populations, suggesting that ethnic undertones can work with gender to further influence an individual's participation in sport. When looking for the root cause of this type of marginalization, however, it is important to consider the extent to which individual choice on the basis of ethnicity is at play. Sport and leisure, for example, may be valued differently within a culture, and nonparticipation does not necessarily indicate that exclusion is taking place.[31]

The influence of race and ethnicity on participation extends far beyond its intersectionality with gender. On a larger scale, the influence of race and ethnicity involves the ways in which the Western world has historically held dominance in sport.[32] Sport and SDP programs specifically are most often rooted in Western cultures and, therefore, may be implicitly infused with values and beliefs derived from them, creating an unintended subliminal cultural curriculum. As an example, consider the communities of Indigenous populations and the ways in which they hold their own independent beliefs, values, and rituals. These communities are often pushed to assimilate into the larger society by seemingly inclusive efforts to advance their development, such as those implemented by means of sport.[33] Given the Eurocentric nature of SDP programs, Lyndsay Hayhurst, Audrey Giles, and Jan Wright[34] described the existence of a fine line that program designers must be aware of that lies between their own values and those that already exist in the Indigenous communities when considering ways in which to use sport as a vehicle for development and change.

Religion

Religion serves as another facet of identity that can influence an individual's participation in sport. This can be attributed to various religious rituals and expectations conflicting with those of the space in which sport is being practiced. The more formalized that sport gets (e.g., a professional league versus community recreation clubs), so do the regulations and codes projected onto those who wish to participate. Regulations, in turn, can work to marginalize those whose religious practices are outward in nature.[35] Sport uniforms, generally speaking, have the tendency to strictly embody what Western societies consider to be appropriate dress, marginalizing those who ascribe to cultures in which religion guides choices in clothing. Muslim women such as Noora, for example, face ongoing challenges in maintaining their religious identity in sport as some organizations have banned headscarves and adhere to strict rules of dress, exemplifying the influence of intersectionality at the crossroads of gender and religion.[36]

Further, on the basis of religion, some cultures do not value sport or physical activity to the same degree that others do in Western communities. In these instances, sport is perceived as unnecessary and an undesirable use of time that could otherwise be spent tending to religious duties and familial obligations.[37] Individuals of such religious beliefs, therefore, may not portray strong engagement when sport is taking place. This can be further evaluated through the lens of gender and the ways in which some religions may perceive gender relations and the appropriateness of mixed-sex activities. Religion may mandate the extent to which male and female participants can engage with another, in addition to involvement with coaches and staff of differing genders, to uphold any beliefs related to modesty.[38]

Familial Status

From childhood to adulthood, an individual's familial status and culture may influence the desire to engage in sport or even the ability to do so. In the early stages of development, family plays an important role in shaping one's values and priorities, such as the salience of sport and physical activity. Socializing children in contexts that value sport, either by exposing them to environments that engage in sport or by providing a role model that values and participates in it, may heighten the perceived importance of sport and, in turn, increase the likelihood of the choice to participate in sport as an adult.[39] Beyond providing opportunities for socialization, parents have the ability to influence sport participation by providing encouragement to engage in it and also a certain degree of freedom for children to explore different areas of sport that interest them. Support and encouragement can manifest as acting as a coach, providing transportation to games and events, or something as simple as attending a game. A lack of these factors, then, may diminish a child's desire to engage in sport later in life; once an individual has reached adolescence, though, opportunities for new socialization expand and therefore the effects of parental influence may subside.[40]

In adulthood, once individuals have a family of their own, the influence of familial status can shift in how and to what extent it impacts sport engagement. Specifically, the presence of children in a household or other dependent relatives presents unique obstacles that can easily push physical activity to the back burner. Research has shown, for example, that time constraints related to childcare and tending for sick or elderly relatives often become first priority for adults and, as such, are the aspects of their lives in which they choose to invest large portions of their time. Further, as households grow, so do familial expenses that have the potential to restrict the ability to invest in sport, especially if a budget already exists for children to engage in sport themselves.[41] The influence of familial status on sport, then, tends to come full circle as various members of a household are shifted to being prioritized for participation.

Socioeconomic Status

Because of the uneven distribution of resources across communities and cultures, socioeconomic status persists as another major predictor of an individual's ability to participate in sport. Research has repeatedly shown that there is a positive correlation between income and level of involvement in recreational activities, particularly in terms of those that are more organized and formal in nature.[42] This can be attributed to the fact that a long-term commitment to participation requires significant financial investments, such as appropriate clothing, league fees, cost of travel, and a cyclical need for updated equipment as standard wear and tear takes place. Additionally, in families where financial constraints exist, having the time to invest in sport may not be a reality as members may need to take on one or more part-time jobs to help make ends meet.[43]

The influence of socioeconomic status on participation in sport has been shown to change over time and has its greatest stronghold in early childhood.[44] Once an individual reaches the adolescent years, though, and has the opportunity to engage in sport through the structures of educational or community-based institutions, many of the aforementioned financial barriers are lifted. Once adulthood is reached, the relationship between socioeconomic status and participation in sport remains mostly dependent on the region in which one lives and proximity to appropriate facilities in which to engage in sport.[45] Neighborhoods composed of groups of a lower socioeconomic status often have limited facilities to house sports, and if they do, their conditions may not be suitable or optimal for use.[46] This then requires individuals to travel to other locations to engage in sport, which may not be financially feasible, perpetuating the cycle of monetary constraint.

STRATEGIES TO PROMOTE INCLUSION IN SDP PROGRAMS

Inclusive sport most certainly encompasses multiple facets of diversity. As such, it is important to recognize that achieving inclusive excellence in SDP programs requires proactive, intentional planning efforts through an intersectional understanding of human identity. The goal of such efforts is to expand meaningful opportunities for a wide range of participants to engage in inclusive sport and internalize values related to diversity, equity, and inclusion as they see them in practice. The potential of a ripple effect of sustainable, global change can emerge as participants carry these core values into their respective communities equipped with plans for action and implementation.[47] This is no simple task for program designers. Strategies to develop holistically inclusive SDP programs need to be mindful of intersectionality and respectful of the communities where they will be applied. Therefore, utilizing Universal Design (UD) and Universal Design for Learning (UDL) as frameworks in program development can optimize the implementation and impact of inclusive practices in SDP programs.

Universal Design

Developed by a team at North Carolina State University, UD is "the design of products and environments to be usable by all people, to the greatest extent possible, without the need for adaptation or specialized design."[48] Essentially, the creators of UD were concerned with proactive, rather than reactive, design to look beyond standard users and meet the needs of individuals with a vast range of abilities. UD reduces, if not eliminates, the need for accommodations and creates designs that benefit all users. As a classic example of UD in the everyday world, consider a curb cut in a sidewalk. Not only do curb cuts make traveling in a city accessible for an individual using a wheelchair, but they also benefit those pushing shopping carts and strollers, in addition to people who are traveling on scooters or bikes.[49] UD aims to make the world as inclusive and equitable as possible, making it a relevant foundation for SDP program designers to set the tone for welcoming a diverse audience of participants.

UD is an ongoing, complex process that starts with first identifying the context in which it is to be applied—in this instance, an SDP program—followed by the audience for which it is intended. Designers begin by anticipating the range of intersecting participant needs based on different aspects of diversity (e.g., gender, race, dis/ability, ethnicity) in order to address them broadly and proactively in program design. It is helpful to involve the participants themselves in this process by inviting their input in program development,[50] which aligns with the emergent expectation that the voices of local community members should drive the program design process.[51] Finally, components of the design should be carefully constructed through the lens of UD to meet needs that have been identified in addition to those that may emerge unexpectedly. By incorporating the principles of UD, SDP program designers can ensure that inclusion is at the program's core and that they are creating an environment that is accessible for all. To give structure to this process, UD has been divided into seven distinct principles for evaluation, although each may not be applicable to every design.

1. Equitable use: The design is useful and marketable to people with diverse abilities.
2. Flexibility in use: The design accommodates a wide range of individual preferences and abilities.
3. Simple and intuitive use: Use of the design is easy to understand, regardless of the user's experience, knowledge, language skills, or current concentration level.
4. Perceptible information: The design communicates necessary information effectively to the user, regardless of ambient conditions or the user's sensory abilities.
5. Tolerance for error: The design minimizes hazards and the adverse consequences of accidental or unintended actions.
6. Low physical effort: The design can be used efficiently and comfortably and with a minimum of fatigue.
7. Size and space for approach and use: Appropriate size and space is provided for approach, reach, manipulation, and use regardless of user's body size, posture, or mobility.[52]

The principles of UD, in the context of SDP programs, can be used as a framework for the design and modification of program locations, selection of means of transportation, the structure of living quarters, development of marketing materials, overall program components or activities, and action planning for future projects. A universally designed SDP program should create an environment that communicates to participants that both diversity and their unique, individual identities are valued. It is important to note that UD is not just a process but also a way of thinking that will take time and repetition for designers to internalize as programs are developed, implemented, and continuously evaluated.[53] Thinking broadly in terms of UD consequently gives way for program designers to utilize the principles of Universal Design for Learning to take inclusion efforts a step further by funneling the concept directly into inclusive sport and other program activities.

Universal Design for Learning

As an extension of UD, UDL is "a framework to improve and optimize teaching and learning for all people based on scientific insights into how humans learn."[54] UDL builds on UD by providing a cross-disciplinary set of guidelines to maximize inclusion, specifically in educational settings such as SDP programs, to meet the needs of diverse learners. UDL is a strategic approach for SDP program designers to use as a framework when developing inclusive sport opportunities in order to provide multiple ways for participants to engage with content, perceive it, and also demonstrate their ideas and knowledge. In modeling this approach in program delivery, action plans based in the principles of UD and UDL can become a vehicle for catalyzing and sustaining change. The framework of UDL is divided into three main principles and further subdivided into nine guidelines, all of which are outlined here with suggestions for their usage within the context of Noora's program.

>   Principle 1: Multiple means of engagement. Individuals vary in their ability to sustain engagement based on differences in personalities, cultural beliefs, level of interest, and motivation. To accommodate such variations, this principle of UDL sets forth guidelines for (a) recruiting interest, (b) sustaining effort, and (c) optimizing self-regulation.[55]
>> a. Options for recruiting interest. Allow participants autonomy and choice, when possible, throughout the duration of the program. For example, incorporate "choose your own adventure" opportunities to allow participants to select the activities and sports that they join. Threats and distractions to participants should also be reduced, which can be accomplished by fostering a sense of predictability in the program itself and creating a high level of perceived support from program staff.[56] Noora's program, for example, plans to have all participants spend one afternoon with a group of major-league trainers in skill-related softball workshops. A UDL-based redesign of this activity could include providing an agenda for what the afternoon will entail, sharing explicit instruction about the relevance and value of each training activity, establishing practice stations with visual reminders of procedure, allowing participants to prioritize participation at specific stations based on their own training needs, and having program staff available for response to questions at each station.
>> b. Options for sustaining effort and persistence. Heighten salience of the SDP program goals to the greatest extent possible and foster a sense of a supportive community in sport. Program goals should emphasize a group's collective beliefs in order to maximize outcomes of group efficacy and

long-term change.[57] Any time Noora's program is facilitating engagement in sport, they should set clear goals, responsibilities, boundaries, and expectations with participants in advance.[58] It may also be helpful for program staff to provide participants with prompts to use when they need to ask for assistance during an activity, such as a hand signal, that their peers will recognize and respond to by providing the requested support (e.g., clarification of rules, reminder of roles).

c. Options for self-regulation. Include structured activities that provide opportunities for self-reflection and goal setting as learning takes place throughout the program. It may be helpful to have program staff model this process or to provide prompts for participants to begin the reflection and goal-setting processes.[59] In alignment with this guideline, it is recommended that the program set aside time at the end of each day for participants to engage in a journaling method of their choice (e.g., writing, video diary, audio reflections) to reflect on what they learned. Optional prompts for this activity should be provided, and program staff should be available to guide or model the reflection process as needed. Sharing impactful experiences could be used to enhance development of community.

Principle 2: Multiple means of representation. Because individuals differ in how they process information, this principle presents guidelines specific to variations in the provision of information. With diversity in mind, UDL presents the following guidelines to develop options for (a) perception, (b) language and symbols, and (c) comprehension.[60]

a. Options for perception. Display information in multiple formats to include any marketing, programmatic, or activity-based materials and ensure that they can be manipulated by participants. Such formats should include visual, auditory, and tactile versions, when possible.[61] Noora's program, for example, has an activity planned where participants will attend an interactive lecture on health and wellness. For the presentation aspect of it, the facilitator should provide copies of the materials used to the audience as both a printout and a digital file that can be accessed and manipulated on a tablet or computer. Additionally, any videos used in the presentation should be captioned.

b. Options for language and symbols. Be mindful of the usage of any slang, idioms, and culturally exclusive phrases. Intentionally connect new terms to participants' prior experiences and knowledge and promote understanding across cultures by making information available in their first language, with visual support where necessary.[62] Whenever possible, the program should have program documents and materials available in the participants' first language and pay careful attention to abstract language being used by program staff. Real-time interpreting support should also be available to ensure participants can access live sessions.

c. Options for comprehension. Tap into participants' background knowledge when making new connections to information. It may be necessary to scaffold instruction (progressively building on what participants already know), especially within the context of new sport, and provide consistent feedback throughout the duration of the program or an activity to accommodate diverse information-processing abilities.[63] When Noora's program teaches participants how to play sitting volleyball as a part of their inclusive sport curriculum, for example, they must keep in mind that this is an activity that will likely be completely new to participants. Suggestions to incorporate this guideline include activating background knowledge of volleyball to begin instruction, bridging its concepts to sitting volleyball, and then regularly checking for understanding as teaching progresses. It will also be helpful if new ideas and concepts were continually reviewed for maximum generalization.

Principle 3: Multiple means of action and expression. The final principle of UDL seeks to accommodate learners in how they share their thoughts, ideas, and knowledge. Variations in ideal modes of expression can come as a result of certain disabilities, diverse languages, executive functioning deficits, and other diverse characteristics. To meet these needs, UDL seeks to provide options for (a) physical action, (b) expression, and (c) executive functions.[64]

a. Options for physical action. Provide a range of physical materials and equipment for participants to access. Create flexibility for the use of assistive devices, when needed, and provide support in access when barriers are present.[65] Within the first week of Noora's program, they have scheduled a team-building session for participants at a local ropes course. Given the fine motor demands typically required for a ropes course, flexibility should be given in the speed of physical action, and alternatives to certain activities may need to be offered.

b. Options for expression and communication. Allow for the use of multimedia for the communication of thoughts and ideas, when possible. Participants may, for example, best express themselves verbally, through writing, by performance, or via other web-based tools.[66] Toward the end of the program, Noora's program will spend an entire day engaging with curriculum that is focused on leading participants to become agents of social change, with one activity involving small groups presenting action plans to the whole group. To align this activity with this guideline of UDL, program staff should allow these small groups to choose the way in which they present their action plans in front of their peers (e.g., a short film, poster presentation, spoken word). The program should provide a variety of materials and equipment so participants can choose to use different presentation formats.

c. Options for executive function. Guide the process of goal setting and strategy development when working with participants. For example, at the conclusion of the SDP program when action plans are being developed, provide checklists, prompts, and guiding questions for self-reflection.[67] In addition, program staff could take this a step further by creating templates for use throughout the program any time writing is taking place, such as for note-taking during presentations or during reflections at the end of each day.

CONCLUSION

In sport-for-development programs, you are literally touching the groups you work with—demonstrating new skills in close proximity to all members of the group when you engage them in a sport activity. It is important to note that this list of strategies is not exhaustive, just as were the range of intersecting identities discussed earlier. There are infinite ways in which the principles of UDL can be intertwined in the implementation of inclusive sport and SDP programs as a whole, and it will take time to address each of the guidelines and principles discussed in this chapter. No matter the specific approach, using UD as a foundation and UDL as a framework for program design will foster environments that, to the greatest extent possible, are designed to meet the needs of the diverse participants of an SDP program, just like Noora. Consequently, this creates opportunities for the engagement in truly inclusive sport and elevates the salience of SDP program goals related to local actions and global change. Designing meaningful and inclusive programs for participants requires careful and collaborative planning in advance with a willingness to adapt to ever-evolving situations.

Questions

1. Analyze an existing SDP program and its efforts related to inclusive sport, including recommendations to enhance its overall inclusion of diverse individuals in the program relative to:
   a. Usage of the principles of Universal Design
   b. Usage of the principles of Universal Design for Learning
   c. Approach to proactive planning
2. Describe the various aspects of "inclusion" and what implications this creates for the development of SDP programs around the world.
3. Using the framework of intersectionality, reflect on your own identity and the ways in which pieces of it work together to influence your day-to-day life, particularly in terms of participation in sport.

Learning Activities

Conduct an identity-mapping activity to create individual identity charts. Start by having the group brainstorm factors that shape who we are, such as gender, race, ethnicity, family, religion, abilities, sport, interests, and hobbies. Consider sharing your own example or building one as a group using a well-known sport figure. Use a starburst model (name at center, arrows radiating out from the center) to have each individual create a personal graphic addressing the question of "Who am I?"

Strategies for Success

1. Include diverse perspectives in the planning process of SDP programs to maximize inclusion efforts.
2. Engage in proactive planning with participants to allow for the careful, intentional development of inclusive sport opportunities.
3. Approach SDP program design through the lens of Universal Design with all participants in mind.

NOTES

1. Alexis Lyras and Jon Welty Peachey, "Integrating Sport-for-Development Theory and Praxis," *Sport Management Review* 14, no. 4 (November 2011): 311–26.

2. Robert E. Baker, Pamela Hudson Baker, Anya Evmenova, and Laura Hayes-Harris, "Perceptions of International Sport Exchange Participants Regarding Inclusive Sport," *International Journal of Sport Management* 16, no. 3 (July 2015): 417–36.

3. Anne Marte Pensgaard and Marit Sorenson, "Empowerment through the Sport Context: A Model to Guide Research for Individuals with Disability," *Adapted Physical Activity Quarterly* 19, no. 1 (January 2002): 48–67.

4. Elaine M. Blinde and Diane E. Taub, "Personal Empowerment through Sport and Physical Fitness Activity: Perspectives from Male College Students with Physical and Sensory Disabilities," *Journal of Sport Behavior* 22, no. 2 (June 1999): 181–202.

5. Robert E. Baker, Pamela H. Baker, Christopher Atwater, and Heather Andrews, "Sport for Development and Peace: A Program Evaluation of a Sport Diplomacy Initiative," *International Journal of Sport Management and Marketing* 16, nos. 1–2 (2015): 52–70, https://doi.org/10.1504/IJSMM.2015.074932.

6. Göran Svensson, "'Glocalization' of Business Activities: A 'Glocal Strategy' Approach," *Management Decision* 39, no. 1 (2001): 6–18, https://doi.org/10.1108/EUM0000000005403.

7. Richard Giulianotti, "The Sport Development and Peace Sector: An Analysis of Its Emergence, Key Institutions, and Social Possibilities," *The Brown Journal of World Affairs* 18, no. 2 (April 2012): 279–93, https://www.jstor.org/stable/24590877.

8. Giulianotti, "The Sport Development and Peace Sector."

9. Baker et al., "Sport for Development and Peace: A Program Evaluation of a Sport Diplomacy Initiative."

10. Giulianotti, "The Sport Development and Peace Sector."

11. Gordon W. Allport, *The Nature of Prejudice* (Cambridge, MA: Addison-Wesley, 1954).

12. Wendy Frisby and Pamela Ponic, "Sport and Social Inclusion," in *Sport Policy in Canada*, ed. Lucie Thibault and Jean Harvey (Ottawa, Canada: University of Ottawa Press, 2013), 381–403, https://www.jstor.org/stable/j.ctt5hjk9x.15.

13. Anne Tjønndal and Jorid Hovden, "'Will God Condemn Me Because I Love Boxing?' Narratives of Young Female Immigrant Muslim Boxers in Norway," *The European Journal of Women's Studies* (August 2020), https://doi.org/10.1177/1350506820954885.

14. Tjønndal and Hovden, "'Will God Condemn Me Because I Love Boxing?'"

15. Frisby and Ponic, "Sport and Social Inclusion."

16. David P. Howe, "Policy on Sport for the Disabled," in *Sport Policy in Canada*, ed. Lucie Thibault and Jean Harvey (Ottawa, Canada: University of Ottawa Press, 2013), 295–316, https://www.jstor.org/stable/j.ctt5hjk9x.15.

17. "About the Ironman Group," Ironman Group, accessed April 2, 2021, https://www.ironman.com/about-ironman-group.

18. "About the Ironman Group," Ironman Group.

19. "Disability Impacts All of Us Infographic," Centers for Disease Control and Prevention, September 16, 2020, https://www.cdc.gov/ncbddd/disabilityandhealth/infographic-disability-impacts-all.html.

20. "Disability and Health," World Health Organization, last modified December 1, 2020, https://www.who.int/news-room/fact-sheets/detail/disability-and-health.

21. World Health Organization and World Bank, *World Report on Disability* (Geneva, Switzerland: World Health Organization, 2011), https://apps.who.int/iris/handle/10665/44575.

22. "Autism Spectrum Disorders," World Health Organization, last modified April 2, 2021, https://www.who.int/news-room/fact-sheets/detail/autism-spectrum-disorders.

23. Robert E. Baker, Pamela H. Baker, Christopher Atwater, and Craig Esherick, "U.S. Sport Diplomacy in Latin America and the Caribbean: A Programme Evaluation," *Journal of Sport for Development* 6, no. 10 (2018): 71–85; Baker et al., "Sport for Development and Peace"; Baker et al., "Perceptions of International Sport Exchange Participants Regarding Inclusive Sport."

24. Eva Válková, "'You're Going to Teach My Son to Be *Viado*': From 'Girling' to *Queering* Sport for Development?" *International Review for the Sociology of Sport* 56, no. 1 (2021): 97–113, https://doi.org/10.1177/1012690219894885.

25. Agnes Elling and Annelies Knoppers, "Sport, Gender, and Ethnicity: Practises of Symbolic Inclusion/Exclusion," *Journal of Youth and Adolescence* 34, no. 3 (June 2005): 257–68, https://doi.org/10.1007/s10964-005-4311-6.

26. Elling and Knoppers, "Sport, Gender, and Ethnicity."

27. Válková, "'You're Going to Teach My Son to Be *Viado*.'"

28. Válková, "'You're Going to Teach My Son to Be *Viado*.'"

29. Válková, "'You're Going to Teach My Son to Be *Viado*.'"

30. Elling and Knoppers, "Sport, Gender, and Ethnicity," 264.

31. Elling and Knoppers, "Sport, Gender, and Ethnicity."

32. Elling and Knoppers, "Sport, Gender, and Ethnicity."

33. Frisby and Ponic, "Sport and Social Inclusion."

34. Lyndsay M. Hayhurst, Audrey R. Giles, and Jan Wright, "Biopedagogies and Indigenous Knowledge: Examining Sport for Development and Peace for Urban Indigenous Young Women in Canada and Australia," *Sport, Education and Society* 21, no. 4 (2016): 549–69.

35. Symeon Dagkas, Tansin Benn, and Haifaa Jawad, "Multiple Voices: Improving Participation of Muslim Girls in Physical Education and School Sport," *Sport, Education and Society* 16, no. 2 (March 2011): 223–39.

36. Tjønndal and Hovden, "'Will God Condemn Me Because I Love Boxing?'"

37. Tjønndal and Hovden, "'Will God Condemn Me Because I Love Boxing?'"

38. Dagkas et al., "Multiple Voices."

39. Marlene A. Dixon, Stacy M. Warner, and Jennifer E. Bruening, "More Than Just Letting Them Play: Parental Influence on Women's Lifetime Sport Involvement," *Sociology of Sport* 25, no. 4 (2008): 538–59.

40. Dixon et al., "More Than Just Letting Them Play."

41. Jane E. Ruseski, Brad R. Humphreys, Kirstin Hallmann, and Christoph Breuer, "Family Structure, Time Constraints, and Sport Participation," *European Review of Aging and Physical Activity* 8, no. 2 (2011): 57–66.

42. Philip White and William McTeer, "Socioeconomic Status and Sport Participation at Different Developmental Stages during Childhood and Youth: Multivariate Analyses Using Canadian National Survey Data," *Sociology of Sport Journal* 29, no. 2 (June 2012): 186–209, https://doi.org/10.1123/ssj.29.2.186.

43. R. Stalsberg and A. V. Pedersen, "Effects of Socioeconomic Status on the Physical Activity in Adolescents: A Systematic Review of the Evidence," *Scandinavian Journal of Medicine and Science in Sports* 20, no. 3 (June 2010): 368–83.

44. White and McTeer, "Socioeconomic Status and Sport Participation."

45. White and McTeer, "Socioeconomic Status and Sport Participation."

46. Stalsberg and Pedersen, "Effects of Socioeconomic Status on the Physical Activity in Adolescents."

47. Baker et al., "Perceptions of International Sport Exchange Participants Regarding Inclusive Sport."

48. North Carolina State University and the Center for Universal Design, "The Principles of Universal Design," April 1, 1997, https://projects.ncsu.edu/ncsu/design/cud/about_ud/udprinciplestext.htm.

49. Sheryl Burgstahler and DO-IT [Disabilities, Opportunities, Internetworking, and Technology], "Universal Design: Process, Principles, and Applications," 2015, https://www.washington.edu/doit/universal-design-process-principles-and-applications#header.

50. Burgstahler and DO-IT, "Universal Design."

51. Nico Schulenkorf, "Managing Sport-for-Development: Reflections and Outlook," *Sport Management Review* 20, no. 3 (2017): 243–51.

52. NC State University and the Center for Universal Design, "The Principles of Universal Design."

53. Burgstahler and DO-IT, "Universal Design."

54. CAST [formerly, Center for Applied Special Technology], "Universal Design for Learning Guidelines Version 2.2," 2018, http://udlguidelines.cast.org.

55. CAST, "Universal Design for Learning Guidelines Version 2.2."

56. CAST, "Universal Design for Learning Guidelines Version 2.2."

57. Lyras and Welty Peachey, "Integrating Sport-for-Development Theory and Praxis."

58. CAST, "Universal Design for Learning Guidelines Version 2.2."

59. CAST, "Universal Design for Learning Guidelines Version 2.2."

60. CAST, "Universal Design for Learning Guidelines Version 2.2."

61. CAST, "Universal Design for Learning Guidelines Version 2.2."

62. CAST, "Universal Design for Learning Guidelines Version 2.2."

63. CAST, "Universal Design for Learning Guidelines Version 2.2."

64. CAST, "Universal Design for Learning Guidelines Version 2.2."

65. CAST, "Universal Design for Learning Guidelines Version 2.2."

66. CAST, "Universal Design for Learning Guidelines Version 2.2."

67. CAST, "Universal Design for Learning Guidelines Version 2.2."

5

Sport, Conflict Resolution, and Diplomacy

Stuart Murray and Shinae Haidley

OBJECTIVES

This chapter will:

- Assess the differences and similarities between sport diplomacy and sport for development and peace.
- Critically analyze the shortcomings of some sport for development efforts.
- Discuss the major stakeholders engaged in sport diplomacy and sport for development and peace.
- Delineate the utility of sport as a diplomatic and development tool.

Throughout history, sport has provided an avenue for people from different nations to peacefully interact. It has a transcendental ability to move beyond politics, religion, and conflict because most humans speak the universal language of sport. Despite the entrenched differences between Israel and Palestine, children from both states can play a game of football together while learning "intrinsic values such as teamwork, fairness, discipline, respect for the opponent and the rules of the game."[1] From 1996 (when they were awarded hosting rights) to 2002, Japan and the Republic of Korea demonstrated they could suspend their frosty diplomatic relationship and work together, organize and co-host the biggest tournament of all—the World Cup. And, while the Islamic Republic of Iran and the United States of America have had no formal diplomatic relationship since 1978, freestyle wrestling provides the faintest sports diplomacy link between the two nations. Speaking on the eve of a controversial 1998 tour of Iran by the American team, Larry Sciacchetano, president of USA Wrestling, noted, "We're not going there as a political pawn. We're going there because we want to compete. Maybe it's too simplistic that sport ought to be above politics. Maybe it's naïve, but that's what I think."[2]

These are but a few of many examples that show the ability of sport to rise above political conflict. However, both the theory and practice of sport and conflict resolution (SCR) attract as much criticism as they do plaudits. From the purview of sociologists and behaviorists, the field is somewhat esoteric and is often accused of being naïve to believe that sport can resolve entrenched conflict. Despite being an interdisciplinary endeavor within sports sciences, SCR is also rather siloed and could engage in more cross-disciplinary activity. It has yet, for example, to incorporate knowledge from international relations (IR) and diplomatic studies, which focus on the structural causes—and solutions—of conflict: politics, the state, and the state system. Furthermore, SCR has a questionable track record in terms of sustaining peace. While cricket may bring India and Pakistan closer together for a day or two, sport pales into insignificance when compared with nuclear security, terrorist attacks, espionage, and which nation the disputed region of Kashmir belongs to. Moreover, SCR is a crowded playing field. Sovereign states, international regimes, nongovernmental organizations (NGOs), businesses, and elite athletes all play the game but lack cohesion, a shared strategy, or a networked approach where best practice, cost, and resources could be shared.

This chapter argues that such criticism could be mitigated via a fresh perspective on SCR: sports diplomacy. This new body of theory and practice contends that sport and politics do mix, all the time. As part of their commitment to the United Nations Agenda for Change 2030, sovereign states are introducing sport for development, conflict, and peace programs as integral parts of their diplomatic strategies and foreign policies. At the same time, sportspeople, clubs, businesses, and regimes are doing more "off the pitch," so to speak. The key to enhancing SCR is to think of the sport as a form of diplomacy and IR as a zero-sum game dominated by powerful, introspective, and—at times—bizarre nation-states. Sport, it turns out, has much to say of diplomacy, and vice versa.

This chapter begins with a literature review of SCR followed by a critique of its practice. This exercise alludes to the strengths and weaknesses of the paradigm and, crucially, the proverbial gaps in what we know, and do not know, about the use of sport as a tool for conflict resolution. The diplomatic quality, power, and character of sport is then established in anthropology and history before the term *sports diplomacy* is broken down, defined, and validated via a number of practical examples. These demonstrate that sports diplomacy and SCR share many similarities, and, working together, could provide a more networked, modern, and effective approach to the use of sport to suspend, mitigate, or sublimate conflict.

Figure 5.1. **Sport brings people together as reflected in this sign created by secondary school students in Moscow during a Russia–America youth ice hockey exchange.** *Credit*: Center for Sport Management at George Mason University

SPORT AND CONFLICT RESOLUTION: HISTORY, THEORY, AND DEFINITIONS

As Nico Schulenkorf, John Sugden, and Jack Sugden[3] note, the origins of SCR stem from Gordon Allport's seminal work *The Nature of Prejudice*.[4] The book, first published in 1954, claimed that instigating contact between opposing groups, through sport or other means, does not "automatically" improve relations between those groups. Building on this concept in the 1960s and 1970s, sociologists argued that sport is often "contested" and therefore serves as a source of conflict within and between societies.[5] Max Gluckman, for example, observed that the "balance [between conflict resolution and instigation] is often delicate," and that games can breed excitement and aggression simultaneously.[6] This understanding of sport parodied the twentieth century, an epoch characterized by war, ideological conflict, and nationalism. Trends in the literature reflected George Orwell's notion that international sport was little more than "war minus the shooting."[7]

However, in 1973, there was a shift toward a more positive view of the role sport could play in terms of peacemaking and conflict resolution. At the Tenth Olympic Congress, a motto was introduced that was radical at the time: "Sport in the service of peace."[8] Such a lofty goal ushered in a new era of scientific inquiry into the concept. In 1982, for example, Günther Lüschen, who wrote extensively on contemporaneous issues in sport, expressed that "conflict resolution or conflict instigation through sport is a functional rather than a causal question,"[9] subjecting the model to deeper analysis. Fred Coalter describes the subsequent interest in sport for development and conflict resolution in the 1990s, as peace and development theorists considered its potential to rectify "perceived failures of top-down economic aid and an increased concern with issues of human and social capital."[10]

At a minimum, these early advocates for SCR demonstrated that sporting activities served as a diversion for warring communities, creating "a haven for the temporary suspension of conflict."[11] Seen through a social constructivist lens, sport provided a relatively safe space to express rivalry, engage in competition, and redirect conflict.[12] Others such as Keith Gilbert and Will Bennett were of the view that grassroots organizations could use sport to increase intergroup contact and peacebuilding in conflict-affected areas.[13] While such ideas were ambitious, they were legitimized by a widespread consensus among academics and practitioners that sport is a force of social good.[14] Therefore, one of the greatest strengths in the theory of sport and conflict resolution is that sport "carr[ies] meaning beyond anything intrinsic to the activity itself."[15]

The body of literature is, however, not without fault. In academic terms, the theory of SCR is "a relatively new stream within the field of international development"[16] and does not yet enjoy substantive discussion beyond the fields of sociology and behavioral studies.[17] It is also difficult to isolate an agreed definition of SCR. Bruce Kidd's commonly cited definition, for instance, describes sport as a development tool, particularly in divided societies or seriously disadvantaged communities.[18] He links the concept of conflict resolution to sport and development, breaking activities of it into three categories:

1. Traditional sports development: the provision of basic sports coaching, equipment, and infrastructure from one country to another, typically undertaken as a form of diplomacy with the potential to forge new friendships or reduce tensions
2. Humanitarian assistance: using funds raised through sport or sponsorship to provide aid to those in conflict-affected areas
3. The sport for development and peace model: locally run projects for individual and community development purposes[19]

Alternatively, Roger Levermore proposes that sport for development and peace is defined by the desired outcomes of those who adopt it, which might include conflict resolution and intercultural understanding; physical and psychological health; and general welfare, economic development, or poverty alleviation.[20] Other scholars position SCR under the broader umbrella of constructivism.[21] By participating in cross-cultural networks and exchanges, often facilitated by sporting matches, private citizens can contribute to the maintenance of peace and community at the international level.[22] Richard Giulianotti, for example, writes that SCR is a positivistic philosophy that assumes that specific societies encounter "objectively identifiable social problems."[23] Sporting NGOs engage in "utilitarian intervention, with a likely commitment to the incremental resolution of social problems" in conflict situations.[24] Considering the contest over the basic meaning of SCR, it is little wonder that the field of studies is frequently described as "ambiguous" in the relevant literature.[25]

SCR: Theory into Practice

A brief, well-known, and practical example of SCR will add practical muscle to the preceding conceptual discussion. Football4Peace ("F4P") was the product of cumulative studies at the University of Brighton confirming "the deep-rootedness of nationalistic and sometimes prejudiced football cultures" in Northern Ireland.[26] In a bid to overcome sectarian violence in Belfast, the organization was founded in the 1990s and sought to integrate different communities into common football teams and coaching groups.[27]

What began as a "sport and integration experiment" expanded to northern Israel, where F4P established coaching camps for Jewish and Arab children, with a policy aim of "peaceful and sustainable coexistence."[28] However, early evaluations of the program found that sport-based contact alone was insufficient to promote enduring mutual understanding. The program was remodeled to remove emphasis on skill acquisition and competition and instead moved toward a coaching curriculum that taught respect, trust, responsibility, equality, and inclusivity, qualities that were later demonstrated back to researchers by participants.

Since its inception, the program has expanded across forty Jewish and Arab communities, and several international governmental organizations, including the European Union, have funded cross-community activities based on the F4P model.[29] One of the organization's successes is its willingness to engage in further research, work with diverse focus groups, write impact case studies backed up by good data, and master the intricacies of practicing SCR at the local level. Considering its history, success, and widespread appeal, F4P clearly demonstrates that sport can create positive, incremental contributions to peacebuilding.[30]

From this example, several practical tenets of SCR can be elucidated. For one, sport "enters into the most varied spheres of life and has numerous social, economic, and cultural interfaces and points of contact. From a development and peace perspective, [it] is . . . the ideal cross-cutting instrument."[31] Another practical strength is that SCR is a "low-cost, high-impact" tool to advance local, national, and global development objectives.[32] And, in conflict and postconflict situations, sport can, more readily than other development initiatives:

1. Strengthen interaction between communities, people, and cultures and thus contribute to the maintenance of a dialogue between the parties in an open or latent conflict situation.
2. Promote identity and solidarity among communities and increase the readiness of individuals to become involved in society.

3. Help to create a constructive outlet for the people affected by the conflict, which is oriented toward the peaceful reduction of aggression and tensions.
4. Assist in managing trauma after armed conflicts or natural catastrophes.[33]

In other words, SCR creates opportunities for intergroup contact and can be adjusted based on a group's needs and cultural history. If executed carefully, SCR can foster a sense of local empowerment and sustainable development for participants.[34]

At the turn of the century, SCR began to attract the attention of the UN. In 2001, the UN appointed a special adviser to the Secretary-General on Sport for Development and Peace, opened the United Nations Office on Sport for Development and Peace (UNOSDP), and commissioned the major report *Sport for Development and Peace: Towards Achieving the Millennium Development Goals* (eventually published in 2003).[35] In 2003 and 2005, the UN then organized the first high-level conferences on sport, conflict resolution, and development. These provided "important rhetorical and symbolic legitimation" for the SCR paradigm.[36]

Despite the closure of the UNOSDP in 2017 as part of Secretary-General António Guterres's sweeping reform agenda, both the theory and practice of sport for development and peace has gone from strength to strength. Significantly, other actors have stepped into fill the void created by the closure of the UNOSDP. These include, but are not limited to:

1. States: The Sport for Development and Peace International Working Group, an intergovernmental advisory body, asserts that the practice of SCR "ultimately depends" on states.[37] As states determine their own development priorities and allocate funding for initiatives, they hold significant power and influence in the sector.
2. Intergovernmental organizations such as the UN, Commonwealth Secretariat, the European Union, and the African Union are instrumental in drawing cohesive, international frameworks and developing regional goals for the practice of SCR.[38]
3. NGOs facilitate grassroots approaches to SCR. By engaging directly with conflict-affected communities, they play an important role in implementing and strengthening existing programs, disseminating information, and influencing policy decisions.[39]
4. Corporations often assist in the practice of SCR for corporate social responsibility purposes, providing valuable financial support in the process.[40]
5. Elite athletes can serve as powerful role models and highly effective advocates in the practice of SCR.[41]

This diverse cast of SCR actors demonstrates that many different institutions are active in the SCR space. However, and akin to its theory, the practice of SCR often attracts criticism. For one, the practical relationships between the players described here are characterized by disconnection, duplication, and estrangement. Actors remain "siloed," and financial burdens, best practices, and intellectual resources are not shared. Where collaboration occurs, it is often on a one-off basis as opposed to a sustainable partnership. There is also no shared vision, theory, or SCR doctrine that—as yet—encourages a plural, sustainable framework amenable to all.

In addition, in its "World Development Report 2007," the World Bank noted that SCR was a "promising but unproven" endeavor.[42] Besides a lack of empirical data, case studies are distorted by the various metrics used to measure the success of programs (as outlined previously) and an often overly optimistic interpretation of a program's performance.[43]

Moreover, SCR programs are rarely introduced by those living in the conflict-affected area.[44] Instead, they are imposed by an impartial "change agent," usually without any political, cultural, or ethnic affiliation to the conflict. Of course, in deeply divided societies, this "outside agent" can act as an objective mediator; however, where the intermediary is not aware of or does not respect cultural norms and traditions, tensions often escalate between groups and jeopardize the program.[45]

In addition, it is difficult to ensure that the "recruitment, training and capacity building of local people and expertise are prioritised over top-down and externally designed and imposed delivery models," especially when funding and volunteers for such programs are sourced externally.[46] Further weaknesses in the SCR model occur when host states encounter difficulties with sport governance, are subject to a lack of regulation in the development sector, experience excessive commercialization and politicization of sport, or are prone to corruption in the sector.[47]

A final concern is that there is a lack of theory on SCR from a diplomatic studies perspective. This field of studies focuses on the relationships between political entities such as sovereign states and nonstate actors as they navigate an extraordinarily complex IR system characterized by both order and anarchy. There is ample opportunity for IR scholars with a deeper understanding of geopolitics, conflict trends, and peacekeeping practices to bring a fresh perspective to SCR. It is also unusual that SCR has not developed in tandem with writings on sports diplomacy. Often described as the missing link between politics and sport, this relatively new area of theory and practice could be the key to enhancing SCR in the twenty-first century.

SPORTS DIPLOMACY

The practice of using sport for diplomatic purposes is ancient; however, the new wave of sports diplomacy scholarship and policy is relatively new, beginning in 2011. Applying best theory and practice from sports diplomacy could counter the weaknesses in SCR described in this chapter. Arguably, this new term better describes the role sport can play in addressing political and diplomatic estrangement between political entities (as opposed to sociological or behavioral divisions within societies). To validate this argument is to first deconstruct the term, starting with diplomacy.

A Crash Course in Diplomacy, the "Business of Peace"

For most, diplomacy is a profession practiced by officially accredited representatives serving their government in overseas embassies, consulates, and commissions. Diplomats, who physically represent their state abroad, communicate their state's core national interests and foreign policy positions to other states, minimize friction in political relationships, and, via bilateral and multilateral channels, negotiate with other diplomats.

Diplomacy is a means to a state's foreign policy ends. As Geoff Berridge, Maurice Keens-Soper, and T. G. Otte note, it is "the term given to the official channels of communication employed by the members of a system of states" whose "chief purpose" is to "enable states to secure the objectives of their foreign policies without resort to force, propaganda, or law."[48] Berridge and colleagues are not alone in stressing diplomacy's peaceful nature. For Sir Ernest Satow and many other distinguished former diplomats, diplomacy is "the conduct of business between states by peaceful means."[49]

For "outsiders," however, a stereotypical view of the "dialogue between states" prevails.[50] According to Seymour Finger, a typical foreign service is made up of "rich young men" who spend "most of their time on high living abroad."[51] Paul Sharp is more sardonic, claiming that "among general publics, a well-developed image exists of a privileged elite pursuing exciting and prestigious careers, without paying parking tickets and with varying degrees of effectiveness."[52] Seminal books in the canon reinforce this trite opinion of diplomacy. Henry Kissinger's 1994 *Diplomacy* tome, for example, is full of "pictures of grand old men at major international conferences that reshaped the contours of our world over the past few centuries."[53]

As with most stereotypes, however, these views are quite far from the truth. While diplomacy does have its issues—it is largely a secret, opaque activity in an era where openness, authenticity, and transparency are the order of the day; in many foreign services the ranks of diplomats are "pale, male, and stale," and, in some countries, diplomacy is bereft of morals—it is vital to the peaceful functioning of the IR system. Raymond Cohen quite rightly describes diplomacy as the "engine room"[54] of international affairs, and Satow as the "best means devised by civilisation for preventing IR from being governed by force alone."[55] Throughout the ages, it is diplomacy—not trade, statecraft, or armed force—that has been the difference between war and peace, chaos and order, suffering and progress.

"Widening" the Business of Peace

While the state and its diplomats are the custodians of diplomacy, they do not own the profession, nor the concept. Diplomacy, in other words, is not axiomatic with the state. Arguably, all humans are all diplomats. We share many complex relationships in a world made up, largely, of strangers. We exchange messages, have core interests, represent something to others, gather and disseminate information, and try to negotiate the anarchy and order of life while, ideally, avoiding major conflicts. In the 1990s, this type of revolutionary way of thinking led several scholars to "widen" the centuries-old understanding of diplomacy.[56] The sovereign state, they argued and empirically demonstrated, did not, and should not, have a monopoly on the core functions of diplomacy: "communication, negotiation, information gathering, the minimisation of friction and representation."[57]

Arguably, nonstate actors are equally placed to carry out these functions because they are not bound by state concerns such as survival, security, and national interests. This is why one of the leading diplomatic scholars, Paul Sharp, redefined *diplomacy* in 2003 as "a theory of how human relations are and might be conducted between groups that seek to live separately from one another and hold this separation to be both good and desirable."[58] For Sharp, and others, our social, cultural, and political landscapes are dominated by a broad range of actors that are fundamentally "estranged" and "alienated."[59] Diplomacy, whether practiced by states, groups, or individuals, is an ancient, civil activity, a system that "mediates" separation created by the institutions that humans form. It is therefore important to "relax the assumption that diplomacy is conducted only by states" and instead view diplomacy as "human beings engaged in a particular kind of social practice."[60]

Such simple yet profound epistemological realizations led to a flood of new ideas into diplomatic studies. Brian Hocking's "multistakeholder" paradigm, where "diplomacy is an activity concerned with the creation of networks, embracing a range of state and non-state actors," aptly describes the character of modern diplomacy.[61] Diplomacy is no longer an exclusive dialogue between officially accredited representatives of states but a plural effort often involving multinational corporations, chief security officers, intergovernmental institutions, and even influential "celebrity diplomats," to borrow Andrew Cooper's term.[62]

Many of these new diplomatic actors coalesce in fluid, ad hoc, and plural networks in an organic, rapidly evolving diplomatic environment. In this dynamic, experimental setting, music, art, sport, and even food have become the subject of inquiry in the theory and practice of diplomacy. All are universal soft-power languages, which facilitate contact among diverse stakeholders at home and abroad. Working in tandem with traditional diplomacy, sport, for example, is no longer below government but an increasingly relevant soft-power tool desperately required to solve a host of old, and new, problems.

The Diplomatic Qualities of Sport

The discerning polymath will already detect similarities between diplomacy and sport, particularly that diplomacy is a conscious device governed by rules and "players" that evolved to bridge divides between separate communities. Sport, too, is one of the oldest, complex institutions created by humans for pleasure, spectacle, and, seen through a diplomatic lens, the sublimation of conflict and the "mediation of estrangement."[63]

Anthropological evidence supports this broad thesis. Games, play, running, sport, and so on are woven into human DNA. Sportspeople all over the world practice the same universal skills: hand-eye coordination, athleticism, physical exertion, organization, and discipline, for example.[64] Nelson Mandela was correct when, in his now famous speech, he argued that sport "has the power to unite people in a way that little else does."[65] While 7.8 billion (and counting) humans remain separated by borders, governments, language, religion, and so on, sport is something they all have in common. This is why people from all walks of life refer to as sport as the "great leveller," something Queen Elizabeth, a keen horse rider and shooting enthusiast in her day, agrees with: "The same rules apply to all; there are no age, racial or cultural barriers to participation. Indeed, enthusiasm for a sport brings together people from every background."[66] It is this very universality of sport that makes it a perfect tool for diplomacy, whose core purpose is to overcome estrangement between political communities via common mechanisms.

Sport and diplomacy connect all human beings, both in a modern and prehistoric sense. Returning to the ancient past, the earliest nations used sport for social, cultural, and diplomatic purposes, especially to avoid intergroup conflict. Sport played a vital role as a "civilizing process" and often reduced the prospect of conflict.[67] Konrad Lorenz, a celebrated zoologist, ethologist, ornithologist, and Nobel Prize winner, notes that because sport "probably originated from highly ritualized, but still hostile fighting . . . it can be defined as a specifically human form of non-hostile combat, governed by the strictest of culturally developed rules."[68]

For Lorenz, sport "contains aggressive motivation," a quality that can be traced back to the "evolution of tribal warfare at the very dawn of culture."[69] An abundance of anthropological and historical evidence adds further credence. First Australians, for example, engaged in sport to avoid conflict. When the British arrived to set up a penal colony in 1788, the First People of Australia numbered around 750,000 and the population was split into roughly five hundred or so clan groups or nations, each with a distinctive culture, belief system, and language.[70] These communities were separated and occasionally hostile to one another; however, they all spoke the common language of sport. *Battendi* (a spear-throwing game), *Marngrook* (a form of football, played with a ball made up of sewn kangaroo or possum skin), and *Koolche* (a ball throwing and hitting game) are good examples of common Aboriginal games that were played between separate political communities.[71]

Sport and games had many different purposes for Indigenous Australians: to "absorb conflict, to increase communication between tribes, to record and celebrate tribal lore"; to teach the "young to ultimately become effective tribal providers"; and, concomitantly, to remind the elders of what skills were required for good statecraft and diplomacy.[72] Some games, such as *Prun*, mimicked warfare and were a shared means of avoiding real, deadly, and serious forms of conflict. Michael Salter describes *Prun* as a

> sort of mock war used as a means to settle disputes between separate groups of aboriginal communities. Brandishing spears, shields and boomerangs, and wearing elaborate dress and body paints, both the men and the women enter the designated "fighting" and the "sport" begins.[73]

Figure 5.2. Teamwork provides the building blocks of change. *Credit*: Ashi Fachler

The game is still played to this day and for much the same reasons. Local clan groups "use the event as an opportunity to settle disputes, to entertain themselves, or simply show off their respective skills."[74]

Throughout most periods of history the diplomatic utility of sport is evident. The Ancient Olympiad, for example, began in 776 BCE "in a religious setting as one of the activities during the festival of Zeus," subsequently morphed into a complex and famous sporting competition, and was finally abolished in 394 CE by the Roman Emperor Theodosius I as part of a campaign to abolish Paganism and impose Christianity as a state religion.[75] The Olympic Truce prevented conflict between Greek city-states and afforded athletes, spectators, and officials protection while traveling to and from the Games. *Ekecheria*, the Greek word for "a staying of the hand," allowed citizens from estranged political entities to travel safely, even while journeying through enemy territory. The ancient Games were also an expression of Panhellenism. While Sparta, Argos, Athens, and others had their military rivalries and political differences, sport was something they all had in common. It transcended politics, in other words.

Sport can also be used to consolidate acrimonious relationships, as was the case with the 1520 meeting between King François I of France and Henry VIII of England.[76] After a century of hostilities, the two kings hosted a summit at the Fields of Cloth of Gold in northern France. For two weeks, François, Henry, and their retinues wrestled, jousted, and competed in archery events as a means of strengthening the bond of friendship after the signing of the Anglo–French Treaty of 1514.[77]

More recently, diplomatically estranged states have used sport as a way of exploring the normalization of diplomatic relations. The best example is, of course, the case of "ping-pong diplomacy" between Chinese and American table tennis players. A visit by the US Table Tennis team to China in 1971, to play a series of exhibition matches, was used as a "vehicle to test whether the public of the two countries would be accepting of a more formal diplomatic opening of frozen relations between the two Cold War adversaries."[78] These games led to the normalization of relations between China and the United States after decades of animosity and paved the way for US national security advisor Henry Kissinger's July 1971 visit and the more famous visit by US president Richard Nixon in February 1972.

States, however, are not the only actors interested in the opiate of the masses. NGOs such as Beyond Sport or Right to Play use sport to raise awareness of social issues or as part of disarmament, demobilization, and reintegration programs in war-torn nations such as Afghanistan. Sport is also extraordinarily useful for augmenting development initiatives, such as the UN's Millennium and Sustainable Development Goals (SDGs). And, not to be forgotten, international sporting regimes such as Fédération Internationale de Football Association (FIFA) are highly visible and often controversial actors in both football and politics. The 2022 World Cup to be held in Qatar could, for example, became a political football match between Iran and Saudi Arabia (and their powerful allies).

Clearly, sport plays a major part in the IR between states, nonstate actors, and people all over the world. For its advocates, sport is a hallmark of civilization, a way to avoid conflict, and a powerful yet neglected diplomatic device that effortlessly brings people closer together. Recently, such realizations created a new field of studies: sports diplomacy.

Sports Diplomacy

As noted, sport has been part of the diplomatic milieu for tens of thousands of years. However, and despite the "profound connections between sport and international affairs," the study of this "mixing" of sport and policy was a "mere backwater," a "peripheral" or "perfunctory aside."[79] This academic neglect ended around the late 1960s. Scholars such as Christopher Chataway and Philip Goodhart in their seminal *War without Weapons*, Richard Espy who wrote the first survey of Olympic Sport and IR, and many others since became epistemic trailblazers for the study of sport and IR.[80] These days, there are plenty of works that focus on sport and IR,[81] sport and war,[82] sport for development and peace,[83] and many other topics with an IR flavor. Far less attention, however, has been paid to the means and processes of such exchanges: sports diplomacy.

An esoteric area of theory, "old" sports diplomacy languished in the bleachers of the canon of diplomatic studies. For decades, all that existed was a collection of anecdotal, sporadic, and case-study articles on important but familiar narratives: ping-pong diplomacy, the role sport played in isolating apartheid South Africa, or the intermittent baseball diplomacy practiced between the United States and Cuba, for instance. Academics, such as Jeremy Goldberg, wrote papers titled "Sporting Diplomacy" but simply rehashed common historical narratives of sport and IR or mentioned tantalizing areas of research without inquiring further.[84]

A new wave of sports diplomacy scholarship and policy began in 2011 with a seminal conference paper presented at the International Symposium on Cultural Diplomacy in Berlin.[85] Several panels at major international conferences followed, four special issues of major academic journals,[86] and, in signs of a growing field, a few research monographs have appeared. Aaron Beacom's *International Diplomacy and the Olympic Movement*, Heather Dichter and Andrew Johns's *Diplomatic Games*, J. Simon Rofe's *Sport and Diplomacy*, and Stuart Murray's *Sports Diplomacy: Origins, Theory and Practice* spring to mind. All of these works allude to fecund intellectual terrain, one that is "at once parochial and universal, unifying and dividing, and has the power to fundamentally affect relations between individuals and nations."[87]

In terms of a theoretical ambit, sports diplomacy focuses on the processes, actors (state, nonstate, and individual) involved where sport, politics, and diplomacy overlap. It is a new term that describes and reconceptualizes an old practice: the use of sport to realize goals, minimize friction, and generally bring strangers closer together. More specifically, it can be defined as the conscious, strategic use of sportspeople and sporting events by state and nonstate actors to engage, inform, and create a favorable image among foreign publics and organizations to shape their perceptions in a way that is (more) conducive to the sending group's goals.[88]

Sports diplomacy encapsulates the notion of "rethinking collaboration,"[89] and the reason behind its growth is simple: It is a new, grand area of theory, strategy, and practice and a metadoctrine that brings greater order to the crowded landscapes of sport *and* politics. As a theory, it encourages mapping, reviewing, and the bespoke application of the best knowledge around the world on harnessing the power of sport to effect change at local, national, and international political levels. Practically, it provides a way of integrating disparate sporting and political systems conducive to improved working relationships and sustainable partnerships for mutual gain.

Sports Diplomacy: Theory into Practice

Many states, regimes, and institutions are turning toward sports diplomacy. Indian and Pakistani leaders often engage in cricket diplomacy as a means of diffusing tensions over Kashmir, terrorist attacks, trade disputes, and any number of security dilemmas. After September 11, 2001, the US Department of State instigated the SportsUnited initiative as a way to engage disenfranchised young Muslims across Africa, the Middle East, and South Asia. More recently, Japan, Croatia, Wales, and the European Commission have launched sports diplomacy policies, working groups, and strategies. In 2019, the United Nations created a UNESCO Chair on Sports Diplomacy and Development; Afghanistan is investigating sports diplomacy as a way of telling a different, more positive story of the war-torn nation; and in 2019 the Australian Minister for Foreign Affairs, Marise Payne, launched the federal *Sports Diplomacy 2030* strategy in order to "support the great work of the sport industry and athletes as they engage across the world, and provide them with the skills and networks to support our broader diplomatic efforts, . . . and [unlock] the opportunities off-field between Australia and the global sports community."[90]

The new federal strategy is a good example of sport driving innovation in diplomacy, as well as bringing government closer to sport and vice versa. The entrance of sovereign states and intergovernmental organizations such as the European Commission into the hallowed realms of sport is nothing new. Political entities, well aware of the opiate of the masses, have been trying to co-opt sport for decades. The difference today is that these entrances are no longer sporadic, opportunistic, and jingoistic. The examples described here are driven by sports diplomacy strategies or policies aimed at creating better, sustainable links between government and sport.

However, as this final section argues, perhaps governments are not the best frontline actors to truly unleash the "power" of sport "to change the world." Indeed, for many lovers of sport, politicians should be kept far away from sport and sporting arenas. A choreographed appearance by a politician at a sporting event is often seen as a cheap stunt designed to win a few votes, a mere photo-op. Moreover, the practice can look rather clumsy and intrusive: fans come to stadiums to watch sport and not to listen to politicians. Words and messages that have some meaning in national and international politics are, therefore, nothing more than "empty sounds . . . after passing through the gates of sport."[91] After all, sport, sportspeople, or sporting events are co-opted by governments only if they provide a direct benefit to a state's national interest or help realize a foreign policy goal.

Moreover, national interests will always trump regional or international interests, and hard-power concerns will always override "low," soft-power initiatives. For governments, sport will always come second to survival, nationalism, trade, and security.

In the era of globalization, one increasingly marked by pluralism, transparency, and innovation, juxtaposed with the Gordian challenges of climate change, terrorism, and toxic national populism, it is time to think differently; time, perhaps, to train an army of nonstate sports institutions and diplomats.

Sports Diplomacy, Conflict Resolution, and Nonstate Actors

In the tumultuous twenty-first century, the opportunity in using sport as a "resource for hope" lies with nonstate sporting actors (NSSAs) working more closely with sovereign states.[92] Players, clubs, sporting NGOs, businesses, and regimes are but five examples of NSSAs that, as this section argues, are far better placed, skilled, and equipped to deliver sports diplomacy, sport for development, and SCR programs. Three arguments in support of this hypothesis are presented as follows.

First, many NSSAs already exhibit diplomatic characteristics, qualities, and capacities. Individually, a regime such as the International Olympic Committee (IOC), for example, has a flag, a charter, policy goals, representatives, and a role—and history—of peacemaking between nations via sport enshrined in the Olympic Truce. Collectively, the IOC works on a daily basis with a wide range of actors, all of whom communicate, negotiate, and engage in diplomatic representation "to make international sporting competition possible" in the first place.[93] Sport is the reason this network exists (playing, organizing, or marketing it, for example), and a unique type of sport-as-diplomacy is the glue that binds it together.

Second, because sport requires stability to function, it is a generally positive phenomenon that minimizes friction in international affairs. In other words, NSSAs are geared for peace and, unlike states, are not hamstrung by national interests; classical political-military agendas; and the stiff, boring "waltz" of the *haute politique*. In the plural, networked, and "flat" era, NSSAs have a far greater role to play than simply organizing sport.[94] This capacity—nay, obligation—is exactly what Mandela meant when he said that sport is "more powerful than government."[95]

Third, and related, NSSAs are vital to realizing *human*—not traditional or state—security. Human security is vital in the twenty-first century because it moves away from "traditional, state-centric conceptions" and "concentrates on the security of individuals, their protection and empowerment."[96] NSSAs are both creators and custodians of a reinvigorated, vital, and positive interface between sport and human "security, development and human rights."[97] If sport cannot "change the world" (and it is a big ask), it can certainly help make humans' lives better as a diplomatic vehicle to the human security and, for example, the SDGs.

A brief example might shed further light on these arguments. In March 2015, the Afghanistan cricket team flew to Australia and New Zealand to participate in their first-ever international tournament, the International Cricket Council (ICC) World Cup. Coming from a nation blighted by conflict since the late 1960s, qualifying for the tournament alone was a remarkable feat. In 2013, when the team beat Kenya to qualify for the 2015 ICC World Cup, the entire nation celebrated, the Taliban included. A fan, Wahidullah Mihakhail, summed the moment up, noting that victory had provided Afghanistan with something that no politician or militant could: "unity to a nation that has had too many years of war."[98]

Similar scenes were repeated two years later when the team, made up of players who grew up in refugee camps, finally made it to the 2015 World Cup. They only managed to win one match—eking out a victory over Scotland in the most dramatic fashion (one wicket in hand and three balls remaining)—but anyone watching could be forgiven for thinking the Afghan team had won the trophy. Some players wept, others did cartwheels or danced, and a few tried to lift Shapoor Zadra, who hit the winning boundary (he's over six and a half feet tall and weighs about 110 kilograms). Several other players did nothing. Paralyzed by disbelief and euphoria they just stood, lost to a sporting trance. Meanwhile, "in the streets of Kabul and Jalalabad, in the provinces of Paktia and Kandahar" the entire nation celebrated.[99] For a moment, a warring country was united by a national team, playing in a tournament 8,380 miles away. The story reverberated around the world, capturing "the imaginations of not only cricket fans, but of people everywhere."[100] In 2017, Afghanistan was offered full ICC membership (and, therefore, Test status), another memorable occasion in the practice of SCR, the sort of fairy-tale, miracle moment that sport regularly delivers.

The triumph of the Afghan cricket team confirms that sport is indeed a form of diplomacy and conflict resolution. History abounds with other examples of sport overcoming estrangement. The First World War Christmas Truce, when some German and British troops exchanged gifts and played football in No Man's Land, is an example of sport *minimizing friction* between enemies in the most warlike of circumstances.[101] Or, in 1966, when the boxer Muhammed Ali defied the draft and refused to fight in the Vietnam War, he *communicated* the way that many Americans felt about the impending war via a simple, famous message of "Man, I ain't got no quarrel with them Viet Cong." And in August 2016, the American football player Colin Kaepernick gained worldwide attention by "taking a knee" while the national anthem was playing in protest of the oppression of people of color in the United States. Kaepernick's silent gesture inspired many other black and white sports stars, and within a matter of months he became the *representative* for "a movement dividing a country."[102]

So far, however, only a few diplomatic scholars have tinkered with this promising area of sports as diplomacy.[103] The framework needs more diplomatic analysis, particularly in terms of what works and what does not. The American soccer star Megan Rapinoe is often held up as a powerful role model and activist, personifying the way many women feel about their role in a patriarchal society thousands of years old. However, a diplomat would suggest that activism, while important, serves only to antagonize a more powerful incumbent. Moreover, what key messages, culture, and values is Rapinoe *communicating*? Considering many women are estranged from men (and vice versa), how does she *negotiate* with her male interlocutors that produce and reproduce an overwhelmingly patriarchal world (remember Politics 101: people in power rarely surrender power).

The same might be said of the remarkable story of Didier Drogba when, after qualifying for the 2006 World Cup (the first time for the country in seventy-six years), Drogba and his Muslim and Christian Ivory Coast teammates played a vital role in ending a brutal five-year civil war. Success on the pitch demonstrated that Ivorians could play in harmony irrespective of their creeds, backgrounds, or religions. Rather than regurgitating the same fascinating story, however, a diplomat might ask: How did this happen? What unique factors do sportspeople have that diplomats, politicians, and peacemakers do not? Why did Ivorians listen to footballers and not the president? Is this a model that can be studied, replicated, and rolled out in other regions suffering conflict? There are many other cases where sport has mixed with politics that, similarly, need to be studied, modeled, and—where possible—replicated.

THE FINAL WHISTLE

If this chapter has proven anything, it is that there are many different players and systems where sport, diplomacy, and conflict resolution overlap. At the moment, however, states, regimes, and NSSAs continue to work largely in isolation. Sports diplomacy is a new way of thinking about the relationships that exist between sport, politics, and conflict resolution. Analogously, we can equate sports diplomacy with the doctrine of Total Football that propelled the Dutch national team to great heights in the 1970s (or, F. C. Barcelona and tiki-taka, for a more recent example, coincidentally introduced by Johan Cruyff). The structure of the game remained the same—twenty-two players still kicked a ball around on a rectangular pitch—but how one of the teams played the game was revolutionary. Sports diplomacy is similar. It is a new way to think about, and play, the sport, politics, and conflict resolution game.

The challenge is to ensure that all players have a common vision, a willingness to learn from one another, and a willingness to accept that they are stronger working together, ideally in sustainable networks. Some sports-mad nations are already doing just that. Somewhat unusually, for these projects are generally in-house, the Australian government's *Sports Diplomacy 2030* strategy was designed after a five-month period of consultation with the sport industry. As one of the architects of the strategy, Caitlin Byrne, noted, "[A] long period of national consultation occurred with the sports industry before a single word of the new strategy was written."[104] Government listened to, and incorporated, the views of sports people, academics, sport-for-development practitioners, sports businesses, administrators, fans, and so on. Rather than barging into the world of sport, as has often been the case in the past, the Australian Government realized that if the strategy were to work, its success depended on a new era of "partnership" with the sports industry.[105]

When it comes to sport and diplomacy, the Australians are exceptionally well qualified. One of the instigators of a new strategic approach to sport and diplomacy is Julie Bishop, the foreign minister of Australia from 2013 to 2018, a keen runner and ardent supporter of the West Coast Eagles Australian Rules Football team. In

2002, long before she entered high office, Bishop served as an election observer in Zimbabwe during the landgrab by Robert Mugabe's war veterans, who had been invading, terrorizing, and trashing white-settler farms. In a remote area near the Mozambique border, Bishop visited a farm and met with some veterans sitting round a campfire. She recalls:

> I was introduced to the leader of the gang—toothless, bike chains around his neck, wearing animal skins, with machetes, guns and weapons. After quickly clarifying I was Australian and not British, the leader of the gang looked me up and down and said . . . you don't know Shane Warne [a legendary Australian cricketer], do you? The moment was saved.[106]

Many people have a story like the former Australian foreign minister, cast abroad to a strange and foreign land where sport provides a bond between strangers, regardless of our position in life, race, creed, or religion. That is both the simplicity and beauty of sports diplomacy, a new, growing method of breathing fresh life into the vital role sport can play in bringing groups of people locked in conflict closer together.

Questions

1. Define *sport diplomacy*.
2. Define *sport for development*.
3. Who are the major stakeholders in the sport for development space?
4. Name some of the soft-power tools used by nations in their diplomatic toolbox.
5. Other than the United States, what nations use sport as a diplomatic tool? How is it used?
6. What parties were involved in the design of Australia's *Sports Diplomacy 2030* initiative?
7. What are some of the major criticisms of organizations that engage in sport for development and peace?

Learning Activity

1. Viewing the websites of three organizations involved in sport for development and peace, compare and contrast these organizations.
    a. What is the mission and purpose of each organization?
    b. Who are the executives?
    c. Who are the sponsors?
    d. Where are they headquartered?
    e. What are the major projects?

NOTES

1. "International Day of Sport for Development and Peace," United Nations, accessed November 22, 2020, https://www.un.org/en/events/sportday/.

2. Daniel Pearl, "Iran Hopes to Use Wrestling to Warm Relations with the U.S.," *Wall Street Journal*, last modified January 12, 1998, https://www.wsj.com/articles/SB884557829174997000.

3. Nico Schulenkorf, John Sugden, and Jack Sugden, "Sport for Conflict Resolution and Peace Building," in *Managing Sport Development: An International Approach*, ed. Emma Sherry, Nico Schulenkorf and Pamm Phillips (New York: Routledge, 2016), 163.

4. Gordon W. Allport, *The Nature of Prejudice* (Cambridge, MA: Addison-Wesley, 1954).

5. See, for example, Pelle Kvalsund, "Sport and Peace Building," 2007, https://www.sportanddev.org/sites/default/files/downloads/sport_and_peace_paper_pelle_kvalsund.pdf; John Sugden, "The Ripple Effect: Critical Pragmatism, Conflict Resolution and Peace Building through Sport in Deeply Divided Societies," in *Global Sport-for-Development: Critical Perspectives*, ed. Nico Schulenkorf and Daryl Adair (London: Palgrave Macmillan, 2013), 79–96.

6. Max Gluckman, "Sport and Conflict," in *Sport in the Modern World: Chances and Problems*, ed. Ommo Groupe, Dietrich Kurz, and Johannes Marcus Teipel (Berlin, Germany: Springer, 1973), 48–54.

7. George Orwell, "The Sporting Spirit," accessed January 13, 2020, http://www.orwell.ru/library/articles/spirit/english/e_spirit.

8. Günther Lüschen, "Sport, Conflict and Conflict Resolution," *International Social Science Journal* 34, no. 2 (1982): 185; The International Olympic Committee, "Promote Olympism in Society," 2019, https://www.olympic.org/the-ioc/promote-olympism.

9. Lüschen, "Sport, Conflict and Conflict Resolution."

10. Fred Coalter, "The Politics of Sport-for-Development: Limited Focus Programmes and Broad Gauge Problems?" *International Review for the Sociology of Sport* 45, no. 3 (2010), 291–314.

11. John Sugden, "Critical Left-Realism and Sport Interventions in Divided Societies," *International Review for the Sociology of Sport* 45, no. 3 (2010): 258–72.

12. Philip Goodhart and Christopher John Chataway, *War without Weapons: The Rise of Class Sport in the Twentieth Century and Its Effect on Men and Nations* (London: W. H. Allen, 1968).

13. Keith Gilbert and Will Bennett, eds., *Sport, Peace and Development* (Champaign, IL: Common Ground, 2012).

14. Samantha Nanayakkara, "Olympism in Practice: An Evaluation of the Effectiveness of an Olympism Education Programme to Resolve Conflicts between Primary School Students in Sri Lanka" (PhD thesis, University of Canterbury, 2012); International Platform on Sport and Development, "Defining Peace and Relationship Building," 2019, https://www.sportanddev.org/en/learn-more/peacebuilding/defining-peace-and-relationship-building; John Sugden, "Critical Left-Realism and Sport Interventions in Divided Societies."

15. Sugden, "Critical Left-Realism and Sport Interventions in Divided Societies."

16. Schulenkorf, Sugden, and Sugden, "Sport for Conflict Resolution and Peace Building."

17. Roger Levermore, "Sport: A New Engine of Development?" *Progress in Development Studies* 8, no. 2 (2008): 183–90.

18. Bruce Kidd, "A New Social Movement: Sport for Development and Peace," *Sport in Society* 11, no. 4 (2008): 370–80.

19. Kidd, "A New Social Movement: Sport for Development and Peace."
20. Levermore, "Sport: A New Engine of Development?"
21. Patrick Thaddeus Jackson and Joshua S. Jones, "Constructivism," in *An Introduction to International Relations*, 2nd ed., ed. Richard Devetak, Anthony Burke, and Jim George (Melbourne, Australia: Cambridge University Press, 2012), 117.
22. Jackson and Jones, "Constructivism."
23. Richard Giulianotti, "Sport, Peacemaking and Conflict Resolution: A Contextual Analysis and Modelling of the Sport, Development and Peace Sector," *Ethnic and Racial Studies* 34, no. 2 (2011): 207–28.
24. Giulianotti, "Sport, Peacemaking and Conflict Resolution."
25. Sugden, "Critical Left-Realism and Sport Interventions in Divided Societies"; Richard Giulianotti, "Sport, Peacemaking and Conflict Resolution."
26. University of Brighton, "Impact Case Study: Football4Peace," Research Excellence Framework 2014, https://ref.ac.uk/CaseStudy.aspx?Id=39771.
27. Schulenkorf, Sugden, and Sugden, "Sport for Conflict Resolution and Peace Building," 164.
28. Schulenkorf, Sugden, and Sugden, "Sport for Conflict Resolution and Peace Building," 164.
29. Football 4 Peace International, "F4P Israel," University of Brighton, 2014, http://www.football4peace.eu/projects/israel/.
30. University of Brighton, "Impact Case Study: Football4Peace."
31. Swiss Agency for Development and Cooperation, "Sport for Development and Peace," 2005, https://www.sportanddev.org/sites/default/files/downloads/44_sport_for_development_and_peace.pdf.
32. Schulenkorf, Sugden, and Sugden, "Sport for Conflict Resolution and Peace Building."
33. Swiss Agency for Development and Cooperation, "Sport for Development and Peace."
34. Schulenkorf, Sugden, and Sugden, "Sport for Conflict Resolution and Peace Building."
35. Sport for Development and Peace International Working Group, "Sport for Development and Peace: From Practice to Policy," Preliminary Report of the Sport for Development and Peace International Working Group, June 2006, https://www.sportanddev.org/sites/default/files/downloads/20__s_for_dev_and_peace__from_practice_to_policy.pdf.
36. Kidd, "A New Social Movement: Sport for Development and Peace."
37. Sport for Development and Peace International Working Group, "Sport for Development and Peace: From Practice to Policy."
38. African Union, "Policy Framework for the Sustainable Development of Sport in Africa (2008–2018)," October 14, 2008, https://au.int/sites/default/files/pages/32902-file-final_sport_policy_framework_for_africa-version_to_be_printed_-_english.pdf.
39. Tom Woodhouse (2016).
40. Richard Giulianotti and Gary Armstrong, "The Sport for Development and Peace Sector: A Critical Sociological Analysis," in *Global Sport-for-Development: Critical Perspectives*, ed. Nico Schulenkorf and Daryl Adair (London: Palgrave Macmillan, 2013), 15–32.
41. Sport for Development and Peace International Working Group, "Sport for Development and Peace: From Practice to Policy"; Woodhouse.
42. The World Bank, "World Development Report 2007: Development and the Next Generation," 2006, http://documents.worldbank.org/curated/en/556251468128407787/pdf/359990WDR0complete.pdf.

43. David R. Black, "The Ambiguities of Development: Implications for 'Development through Sport,'" *Sport in Society* 13, no. 1 (2010): 121–29.

44. Nico Schulenkorf, "The Roles and Responsibilities of a Change Agent in Sport Event Development Projects," *Sport Management Review* 13, no. 2 (May 2010): 118–28.

45. Schulenkorf, Sugden, and Sugden, "Sport for Conflict Resolution and Peace Building."

46. Schulenkorf, Sugden, and Sugden, "Sport for Conflict Resolution and Peace Building."

47. Sport for Development and Peace International Working Group, "Sport for Development and Peace: From Practice to Policy."

48. Geoff R. Berridge, Maurice Keens-Soper, and T. G. Otte, *Diplomatic Theory from Machiavelli to Kissinger* (New York: Palgrave, 2001), 1.

49. Sir Ernest Satow, *A Guide to Diplomatic Practice*, 4th ed. (London: Longmans, Green and Co., 1957), 3.

50. Adam Watson, *Diplomacy: The Dialogue between States* (London: Eyre Methuen, 1982), 10.

51. Seymour Maxwell Finger, *Inside the World of Diplomacy: The US Foreign Service in a Changing World* (Portsmouth, NH: Greenwood, 2002), 1.

52. Paul Sharp, "For Diplomacy: Representation and the Study of International Relations," *International Studies Review* 1, no. 1 (1999): 40.

53. Peter Varghese, "Australian Diplomacy Today," accessed January 13, 2020, http://dfat.gov.au/news/speeches/Pages/australian-diplomacy-today-symposium.aspx.

54. Raymond Cohen, "Putting Diplomatic Studies on the Map," *Diplomatic Studies Program Newsletter* (Leicester University, 1988), 1.

55. Satow, *A Guide to Diplomatic Practice*, 1.

56. Stuart Murray, Paul Sharp, Geoffrey Wiseman, David Criekemans, and Jan Melissen, "The Present and Future of Diplomacy and Diplomatic Studies," *International Studies Review* 13, no. 4 (December 2011): 709–28.

57. Hedley Bull, *The Anarchical Society: A Study of Order in World Politics* (New York: Columbia University Press, 1977), 171–75.

58. Paul Sharp, "Herbert Butterfield, the English School and the Civilizing Virtues of Diplomacy," *International Affairs* 79, no. 4 (2003): 857.

59. James Der Derian, "Mediating Estrangement: A Theory for Diplomacy," *Review of International Studies* 13, no. 2 (1987): 91–110.

60. Paul Sharp, "Diplomacy in International Relations Theory and Other Disciplinary Perspectives," in *Diplomacy in a Globalizing World*, ed. Pauline Kerr and Geoffrey Wiseman (London: Oxford University Press, 2012), 65.

61. Brian Hocking, "Multistakeholder Diplomacy: Forms, Functions and Frustrations," in *Multistakeholder Diplomacy: Challenges and Opportunities*, ed. Jovan Kurbalija and Valentin Katrandjiev (Malta: DiploFoundation, 2006), 13.

62. Andrew F. Cooper, *Celebrity Diplomacy* (London: Routledge, 2015).

63. Der Derian, "Mediating Estrangement," 91.

64. Klaus V. Meier, "On the Inadequacies of Sociological Definitions of Sport," *International Review of Sport Sociology* 16, no. 2 (1981): 79–102.

65. Nelson Mandela, "Address to the 1st Laureus World Sports Award," accessed January 15, 2020, http://www.laureus.com/content/nelson-mandela-speech-changed-world.

66. BBC, "Queen Hails Sport as 'Great Leveller,'" accessed January 15, 2020, http://news.bbc.co.uk/2/hi/uk_news/63367.stm.

67. Eric Dunning, "Sociological Reflections on Sport, Violence and Civilization," *International Review for the Sociology of Sport* 25, no. 1 (1990): 66.
68. Konrad Lorenz, *On Aggression* (New York: MJF Books, 1966), 271.
69. Lorenz, *On Aggression*.
70. Robert Hughes, *The Fatal Shore* (New York: Vintage Books, 1988), 47.
71. Kendall Blanchard, *The Anthropology of Sport: An Introduction* (Westport, CT: Praeger, 1995).
72. Michael A. Salter, "Play: A Medium of Cultural Stability," in *Beiträge zur Geschichte der Leibeserziehung und des Sports*, ed. Hans Groll (Vienna: Universitat Wien, 1974), 5–16.
73. Salter, "Play."
74. Blanchard, *The Anthropology of Sport*, 144.
75. Hugh M. Lee, "The Ancient Olympic Games: Origin, Evolution, Revolution," *Classical Bulletin* 74, no. 2 (1998): 129.
76. Stuart Murray and Geoffrey Allen Pigman, "Mapping the Relationship between International Sport and Diplomacy," *Sport in Society* 17, no. 9 (2014): 1102.
77. Garrett Mattingly, "An Early Nonaggression Pact," *The Journal of Modern History* 10, no. 1 (1938): 1–30.
78. Murray and Pigman, "Mapping the Relationship between International Sport and Diplomacy."
79. Barbara Keys, "International Relations," in *Routledge Companion to Sports History*, ed. S. W. Pope and John Nauright (London: Routledge, 2009), 248–67.
80. Keys, "International Relations."
81. Adrian Budd and Roger Levermore, eds., *Sport and International Relations: An Emerging Relationship* (London: Routledge, 2004).
82. Kevin Blackburn, *War Sport and the Anzac Tradition* (London: Palgrave Macmillan, 2016).
83. Lyndsay Hayhurst, Tess Kay, and Megan Chawansky, eds., *Beyond Sport for Development and Peace: Transnational Perspectives on Theory, Policy and Practice,* (London: Routledge, 2016).
84. Jeremy Goldberg, "Sporting Diplomacy: Boosting the Size of the Diplomatic Corps," *Washington Quarterly* 23, no. 4 (2000): 63–70.
85. Stuart Murray, "The Two Halves of Sports Diplomacy," *Diplomacy and Statecraft* 23, no. 3 (2012): 576–92.
86. *The Hague Journal of Diplomacy* (2013), *Sport and Society* (2014), *Diplomacy and Statecraft* (2016), and *Place Branding and Public Diplomacy* (2019).
87. Heather Dichter and Andrew L. Johns, eds., *Diplomatic Games: Sport, Statecraft, and International Relations since 1945* (Lexington: University Press of Kentucky, 2014), 3.
88. Stuart Murray, "Sports Diplomacy in the Australian Context: Theory into Strategy," *Politics and Policy* 45, no. 5 (2017): 845.
89. Stuart MacDonald of International Cultural Relation Research, London, must be credited for this phrase.
90. "Sports Diplomacy 2030," accessed January 12, 2020, https://dfat.gov.au/sites-default/files/sports-diplomacy-2030.pdf.
91. Robert Redeker, "Sport as an Opiate of International Relations: The Myth and Illusion of Sport as a Tool of Foreign Diplomacy," *Sport in Society* 11, no. 4 (2008): 498.

92. Grant Jarvie and Erik Leaver, "Sport as a Resource of Hope," August 18, 2008, FPIF (Foreign Policy in Focus), accessed January 15, 2020, http://fpif.org/sports_as_a_resource_of_hope/.

93. Murray and Pigman, "Mapping the Relationship between International Sport and Diplomacy," 1099.

94. Thomas L. Friedman, *The World Is Flat: A Brief History of the Twenty-First Century* (New York: Picador, 2007).

95. Nelson Mandela, "Address to the 1st Laureus World Sports Award."

96. "Human Security in Theory and Practice," Human Security Unit, Office for the Coordination of Humanitarian Affairs, UN, accessed January 12, 2020, http://www.un.org/humansecurity/sites/www.un.org.humansecurity/files/human_security_in_theory_and_practice_english.pdf.

97. "Human Security in Theory and Practice."

98. BBC News, "Afghanistan Celebrates Cricket World Cup Qualification," accessed January 12, 2020, http://www.bbc.com/news/world-asia-24404178.

99. ICC-Cricket, "Afghanistan Dare to Dream in Debut Win," accessed January 13, 2020, http://www.icc-cricket.com/cricket-world-cup/news/2015/features-and-specials/86217/afghanistan-dare-to-dream-in-debut-win.html.

100. ICC-Cricket, "Afghanistan Dare to Dream in Debut Win."

101. Colin Veitch, "'Play Up! Play Up! and Win the War!' Football, the Nation and the First World War 1914–15," *Journal of Contemporary History* 20, no. 3 (1985): 363–78.

102. Patrick Jennings, "Colin Kaepernick: From One Man Kneeling to a Movement Dividing a Country," accessed January 14, 2020, http://www.bbc.com/sport/american-football/41530732.

103. Aaron Beacom, *International Diplomacy and the Olympic Movement: The New Mediators* (London: Palgrave Macmillan, 2012); Murray and Pigman, "Mapping the Relationship between International Sport and Diplomacy"; J. Simon Rofe, ed. *Sport and Diplomacy: Games within Games* (Manchester, UK: Manchester University Press, 2018); Stuart Murray, *Sports Diplomacy: Origins, Theory and Practice* (London: Routledge, 2018).

104. Caitlin Byrne, "Consultation Process for the Australian *Sports Diplomacy 2030* Strategy," interview by author, Bond University, September 29, 2019.

105. Australian Government, "Sports Diplomacy Strategy 2030" (2015), 18, https://dfat.gov.au/about-us/publications/Documents/sports-diplomacy-2030.pdf.

106. Australian Associated Press, "Bishop Hails Sport in the Art of Diplomacy," Sky News, June 25, 2015, http://www.skynews.com.au/news/politics/national/2015/06/25/bishop-hails-sport-in-the-art-of-diplomacy.html.

6

Sport's Economic Utility

The Essential Place of Economic Development in Sport-for-Development Programs

Laurence Chalip

OBJECTIVES

This chapter will:

- Explore the vital role of economic development in sport for development.
- Describe ways that sport can contribute to economic development.
- Demonstrate that sport's utility for economic development depends on how programs and facilities are designed, managed, and marketed.
- Explain how to use sport effectively as an economic development tool.

Throughout the first two decades of the twenty-first century, scholars and practitioners have focused increasing attention on the uses sport might have for development. The expanding interest has been accompanied by exponential growth in organizations and agencies. The result is that there are more than 950 organizations claiming to use sport for development[1]—ranging from those that operate locally or target specific at-risk populations to multifaceted international agencies such as the United Nations and United States Agency for International Development (USAID). What is particularly interesting about these organizations and the academic discourse about sport for development is that the focus is nearly always on social well-being or health.[2] Sport for development research and theory have treated the economic uses of sport as secondary or have ignored the economic relevance altogether. It is as if social well-being and health were independent of their economic context.

The marginalization of economic development in sport-for-development discourse is surprising as the close association between economic conditions, on the one hand, and well-being on the other has been demonstrated across ethnic, cultural, and national contexts.[3] Economic conditions are acutely important across demographic groups but especially for young people. Research demonstrates both direct and indirect negative effects of economic disadvantage on the quality of child-rearing and consequent child development.[4] Those effects then flow on to adult health and well-being.[5] This is not to suggest that improved economic conditions are sufficient to improve social well-being or health, as cultural, political, and environmental factors also matter.[6] So economic development can be necessary for enhancement of social and physical well-being even if economic gains are insufficient in and of themselves. In other words, attention to the economic uses of sport is essential when using sport for development, and those economic uses may need to be combined with social, political, or public health interventions to enable desired impacts.

There is a further reason for incorporating economic development into sport-for-development intervention planning. In democratic societies, policymakers pay careful attention to the economic objectives and outcomes from interventions because economic trends and conditions play a significant role in election results.[7] Totalitarian leaders are also concerned about economic conditions because improved economic conditions reduce the costs and challenges for remaining in power.[8] Consequently, access to funding, institutional support, and target populations are enhanced when economic development is incorporated into an intervention.

SPORT'S POTENTIAL FOR ECONOMIC DEVELOPMENT

There has been substantial study of sport economics, including the economic impacts that sport can have. That work demonstrates clearly that sport's value to the economy is not always demonstrable, or even positive. Despite political claims to the contrary, building a sport facility does not necessarily attract events,[9] bring teams and fans,[10] or guarantee attractive programming for sport participants.[11] Even when it does, the economic gains may be marginal at best,[12] or even negative,[13] especially when opportunity costs are considered. So the mere fact of sport provision, whether as an entertainment or a participative opportunity, does not imply economic value.

What matters is how sport is used. Although much of the research on sport's economic impact has treated sport as if its effect were intrinsic, research consistently demonstrates that the economic impact of sport depends on how it is implemented and how it is coordinated with other elements of the community's or region's product and service mix.

Figure 6.1 illustrates the ways that sport has been used in economic development. The top portion of the model identifies elements that can contribute to the quality of life for residents. Six of these—neighborhood amenities, adventure sport amenities, playing fields, sport entertainment facilities, special events, and teams—are sport-specific. The remaining element, downtown development, can be enhanced by sport entertainment facilities. Jointly and separately, these elements can enhance property values, tourism, place branding, and the business environment. Those can, in turn, create jobs and increase wealth, thereby expanding the tax base. Research exploring those linkages is reviewed in this chapter, and implications for managing the implementation of sport for development are noted.

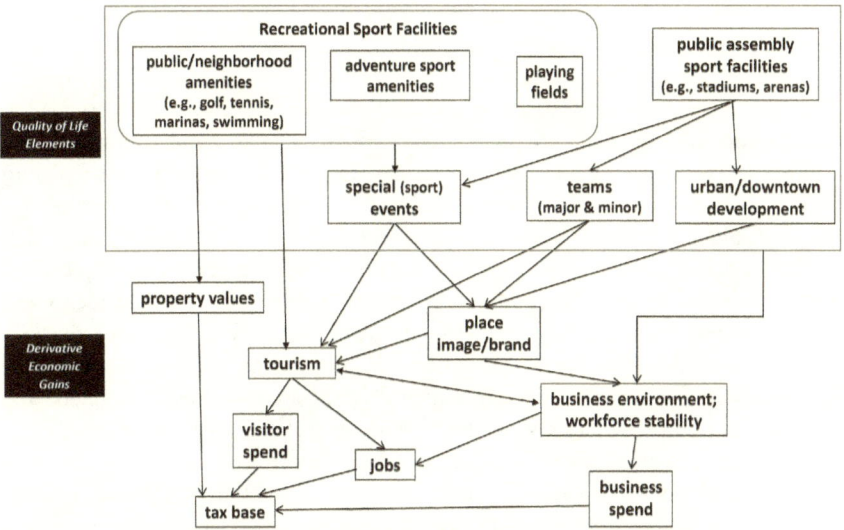

Figure 6.1. Facets and potential outcomes of sport as an economic engine.

Effects of Recreational Sport Facilities on Property Values and Tax Revenues

The impact that recreational sport facilities can have on the desirability of neighborhoods and communities has been of interest to developers for several decades. That is one reason that swimming pools have been included in so many community developments since the late nineteenth century.[14] By the mid-1980s, the Urban Land Institute recommended that developers consider including marinas, golf courses, or tennis courts in their developments to enhance property values, and it also pointed out that ski fields can be used for the same purpose.[15] The value of playing fields, especially in the context of public parks, has also been noted.[16] More recently, the value of adventure (a.k.a. *action* or *extreme*) sports amenities has been considered.[17] Enabling convenient participation in recreational sport can enhance perceptions of life quality, which can increase the price people are willing to pay for homes, condominiums, and apartments in the area. Since communities rely on property taxes to support public services, the increase in property values also enhances public revenues.[18]

Much of the empirical work on recreational sport amenities has focused on golf. One of the key findings is that, although golf courses can have positive economic effects, their effects can also be negative.[19] The aesthetics of golf course design,[20] as well as location and configuration,[21] account for much of the variation in economic value. In other words, the mere fact that a golf course is provided does not ensure that property values and consequent taxation revenues will benefit. Rather, the ways that golf courses are designed and managed are what matter. Strategic analysis and planning are required to render the desired effect.

The predominant empirical focus on golf may have led to overdevelopment of golf courses. Although golf was once a preferred game for white-collar residents, its popularity has been waning in recent years.[22] Many courses have consequently become unsustainable despite the golf industry's efforts to resuscitate demand for the sport.[23] There are numerous alternatives to golf facilities. In the presence of segmented markets and shifting consumer preferences, it is necessary to build a range of sport facilities and to identify local preferences and market trends when choosing which to build.[24] Indeed, it is clear that the potential utility of recreational sport amenities for property values and consequent tax revenues extends well beyond golf.[25]

The fundamental value that sport facilities can have seems to be a consequence of both aesthetic value and the opportunities those facilities afford local residents and tourists to enjoy an active lifestyle. Although the opportunity to build an active lifestyle can have demonstrably positive effects on property values[26]—especially when those facilities are substantial,[27] convenient,[28] and safe[29]—evidence suggests that sport facilities can have negative effects if residents feel that they are unaffordable[30] or aesthetically unattractive.[31] The challenge is to choose a portfolio of sport facilities that cater to local preferences and to integrate them strategically with tourism planning,[32] as well as with nonsport facilities and social services,[33] while providing recreational sport programming that meets local needs and interests.[34] Social interventions using sport could certainly be among those programs.

Yet sport providers are too often mired in sport offerings and modes of program management and marketing that are traditional, even when such programs are suboptimal for target users[35] or the delivery is downright dysfunctional.[36] Standard injunctions for effective marketing[37] dictate that in order for the social and economic value of sport to be optimized, it is essential to develop facilities and programs designed to meet user wants and needs and to do so in a manner that is both efficient and effective. Simply following traditional choices for facilities, programs, and their administration undermines the necessary strategic research and planning. Once again, it matters less that sport facilities and programs are offered than it does that facilities and programs are planned, implemented, and managed so that they address local wants and needs, even if those differ substantially from past sporting practice.

This is amply illustrated by adventure sports—that is, sports with a high degree of action and even risk, such as paragliding, BMX (bicycle motocross), parkour, highlining, ice cross, mountain boarding, kite boarding, and street luge. Adventure sport participation has grown substantially in recent years precisely because such sports offer sensations and risks that traditional sports rarely enable.[38] Adventure sports clearly have growing economic value, but their facilities, programming, and management can differ substantially from what is typical for traditional sports.[39] Furthermore, adventure sports amplify the utility of recreation facilities for the development of tourism.⁴⁰ The emergence and growth of adventure sports clearly demonstrates the necessity of a broad portfolio of sport facilities and programming.

There is no one best practice when using recreational sport facilities and programs to enhance economic development. If there were one best way to do it, then every community's sport facilities and programs would be identical, or nearly so. In practice, the community context, goals for development, and preferences of the multiple resident segments must shape the design and implementation of facilities and programs. Design, redesign, and development of facilities must include a programming, managing, and marketing plan. Since multiple uses must often be accommodated, planning for sport must take place within the context of the full range of recreational activities to be accommodated. Eight strategic questions (including subquestions) to guide recreational sport planning and programming are:

1. What are the demographic and psychographic community and tourist segments (i.e., different groups of people) to be served?
2. What are the wants and needs of those segments?
3. What trends need to be considered now and for the future?
4. What spaces, equipment, and lighting are needed to meet community and tourist segments' wants and needs now and into the future?
5. Where can facilities and the programs they house be placed to optimize accessibility across the community and tourist segments being served?
6. What conflicting demands might potentially arise between and within community segments for spaces, equipment, and programs, and how can design and implementation eliminate or manage conflicting demands?
7. How can the aesthetic quality of facilities and their programs be optimized?
    a. How will the look and feel of the facility blend with its surrounding environs and contribute to the area's overall beauty?
    b. How will traffic and pedestrian flows be managed to facilitate access and avoid congestion for local residents?
    c. What can be done to minimize noise beyond the facility from users and programs, including from their arrival and departure?
8. What will be done to optimize security for users and nearby residents?

Public Assembly Sport Facilities and Urban Economic Development

Public assembly sport facilities (i.e., stadiums and arenas intended to house sport as entertainment rather than as a place for the public to participate in sport) are expensive to build and are routinely advocated by developers and team owners as sources of economic advantage for the host community. A modern American stadium costs more than $680 million on average, while a modern American sports arena costs over $425 million on average,⁴¹ some or all of which typically comes directly or indirectly from public monies.⁴² To unpack the rhetoric supporting public investment in such facilities, it is useful to recognize who the stakeholders are and the influence they wield. The most visible are owners of professional franchises who stand to benefit from public subsidy to the stadiums in which their teams play.[43] They wield two key sources of influence. First, they can threaten to shift the team away from the city. Few elected officials are prepared to be labeled as the person who cost their community its team. Second, they can hire economic consultants to provide economic forecasts touting the value of the team and its facility. Despite the credibility of those expert economists, their forecasts are much more political rhetoric than they are accurate forecasts, as there are myriad ways to manipulate the data to guarantee a positive finding.[44] Indeed, independent economic studies conducted after facilities have been built demonstrate that public assembly sport facilities provide little public economic benefit[45] but are more beneficial to a team's value than is winning,[46] which is one reason that team owners advocate for them so adamantly. Yet the opportunity costs resulting from investing in sport facilities rather than schools, roads, hospitals, and other public goods can be downright harmful to the community.[47]

None of that could occur without the connivance of public officials advocating those facilities for reasons beyond the economic gain to the community that they claim will accrue. There are personal benefits for them when a facility is being planned and developed. First, the facility enhances their status, as its presence in the community is a tangible legacy of their administration.[48] Second, developing the facility enables interaction with high-status individuals, including team owners and athletes.[49] Thus creation of sport facilities can be advantageous to politicians even if the economic promises legitimizing their construction are fallacious.

The fact that facilities built to house sport as entertainment do not typically render a discernable economic benefit to the community does not mean that they could not do so if appropriate plans for design, management, and strategic leverage are put into place.[50] The core problem has been that facility development is typically founded on political promises that it will inexorably deliver economic benefits. Those promises militate against the requisite strategic planning for design, management, and policy utilization. Public assembly sports facilities can be economically beneficial if planning incorporates design elements that complement or enhance the community's look and feel, especially if planning incorporates strategies to raise the value of surrounding real estate and build foot traffic to boost local retail sales. Increases in local real estate values and retail sales can enhance local tax revenues, while the facility itself can help to build the community's brand, thereby fostering job creation through tourist attraction, workforce stability, and businesses locating to the area.[51] This is not to say that public assembly sport facilities or the teams they house are either necessary or sufficient for economic development. Rather, such facilities and their teams can aid economic development if used in conjunction with other amenities and assets for purposes of urban development, destination branding, and place marketing. Integrated strategic planning and implementation are required. A core reason that the economic consensus has been that stadia and arenas are poor public investments has been that the requisite strategic planning has been missing.[52] Sport has been the sole focus, as if the sport facility were an end in itself. Rather, the uses of the sport facilities and services within the overall matrix of retail, hospitality, and cultural activities need to be incorporated into facility design and management. To guide this process, eight subsequent strategic questions (including subquestions) for planning and management of a public assembly sport facility are:

1. How can the facility contribute to the overall urban plan, including real estate development?
2. Where can the facility be located so that it contributes optimally to entertainment, tourism, and cultural activities in its immediate vicinity?
3. How will vehicle and pedestrian traffic flows be managed to and from the facility?
4. What regional businesses can the facility help to support, and how?
5. What business alliances and partnerships need to be struck to enable the facility to remain complementary (rather than competitive) to local and regional business development?
6. What business elements beyond sport might complement attractions to the area for locals and tourists?
   a. Museum?
   b. Merchandising?
   c. Hospitality?
   d. Nonsport entertainment?
7. How will the facility's design blend into the local environment?
   a. Look and feel?
   b. Fostering foot traffic to local retail, bars, and restaurants?
8. How will security be managed?

It is also arguable that economists' preoccupation with facilities is too narrow. Although an iconic sport facility can become a tourist attraction,[53] especially if it includes a sport museum,[54] it is fundamentally a home for sport competitions. Its effects come from social interactions among fans,[55] the sense of community a team can generate because of its iconic representation of place,[56] and the team's contribution to a community's brand through the media it generates.[57] Appropriately utilized, these can contribute to local economic development,[58] including tourism.[59] Nevertheless, the mere presence of a professional sport franchise is insufficient to render a desired economic benefit to the community.[60] The requisite strategies for integrating a professional franchise into the community's social and business development have been understood for some time[61] but are implemented only haphazardly, if at all. Indeed, for economic development purposes, professional sport entertainment is treated separately from the rest of the economy. Sport's tactical utilization for economic development is relegated to sport-specific planning, as in Europe,[62] or quasi-independent sports commissions, as in the United States.[63] That separation militates against the essential strategic integration of professional sport into an overall vision for community and regional development. When formulating and implementing economic development tactics, institutional separation of sport from other elements of the community's product and service mix undermines sport's utility.[64] Six questions that can focus strategic planning to integrate and apply professional sport franchises in economic development are:

1. How can the team and its activities be incorporated into marketing communications to build the host community's brand?
   a. In external markets?
   b. Among local residents?
2. How can the team be used to attract businesses to locate to the host community and to remain?
3. How can residents' identification with the team be fostered and then used to stabilize the local workforce?
4. How can employment with the team be used to enhance local workers' skill levels?
5. How can fanship and fan groups be used to build identification with the community among local residents?
6. How can the team be incorporated into tourists' itineraries to lengthen their stays and increase their aggregate spend?

Sport Events for Economic Development

Sport facilities intended to enable recreational participation and those intended to house sport as an entertainment provide opportunities to host special events. Communities are turning increasingly to special events as a means to build their brand and to attract tourists, especially to fill hotel and motel spaces that might otherwise be empty. Thus communities are building event portfolios that can enhance their image while optimizing the reach and frequency of exposure through media.[65] In some instances, communities are building sport facilities specifically to attract and host participative sport events, which can expand the range and quality of recreational sport facilities provided to residents.

Of course, not all events require dedicated sport facilities. For example, triathlons, distance running events, and car or motorcycle rallies can make use of nonsport infrastructure and local geographic features. Similarly, large tournaments can take place in convention centers. Conversely, sport facilities can accommodate nonsport events, such as concerts, weddings, and conventions. So although sport facilities provide useful event infrastructure, they are not essential for a community to host events.

There has been a great deal of interest in recent years regarding the legacies that events (particularly large events) leave in their wake. However, the legacy framework has been found to be problematic insomuch as it distracts from the strategic planning that is required for events to render optimal economic value.[66] Each event needs to be tactically leveraged, and the requisite means to do so are well established.[67] As

Figure 6.2. Shared experiences, such as this Special Olympics event attended by a group of Sports Visitors from Egypt, can unify participants around common goals. *Credit*: Sports Diplomacy Division, US Department of State

with other sport assets, the key is to build each event into the host community's product and service mix.

However, the politics of special events (especially when they are large) prompts advocates to promise outcomes that are treated as intrinsic to the event.[68] Strategic planning consequently seems less important than organizing and marketing the event. The distraction is aggravated because the political discourse then focuses on the event apart from the product and service mix of the host community. Consequently, strategic leveraging of events becomes inadequate.

A related challenge derives from the economic impact assessments applied. Of course, economic assessments are political, so there is political pressure to find a positive result.[69] The most common method for estimating an event's economic impact is input-output (I/O) analysis. I/O models estimate visitor spend and then apply a multiplier to represent impacts of that money being respent in the economy. Even if event expenses are subtracted, the method tends to yield positive estimates of impact. Opportunity costs, downstream economic effects, and crowding out of other economic activity are not considered. When those factors are incorporated into more rigorous cost-benefit event analysis, strongly positive estimates of impact are not merely reduced; they can become negative.[70] The overly positive estimates from I/O modeling undermine incentives to leverage events, but more realistic cost-benefit analysis demonstrates that leveraging is essential if events are intended to boost the local economy.

As with sport facilities and professional sport teams, effective utilization of events for economic development purposes requires inclusive and multifaceted strategic planning. The following eight questions can be used when seeking to leverage one or more events for purposes of economic development:

1. What can be added into the event to lengthen visitors' stay in the host community or region?
2. What tourist excursions and activities before and after the event can be bundled into event visitors' itineraries?
3. What can local businesses do to optimize sales to event visitors?
4. How can we optimize local supply of materials and services for the event?
5. How can local businesses use the event to create or enhance relationships with government and business leaders who attend the event?
   a. Identify and meet government and business leaders?
   b. Use event hospitality to strengthen current relationships?
6. Where should the event be located to best showcase the host destination?
7. How can the host destination's brand be enhanced through mentions and visuals in event media and advertising?
8. How can event visuals and mentions be built into the host destination's marketing communications?

PROCESSES WHEN USING SPORT FOR ECONOMIC DEVELOPMENT

The foregoing analysis notes ways that sport programs, events, and facilities can contribute to economic development but stresses that sport's utility for economic development depends entirely on the quality of strategic planning and application. Sport can have positive effects, negative effects, or no effect at all. The economic consequences of sport depend on sport's tactical utilization in combination with other local assets. When sport is intended to contribute strategically to urban design, quality lifestyles, business development, or tourism marketing, the value that sport can add to other elements of the local product and service mix must steer policy formulation and implementation.

For that to occur, sport cannot be treated as an end in itself. Strategic use of sport for economic development is less about having more sport or better sport than it is about the wide-ranging value sport can have. Yet the frames of reference and resulting contingencies confronting sport managers are grounded in more and better sport rather than sport's potential contributions to the broader economy. Consequently, when sport's value to the economy is referenced by sport managers and marketers, its economic relevance is typically asserted through declarations intended to legitimize sport's claim on the public purse but with little or no reference to the essential integration of sport infrastructure and programs with the overall economy. Sport is treated as if it were intrinsically beneficial. The means to enable broad economic contributions are consequently set aside. That is why sport's advocates have fallaciously presented sport as if its mere presence were intrinsically beneficial, and why economic impact claims from the sport industry have been misleadingly optimistic,[71] with the long-term result that those claims have undermined sport's credibility as an economic development tool.[72]

The strategic separation of sport from its broader economic development context has detrimental effects for sport, just as it does for the economy as a whole. For example, sport's contributions to tourism have caused sport tourism to become one of the fastest growing facets of both sport and tourism.[73] Nevertheless, the institutional separation of sport training and practice from tourism training and practice has impaired the strategic combination of sport with tourism, resulting in substantial loss of economic opportunity.[74] Similarly, sport development has routinely relied on facilities and programs provided through public recreation.[75] However, recreation training, practice, and discourse have increasingly become separated. One result is that many public recreation agencies contract private companies to provide sport programming using public facilities.[76] In other words, public funding of facilities often subsidizes private providers of sport services, with the result that working-class families are increasingly priced out of participation, yielding an overall decline in youth sport participation.[77] Clearly then, an encompassing grasp of sport's contributions to economic development could enhance the quality of sport development.

This sounds simpler than it is. Development is about change, which makes it intrinsically political.[78] The politics affect who has voice in the formulation and implementation of development tactics and how much influence that voice has. Indeed, aggregate economic gain does not mean that everyone benefits from sport's economic impacts. Quite often, the economic benefits from sport are the result of income transfers from taxpayers[79] or consumers[80] to those who own or administer sport. When using sport for economic development, the politics of distribution need to be thought through—not merely because so doing is ethically incumbent but because income transfers can undermine political support.

The political consequences of economic development highlight a fundamental point: economic development and social development are conjoined.[81] Sport-for-development programs benefit when they encompass both. Incorporating economic objectives with social purpose can improve program efficacy as well as access to resources.

Questions

1. Describe several factors that can enhance the economic impact of a sport event.
2. Discuss the economic impact of a sport event or team in a community of your choosing.
3. How can sport impact economic development in a community?

4. When locating a public assembly sport facility in a community, describe factors to consider to enhance economic development.
5. Develop a plan to utilize sport as an effective development tool in a community of your choosing.
6. Discuss the role of economic development in sport-for-development endeavors.

NOTES

1. Per G. Svensson and Hilary Woods, "A Systematic Overview of Sport for Development and Peace Organisations," *Journal of Sport for Development* 5, no. 9 (September 2017): 36–48.

2. Holly Collison, Simon C. Darnell, Richard Giulianotti, and P. David Howe, eds., *Routledge Handbook of Sport for Development and Peace* (New York: Routledge, 2019).

3. Bruno S. Frey and Alois Stutzer, *Happiness and Economics: How the Economy and Institutions Affect Human Well-Being* (Princeton, NJ: Princeton University Press, 2002).

4. Rand D. Conger, Katherine J. Conger, and Monica J. Martin, "Socioeconomic Status, Family Processes, and Individual Development," *Journal of Marriage and Family* 72, no. 3 (June 2010): 685–704.

5. Janet Currie and Maya Rossin-Slater, "Early-Life Origins of Life-Cycle Well-Being: Research and Policy Implications," *Journal of Policy Analysis and Management* 34, no. 1 (Winter 2015): 208–42.

6. Gheorghe H. Popescu, "Does Economic Growth Bring About Increased Happiness?" *Journal of Self-Governance and Management Economics* 4, no. 4 (2016): 27–33.

7. Michael S. Lewis-Beck and Mary Stegmaier, "Economic Determinants of Electoral Outcomes," *Annual Review of Political Science* 3, no. 1 (2000): 183–219.

8. Ronald Wintrobe, "The Tinpot and the Totalitarian: An Economic Theory of Dictatorship," *American Political Science Review* 83, no. 3 (September 1990): 849–72.

9. Glen Searle, "Uncertain Legacy: Sydney's Olympic Stadiums," *European Planning Studies* 10, no. 7 (2002): 845–60; Benjamin Siegel, "Playing Host Is Hard to Do: The Allure of the World Stage and Shiny New Stadiums," *World Policy Journal* 27, no. 4 (2010/2011): 59–66.

10. Kenneth L. Shropshire, *The Sports Franchise Game: Cities in Pursuit of Sports Franchises, Events, Stadiums, and Arenas* (Philadelphia: University of Pennsylvania Press, 1995).

11. Pamela Wicker, Kirstin Hallmann, and Christoph Breuer, "Micro and Macro Level Determinants of Sport Participation," *Sport, Business and Management* 2, no. 1 (2012): 51–68.

12. John Siegfried and Andrew Zimbalist, "The Economic Impact of Sports Facilities, Teams, and Mega-Events," *Australian Economic Review* 39, no. 4 (February 2006): 420–27.

13. Marijke Taks, Stefan Kesenne, Laurence Chalip, and B. Christine Green, "Economic Impact Analysis versus Cost Benefit Analysis: The Case of a Medium-Sized Sport Event," *International Journal of Sport Finance* 6, no. 3 (2011): 187–203.

14. Jeff Wiltse, *Contested Waters: A Social History of Swimming Pools in America* (Chapel Hill: University of North Carolina Press, 2007).

15. Patrick L. Phillips, *Developing with Recreational Amenities: Golf, Tennis, Skiing, Marinas* (Washington, DC: Urban Land Institute, 1986).

16. John L. Crompton, "The Impact of Parks on Property Values: Empirical Evidence from the Past Two Decades in the United States," *Managing Leisure* 10, no. 4 (2005): 203–18.

17. Heike Puchan, "Living 'Extreme': Adventure Sports, Media and Commercialization," *Journal of Communication Management* 9, no. 2 (2004): 171–78.

18. David Brunori, *Local Tax Policy: A Primer*, 4th ed. (Lanham, MD: Rowman & Littlefield, 2020).

19. Paul K. Asabere and Forrest E. Huffman, "Negative and Positive Impacts of Golf Course Proximity on Home Prices," *The Appraisal Journal* 64, no. 4 (January 1996): 351–55.

20. Stephen Shmanske, "The Economics of Golf Course Condition and Beauty," *Atlantic Economic Journal* 27, no. 3 (1999): 301–13.

21. John L. Crompton, "Designing Golf Courses to Optimize Proximate Property Values," *Managing Leisure* 5, no. 4 (2000): 192–99.

22. Joseph F. Beditz and James R. Kass, *Golf Participation in America*, 2010–2020 (Jupiter, FL: National Golf Foundation, 2010).

23. Brenda Hayden Sheets, Joy Roach-Humphreys, and Timothy Johnston, "Turnaround Strategy: Overview of the Business and Marketing Challenges Facing the Golf Industry and Initiatives to Reinvigorate the Game," *Business Education Innovation Journal* 8, no. 2 (December 2016): 161–71.

24. Phillips, *Developing with Recreational Amenities*.

25. Justin D. Benefield, "Neighborhood Amenity Packages, Property Price, and Marketing Time," *Property Management* 27, no. 5 (October 2009): 348–70; Özer Sari Ferika, "In-Depth Analysis of Marinas," *International Journal of Social Sciences and Humanity Studies* 4, no. 2 (2012): 199–205; M. Alexander Gabrielsen and Ralph L. Johnson, "A Professional Challenge: Swimming Pool Safety," *Journal of Physical Education and Recreation* 50, no. 6 (June 1979): 43–46.

26. Rainer vom Hofe, Oana Mihaescu, and Mary Lynne Boorn, "Are Homeowners Willing to Pay More for Access to Parks? Evidence from a Spatial Hedonic Study of the Cincinnati, Ohio, USA Park System," *Journal of Regional Analysis and Policy* 48, no. 3 (2018): 66–82.

27. Neelam C. Poudyal, Donald G. Hodges, and Christopher D. Merrett, "A Hedonic Analysis of the Demand for and Benefit of Urban Recreation Parks," *Land Use Policy* 26, no. 4 (October 2009): 975–83.

28. Steven C. Deller, David W. Marcouiller, Donald B. K. English, and Victor Lledo, "Amenities and Rural Development: Theory, Methods and Public Policy," in *Regional Economic Growth with a Focus on Amenities*, ed. Gary Paul Green, Steven C. Deller, and David W. Marcouiller (Cheltenham, UK: Edward Elgar, 2005), 129–52.

29. Austin Troy and J. Morgan Grove, "Property Values, Parks, and Crime: A Hedonic Analysis in Baltimore, MD," *Landscape and Urban Planning* 87, no. 3 (September 2008): 233–45.

30. Steven C. Deller, Tsung-Hsiu Tsai, and Donald B. K. English, "The Role of Amenities and Quality of Life in Rural Economic Growth," *American Journal of Agricultural Economics* 83, no. 2 (May 2001): 352–65.

31. I-Hui Lin, Changshan Wu, and Christopher De Sousa, "Examining the Economic Impact of Park Facilities on Neighboring Residential Property Values," *Applied Geography* 45 (December 2013): 322–31.

32. Patrick T. Long and Sarah L. Richardson, "Integrating Recreation and Tourism Development in Small Winter Cities," *Journal of Physical Education, Recreation and Dance* 60, no. 8 (1989): 58–61.

33. Paul D. Gottlieb, "Amenities as an Economic Development Tool: Is There Enough Evidence?" *Economic Development Quarterly* 8, no. 3 (1994): 270–85.

34. Christopher R. Edginton, Samuel Lankford, Rodney B. Dieser, and Christopher L. Kowalski, *Recreation and Leisure Programming: A 21st Century Perspective* (Champaign, IL: Sagamore-Venture, 2018).

35. Laurence Chalip and B. Christine Green, "Establishing and Maintaining a Modified Youth Sport Program: Lessons from Hotelling's Location Game," *Sociology of Sport Journal* 15, no. 4 (December 1998): 326–42.

36. Laurence Chalip and E. Philip Scott, "Centrifugal Social Forces in a Youth Sport League," *Sport Management Review* 8, no. 1 (May 2005): 43–67.

37. Robert W. Palmatier and Shrihari Sridhar, *Marketing Strategy Based on First Principles and Data Analytics* (London: Palgrave, 2017).

38. Gunnar Breivk, "Trends in Adventure Sports in a Post-Modern Society," *Sports in Society* 13, no. 2 (March 2010): 260–73; Catherine Palmer, "'Shit Happens': The Selling of Risk in Extreme Sport," *Australian Journal of Anthropology* 13, no. 3 (2002): 323–36.

39. Pamm Kellett and Roslyn Russell, "A Comparison between Mainstream and Action Sport Industries in Australia: A Case Study of the Skateboarding Cluster," *Sport Management Review* 12, no. 2 (May 2009): 66–78.

40. Tracey J. M. McKay, "Leaping into Urban Adventure: Orlando Bungee, Soweto, South Africa," *African Journal for Physical Health Education, Recreation and Dance* 19, supplement 2 (September 2013): 55–71; Marta K. Moorman and Kathleen English, "Adventure Racing for the Rest of Us," *Journal of Physical Education, Recreation and Dance* 86, no. 2 (February 2015): 14–21.

41. Brookings Institution, *Average Construction Costs of Professional Sports Arenas/Stadiums Built since 2000 (in Millions of U.S. Dollars), by League* (Washington, DC).

42. Dennis Coates and Craig A. Depken, "Tax Schemes for Sports Venues," in *For Your Own Good: Taxes, Paternalism, and Fiscal Discrimination in the Twenty-First Century*, ed. Adam J. Offer and Todd Nesbit (Arlington, VA: Mercatus Center, 2018), 244–62.

43. Dennis Coates and Brad R. Humphreys, "The Stadium Gambit and Local Economic Development," *Regulation* 23, no. 2 (2000): 15–20.

44. John L. Crompton, "Economic Impact Studies: Instruments for Political Shenanigans?" *Journal of Travel Research* 45, no. 1 (August 2006): 67–82; Ian Hudson, "The Use and Misuse of Economic Impact Analyses: The Case of Professional Sports," *Journal of Sport and Social Issues* 25, no. 1 (February 2001): 20–39.

45. David Schein, James Phillips, and Caroline Rider, "American Cities Held Hostage: Public Stadiums and Pro Sport Franchises," *Richmond Public Interest Law Review* 20, no. 1 (2017): 62–110.

46. Zach Muetzel, Peter Titlebaum, Ron Dick, and Steve Chen, "Analyses of National Football League 2011–2017 Team Values: Stadium Renovation and Construction Trumps Winning," *KAHPERD* [Kentucky Association for Health, Physical Education, Recreation, and Dance] *Journal* 56, no. 2 (2019): 39–50.

47. Coates and Humphreys, "The Stadium Gambit and Local Economic Development."

48. Kevin J. Delaney and Rick Eckstein, *Public Dollars, Private Stadiums: The Battle over Building Sports Stadiums* (New Brunswick, NJ: Rutgers University Press, 2003).

49. Graeme Turner, *Understanding Celebrity* (Newbury Park, CA: Sage, 2013).

50. Mark S. Rosentraub, *Reversing Urban Decline: Why and How Sports, Entertainment, and Culture Turn Cities into Major League Winners*, 2nd ed. (Boca Raton, FL: CRC Press, 2014).

51. Roland V. Anglin, *Promoting Sustainable Local and Community Economic Development* (New York: Routledge, 2017); Maury D. Granger and Glenn C. Blomquist, "Evaluating the

Influence of Amenities on the Location of Manufacturing Establishments in Urban Areas," *Urban Studies* 36, no. 11 (1999): 1859–73; Jillian M. Rickly-Boyd, Daniel C. Knudsen, and Lisa C. Braverman, *Tourism, Performance, and Place: A Geographic Perspective* (London: Routledge, 2014).

52. Rosentraub, *Reversing Urban Decline.*

53. Heetae Cho, Er Chin Khoo, and Hyun-Woo Lee, "Nostalgia, Motivation, and Intention for International Football Stadium Tourism," *Asia Pacific Journal for Tourism Research* 24, no. 9 (2019): 912–23; Gregory Ramshaw and Sean J. Gammon, "Towards a Critical Sport Heritage: Implications for Sport Tourism," *Journal of Sport & Tourism* 21, no. 2 (2017): 115–31.

54. Greg Ramshaw and Sean Gammon. "More Than Just Nostalgia? Exploring the Heritage/Sport Tourism Nexus," *Journal of Sport & Tourism* 10, no. 4 (2005): 229–41.

55. Chad Seifried and Aaron W. Clopton, "An Alternative View of Public Subsidy and Sport Facilities through Social Anchor Theory," *City, Culture and Society* 4, no. 1 (March 2013): 49–55.

56. Patricia Vertinsky and John Bale, eds., *Sites of Sport: Space, Place and Experience* (New York: Routledge, 2004).

57. Laurence Chalip, "Marketing, Media, and Place Promotion," in *Sport Tourism Destinations: Issues, Opportunities and Analysis,* ed. James Higham (Oxford, UK: Butterworth-Heinemann, 2005), 162–76.

58. James Midgley and Michelle Livermore, "Social Capital and Local Economic Development: Implications for Community Social Work Practice, *Journal of Community Practice* 5, nos. 1–2 (1998): 29–40.

59. Michael J. Gross and Graham Brown, "An Empirical Structural Model of Tourists and Places: Progressing Involvement and Place Attachment into Tourism," *Tourism Management* 29, no. 6 (December 2008): 1141–51.

60. Robert A. Baade, "Professional Sports as Catalysts for Metropolitan Economic Development," *Journal of Urban Affairs* 18, no. 1 (1996): 1–17.

61. Emily Sparvero and Laurence Chalip, "Professional Teams as Leverageable Assets: Strategic Creation of Community Value," *Sport Management Review* 10, no. 1 (May 2007): 1–30.

62. Leo van den Berg and Erik Braun, *Sports and City Marketing in European Cities* (London: Rutledge, 2002).

63. National Association of Sports Commissions, *Sports Commissions 101* (Cincinnati, Ohio).

64. Mihalis Kavaratzis, "From 'Necessary Evil' to Necessity: Stakeholders' Involvement in Place Branding," *Journal of Place Management and Development* 5, no. 1 (2012): 7–19.

65. Vassilios Ziakas, *Event Portfolio Planning and Management: A Holistic Approach* (London: Routledge, 2014).

66. Laurence Chalip, "Trading Legacy for Leverage," in *Legacies and Mega Events: Fact or Fairy Tales?* ed. Ian Brittain, Jason Bocarro, Terri Byers, and Kamilla Swart (Abingdon, UK: Routledge, 2017), 25–42.

67. Laurence Chalip, "Beyond Impact: A General Model for Sport Event Leverage," in *Sport Tourism: Interrelationships, Impacts and Issues,* ed. Brent W. Ritchie and Daryl Adair (Clevedon, UK: Channel View, 2004), 226–52.

68. Stacy-Lynn Sant and Daniel S. Mason, "Framing Event Legacy in a Prospective Host City: Managing Vancouver's Olympic Bid," *Journal of Sport Management* 29, no. 1 (January 2015): 42–56.

69. Crompton, "Economic Impact Studies."

70. Taks, Kesenne, Chalip, and Green, "Economic Impact Analysis versus Cost Benefit Analysis."

71. Crompton, "Economic Impact Studies"; Hudson, "The Use and Misuse of Economic Impact Analyses."

72. Coates and Humphreys, "The Stadium Gambit and Local Economic Development"; Taks, Kesenne, Chalip, and Green, "Economic Impact Analysis versus Cost Benefit Analysis."

73. James Higham and Thomas Hinch, *Sport Tourism Development*, 3rd ed. (Bristol, UK: Channel View, 2018).

74. Mike Weed, "Why the Two Won't Tango: Explaining the Lack of Integrated Policies for Sport and Tourism in the UK," *Journal of Sport Management* 17, no. 3 (2003): 258–63; Mike Weed, "Is Tourism a Legitimate Legacy from the Olympic and Paralympic Games? An Analysis of London 2012 Legacy Strategy Using Programme Theory," *Journal of Sport and Tourism* 19, no. 2 (2014): 101–26.

75. Edginton, Lankford, Dieser, and Kowalski, *Recreation and Leisure Programming*.

76. Eric Legg, Gareth J. Jones, and Misha White, "Whose Job Is It Anyway? Public-Private Partnerships in Youth Sport," *Managing Sport and Leisure* 23, nos. 4–6 (2018): 261–76.

77. Derek Thompson, "American Meritocracy Is Killing Youth Sports," *The Atlantic*, November 6, 2018, https://www.theatlantic.com/ideas/archive/2018/11/income-inequality-explains-decline-youth-sports/574975/.

78. Gunnar Myrdal, *The Political Element in the Development of Economic Theory* (Cambridge, MA: Harvard University Press, 1954).

79. Trevor Mules, "Taxpayer Subsidies for Major Sporting Events," *Sport Management Review* 1, no. 1 (November 1998): 25–43.

80. William P. Putsis, Jr., "Winners and Losers: Redistribution and the Use of Economic Impact Analysis in Marketing," *Journal of Macromarketing* 18, no. 1 (1998): 24–33.

81. Santosh Mehrotra and Richard Jolly, eds., *Development with a Human Face: Experiences in Social Achievement and Economic Growth* (Oxford: Oxford University Press, 2000).

7

Corporate Social Responsibility and Sport for Development and Peace

New Media, Communication, and Engagement for Greater Impact

Kathy Babiak and Javier Abuín-Penas

OBJECTIVES

This chapter will:

- Identify the dimensions of effective communication used by sport for development and peace organizations to engage with stakeholders and participants.
- Illustrate the communication channels used by companies that are engaged in sport for development activities.
- Evaluate the challenges facing international organizations when they are formulating their communication messages in the sport for development space.
- Propose a communication strategy for sport for development and peace organizations and companies engaged in this activity.

Corporate social responsibility (CSR) has emerged as a core strategic activity for companies around the world. The central premise of CSR is that businesses engage in activities—sometimes beyond their business focus—to address and ameliorate pressing social issues. *CSR* is defined as a company's voluntary integration of social and environmental "commitment to improve (individual), community (and global) well-being through discretionary business practices and contributions of corporate resources."[1] A growing number of companies (national and transnational) are using sport as a vehicle to engage in socially responsible practices globally.[2] In doing so, companies often partner with sport properties (such as professional sport teams or leagues, national and international sport governing bodies, and global sport agencies such as the International Olympic Committee [IOC]) to deliver on their CSR strategies. Increasingly, companies are seeking deeper, more meaningful, and impactful social change efforts through the platform of sport for development and peace

(SDP). This strategic orientation offers benefits to both SDP organizations and the companies themselves, as together they are able to connect deeply with communities, provide an entree into new markets, and generate branding and image enhancement benefits, as well serve more socially oriented justifications (addressing social aims and mission-focused activities such as gender equity, health and well-being, education, sustainability, community development, etc.).

Matthew Walker, Aubrey Kent, and John Vincent argued that communicating and articulating CSR efforts is central for sport organizations to attain the desired potential relational (e.g., reputation) and transactional (e.g., patronage) business and social outcomes (e.g., positive social impact and change).[3] Given this shifting role of CSR to a more central strategic function, and considering the intended benefits organizations aim to receive, the communication and articulation of CSR efforts become critical for both a corporate entity and any nonprofit or nongovernmental partners it works with. In general, the reporting of CSR has as its target audience society at large, but also targeted stakeholders such as investors, actual and potential employees, partners, sponsors, funders, nongovernmental organizations, local governments, beneficiaries, program participants, and customers.[4] As new media become critical channels of communication for these efforts,[5] we argue in this chapter that effective and strategic approaches to communication of these activities can help to generate greater awareness and encourage participation, engagement, and support of the causes addressed in the SDP sector.

Our aim is to provide an overview of the role of CSR in sport and discuss its benefits, challenges, and strategic outcomes in general. We hone in specifically on the role of CSR in SDP initiatives and discuss how communication of these efforts is reflected and integrated through new media channels (e.g., Twitter) by providing examples of companies and SDP organizations that have incorporated a social media communication strategy for their sport for development oriented CSR efforts. The chapter concludes with suggestions for both practitioners and scholars interested in exploring this phenomenon.

STRATEGIC AND SOCIAL PERSPECTIVES

Wicked social problems around the globe are emerging, and, increasingly, international agencies, governments, nongovernmental organizations, and companies are bringing to bear their energies, attention, and resources to solve them.[6] These issues pose challenges because there is either incomplete or contradictory knowledge about them, the number of constituencies and opinions involved is significant, there is a large economic burden, and often these problems are interconnected with other problems.[7] As one emerging sector, SDP organizations aim to address these significant problems such as peacebuilding and conflict resolution, equality, health, education, community regeneration, or environmental sustainability.[8] SDP programs and interventions "aim to facilitate social, economic, environmental, and political change through structured physical activity and sporting-based activities."[9] These efforts are amplified through collaboration, partnerships, and alliances. Significant relationships are being forged by SDP organizations with companies through the guise of CSR.[10] Multinational corporations (e.g., Microsoft, Ikea, Mercedes Benz, Nike, Adidas, and Under Armour) have begun developing, supporting, and promoting sport-based, community-driven programs and initiatives such as the Mathare Youth Sports Association, Magic Bus (in Mumbai, India), and Right to Play as part of their CSR agendas.[11]

The term *CSR* has been referred to as a "tortured concept"[12] and has received growing attention in the development world since the "discourse of international development has shifted from state-led development initiatives towards market-driven solutions. . . . [H]owever[,] . . . CSR as a business tool is distinct from CSR as a development tool—which has yet to be fully understood."[13] From a development perspective, the term *global corporate social engagement* has been suggested to represent corporate efforts to address issues related to underdevelopment.[14] Thus, while SDP nonprofits might be driven to consider engaging in partnerships with corporate (or private sport) firms, many uncertainties exist in the nature and form of these relationships—primarily that of how companies are really impacting the development objectives of the partnership through their CSR platforms.

An emerging line of scholarly inquiry explores how businesses collaborate with nonprofit organizations as a vehicle to implement social responsibility programs.[15] In terms of CSR implementation and execution, some companies develop their own resources and capabilities to deliver their proprietary in-house CSR programs or projects.[16] A second tactic adopted by some firms is to outsource CSR and charitable giving through a partnership approach that reflects a more strategic orientation.[17] Both of these approaches aim to deliver a CSR agenda for the corporate or private entity and to help advance the mission and goals of the partner (SDP program, etc.) ultimately to create social value and impact.

CSR activities are fundamentally grounded in the concept of philanthropy (i.e., altruistic and noble actions); however, many have also evolved into more complex and strategic forms often aiming to integrate threads of innovation and shared value. Emerging from Michael Porter and Mark Kramer's[18] work, this concept of shared value suggests the aim of both economic value through a firm's competitiveness development and creating social value (social good, impact, and other positive outcomes) for partners in communities that the company serves or operates.[19]

The nexus of corporate involvement and SDP organizations and networks is a significant dynamic in program delivery; however, these relationships are also critical in communicating, connecting, and engaging with a broad array of both internal and external stakeholders.[20] We contend in this chapter that the advancement of SDP efforts via CSR partnerships necessitates a strong and strategic communication platform to achieve the intended objectives.[21] To attain goals such as community connectedness, social issue awareness, collective action or volunteerism, program impact and outcomes, fundraising objectives, or partner solicitation, strategically

Figure 7.1. Corporate programs, such as this NBA Cares initiative in Tanzania, can impact communities in a variety of meaningful ways. *Credit*: Sports Diplomacy Division, US Department of State

designed communication strategies are critical.[22] Even if SDP organizations have limited resources, through their partnerships with companies they may strategically aim to engage people through social media channels in the hopes of generating increased offline support.[23] Thus, given their limited resources, new media platforms are a highly appealing tool for CSR partnerships with nonprofits, including SDP organizations.[24] In the next section, we discuss and describe the relationship between CSR and communication and highlight in particular its value for SDP organizations.

CSR-SDP COMMUNICATION

As CSR has become increasingly important in management, CSR communication has also become a central strategic topic.[25] To achieve their goals, corporations and their partners should not only engage in socially responsible practices but also communicate their CSR activities strategically.[26] Authentic communication about CSR that is aligned with corporate values has been found to satisfy the expectations of stakeholders, influence consumer attitudes and perceptions (e.g., skepticism), and build trusting relationships with other various publics.[27]

However, CSR communication is not easily undertaken as it poses several challenges to socially responsible initiatives such as lack of awareness or stakeholder skepticism. Usually, stakeholders (external as well as internal) do not have an extensive knowledge about CSR activities carried out by companies and their partners.[28] In addition, in many cases, excessive communication of CSR activities could generate skepticism by consumers or the general public.[29] Alternately, there are several researchers who agree that effective communication of CSR could improve awareness, engagement, trust, commitment, and perceptions of corporate reputation while reducing consumer skepticism.[30]

Basing their work on the research of the authors noted previously, Sara Kim and Mary Ann Ferguson identified eight possible dimensions that might contribute to effective CSR communication: *informativeness* (CSR communication should contain detailed information), *third-party endorsement* (credibility of third parties can be transferred onto the organization), *personal relevance* (companies should relate stakeholders to their CSR messages by including personally relevant examples), *self-efficacy* (related to people's belief that the suggested behavior will lead to a desirable outcome), *self-promotional message tone* (self-promotional or self-congratulatory tone is highly related to public skepticism), *consistency* (how steadily the company communicates about its CSR goals), *frequency* (frequent communication on a topic can increase public awareness of the topic), and *transparency* (openness of CSR information disclosure including both good and bad).[31] In another recent study, Kim showed that when the public perceived the presence of the previously mentioned factors in CSR communication, better relations and affective cognitive responses were generated with stakeholders, and at the same time, the knowledge and awareness of corporate social efforts and impact were increased. This can lead to greater trust in the company, which translates into reputation enhancement.[32]

Nowadays, companies and other social impact organizations use a wide range of channels to communicate about their socially oriented activities and outcomes, such as social reports, codes of conduct, websites, internal channels, events, product packaging, and advertising. Social media platforms (such as Twitter, Instagram, Facebook) have emerged as one of the most prominent channels for reaching key stakeholders on CSR communication.[33] Shuili Du, C. B. Bhattacharya, and Sankar Sen point to social media platforms as a great opportunity to amplify word-of-mouth communication among stakeholders.[34] Similarly, Daniel Korschun and Du suggest that CSR communication through digital channels is different from traditional media because it creates a space for information exchange and allows engagement with multiple stakeholders.[35] On social media, the possibilities to generate more interactive communication (participation and dialogue) with stakeholders may lead to the biggest benefits of the CSR communication strategy.[36]

In the SDP milieu, several scholars have noted that many SDP organizations vary greatly in size and economic power, with most SDP organizations being characterized by having limited resources[37] and varied organizational capacity.[38] Scholars have suggested that SDP organizations aim to involve people and partners through social networks with the intention of achieving more support than through traditional media.[39] In this same study, Holly Thorpe and Robert Rinehart indicated that SDP organizations have been using social media to overcome these economic or resource limitations that narrow their scope, messaging, and impact. Thus, it is critical for SDP organizations to be able to effectively communicate about their efforts and mission—in particular, using CSR partnerships and platforms may help to amplify those messages to broader audiences. Social media platforms such as Twitter may be particularly suited to SDP organization communication, given their low cost, ability to foster dialogue, and content diffusion.[40] Twitter has the potential to raise awareness of a company's CSR-SDP initiatives by actively promoting CSR efforts and at the same time minimizing stakeholder skepticism through more dialogical and personalized interaction as favorably applied by the engagement strategy. As an additional communication channel, Twitter increases the degree of interaction facilitating the sharing of (CSR-related) information with stakeholders and the development of relationships.

To uncover how these approaches are implemented in practice, we offer some examples of the communication of collective action around SDP social movements and companies' CSR efforts next.

APPLIED EXAMPLES OF SDP AND CSR SOCIAL MEDIA COMMUNICATION PRACTICES

Here, we present some applied examples of SDP- and CSR-related communication strategies. Given that there has been little research in this area,[41] we highlight how some companies communicate their CSR around SDP on Twitter. Following Per Svensson, Tara Mahoney, and Marion Hambrick's approach,[42] we selected a sample of organizations recognized by Beyond Sport (a "global organisation that promotes, supports and celebrates the use of sport to address social issues in communities around the world convening, supporting and advising business or governments on how sport can be used as a tool to achieve both social and business objectives") as delivering the best CSR campaign or initiative in the sport and social impact space in its Beyond Sport Global Awards.[43]

We gathered data from those organizations' Twitter accounts and used Python to retrieve the stream of tweets from Twitter pages posted during 2018. In total, 7,853 tweets were collected for the seventeen organizations we identified, with the actual numbers of collected tweets ranging from 52 to 1,956 for each organization. In addition, we collected data on organizational characteristics from the member profile pages on the Beyond Sport platform, including company name, award result, year of participation, country where the SDP program operates, project's name, focal sport, and funding supporters and other charity partners with which these companies collaborate.

Our aim was to highlight some of Kim and Ferguson's[44] dimensions of CSR communication effectiveness around SDP initiatives, including the level of information diffusion (measured as the number of retweets), and the level of endorsement (measured as the number of likes) that each tweet received. The seventeen corporate campaigns we examined include those listed in table 7.1. Some of the campaigns were established and implemented by SDP organizations working with corporate partners and others were led by corporate entities in partnership with SDP organizations. Next, we briefly describe three of these initiatives.

Football Club Barcelona, in Barcelona, Spain, is one of the most popular professional sports teams in the world. The team's foundation, the Football Club Barcelona Foundation (Fundacio FCB), seeks to promote and encourage work with vulnerable children and adults through the promotion of the values and practice of sport. As the owner of the foundation, the Football Club Barcelona understands that sport is a powerful and effective tool to give visibility to disadvantaged groups and aims to become an agent of social transformation. In 2018, the Football Club Barcelona Foundation received the "Best Corporate Campaign or Initiative in Sport for Good" award by Beyond Sport through its "Nujeen's Dream: FC Barcelona's Holiday Campaign." This initiative highlights the team's commitment to the refugee population, especially to refugee children, and gives visibility to a social problem through sport. Through its communications on Twitter, the Football Club Barcelona Foundation and the team generate visibility for this and other similar projects, communicating key alliances, collaborations, and campaigns with other organizations. In reviewing the foundation's Twitter communication over a one-year period, some key markers of effective communication[45] were evident, such as the following: informativeness (they include as much data as possible about their SDP activities), third-party endorsement (they usually mention organizations that they collaborate with or that they support), personal relevance (they explain the reason why they are involved in each particular cause and why it might affect fans and followers), message tone (they do not include promotional messages about non-SDP-relevant issues), consistency (they regularly publish reminders about their SDP and CSR activity), and frequency (they publish a large number of messages on Twitter in relation to the other companies analyzed).

Under Armour, an American company that manufactures sports and casual apparel, also believes that sports can inspire, unite, and even change the world. Through various partnerships with nonprofit organizations and through initiatives such as #WeWill Baltimore, this company has committed to create change through sport, education, activity, and mentorship. This initiative was also recognized with one of the "Best Corporate Campaign or Initiative in Sport for Good" awards by Beyond Sport. Under Armour's commitment is reflected in grants of up to $25,000 to twenty-four schools that improve the quality, safety, and accessibility of athletic, academic, and recreation facilities, with a particular focus on improving student wellness. In this example of CSR through sport, Under Armour uses their Twitter account to communicate to their followers mainly about what they support. Based on a review of Under Armour's posts, many focus on equity issues related to race, culture, and gender and transgender identity and were connected to access and participation in sport. The focus of the communication is primarily around promotion of sport (and Under Armour's products), personal relevance, and inspiration as well as to some of the partnerships and collaborations they establish in their CSR efforts. Some examples of the content of the posts reflect the inspirational athletic performance of athletes with disabilities at the Warrior Games ("@warriorgames are

Table 7.1. Followers and following data

Company	Industry	Tweets	Followers	Following	Ratio	Hashtags	%Hashtags	Mentions	%Mentions
CentreBell	Sport and Entertainment Complex	52	1988	7	284,00	6	12%	21	40%
ChevronSTEMZone	Oil Industry Company	300	7474	254	29,43	199	66%	117	39%
ESPNCitizenship	Sport Media	121	2625	865	3,03	93	77%	97	80%
FundacioFCB	Professional Sport Club	561	46072	139	331,45	307	55%	331	59%
GeneracionDTV	Satellite Television Company	285	5520	777	7,10	188	66%	180	63%
GRNsportswear	Sports Apparel	317	1291	1330	0,97	102	32%	139	44%
ImpactMarathons	Sport Event	158	3217	2472	1,30	61	39%	64	41%
MLSEFoundation	Sport and Entertainment Company	512	13984	1780	7,86	388	76%	440	**86%**
NRLCommunity	Sport League	233	6319	401	15,76	215	**92%**	109	47%
BoksKids	Sports Apparel	337	1754	3811	0,46	203	60%	154	46%
SAP4good	Software Company	972	18052	4880	3,70	837	86%	566	58%
SlumSoccer	Sport Foundation	631	5825	643	9,06	526	83%	381	60%
SportChanges	Sport Foundation	400	2131	2652	0,80	121	30%	52	13%
SustainableDXB	CSR Consulting Agency	130	289	529	0,55	45	35%	75	58%
TheOceanRace	Sport Event	1956	968277	1127	859,16	**1470**	75%	**1326**	68%
UnderArmour	Sports Apparel	489	42385	82	516,89	419	86%	326	67%
UnileverBrasil	Consumer Goods Company	399	100792	301	334,86	144	36%	118	30%
TOTAL		7853	1227995	22050		5324		4496	
MEAN		461,94	72235	1297,06	141,55		68%		57%
MEDIAN		337	5825	777	7,86				

as much about camaraderie as they are competition. After winning the 400m race, @USMC Sgt Robert Jones returned to run alongside @USNavy Anthony Dieli and encouraged him to finish strong. #WillFindsAWay").

Unilever, a multinational company headquartered in Brazil, has more than four hundred brands in categories as diverse as food, drinks, home, and personal and animal care. Although it seems that a company with these characteristics may not have much to do with sport, it carried out a project called "Conectados pela Cidade" in 2017 through which they used sport as a main connector of people and organizations to reach other latent social problems in underprivileged communities of Rio de Janeiro.[46] Unilever developed a sport environment to engage people, using its brands with a sustainability purpose. Although in this case the sport-for-development initiative was considered successful (being recognized as 2017's Best Corporate Campaign or Initiative in Sport for Good granted by Beyond Sport) within its CSR program, the CSR social media communication generated by Unilever Brasil did not generate a strong impact based on the dimensions established by Kim and Ferguson.[47] Neither the frequency nor the consistency of the messages on Twitter was high. The content (informativeness) and the personal relevance dimensions did not have prominence in these publications. In addition, although they did have third-party endorsements with those who collaborated to perform this type of activity, they did not often mention them in their tweets, which may potentially lead to skepticism from stakeholders and consumers. This skepticism is also increased by the fact that Unilever Brasil regularly publishes content that could be considered "self-promotional message tone," so that a self-congratulatory or promotional message tone in CSR communication may be viewed as too conspicuous, resulting in higher public skepticism.[48]

These examples reflect the varied approaches, focus, and nature of not only the type of SDP initiatives and programming but also the broad range of social media communication efforts in the delivery of CSR- and SDP-oriented initiatives. Next, we discuss some of the unique constraints and considerations that SDP organizations as well as corporate partners need to consider in establishing a coordinated and impactful communication strategy.

Strategic Communication of SDP and CSR

Given the unique context of CSR and SDP initiatives noted previously (e.g., varied sizes and budgets, social issue focus, geographic dispersion, capacity for CSR-oriented partnerships), several factors should be considered in the implementation and communication of CSR partnership initiatives. In this section, we discuss these factors and provide support from the literature to enhance insights and identify areas of opportunity. Specifically, we focus on SDP-CSR communication aspects including communication across borders, creating an audience, and objectives of communication.

Communication across Borders

SDP programs and projects are delivered throughout the world and SDP-CSR initiatives engage with many international stakeholders. In many cases, SDP organizations have office headquarters situated in locales far from programming activities. Additionally, corporate partners may also be geographically dispersed, both from proximity to the SDP organization or office or initiative as well as from programming activities.[49] This poses unique challenges to ensuring that communication is coordinated and consistent for both parties (i.e., the SDP organization and the corporate partner) and in making certain that the targets of the communication are receiving timely and appropriate messaging.[50] Adding a layer of complexity, using social media as a tool for CSR-SDP communication may be effective in targeting certain key stakeholders (such as corporate customers, funders, other potential partners); however, it may not be an appropriate channel to connect with program participants who are often underserved and may not have access to digital technology to learn or interact.

Other key issues with global CSR-SDP communication are the cultural dimensions at play. Research on CSR and social engagement has revealed differences in stakeholder values, intentions, responses, attitudes, and engagement related to CSR across borders.[51] For SDP organizations and initiatives partnering with companies, this may impact the nature of dialogue and engagement with stakeholders and needs to be a key factor in the content and focus of communications. Language issues are also a key consideration in CSR-SDP communication. For example, many of the posts we analyzed were communicated in different languages (including Portuguese, Spanish, German, and English). Creating a common platform for communication across geographical boundaries is challenging, particularly for global SDP-CSR efforts.

Targeting and Engaging an Audience

Another important factor in CSR-SDP communication is creating and engaging an audience. As noted earlier, audiences of CSR-SDP communication may include global stakeholders such as transnational companies, participants, funders, and partners from different sectors. Having a targeted audience that values—and can take action on—the communication of the CSR-SDP initiatives is critical. The appropriate audience receiving messaging can add value to both the corporate partner (e.g., create legitimacy, expand market reach, build socially responsible brand name) and the SDP initiative or organization (e.g., create legitimacy, create deeper cause awareness, access larger networks). The data we collected showed a large variance in the size of audience (or followers) of SDP campaigns, with some reaching nearly one hundred thousand followers (e.g., The Ocean Race) and others fewer than three hundred followers (e.g., Sustainable DXB). Our sample of SDP-CSR initiatives had a median of 5,825 followers. This is relevant in terms of messaging and communicating about the socially responsible initiatives of SDP programs. The larger the number of social network members (followers and following), the more visibility, awareness, and relationship- and legitimacy-building opportunities arise.[52] Meaningful interactions, exchanges, and engagement with the public are based on frequency and consistency of messaging as well as personal relevance. For SDP-CSR initiatives, having a corporate partner who often has a larger network to reach via communication (e.g., Under Armour has 971,000 followers whereas Slum Soccer has 6,038 followers) can amplify messaging to broader audiences. Having access to larger audiences around the world may be beneficial for creating awareness, harnessing interest, and generating action around the social issues addressed by SDP-CSR efforts.[53]

In terms of engagement and communication dynamics (an important metric in social media communication as it may serve as an indicator of interest and awareness and reinforce the significance of an initiative),[54] one measure of interaction is the number of retweets. In our sample, the total tweets (7,853) generated almost 80,000 retweets (although almost 35,000 of those correspond to The Ocean Race tweets) and over 300,000 favorites. The companies that accumulated the most favorites in their tweets were Under Armour and The Ocean Race, with more than 100,000. While Under Armour and The Ocean Race generated more interaction in absolute terms by far, the engagement they got from The Ocean Race is the third lowest in the entire sample (along with Center Bell and Unilever Brasil).

Creating an audience and segmenting messaging to key stakeholders is a critical component of communication for CSR-SDP partnerships. Through strategic messaging, a CSR-SDP partnership can explain in detail the value of focus on the social issue they support, the role that sport plays in addressing the issue, why it needs support, how long the partners have been involved, and the impact they have made, and ultimately can enhance legitimacy as a supportive social citizen. Strategic messaging ensures that important information about programs, events, funding and fundraising opportunities, partnerships, outcomes, impact, and other relevant news can create awareness, generate interest, foster loyalty, and instill supportive behaviors (e.g., volunteering, donations, and other means of cause support) for both an SDP organization and its corporate partners.[55] Strengthening the "personal relevance" in a message can help to increase public acceptance of CSR communication.[56]

Objectives of Communication

Clearly identifying the objectives and aims of a communication engagement strategy is a significant aspect of ensuring maximum impact from any CSR communications. The literature on CSR communication and social media in particular has identified call-to-action (CTA) posts (using "you" or "your" on the text and using "tu" or "tus" for accounts that tweet in Spanish or Portuguese) as engaging strategy. In our sample, for example, more than 25 percent of tweets were considered CTA messages (figure 7.2). These messages were directed at audiences to take action—such as engaging in volunteer opportunities, encouraging donations and charitable giving, purchasing cause-branded products, participation in programs, and helping with content creation (retweeting), and "faving" or "liking."

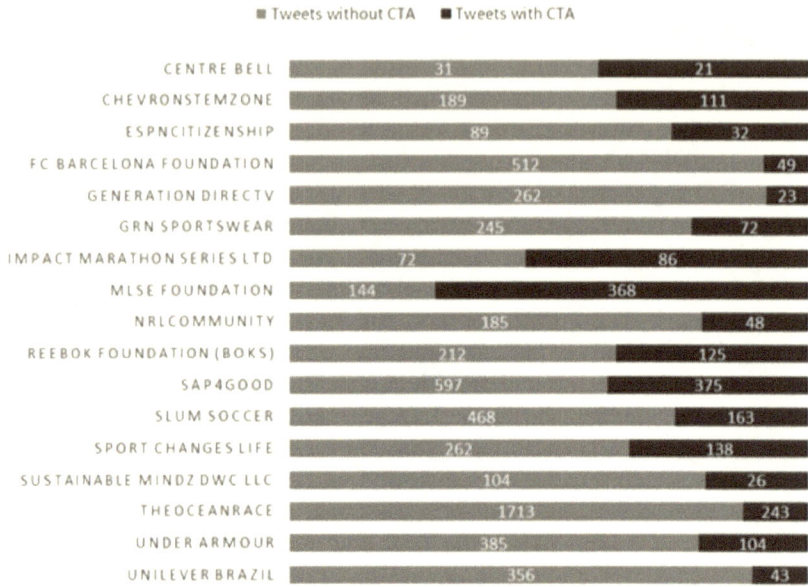

Figure 7.2. Call-to-action presence on tweets.

In some cases, in coordinating SDP programming among a company, an SDP organization, and other partners, diverging interests may influence the focus, frequency, and nature of the messaging around SDP efforts. For example, the commercial interests of a corporate partner may be a priority for CSR communication for a business. Companies may want to drive product purchase through cause-related marketing efforts. These types of communications run the risk of high skepticism from followers.[57] Sometimes, as was the case of some organizations in our sample (e.g., Under Armour), corporate partners may have more followers than SDP organizations on their social media accounts. This may, however, be a strategic advantage that allows SDP organizations to amplify their messaging to broader audiences. For SDP organizations, having endorsements from legitimate companies through CSR partnerships as well as support from credible third parties can help to reinforce the social impact work being carried out. Seung Lee and Kathy Babiak[58] noted that support from experts (credible third parties such as partners, government agencies, as well as highly regarded evaluators) can lower levels of public skepticism and lend credence to the work being done.[59]

Integration of CSR messaging with other messaging may dilute the focus and impact of SDP-CSR communication. Indeed, in looking at Under Armour's Twitter posts, it is evident that the blend of product, athlete promotion, and social impact communications are intermingled. In communicating about social impact efforts using sport as a platform, narratives and storytelling about the outcomes of these initiatives and organizations are critical. Corporate and SDP partners must determine the right approach and balance for message content, purpose, and action.

CONCLUSIONS AND RECOMMENDATIONS

Social media has emerged as an ideal platform for sharing corporate responsibility efforts with stakeholders given its potential for authenticity, ability for consistent and frequent interactions, potential to target specific audiences, and, importantly, its interactivity.[60] In the SDP landscape, where CSR efforts via strategic partnerships between companies and SDP organizations and initiatives are emerging,[61] communication and awareness building around these efforts are critical. There are strategic opportunities for both companies and SDP organizations in this area.

Denise Bortree noted that CSR engagement has shifted in focus and slowly evolved from one-way communication, which framed messages and primed audiences, to two-way communication, which engaged with them, attracted attention, and encouraged greater involvement.[62] Academic investigations into the communication of CSR initiatives in sport have only recently begun to emerge,[63] and research into the nexus of CSR-SDP initiatives and communication has not received much scholarly attention. However, we expect, given the growth and increased prominence of SDP programs, initiatives, and organizations around the world, that communication via different channels—including through social media—will take on greater strategic significance, help raise awareness, and foster greater support and engagement from a range of stakeholders. We believe there are unique aspects of this sport sector that have potential for further exploration.

While social media is a low-cost and easily accessible communications tool for CSR and SDP initiatives, using this tool effectively requires organizational resources of time and money.[64] With SDP-related organizations "increasingly engaging social media in an effort to understand the needs of and efficiently communicate their programs and services with stakeholders,"[65] there is a need for further research in this area. Matthew Walker and Bob Heere argue that both the awareness of CSR and the positive evaluation of CSR held by consumers are critical in determining their behavioral response.[66] This may be a critical question to explore in the SDP domain. How can the communication of these actions create greater interest, engagement, and ultimately a behavioral response (for example, support for volunteering, giving, networking) to advance the SDP organization's mission? Another focus for future research and practice may explore global CSR-SDP communication. Given the global focus of many SDP initiatives and the transnational nature of corporate partners, exploring the cross-cultural application of SDP-CSR communication may provide insights as to how to maximize impact.

From a practical perspective, we believe that the convergence of SDP and CSR may provide many potential opportunities as well as challenges to companies and SDP programs and organizations. We note that one challenge facing SDP organizations, initiatives, and companies will be finding ways to connect CSR initiatives in a meaningful way with the interests of society. There may also be differences in the ways companies design their strategic communications around their SDP partnerships depending on whether their main industry is sport based (e.g., sport apparel manufacturers, professional sport teams) or whether they operate in a different sector (e.g., automobile, finance, technology). Developing a strategy for how to maximize communication messaging and interactions is also a key consideration. This should integrate communication frequency, target audience, interaction objectives, authentic fit between the partner company's brand and the SDP organization or initiative. Resources (such as people, time, and financial capital) should be dedicated to the communication of CSR partnerships, activities, and outcomes in the SDP sector. As noted previously, however, coordinating synergistic messaging between a corporate partner and an SDP organization requires open communication and management. Finally, the importance of Kim and Ferguson's dimensions of effective communication via social media should be kept in mind for any messaging around CSR and SDP initiatives.[67] While communication and promotion of initiatives is important for varied audiences, often SDP organizations operate in remote locations and target populations that do not have access to social media channels or other internet availability. Thus communication around CSR and SDP efforts tends to be perhaps more commercially oriented, in particular when focused on locations where the companies and SDP organizations are based.

This chapter provides some initial insights into a key area of managing partnerships around SDP entities and companies under the guise of CSR. Our aim has been to introduce relevant factors in ensuring effective communication, provide some examples around how these efforts are currently using social media to communicate about various facets of the relationship, and provide some practical and academic insights for future areas of opportunity.

Questions

1. Name some of the partners companies use to deliver CSR programs in the sport for development space.
2. What social problems have SDP organizations, with their corporate partners, tried to address?
3. List Kim and Ferguson's seven dimensions of effective CSR communication.
4. List the channels used by companies and their SDP partners to communicate information about their activities.

Learning Activity

1. Pick three SDP organizations from a search of the internet. What social media do these companies use? Find recent communications on these platforms and critique the messaging, using the Kim and Ferguson model.

NOTES

1. Philip Kotler and Nancy Lee, *Corporate Social Responsibility: Doing the Most Good for Your Company and Your Cause* (Hoboken, NJ: John Wiley & Sons, 2005), 3.

2. Kathy Babiak and Richard Wolfe, "Perspectives on Social Responsibility in Sport," in *Handbook of Sport and Corporate Social Responsibility*, ed. Juan Luis Paramio Salcines, Kathy Babiak, and Geoff Walters (London: Routledge, 2013), 17–34; Kathy Babiak and Daniel Yang, "Toward Developing Strategic Partnerships between SDP and Corporate Organizations: Elements of Effective Partnership Interactions," in *Partnerships and Alliances in Sport for Development and Peace*, ed. Jon Welty Peachey, B. Christine Green, and Laurence Chalip (Urbana, IL: Sagamore Venture, 2020), 189–216.

3. Matthew Walker, Aubrey Kent, and John Vincent, "Communicating Socially Responsible Initiatives: An Analysis of US Professional Teams," *Sport Marketing Quarterly* 19, no. 4 (2010): 187–95.

4. Stuart Esrock and Greg Leichty, "Social Responsibility and Corporate Web Pages: Self-Presentation or Agenda-Setting?" *Public Relations Review* 24, no. 3 (Autumn 1998): 305–19.

5. Melanie Formentin and Kathy Babiak, "Communicating Corporate Social Responsibility in Sport Organizations: Incorporating New Media," in *Routledge Handbook of Sport and New Media*, ed. Andrew C. Billings and Marie Hardin (Abingdon, UK: Routledge, 2014), 207–17.

6. Michael P. Sam, "The Public Management of Sport: Wicked Problems, Challenges and Dilemmas," *Public Management Review* 11, no. 4 (2009): 499–514.

7. Horst Rittel and Melvin Webber, "Wicked Problems," in *Man-Made Futures: Readings in Society, Technology, and Design*, ed. Nigel Cross, David Elliot, and Robin Roy (London: Hutchinson Educational/Open University Press, 1974), 272–80.

8. Cora Burnett, "Engaging Sport-for-Development for Social Impact in the South African Context," *Sport in Society* 12, no. 9 (2009): 1192–205, https://doi.org/10.1080/17430430903137852; Lyndsay M. C. Hayhurst, Brian Wilson, and Wendy Frisby, "Navigating Neoliberal Networks: Transnational Internet Platforms in Sport for Development and Peace," *International Review for the Sociology of Sport* 36, no. 3 (September 2011): 315–29.

9. Hayhurst, Wilson, and Frisby, "Navigating Neoliberal Networks," 317.

10. Babiak and Yang, "Toward Developing Strategic Partnerships between SDP and Corporate Organizations."

11. Fred Coalter, *Sport for Development: What Game Are We Playing?* (New York: Routledge, 2013).

12. Paul Godfrey, "Corporate Social Responsibility in Sport: An Overview and Key Issues," *Journal of Sport Management* 23, no. 6 (November 2009): 698–716.

13. Courtney Szto, "Serving Up Change? Gender Mainstreaming and the UNESCO–WTA Partnership for Global Gender Equality," *Sport in Society* 18, no. 8 (2015): 895–908.

14. Hayhurst, Wilson, and Frisby, "Navigating Neoliberal Networks," 315–29.

15. Omar Al-Tabbaa, Desmond Leach, and John March, "Collaboration between Nonprofit and Business Sectors: A Framework to Guide Strategy Development for Nonprofit Organizations," *VOLUNTAS* 25, no. 3 (2014): 657–78.

16. Babiak and Yang, "Toward Developing Strategic Partnerships between SDP and Corporate Organizations."

17. Bryan W. Husted, "Governance Choices for Corporate Social Responsibility: To Contribute, Collaborate or Internalize?" *Long Range Planning* 36, no. 5 (October 2003): 481–98.

18. Michael Porter and Mark Kramer, "Creating Shared Value: How to Reinvent Capitalism—and Unleash a Wave of Innovation and Growth," *Harvard Business Review* 89, nos. 1–2 (January–February 2011): 1–17.

19. Babiak and Yang, "Toward Developing Strategic Partnerships between SDP and Corporate Organizations."

20. Burnett, "Engaging Sport-for-Development for Social Impact in the South African Context"; Fred Coalter, "Sport-in-Development: Accountability or Development?" in *Sport and International Development*, ed. Roger Levermore and Aaron Beacom (London: Palgrave Macmillan, 2009), 55–75.

21. Seung P. Lee and Kathy Babiak, "Measured Societal Value and Its Impact on Donations and Perception of Corporate Social Responsibility: An Experimental Approach," *Nonprofit and Voluntary Sector Quarterly* 46, no. 5 (2017): 1030–51.

22. Chao Guo and Gregory D. Saxton, "Tweeting Social Change: How Social Media Are Changing Nonprofit Advocacy," *Nonprofit and Voluntary Sector Quarterly* 43, no. 1 (2014): 57–79.

23. Holly Thorpe and Robert Rinehart, "Action Sport NGOs in a Neo-Liberal Context: The Cases of Skateistan and Surf Aid International," *Journal of Sport and Social Issues* 37, no. 2 (2013): 115–41.

24. Per G. Svensson, Tara Q. Mahoney, and Marion E. Hambrick, "Twitter as a Communication Tool for Nonprofits: A Study of Sport-for-Development Organizations," *Nonprofit and Voluntary Sector Quarterly* 44, no. 6 (2015): 1086–106.

25. Jennifer L. Bartlett, "Public Relations and Corporate Social Responsibility," in *The Handbook of Communication and Corporate Social Responsibility*, ed. Øyvind Ihlen, Jennifer L. Bartlett, and Steve May (Malden, MA: John Wiley & Sons, 2011), 67–86; Michael L. Kent and Maureen Taylor, "From Homo Economicus to Homo Dialogicus: Rethinking Social Media Use in CSR Communication," *Public Relations Review* 42, no. 1 (March 2016): 60–67; Angeles Moreno and Paul Capriotti, "Communicating CSR, Citizenship and Sustainability on the Web," *Journal of Communication Management* 13, no. 2 (2009): 157–75.

26. Peggy Brønn and Albana Vrioni, "Corporate Social Responsibility and Cause-Related Marketing: An Overview," *International Journal of Advertising* 20, no. 2 (2001): 207–22; Jeffrey Unerman and Mark Bennett, "Increased Stakeholder Dialogue and the Internet: Towards Greater Corporate Accountability or Reinforcing Capitalist Hegemony?" *Accounting, Organizations and Society* 29, no. 7 (October 2004): 685–707.

27. Lee and Babiak, "Measured Societal Value and Its Impact on Donations and Perception of Corporate Social Responsibility"; Sandra Waddock and Bradley Googins, "The Paradoxes of Communicating Corporate Social Responsibility," in *The Handbook of Communication and Corporate Social Responsibility*, ed. Øyvind Ihlen, Jennifer L. Bartlett, and Steve May (Malden, MA: John Wiley & Sons, 2011), 23–43.

28. Shuili Du, C. B. Bhattacharya, and Sankar Sen, "Maximizing Business Returns to Corporate Social Responsibility (CSR): The Role of CSR Communication," *International Journal*

of Management Reviews 12, no. 1 (January 2010): 8–19; Kristen Lovejoy and Gregory Saxton, "Information, Community, and Action: How Nonprofit Organizations Use Social Media," *Journal of Computer-Mediated Communication* 17, no. 3 (2012): 337–53.

29. Mark R. Foreh and Sonya Grier, "When Is Honesty the Best Policy? The Effect of Stated Company Intent on Consumer Skepticism," *Journal of Consumer Psychology* 13, no. 3 (2003): 349–56; Yeosun Yoon, Zeynep Gürhan-Canli, and Norbert Schwarz, "The Effect of Corporate Social Responsibility (CSR) Activities on Companies with Bad Reputations," *Journal of Consumer Psychology* 16, no. 4 (2006): 377–90.

30. Du, Bhattacharya, and Sen, "Maximizing Business Returns to Corporate Social Responsibility (CSR)"; Mette Morsing and Majken Schultz, "Corporate Social Responsibility Communication: Stakeholder Information, Response and Involvement Strategies," *Business Ethics: A European Review* 15, no. 4 (2006): 323–38; Alan Pomering and Sara Dolnicar, "Assessing the Prerequisite of Successful CSR Implementation: Are Consumers Aware of CSR Initiatives?" *Journal of Business Ethics* 85, no. 2 (2009): 285–301; Bodo B. Schlegelmilch and Irene Pollach, "The Perils and Opportunities of Communicating Corporate Ethics," *Journal of Marketing Management* 21, nos. 3–4 (2005): 267–90.

31. Sora Kim and Mary Ann T. Ferguson, "Dimensions of Effective CSR Communication Based on Public Expectations," *Journal of Marketing Communications* 24, no. 6 (2018): 549–67.

32. Yeonsoo Kim, "Consumer Responses to the Food Industry's Proactive and Passive Environmental CSR, Factoring in Price as CSR Tradeoff," *Journal of Business Ethics* 140, no. 2 (2017): 307–21.

33. Theo Araujo and John Kollat, "Communicating Effectively about CSR on Twitter: The Power of Engaging Strategies and Storytelling Elements," *Internet Research* 28, no. 2 (2018): 419–31; Du, Bhattacharya, and Sen, "Maximizing Business Returns to Corporate Social Responsibility (CSR)."

34. Du, Bhattacharya, and Sen, "Maximizing Business Returns to Corporate Social Responsibility (CSR)."

35. Daniel Korschun and Shuili Du, "How Virtual Corporate Social Responsibility Dialogs Generate Value: A Framework and Propositions," *Journal of Business Research* 66, no. 9 (September 2013): 1494–504.

36. Paul Capriotti, "Communicating Corporate Social Responsibility through the Internet and Social Media," in *The Handbook of Communication and Corporate Social Responsibility*, ed. Øyvind Ihlen, Jennifer L. Bartlett, and Steve May (Malden, MA: John Wiley & Sons, 2011), 358–78; Korschun and Du, "How Virtual Corporate Social Responsibility Dialogs Generate Value"; Walker, Kent, and Vincent, "Communicating Socially Responsible Initiatives."

37. Richard Giulianotti, "The Sport, Development and Peace Sector: A Model of Four Social Policy Domains," *Journal of Social Policy* 40, no. 4 (October 2011): 757–76; Bruce Kidd, "A New Social Movement: Sport for Development and Peace," *Sport in Society* 11, no. 4 (July 2008): 370–80; Iain Lindsey, "Community Collaboration in Development Work with Young People: Perspectives from Zambian Communities," *Development in Practice* 23, no. 4 (June 2013): 481–95.

38. Fred Coalter, "Sport-for-Development: Going beyond the Boundary?" *Sport in Society* 13, no. 9 (November 2010): 1374–91.

39. Thorpe and Rinehart, "Action Sport NGOs in a Neo-Liberal Context."

40. Svensson, Mahoney, and Hambrick, "Twitter as a Communication Tool for Nonprofits."

41. Hayhurst, Wilson, and Frisby, "Navigating Neoliberal Networks," 315–29.

42. Svensson, Mahoney, and Hambrick, "Twitter as a Communication Tool for Nonprofits."

43. Beyond Sport, "About Us," accessed July 19, 2019, https://www.beyondsport.org/About-Us.

44. Kim and Ferguson, "Dimensions of Effective CSR Communication Based on Public Expectations."

45. Kim and Ferguson, "Dimensions of Effective CSR Communication Based on Public Expectations."

46. Beyond Sport, "About Us."

47. Kim and Ferguson, "Dimensions of Effective CSR Communication Based on Public Expectations."

48. Kim and Ferguson, "Dimensions of Effective CSR Communication Based on Public Expectations."

49. Babiak and Yang, "Toward Developing Strategic Partnerships between SDP and Corporate Organizations."

50. Gasha Abeza and Norm O'Reilly, "Social Media Platforms' Use in Building Stakeholder Relationships," *Journal of Applied Sport Management* 6, no. 3 (Fall 2014): 103–26.

51. Frank de Bakker, "Exporting Knowledge and Values: A Discussion of Managerial Challenges When Attempting to Diffuse CSR across Company and National Borders," in *Managing Corporate Social Responsibility in Action*, ed. Frank de Bakker and Frank den Hond (Abingdon, UK: Routledge, 2016), 141–60; David Katamba, Christoph Zipfel, David Haag, and Charles Tushabomwe-Kazooba, eds., *Principles of Corporate Social Responsibility (CSR): A Guide for Students and Practicing Managers in Developing and Emerging Countries* (Houston, TX: Strategic Book Publishing, 2012).

52. Araujo and Kollat, "Communicating Effectively about CSR on Twitter"; Du, Bhattacharya, and Sen, "Maximizing Business Returns to Corporate Social Responsibility (CSR)."

53. Araujo and Kollat, "Communicating Effectively about CSR on Twitter."

54. Elanor Colleoni, "CSR Communication Strategies for Organizational Legitimacy in Social Media," *Corporate Communications: An International Journal* 18, no. 2 (2013): 228–48.

55. Denise S. Bortree, "The State of CSR Communication Research: A Summary and Future Direction," *Public Relations Journal* 8, no. 3 (2014): 1–8.

56. Kim and Ferguson, "Dimensions of Effective CSR Communication Based on Public Expectations."

57. Kim and Ferguson, "Dimensions of Effective CSR Communication Based on Public Expectations."

58. Lee and Babiak, "Measured Societal Value and Its Impact on Donations and Perception of Corporate Social Responsibility."

59. Kim and Ferguson, "Dimensions of Effective CSR Communication Based on Public Expectations."

60. Abeza and O'Reilly, "Social Media Platforms' Use in Building Stakeholder Relationships."

61. Babiak and Yang, "Toward Developing Strategic Partnerships between SDP and Corporate Organizations."

62. Bortree, "The State of CSR Communication Research."

63. Lee and Babiak, "Measured Societal Value and Its Impact on Donations and Perception of Corporate Social Responsibility"; Joon K. Kim, Holly Overton, Kevin Hull, and Minhee Choi, "Examining Public Perceptions of CSR in Sport," *Corporate Communications: An International Journal* 23, no. 4 (2018): 629–47; Dimitrios Kolyperas and Leigh Sparks, "Corporate

Social Responsibility (CSR) Communications in the G-25 Football Clubs," *International Journal of Sport Management and Marketing* 10, nos. 1–2 (November 2011): 83–103.

64. Seungahn Nah and Gregory D. Saxton, "Modeling the Adoption and Use of Social Media by Nonprofit Organizations," *New Media and Society* 15, no. 2 (2013): 294–313; Richard D. Waters, Kimberly A. Burke, Zachary H. Jackson, and Jamie D. Buning, "Using Stewardship to Cultivate Fandom Online: Comparing How National Football League Teams Use Their Web Sites and Facebook to Engage Their Fans," *International Journal of Sport Communication* 4, no. 2 (2011): 163–77; Richard D. Waters and Kristen L. Feneley, "Virtual Stewardship in the Age of New Media: Have Nonprofit Organizations Moved beyond Web 1.0 Strategies?" *International Journal of Nonprofit and Voluntary Sector Marketing* 18, no. 3 (August 2013): 216–30.

65. Abeza and O'Reilly, "Social Media Platforms' Use in Building Stakeholder Relationships," 128.

66. Matthew Walker and Bob Heere, "Consumer Attitudes toward Responsible Entities in Sport (CARES): Scale Development and Model Testing," *Sport Management Review* 14, no. 2 (May 2011): 153–66.

67. Kim and Ferguson, "Dimensions of Effective CSR Communication Based on Public Expectations."

8

Linking Sport Events with Sport Participation and Development

Marijke Taks and Georgia Teare

OBJECTIVES

This chapter will:

- Describe sport participation as one of the various impacts of sport events.
- Distinguish between tangible and intangible impacts of sport events.
- Impart that sport participation and development are considered intangible impacts from events.
- Recognize ways in which sport facilities, as tangible impacts from sport events, affect participation and sport development (or not).
- Discuss how event size (large vs. small) affects sport participation.
- Define and illustrate the concepts of impact, legacy, and leveraging in the context of sport events and sport participation.

Sport is at the core of sport events. Therefore, it is not unreasonable to expect that sport participation could be a major outcome of hosting sport events. In addition, reducing physical inactivity is a desired outcome of the investment that accompanies staging sport events that resonates with policymakers worldwide. Increasing physical activity through events has been referred to in the literature as "trickle-down effects," "inspiration effects," and "demonstration effects," which all propose that elite athletes or elite sport events have the power to inspire spectators to become more active sport participants.[1] The question is: Can sport events deliver this so-called trickle down, inspiration, or demonstration effect?[2] To date, there is little research to support that sport events stimulate new participation in sport or sport development more generally.[3] In fact, if an effect is apparent, it is among those who are already (or have been) involved in sport who may participate a little more.[4]

Moreover, most sport event research to date has focused on planned and tangible legacies of mega-events (both positive and negative). However, there is a shift in focus into three directions: (1) from tangible to intangible impacts;[5] (2) from large to small events;[6] and (3) from legacy to leverage.[7] This chapter illustrates these three trends broadly and then discusses how they are specific to sport participation associated with sport events. Through outlining the current research trends, this chapter acts as a guide to develop a future research agenda to enhance our understanding of how sport events can be used and strategically planned to enhance sport participation and development.

SPORT EVENT IMPACTS: RESEARCH TRENDS

From Tangible to Intangible Impacts

Sport events have a variety of impacts, including economic, tourism, social, and sport participation.[8] Given the lack of substantial economic and sustainable tourism outcomes from events to justify major public funding, there has been a shift in research attention toward more social and sport participation outcomes from events.[9] Generally, economic and tourism impacts are considered to be more *tangible* while social and sport participation impacts are more *intangible* in nature.[10] However, as shown in table 8.1, each of these event impact dimensions have both tangible and intangible aspects, in which tangible impacts are relatively easy to measure, while intangible impacts are easy to see but more challenging to measure. The focus of this contribution is on the tangible and intangible impacts of sport events on sport participation (highlighted in gray) and will be elaborated on further throughout this chapter.

From Large to Small Events

There are no universal definitions or typologies of events; however, Donald Getz[11] defined a *mega sport event* (MSE) as an event that generates "very high levels of tourism, media coverage, prestige or economic impact for their host community," although their impact and meaning reaches far beyond the event and the host city. There is consensus among researchers that the Summer Olympic Games and the FIFA World Cup are mega-events, but there is less consensus about events such as the Commonwealth Games, Euro football cup, and Winter Olympics, which also are labeled as *second-tier events*.[12]

Regardless of *mega* status, major events have a significant impact on the host community. In the context of this chapter, non-mega sport events are one-off sport events, of short duration and *out of the ordinary, significant,* and *special* for the host community where they are being hosted but are considered to be more so the *little brother or sister* of the MSE. They are generally acquired by host communities based on a bidding

Table 8.1. **Examples of tangible and intangible impacts of sport events**

Type of impact	Tangible	Intangible
Economic	• Dollar amounts	• Consumer surplus[1] • Public good value[2] • Psychic income[3] • Opportunity costs[4]
Tourism	• Number of tourists • Sustained tourism adding to economic development[5]	• Destination image (potentially stimulating future tourism[6]) • City marketing
Social	• Physical social spaces[7] (temporary or permanent)	• Social cohesion[8] • Social capital[9] • Community spirit[10] • Happiness[11]
Sport	• Sport facilities and infrastructure • Number of sport participants, coaches, and volunteers	• Sport participation and skill development • New participation • Quality of participation experiences

Note: Specific impacts synthesized from multiple sources: Chalip and Costa (2005), Gibson et al. (2014), Johnson et al. (2001), Kaplanidou (2012), Taks et al. (2009), Taks et al. (2011), Taks et al. (2016)

process and require a substantial amount of public funding. Clearly, they are smaller in size, scale, scope, and reach than their mega counterparts; however, they maintain the same issues faced by host communities of mega events. For instance, Martin Müller identified the *mega-event syndrome* to encompass common issues faced by mega events, as well as their major counterparts. The syndrome includes: (1) the bid to host the event overpromising benefits to the host community; (2) underestimation of costs and the presence of unexpected expenses; (3) event takeover, where the event overshadows any other development priorities of the host community; (4) public risk taking, when private firms reap the rewards; (5) rule of exception, which involves suspension of normal laws and typically benefits corporations and hinders citizens; (6) elite capture, where large firms are favored over local vendors; and (7) event fix, where the event is framed as a solution to a host community's planning challenges.[13]

Based on the notion that events require investments of human, financial, and physical resources from communities that stage them, we prefer to define event size in terms of event resource demand (ERD);[14] more specifically, large events are those events with high ERD and small events have a low ERD. We acknowledge that there are an infinite number of events that fall on the ERD continuum. Thus, instead of using the previous event typologies or event outcomes, we refer to a large event as an event with a high ERD and a small event refers to one with a low ERD. Examples of smaller events are the International Children's Games or the European Junior Swimming Championships.

Large events are under scrutiny for multiple reasons, including financial debacles, corruption, and their questionable sustainable impact. This is evident from cities deciding not to bid for the Olympic Games (e.g., Boston and Toronto for the 2024 Games), withdrawing a bid (e.g., Budapest for the 2024 Games), or choosing not to host when awarded the ability to do so (e.g., Durban for the 2022 Commonwealth Games in South Africa). This has led toward a push for more research on smaller events, which may have greater potential for beneficial and sustainable outcomes for host communities, partially because of tighter social connections and a greater probability for a bottom-up strategy.[15]

From Legacy to Leverage

Special *one-off* sport events are temporal and can trigger a variety of short- or long-term, positive or negative impacts, which lead to positive or negative outcomes; if sustained, these outcomes have been called *legacies*. *Event leveraging* refers to the strategic planning for event outcomes, well in advance of the event, or even bidding for the event to strategically use available resources to meet predetermined goals. The concept and development of event leveraging is further expanded on in the following section on sport participation and events.

SPORT PARTICIPATION IMPACTS FROM SPORT EVENTS: RESEARCH TRENDS

The following sections discuss the research trends described previously as applied to the specific impacts from sport events on sport participation. We look at the collective trends and illustrate tangible and intangible sport participation impacts for both large and small events. This section concludes with a discussion of the third research trend of legacies to leveraging and illustrates the need for deliberate planning when it comes to the facilitation of sport participation impacts from events.

Tangible Sport Participation Impacts

Tangible Impacts and Large Events

Sport facilities are considered the *tangible* component of sport events stimulating sport participation. MSEs usually require expensive, high-end facilities. There are multiple examples of facilities that cost a fortune to build and were abandoned postevent. These so-called white elephants are a detrimental outcome of MSEs;[16] these facilities remain unused postevent because of high maintenance costs and because they do not meet community needs. Examples include most football stadiums following the 2010 FIFA World Cup in South Africa; the Olympic facilities following the 2004 Olympic Games in Athens; and, most recently, the facilities built for the 2016 Olympic Games in Rio de Janeiro. The problem is that these facilities are generally not built with the sport participation needs of the host community in mind. For instance, the facilities from the 1988 Calgary Winter Olympics became a high-end national training center for speed skating postevent to serve high-performance athletes (i.e., those who are already involved with sport), contributing to elite sport development but not necessarily serving the local community or stimulating new participation in sport. In contrast, the Richmond Oval, built for the 2010 Winter Olympics in Vancouver, was first built to serve the Olympic Games but was resized postevent to better serve the community. Of course, building this facility to meet Olympic standards and bringing it down to meet the community needs afterward came at an extravagant cost, which could have been avoided if the city had decided to build a community facility only rather than also staging the Olympic Games. This would have saved a substantial amount of money that could have otherwise been spent to stimulate participation in sport if that was a goal of the local community. In contrast, the facilities built for the 1972 Olympic Games in Munich have served the community very well all these years. There is a current gap in the literature regarding evaluating community usage of multiple post–Olympic Games and World Cup facilities that should be addressed to understand what strategies were effective and why.

Tangible Impacts and Small Events

Occasionally, facilities are upgraded or even newly built for smaller-scale events. Examples of sport events held in Windsor, Ontario, illustrate this point. First, hosting the 2005 Pan American Junior Athletics Championships led to a new stadium that was built at the University of Windsor, a facility that was needed by both the host university and community. Thus the stadium was an expected and intended legacy of hosting the event. Seven years after the fact, Marijke Taks, B. Christine Green, Laura Misener, and Laurence Chalip,[17] evaluated the outcome of this facility among key stakeholders in the community. The new facility provided more and better access to athletics for the community and, with the addition of the infield turf, helped to develop other sports such as soccer and American football. Again, there is evidence for sport development, namely important improvements for those already involved in sport.

Windsor, Ontario, was also the host city of the 2013 International Children's Games that led to the creation of the $78 million aquatic center. The building of this facility required the closure of four smaller local pools, greatly affecting the swimming ability for low-income community members for two reasons: lack of accessibility and price increases to use the new facility.[18] Residents questioned whether this *legacy* benefited the needs of the few over the needs of the many. Moreover, the operational costs for the aquatic complex highly surpassed the estimations, negatively impacting the annual city budgets. This financial burden, with an unintended $3 million deficit per year,[19] is an unexpected outcome that put even the lowest-paying temporary city jobs in jeopardy.[20]

City Council assumed that hosting events and building an aquatic complex would make residents more active. However, in the absence of a benchmark measure of swimming levels in the community, it is impossible to evaluate if swimming participation increased, decreased, or remained the same because of the building of the aquatic center in the community. In fact, there is no record of anybody being held responsible for following up on whether residents have become more active as a result of building the aquatic complex. There is, however, evidence for sport development: The construction of the aquatic complex enabled Windsor to host other international events such as the FINA (International Swimming Federation) World Diving Championships and, to some extent, the FINA 2016 World Swimming Championships. Hosting these events again, however, came at a high additional cost for the city without substantial economic return. Moreover, a local diving club was established in January 2016 and received preferential treatment over other community sport organizations. In 2017, City Council approved a motion to waive aquatic complex fees up to $75,000 over three years for the Windsor Diving Club; however, it denied other swimming clubs the same request.[21] This triggered hostile feelings from these sport clubs toward the City Council as they struggled to afford the high rental costs of the aquatic complex, jeopardizing the viability of their programs.

Tangible Sport Participation Impacts and Implications for Future Research

From this overview of sport facilities built in relation to sport events, we learned that residents' needs are central in the case of building or upgrading sport facilities. Moreover, addressing these needs ensures long-term use, which is central for sustainable community development. Thus, future research should focus on: (1) determining community needs in advance of bidding for an event; (2) learning to accurately determine and estimate community needs; (3) understanding the budgetary implications from building before and maintaining facilities after events; (4) benchmarking participation and physical activity levels in advance of new and upgraded facilities to be able to evaluate their impact; (5) evaluating impact after the facility is built; and (6) learning from past experiences.

Intangible Sport Participation Impacts

Intangible Impacts and Large Events

The 2012 London Olympic Games will likely be remembered as the flagship event for bringing the *sport participation* legacy explicitly to the forefront.[22] Never before has there been an Olympic Games that put such a strong emphasis on leaving a legacy for sport participation and development.[23] This emphasis has had a far-reaching impact on public policy agendas. Sport England, for example, justified this legacy goal because "the promotion of general physical activity and the wider social, community and economic well-being agenda has been marginalized in favour of a concentration on sports for sports sake and sporting excellence."[24] The intention of delivering successful Olympic and Paralympic Games that create "a sustainable legacy and get more children and young people taking part in high quality PE and sport"[25] was at the forefront of the London bid and subsequent public relations campaigns. In their overview of systematic reviews, Kamal Ram Mahtani and colleagues[26] found no evidence of sustained increase in sport participation among the English population or any other associated health outcomes as a result of the London 2012 Olympic Games. Moreover, when speaking to the English population directly, Russell Carter and Theo Lorenc[27] found that sedentary adults were, in fact, discouraged to participate in physical activity after watching Olympic athletes.

In the context of the 2010 Winter Olympic Games in Vancouver, Cora Craig and Adrian Bauman[28] performed rigorous measurements of sport and physical activity levels among five- to nineteen-year-old (n = 19,862) Canadian children between August 2007 and July 2011 (including the use of pedometers). The authors found no impact on objectively measured physical activity or the prevalence of overall sport participation among Canadian children. Similarly, using nationally representative data, Luke Potwarka and Scott Leatherdale found no significant change in physical activity rates among youth at the national (Canada) and provincial (British Columbia) levels. Changes were, however, found at the regional levels of North Shore and Richmond, British Columbia, among female youth. These changes were found in regions that housed Olympic venues that saw female Canadian athletes reach the podium.[29] It was not, however, indicated whether these increases in participation were from new participants or those who were already active participating a little more.

Gertrud Pfister, Marie-Luise Klein, and Nina Tiesler[30] studied the overall impact of the 2011 Women's World Cup on the development of women's soccer in Germany. Since 2007 (the beginning of the application process), the Deutsche Fussball Bund (DFB) launched multiple initiatives to stimulate girls' soccer development in Germany. The authors noted an increase in female membership rates in the DFB immediately after Germany hosted the 2011 Women's World Cup, following a general trend that effects are usually seen in the first *postevent period*. However, the authors noted that membership rates do not accurately reflect soccer involvement. The number of girls' and women's teams is a more accurate measure to estimate participation rates, and these numbers had already started to decline in 2010 (prior to hosting the 2011 Women's World Cup) and continued to decline postevent. The authors concluded that "the World Cup has not triggered an increase in the number of girls taking up soccer."[31] However, the overall quality of women's soccer has drastically improved, pointing out evidence for sport development rather than new participation in sport.

Pamela Wicker and Popi Sotiriadou[32] analyzed the trickle-down effect of the 2006 Melbourne Commonwealth Games, and specifically focused on various population groups benefiting from hosting major sport events. The authors found the overall effects to be relatively small, with only 5.9 percent of the respondents taking up a new activity, and 6.9 percent spending more time participating in sport and physical activity; various groups who benefited were younger people, less educated people, females, people of Aboriginal or Torres Strait Islander origin, and the locals. Note that *taking up a new activity* is not necessarily *new participation*; people may have simply switched sports.

In another study, Frick and Wicker[33] analyzed the long-term effects of the performance of the German national football team on German football participation from 1950 to 2014. The results indicated that only the wins of the World Cup titles of the men's national team had a positive and significant effect on the number and percentage change in individual club membership. Similar effects were not found for the European Championships of the men, nor for the World Cup and European Championships of the women. In fact, this study confirms the temporary peak that can be seen among other sports every four years following the mega-events' cycles because the increases were not sustained. Moreover, it was surprising to not see any results on the variance explained in the regressions.

A cohort analysis executed by Kurumi Aizawa, Ji Wu, Yuhei Inoue, and Mikihiro Sato[34] on the long-term effect of the Tokyo 1964 Olympic Games revealed that the Japanese residents who are currently between sixty and sixty-nine years old (those who were between twelve and nineteen years old during the 1964 Tokyo Olympic Games) participate in sport more frequently than other cohorts. The authors explain this phenomenon through the sleeper effect, where subtle persuasive messages take effect on behavior over time. Though this is an intriguing notion, the sleeper effect can equally explain why younger cohorts are currently not participating more frequently, raising questions about the true effect of the Olympic Games. Moreover, many other initiatives such as policies and sport infrastructure were put in motion in the years leading up to and following Olympic Games, making it extremely difficult to attribute the findings to hosting the 1964 Olympic Games. What if these initiatives were put into place without hosting the Olympic Games and more funds were put into sport participation initiatives instead?

A last example of long-term sport participation effects is from the 1984 Los Angeles Olympic Games. The unexpected profits postevent led to political consensus to give it back to *youth sport* and the establishment of the Foundation LA84. This foundation distributes $225 million USD annually to support 2,200 youth sport organizations in southern California. Unfortunately, there were no benchmark data, but participation rates are significantly higher than the general population.[35]

Intangible Impacts and Small Events

Much of the research on sport participation impacts from sport events has focused on larger events, leaving the power of smaller events to generate sport participation largely under-researched. We present some research conducted on and evaluations of two past events: the 2005 Pan American Junior Athletic Championships (Windsor, Ontario), and the 2005 Canadian National Figure Skating Championships (London, Ontario).[36] Document and media analyses, as well as retrospective interviews (n = 21 and n = 14, respectively) with key stakeholders (i.e. local organizing committee, local sport organization, facility managers, athletes) were conducted six years after the events. Key stakeholders of sport events supported the idea that increasing sport participation through events is a worthwhile endeavor. There was an overarching assumption that the events in and of themselves, through the process of *creating awareness*, were sufficient to engender participation outcomes. However, participation effects in the absence of leveraging are negligible. The authors found no evidence for defined strategic intentions or plans to leverage events to foster sport participation; the leverage occurrences were more coincidental. In the case of the 2005 Pan American Junior Athletic Championships, a coaching clinic and a new facility were two intended tactics expected to intentionally trigger increases in sport participation. The coaching clinic was not well attended and therefore did not attain the intended outcome. As indicated earlier, the building of the new stadium stimulated development for those already involved in sport.[37] The 2005 Canadian National Figure Skating Championships implemented an educational program through schools and organized demonstrations during event breaks. Flyers were handed out on site for both events. No partnerships were activated to serve sport development. Despite the general belief that it would be a good idea to increase the number of new participants, the focus for any sport development efforts or ideas was clearly on individuals already in the sport system rather than any attempts to get new participants into the sport.[38]

In summary, the examples provided here for both large and small events confirm what Mike Weed and colleagues[39] found in their systematic review of large events: (1) those who already do a little sport can be inspired to do a little more; (2) those who have played sport before can be inspired to play again; and (3) some people might give up one sport to try another. Moreover, there is no evidence to support the notion that new participation was generated. Indeed, sport club registration may have increased in the immediate aftermath of an event; however, the use of national data sets or club membership does not indicate if this temporary increase in participation is made up of new sport participants. Furthermore, there is a dearth of investigations that have addressed the quality of these participation experiences. It is suggested that many of the community sport clubs that are tasked with taking on the increase in participation are not equipped to do so,[40] thus potentially leaving participants dissatisfied with their experiences. Clearly, sport events are unlikely in and of themselves to generate increases in sport participation. This raises the question: What can be done to create sport participation from events? Here is where the notion of event leveraging comes into play.

From Legacy to Leveraging Sport Events for Participation

Events are hosted and create outcomes. Usually there is very little strategic planning for event outcomes; therefore legacies are typically "expected" or at least hoped for.[41] Leveraging is different from legacy planning because it focuses attention on the means to obtain desired outcomes (in this case, sport participation objectives), by integrating each event into the community's existing marketing and management strategies.[42] Thus, the focus is on strategy formulation and implementation throughout event planning and implementation processes. Taks, Green, Misener, and Chalip[43] undertook a series of studies to examine and develop how to effectively manage the event leveraging process. Their efforts in the context of the 2013 International Children's Games (hosted in Windsor, Ontario) are detailed here, beginning with the planning phase and followed by the implementation phase. We conclude this section with examples from other scholars' work on leveraging sport events for sport participation.

The Planning Phase

For the planning phase, a task force was created to consider the challenges and prospects for leveraging sport events for sport development. The panel of experts was composed of twelve practitioners and academics from a variety of organizations that would (or could) be involved in (and benefit from) leveraging sport events for participation (e.g., sports policy, event management, facility management, coaching, tourism, marketing, education, and community development). Brainstorming and nominal group techniques were used to collect the data, which resulted in a framework for leveraging sport events to build sport participation (figure 8.1).

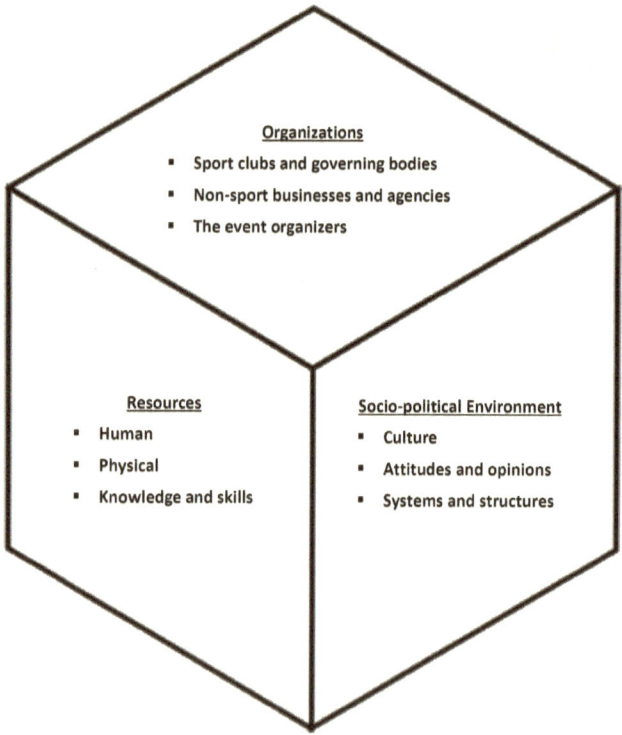

Figure 8.1. Elements to be managed when leveraging sport events to build sport participation. *Credit*: Laurence Chalip

The model, as illustrated in figure 8.1, consists of three elements: (1) the context or environment (culture, opinions and attitudes, systems and structures); (2) three types of organizations with a stake in the leveraging process (event, sport, and nonsport entities); and (c) resources needed (human, physical, and knowledge). The model encompasses core elements necessary for the leveraging effort to enable pursuit of sport participation goals. Each of the factors in the model can enhance or hinder leveraging strategies and tactics. Sport events can be leveraged to enhance sport participation if the necessary alliances among sport organizations, event organizers, and nonsport stakeholders are forged to integrate each event into the marketing mix of sport organizations. Potential barriers need to be addressed; for example, the lack of available capacity to absorb new participants, crowding out of local participation by the event, and the disincentives resulting from elite performances that seem outside the reach of aspiring participants.

The Implementation Phase

For the implementation phase, an international youth sport event (2013 International Children's Games) was selected as the event to be leveraged, and athletics and gymnastics were selected as the two sports to be stimulated.[44] The first step consisted of a one-day workshop six months prior to the event to scope, discuss, and develop an action plan for leveraging. The next steps evaluated processes and outcomes through participant observation and casual meetings during the event, a postevent workshop one month after the event, and reflective interviews (n = 9) one year after the event.

The sport communities (athletics and gymnastics) were unable to implement the ideas and initiatives that had been developed in the six months leading up to the event. Only some isolated tactics were implemented (e.g., handing out posters and flyers in schools prior to the event, flyers during the events). Challenges to implement the developed strategies and tactics seemed to be a lack of human resources (in the case of athletics), and a lack of *community* to enable collaborative actions among a variety of clubs (in the case of gymnastics). One year after the event, stakeholders revealed some evidence of an *inspiration effect*; for those already involved in the sport, competing in an international context at this level and age was very attractive and rather unique. However, there is no evidence of increased participation in either sport. Without evidence of tangible outcomes, the key stakeholders displayed no efforts to sustain any positive impacts. Although stakeholders feel that lessons can be learned from the unsuccessful leveraging effort, what is being done to retain and capitalize on what was learned is unclear at this stage. Based on their empirical work, Taks and colleagues[45] developed an event leveraging framework, presented in figure 8.2.

The major findings from this action research approach are that (1) local sport organizations lack the necessary skills and resources to leverage sport events; (2) local sport organizations have their ways of doing things; and (3) events can help local

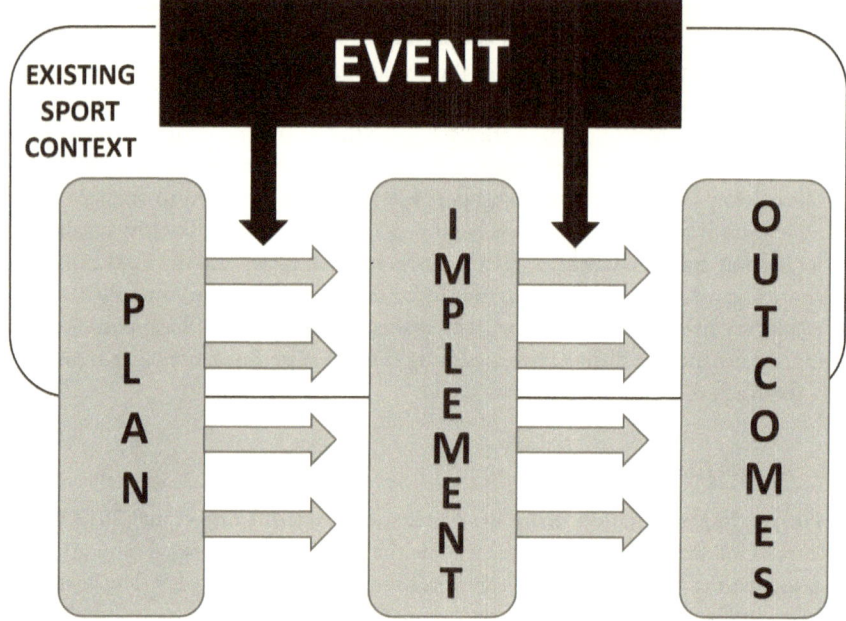

Figure 8.2. Event leverage framework.

sport organizations to build their sport. One of the major questions in terms of creating sport participation outcomes through events is, however, *who* or *which entity* is going to take responsibility for making this happen? (This entity can vary according to the specific context; see leveraging model presented earlier.)

Additional Examples of Leveraging Sport Events for Sport Participation

Although limited, other research teams have attempted to implement leveraging initiatives for sport events to generate sport participation in the context of large and small events. Shushu Chen and Ian Henry[46] evaluated a leveraging for sport participation initiative associated with the London 2012 Olympic Games. The leveraging initiative was partnered with a workplace and aimed at engaging employees in physical activity in regions outside of the Olympic host city (East Midlands and Leicestershire). Although not effective for all individuals in all organizations, the program was found to be an overall successful way of engaging some groups of employees in physical activity in some organizations.

In the context of local sport clubs, when attempting to leverage a series of medium-sized, elite tennis events in Auckland, New Zealand, Katharine Hoskyn, Geoff Dickson, and Sotiriadou[47] employed an action research method to include local sport clubs in the leveraging process. The research team worked with the local tennis clubs to facilitate an offering of free tennis lessons given away at the tennis events that spectators would be able to redeem at a club close to them. Although there was some uptake of the offer, it was limited. In contrast, Potwarka and colleagues[48] provided a voucher for a free trial of the velodrome facility built for the 2015 Pan American Games to spectators after they had watched the competition. The authors found that in the context of a novel participation opportunity, as none of the spectators previously had the opportunity to participate in track cycling before the facility had been constructed for the sport event, the provision for a free-trial voucher stimulated a few to try the sport, but there was no evidence of sustained participation.

In the context of the Tour de Flanders, an elite road cycling event in Flanders, Belgium, local organizations took ownership of implementing the *Village of the Tour*, where youth and current cyclists were targeted for cycling promotion strategies and activities.[49] Although the initiatives were effective in engaging host residents in cycling, the strategies may not be effective in engaging those who did not already participate in cycling. Furthermore, the research team found that resources were limited at the local level, and if the levels of government would be more streamlined in their leveraging approaches, local leveraging initiatives could be more effective.

CONCLUSIONS AND FUTURE RESEARCH

The results of the studies described in this chapter suggest that sport organizations' capacity to market themselves to participants is a prerequisite for effective leveraging of events to build participation, and that capacity building must take place well in advance of an event so that the necessary skills and resources are adequately established. Future research should examine how local sport organizations can build that capacity and evaluate processes and outcomes to determine to what degree adding an event into a well-developed marketing strategy will benefit local sport organizations in building participation in their sport.

It is imperative for future research to evaluate processes and outcomes and create tools to accurately measure changes in sport participation and development. These evaluations should also be applied longitudinally to evaluate the sustainability of any strategies and actions taken. Moreover, based on the event leveraging framework proposed by Taks and colleagues,[50] more strategies and tactics that work to leverage sport events for sport participation and development should be identified, as well as to find pathways to implement strategies and tactics.[51]

Furthermore, it is imperative to take into account the specific context of a sport event; this requires knowledge of the host's available resources and social needs, including which types of events generate the best sport participation outcomes, whether a participant or spectator event should be used, whether a one-sport or multisport event should be held, how long the event should be (one day or multiday), and what age groups should be included in the event (youth, senior, master). We need to find out how these requirements can be added to the policies for hosting sport events, be it at the federal level (e.g., federal policy for hosting international sport events) or the provincial or the local levels (for smaller events).

Although there is evidence of sport development outcomes from sport events for those who are already active sport participants, overall, there is little evidence for new sport participation outcomes from hosting events. We need a better understanding of (1) how sport facilities can become better strategic tools to increase sport participation; (2) how large and small events can grow sport participation and impact the quality of sport participation experiences; (3) what strategies and tactics work to leverage events for sport participation purposes; and (4) how researchers can help local sport organizations to leverage events to increase participation in their sport.

Questions

1. What are the three research trends for studying sport events' impacts on sport participation?
2. What type and size of event would be appropriate for your current city or town to host? What infrastructure is available for that event? What strategies would you employ to leverage that event to increase sport participation in your community? What key performance indicators will you use to measure the sport participation outcome(s)?
3. Why do you think proponents of sport events continue to claim that there is an inherent association between large sport events and sport participation despite the lack of evidence to support this claim?

Learning Activity

1. Find examples of "white elephants" online. Brainstorm ideas of how the white elephants could have been avoided.

Strategies for Success

1. Engage local partners in planning and implementation efforts early and often.
2. Design facilities for efficient conversion from mega-event use to legacy use (avoid white elephants).
3. Explicitly leverage events for increased participation of local residents at a variety of levels (recreational through elite) and collect data to document impact.

NOTES

1. Laura Misener, Marijke Taks, Laurence Chalip, and B. Christine Green, "The Elusive 'Trickle-Down Effect' of Sport Events: Assumptions and Missed Opportunities," *Managing*

Sport and Leisure 20, no. 2 (2015): 135–56; Mike Weed, Coren Esher, Jo Fiore, Ian Wellard, Dikaia Chatziefstathiou, Louise Mansfield, and Suzanne Dowse, "The Olympic Games and Raising Sport Participation: A Systematic Review of Evidence and an Interrogation of Policy for a Demonstration Effect," *European Sport Management Quarterly* 15, no. 2 (2015): 195–226.

2. Misener et al., "The Elusive 'Trickle-Down Effect' of Sport Events: Assumptions and Missed Opportunities."

3. Marijke Taks, B. Christine Green, Laura Misener, and Laurence Chalip, "Evaluating Sport Development Outcomes: The Case of a Medium-Sized International Sport Event," *European Sport Management Quarterly* 14, no. 3 (2013): 213–37; Weed et al., "The Olympic Games and Raising Sport Participation."

4. Weed et al., "The Olympic Games and Raising Sport Participation."

5. Holger Preuss, "The Conceptualisation and Measurement of Mega Sport Event Legacies," *Journal of Sport and Tourism* 12, nos. 3–4 (2007): 207–28.

6. Marijke Taks, "Social Sustainability of Non-Mega Sport Events in a Global World," *European Journal for Sport and Society* 10, no. 2 (2013): 121–41.

7. Laurence Chalip, "From Legacies to Leverage," in *Leveraging Legacies from Sports Mega-Events: Concepts and Cases*, ed. Jonathan Grix (Basingstoke, UK: Palgrave Macmillan, 2014), 2–12.

8. Marijke Taks, Laurence Chalip, and B. Christine Green, "Impacts and Strategic Outcomes from Non-Mega Sport Events for Local Communities," *European Sport Management Quarterly* 15, no. 1 (2015): 1–6.

9. Taks, "Social Sustainability of Non-Mega Sport Events in a Global World."

10. Preuss, "The Conceptualisation and Measurement of Mega Sport Event Legacies."

11. Donald Getz, "Event Studies: Discourses and Future Directions," *Event Management* 16, no. 2 (2012): 171–87.

12. Floris Muller, Liesbet van Zoonen, and Laurens de Roode, "The Integrative Power of Sport: Imagined and Real Effects of Sport Events on Multicultural Integration," *Sociology of Sport Journal* 25, no. 3 (2008): 387–401; Jonathan Grix, ed. *Leveraging Legacies from Sports Mega-Events: Concepts and Cases* (Basingstoke, UK: Palgrave Macmillan, 2014).

13. Martin Müller, "The Mega-Event Syndrome: Why So Much Goes Wrong in Mega-Event Planning and What to Do about It," *Journal of the American Planning Association* 81, no. 1 (2015): 6–17.

14. Nola Agha and Marijke Taks, "A Theoretical Comparison of the Economic Impact of Large and Small Events," *International Journal of Sport Finance* 10, no. 3 (2015): 199–216.

15. Taks, "Social Sustainability of Non-Mega Sport Events in a Global World."

16. Marijke Taks, "The Rise and Fall of Mega Sport Events: The Future Is on Non-Mega Sport Events," in *Ethics and Governance in Sport: The Future of Sport Imagined*, ed. Yves Vanden Auweele, Elaine Cook, and Jim Parry (London: Routledge, 2016), 84–93.

17. Taks et al., "Evaluating Sport Development Outcomes."

18. James Anderson and Marijke Taks, "Urban Governance of Non-Mega Sport Events: A Socio-Political Discourse Analysis," in *Research Handbook on Sports Governance*, ed. Mathieu Winand and Christos Anagnostopoulos (Cheltenham, UK: Edward Elgar Publishing, 2019).

19. Craig Pearson, "Council Waives Fees for Diving Club—but No One Else," *Windsor Star*, February 23, 2017, https://windsorstar.com/news/local-news/council-waives-fees-for-diving-club-but-no-one-else.

20. Anne Jarvis, "Jarvis: 'It's Demeaning,' City Employee Says of Pay Cut to Help Aquatic Centre Bottom Line," *Windsor Star*, June 24, 2017, https://windsorstar.com/opinion/columnists/jarvis-its-demeaning-city-employee-says-of-pay-cut-to-help-aquatic-centre-bottom-line.

21. Pearson, "Council Waives Fees for Diving Club—but No One Else."

22. Weed et al., "The Olympic Games and Raising Sport Participation."

23. Vassil Girginov and Laura Hills, "A Sustainable Sports Legacy: Creating a Link between the London Olympics and Sports Participation," *The International Journal of the History of Sport* 25, no. 14 (2008): 2091–116.

24. Stephen Brookes and Jay Wiggan, "Reflecting the Public Value of Sport: A Game of Two Halves?" *Public Management Review* 11, no. 4 (July 2009): 401–20.

25. Brookes and Wiggan, "Reflecting the Public Value of Sport: A Game of Two Halves?"

26. Kamal Ram Mahtani, Joanne Protheroe, Sarah Patricia Slight, Marcelo Marcos Piva Demarzo, Thomas Blakeman, Christopher A. Barton, Bianca Brijnath, and Nia Roberts, "Can the London 2012 Olympics 'Inspire a Generation' to Do More Physical or Sporting Activities? An Overview of Systematic Reviews," *BMJ Open* 3, no. 1 (2013).

27. Russell Vincent Carter and Theo Lorenc, "A Qualitative Study into the Development of a Physical Activity Legacy from the London 2012 Olympic Games," *Health Promotion International* 30, no. 3 (2015): 793–802.

28. Cora Craig and Adrian Bauman, "The Impact of the Vancouver Winter Olympics on Population Level Physical Activity and Sport Participation among Canadian Children and Adolescents: Population Based Study," *International Journal of Behavioral Nutrition and Physical Activity* 11, no. 1 (2014), article 107.

29. Luke R. Potwarka and Scott T. Leatherdale, "The Vancouver 2010 Olympics and Leisure-Time Physical Activity Rates among Youth in Canada: Any Evidence of a Trickle-Down Effect?" *Leisure Studies* 35, no. 2 (2016): 241–57.

30. Gertrud Pfister, Marie-Luise Klein, and Nina Clara Tiesler, "Momentous Spark or Enduring Enthusiasm? The 2011 FIFA Women's World Cup and Its Impact on Players' Mobility and on the Popularity of Women's Soccer in Germany," in *Women, Soccer and Transnational Migration*, ed. Marie-Luise Klein and Nina Clara Tiesler (New York: Routledge, 2014).

31. Pfister, "Momentous Spark or Enduring Enthusiasm?" 147.

32. Pamela Wicker and Popi Sotiriadou, "The Trickle-Down Effect: What Population Groups Benefit from Hosting Major Sport Events?" *International Journal of Event Management Research* 8, no. 2 (2013): 17.

33. Bernd Frick and Pamela Wicker, "The Trickle-Down Effect: How Elite Sporting Success Affects Amateur Participation in German Football," *Applied Economics Letters* 23, no. 4 (2016): 259–63.

34. Kurumi Aizawa, Ji Wu, Yuhei Inoue, and Mikihiro Sato, "Long-Term Impact of the Tokyo 1964 Olympic Games on Sport Participation: A Cohort Analysis," *Sport Management Review* 21, no. 1 (2018): 86–97.

35. Laurence Chalip, B. Christine Green, Marijke Taks, and Laura Misener, "Creating Sport Participation from Sport Events: Making It Happen," *International Journal of Sport Policy and Politics* 9, no. 2 (2017): 257–76.

36. Misener et al., "The Elusive 'Trickle-Down Effect' of Sport Events."

37. Taks et al., "Evaluating Sport Development Outcomes."

38. Misener et al., "The Elusive 'Trickle-Down Effect' of Sport Events."

39. Weed et al., "The Olympic Games and Raising Sport Participation."

40. Taks et al., "Impacts and Strategic Outcomes from Non-Mega Sport Events for Local Communities."

41. Taks et al., "Impacts and Strategic Outcomes from Non-Mega Sport Events for Local Communities."

42. Chalip, "From Legacies to Leverage;" Taks et al., "Impacts and Strategic Outcomes from Non-Mega Sport Events for Local Communities."

43. Chalip et al., "Creating Sport Participation from Sport Events;" Marijke Taks, B. Christine Green, Laura Misener, and Laurence Chalip, "Sport Participation from Sport Events: Why It Doesn't Happen?" *Marketing Intelligence & Planning* 36, no. 2 (2018): 185–98.

44. Taks et al., "Sport Participation from Sport Events: Why It Doesn't Happen?"

45. Taks et al., "Sport Participation from Sport Events: Why It Doesn't Happen?"

46. Shushu Chen and Ian Henry, "Evaluating the London 2012 Games' Impact on Sport Participation in a Non-Hosting Region: A Practical Application of Realist Evaluation," *Leisure Studies* 35, no. 5 (2016): 685–707.

47. Katharine Hoskyn, Geoff Dickson, and Popi Sotiriadou, "Leveraging Medium-Sized Sport Events to Attract Club Participants," *Marketing Intelligence & Planning* 36, no. 2 (2018): 199–212.

48. Luke R. Potwarka, Ryan Snelgrove, David Drewery, Jordan Bakhsh, and Laura Wood, "From Intention to Participation: Exploring the Moderating Role of a Voucher-Based Event Leveraging Initiative," *Sport Management Review* 23, no. 2 (2020): 302–14.

49. Inge Derom and Robert VanWynsberghe, "Extending the Benefits of Leveraging Cycling Events: Evidence from the Tour of Flanders," *European Sport Management Quarterly* 15, no. 1 (2015): 111–31.

50. Taks et al., "Sport Participation from Sport Events."

51. Laura Misener, "Leveraging Parasport Events for Community Participation: Development of a Theoretical Framework," *European Sport Management Quarterly* 15, no. 1 (2015): 132–53.

9

Evaluation and Analytics in Sport for Development and Peace

Bill Gerrard and Robert E. Baker

OBJECTIVES

This chapter will:

- Describe how the purpose of sport for development and peace impacts program evaluation.
- Describe what program evaluation entails.
- Contrast formative and summative evaluation in sport for development and peace.
- Describe data analytics.
- Identify the five stages of analytics.
- Connect the use of data analytics to the sport for development and peace program evaluation process.
- Deconstruct how data analytics impacts decision making in sport for development and peace.
- Discuss how systems thinking and complexity science are related to the logic model of program evaluation in sport for development and peace.
- Compare practice-led versus discipline-led analytics.
- Distinguish between open- and closed-system ontologies.

Evaluation processes in sport for development and peace (SDP) have been disparaged for a lack of depth and for supplying limited evidence of program impact.[1] Skepticism abounds, evolving from overstated assertions of the benefits of SDP programs without corresponding evidence.[2] Roger Levermore asserted that the dearth of compelling evaluation practices casts doubt on SDP endeavors.[3] Providing evidence of program efficacy and enhancing the conduct of SDP programs via evaluation is essential.[4] SDP has unique characteristics that inform the manner of evaluation appropriate for such programs. Large-scale SDP programs can have, on one hand, a goal to serve as a wide-ranging change agent wherein they purposefully use sport to impact social change on a broad scale. On the other, sport can be used to facilitate grassroots impacts based on local interests. In either case, the use of evaluation procedures is often driven by the purpose of the SDP program being assessed.

The very nature of SDP initiatives is conceptually grounded in double- or multi-bottom line considerations, including numerous socioeconomic and political objectives, as well as the reality of fiscal considerations.[5] Sport, as a universal language, serves as a vehicle through which to facilitate effects beyond sports.[6] SDP initiatives are, at their core, attempting to enact change. Social change objectives might include women's empowerment, inclusion (ability, ethnicity, religion, orientation, etc.), social capital, education, sustainability, and economic or community development. Political objectives can include conflict resolution, peacebuilding, and multitrack diplomatic strategies.

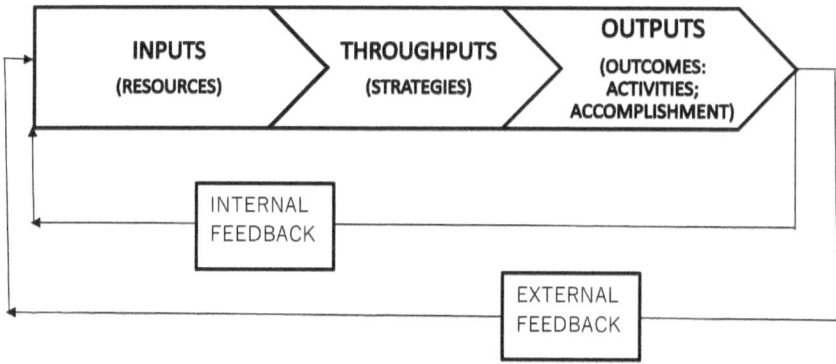

Figure 9.1. The logic model of evaluation and systems thinking in SDP programs.

The interaction of social, political, and economic interests is inescapable. Socioeconomic objectives can include broad external economic impacts. Localized fiscal objectives generally revolve around the ability of the SDP program to sustain its capacity to meet its social objectives. Fiscal interests are influenced by the program's status as for-profit versus not-for-profit. For example, self-sufficiency can be generated through social entrepreneurship in for-profit enterprises, whereas external funding in support of a not-for-profit SDP initiative is typically generated through governments, foundations, nongovernmental organizations, corporations, or individual support.

SDP engages an array of diverse stakeholders with a multitude of diverse interests. Program evaluations should take into account these diverse objectives. Scarvia Anderson and Samuel Ball noted that program evaluation typically has multiple purposes, such as (1) generating evidence to rally support or opposition to a program feature;

(2) informing decisions relative to program installation, continuation, expansion, certification, and modifications; and (3) enhancing understanding of processes.[7] These various purposes are not mutually exclusive, and they can inform program evaluation procedures in SDP. Evaluation of SDP programs must account for the broad interests of stakeholders, which might include large-scale sociopolitical entities, funding agencies, program participants, and local communities, among many others.

Evaluation

There are many purposes and approaches to evaluation in SDP. At an underlying level, evaluation includes using available evidence to inform a value judgment.[8] Some have questioned the value of evaluations, noting expenses, time requirements, technical complexity, misdirected evidence, limited data quality, lack of analytical rigor, delayed findings, and the lack of dissemination and impact.[9] However, the concern over the lack of effectual program evaluations in SDP notwithstanding,[10] the varied interests, diverse stakeholders, and myriad methods have yielded an increase in evaluation over time.[11]

As a rational and objective process, program evaluation in SDP is defined as the "systematic collection and analysis of information related to the design, implementation, and outcomes of a program, for the purpose of monitoring and improving the quality and effectiveness of the program."[12] Given that SDP programs are intended to facilitate change, the program evaluation process should be devised to ascertain if and how change has occurred. Program evaluation uses systematic, repetitive, intentional data collection to provide insights, enhance understanding, and reveal contributing factors in the success of the program while also informing future actions through the evaluation evidence.[13] The influence of reductionist theory, complexity, and system theory provides further insights into program evaluation.[14]

Reductionist theory provides a framework for program evaluation in that it attempts to isolate specific elements and their relationship to or influence on program outcomes.[15] In turn, complexity theory accommodates the uncertainty and ambiguity in SDP programs relative to evaluation. Complexity examines interactions among multiple agents, making it appropriate for the "emergent, messy, nonlinear uncertainty" of systems that generates a relationship that is more than the sum of its parts.[16] SDP program evaluation identifies both internal and external influences on program outcome variation, simultaneously determining the desirability of the influences and the outcomes. Carol Weiss describes program evaluation as the "systematic assessment of the operations and/or outcomes of a program, compared to a set of explicit or implicit standards, as a means of contributing to the improvement of the program."[17] Furthermore, program evaluation addresses both effectiveness and efficiency while also ensuring accountability and quality.[18]

Program evaluation is about deepening our understanding of the SDP program through a repeatable, systematic, and deliberate gathering of information to reveal or recognize what factors contribute to the achievements of the program and what actions need to be taken to address the conclusions of the evaluation process.[19] In this sense, program evaluation involves reviewing, analyzing, and judging the significance of the information gathered using assessment measures directed toward program objectives. The measurement of results is central to program evaluation. The program evaluation process that was used shapes the measurement that yields the information necessary for program evaluation. Choices of specific measurement tools, strategies, or assessments for program evaluation are guided by many factors, including specific mission-informed questions that define the desired awareness of program efficacy or deficiency. Driven by the purpose of the SDP program, manifested in its double bottom line, appropriate measures must be derived. Everything is measurable and this essential element of evaluation must accurately reflect and inform the evaluation process relative to the program objectives. Evaluation in SDP must be intentional; it begins with the mission and is driven by the intended purpose of the SDP program. While complex interests and double or multiple bottom lines are commonplace in SDP programs, each program must establish clear, mission-based program goals and objectives. The desired social and financial outcomes should inform not only these objectives but also the measures used to assess them. Often referred to as *key performance indicators* (KPIs), these measures are directly tied to the program's mission-informed objectives.

There are several broad purposes for evaluation. First, evaluation provides evidence to determine program effectiveness. Evaluation also informs processes to allow for, or even inspire, improvement. Further, evaluation data undergird strategies and informs decision making. Directed toward these purposes, there are two distinctive approaches to evaluation: summative and formative evaluation. *Summative* evaluations, or summative assessments, focus on the outcomes of a program or KPI. Like the final score of a contest, these summative results are measures of success or failure. Summative evaluations can draw conclusions about areas in need of improvement, and they can yield programmatic strategies and drive program decisions. *Formative* evaluations, or formative assessments, focus on outcomes at a specific time in a process of continual improvement. For example, an SDP program may demonstrate limited effectiveness through a formative evaluation, and be provided additional tools to enhance program effectiveness, to assist in decision making enhancing program improvement and to inform strategies for ongoing program development. Both summative and formative evaluations are connected to data analyses in that they are evidentiary metrics and used to determine program or participant effectiveness. The emphasis on data allows decision makers to focus on evidence and continual improvement. The application of data analytics in the form of program evaluations and KPI assessments ensures that organizations and participants are doing what they say they are doing and determines how well they are doing it. In the pursuit of effective evaluation, SDP programs can be viewed as learning organizations that employ evidentiary assessments to pursue continuous improvement.

Systems Evaluation and Analytics

Learning organizations are a key concept in systems thinking.[20] Systems are composed of inputs, throughputs, and outputs and are further informed by feedback loops wherein the collection and analyses of relevant data is used to disclose organizational effectiveness. System theory embraces the concept that change is an inherent part of a system. Framing an SDP program as a system suggests that measures are developed that yield accurate data to inform programmatic strategies and decisions. While ideally guided by an explicit purpose, SDP programs are often complex, with multiple interactions among participants and the environment and multiple bottom lines such that a system theory framework may be well suited to informing program evaluation.[21] Assessment measures inform the system. Data analyses, and their application to decision making, are also central to systems thinking. The logic model of evaluation aligns with systems thinking.[22] This framework defines the intended links between the program resources (or inputs), program strategies or treatments (or throughputs), the immediate results of program activities (or outputs), and the desired program accomplishments (or goal-related outcomes). Systems are influenced by internal (proximate) and external (distal) environmental factors.

Figure 9.2. Education is the foundation for development as shown with this group of participants in India. *Credit*: J. D. Walsh

Peter Senge[23] contended that every system is perfectly designed to yield the results that are seen. Using the systems framework of input-throughput-output and feedback, both internal and external, the use of data analytics is an essential tool to obtain accurate and informative results. If SDP programs are framed as learning organizations seeking continuous improvement (i.e., systems), they are inextricably linked to data analyses in the evaluation process. While evaluation is commonly perceived to be focused on simply measuring program outcomes,[24] systems thinking and its concern for continual improvement prompts evaluation of SDP program processes as well. While everything can be measured, measuring the necessary elements using the appropriate measurement mechanisms is essential to establishing effective evidence with which to inform the SDP system. The appropriate acquisition, analysis, and application of data-based information provide the evidentiary procedures necessary for program evaluation to generate informed decision making and strategy development.

Analytics and Strategic Planning

Strategy is a wide-ranging, deliberate, enduring plan of action directed toward a desired result. It is distinct from the tactics, or actions, employed in pursuit of the strategy. Sun Tzu noted in *The Art of War* that "[s]trategy without tactics is the slowest route to victory. Tactics without strategy is the noise before defeat."[25] Evaluation in SDP programs is connected to planning as an essential managerial function. Strategic management suggests the use of properly applied data analysis in the strategic planning process to inform evaluation. Strategic planning is used to determine objectives, strategies, and evaluation systems directed toward the SDP program mission and intended outcomes. Based on organizational mission, strategic plans provide direction to programs, help in avoiding distractions, and inform the resource needs in pursuit of identified goals. SMART goals, based on the mission, guide organizational objectives and inform decisions. SMART goals are Specific; Measurable; Achievable, Action-oriented, and Agreed-upon; Realistic, Relevant, and Result-oriented; and Time-based, Tangible, and Trackable.

While each SDP program is a unique organizational system with its own discrete mission and goals, establishing a contextual framework for the strategic planning process is based on the program mission and vision. The program vision and mission not only guide the strategic plan, but they also determine the evaluation mechanisms and procedures. In developing a strategy-based SDP program, a SWOT (strengths, weaknesses, opportunities, threats) or SOAR (strengths, opportunities, aspirations, results) assessment is often conducted to inform the planning and subsequently the evaluation processes.[26] Internal or external stakeholders can contribute to the assessments, which inform the data analytics mechanisms necessary to develop an informed strategy. This includes the methods employed for collection of information, the analyses used, and the process used to inform decision making. Emergent program strategies will reflect the SWOT or SOAR assessment and the mission-based SMART goals that ultimately yield action plans, inform resource needs, and establish evaluation and assessment procedures. To close the loop in the evaluation process, mechanisms to inform strategy require appropriate information collection, measurement, and dissemination. This includes the identification of data sources relevant to the program mission, data analysis protocols, and mechanisms used to measure progress. These analysis and evaluation features provide critical feedback to inform strategies and guide managerial decision making.

Effective strategic planning in SDP, in which program evaluation is a component, is built on the analysis of data. In establishing a data analytics process to support strategic management and effective program evaluation, an SDP system must involve the appropriate stakeholders. For example, individuals or programs responsible for each SDP strategy should be accountable for the mission-based KPIs within the evaluation model employed. SDP managers must have a functional knowledge of the KPIs and should utilize them to support decisions. Managers planning for an effective evaluation that informs program strategy will ask questions that guide decisions. For example: (1) What do we do well with respect to our SDP goals? (2) What KPI, or SDP outcomes, do we need to improve on? (3) Where do we want our SDP program to be in year two, three, and so on? (4) What tactics will we employ to get to our intended SDP outcomes? (5) Who is accountable for each strategic action and outcome? (6) How will programmatic success be measured? (7) What data is needed to inform our strategies and tactics? (8) What SDP program stakeholders need to be involved?

The impact of program evaluation on stakeholders encourages broad involvement in the evaluative process. An SDP program evaluation design that acknowledges participant interests in the pursuit of program goals aligns with the empowerment evaluation model, wherein evaluation authority is transferred from a formal evaluator to the program participants and staff.[27] Empowerment evaluation is suitable for SDP program evaluation where systems are guided by double bottom lines or promote development and social justice goals.

The acquisition of evaluation authority by participants and staff encourages their investment in the SDP program. Empowerment evaluation principles necessitate involvement of SDP program staff and participants in the implementation and evaluation of the program.[28] While SDP program managers, along with sponsoring agencies, often determine the sought-after SDP goals, participants selected in alignment with these goals engage with SDP staff in implementing the evaluation process. SDP program participants, as stakeholders in the strategic assessment process, contribute to the systematic SWOT or SOAR process. Yet to further align with the empowerment evaluation model, program participants themselves can be involved in SDP goal setting. Self-determination of evaluation activities, such as postprogram follow-on, is significant for SDP participants and consistent with empowerment evaluation concepts.[29] Participant affiliation and investment in SDP program goals result from such involvement and can impact future strategies and outcomes. The empowerment evaluation model fosters commitment among all SDP stakeholders toward systemic goals and enhances the sustainability of the SDP program.[30] For those stakeholders in SDP who are seeking quantifiable data to demonstrate the efficacy of programming through reliable program evaluation, the empowerment evaluation model, along with frameworks such as reductionist, complexity, and systems theory, has applications for SDP.[31]

Tactically, SDP programs should employ evaluation procedures that support the gathering and analyses of appropriate data to support the program evaluation. The evaluation processes should employ appropriate predetermined mechanisms for collection and analysis. Everything is measurable—if properly conceived and implemented. Properly conceived SDP program evaluation entails the appropriate application of data analytics to inform the SDP system strategy and decision making. SDP systems must have analytical procedures guided by mission-driven goals and desired outcomes, or KPIs, to enhance evaluation efficacy. Revealing progress toward intended SDP outcomes, KPIs can measure individual performance or systemic performance. For SDP systems serving a double bottom line pursuing two outcomes (e.g., fiscal stability and social responsibility), analyses of multiple data aligned to measure KPIs related to diverse program outcomes are required. SDP program managers must therefore be able to identify relevant KPI. While not necessarily responsible for data analyses, it is important for program stakeholders to understand the SDP system, the KPIs that inform program strategies, the questions that prompt data collection and analysis, and how available data analyses inform decisions in pursuit of strategic SDP initiatives.

SDP program managers and participants are responsible to make data-driven, data-informed, or data-inspired decisions where appropriate. They must also employ appropriate processes in data collection and analyses while basing decisions on applicable measures. Appropriately applied measures yield SDP program data that is collected, analyzed, and used to guide decisions. While analysts collect and process data, managers must both contextualize the analyses and use the data to guide decisions. All stakeholders in the evaluation process must communicate, translating data needs and analyses to accurately reveal program efficacy and yield better decisions. SDP managers who utilize analytical tools within the program context systemically enhance the decision-making process.

Data-driven, Data-informed, and Data-inspired Decision Making in SDP

Shayna Stewart[32] identified the distinction between data-driven, data-informed, and data-inspired interactions in decision making. *Data-driven* decision making requires the precise data needed to make a decision, yielding an exact answer. *Data-informed* decision making requires an awareness of the current metrics to inform strategies. *Data-inspired* decision making requires predictive interpretation and trend spotting derived from multiple data sources.

Data-driven decision making is based on data collected and analyzed to answer a specific question. Data-driven analyses suggest that the data needed to ascertain the specific outcome is accessible. Data-driven decision making uses highly specific metrics and is very rigid in its use of data. The specific data to be analyzed is predetermined, as is the methodology employed. Knowledge of statistical methodologies is essential for a properly implemented data-driven plan.[33]

Data-informed decision-making strategies entail data analyses in combination with experiential and other factors in the decision process. Data-informed decision making in SDP requires a direct knowledge of KPIs. Data informs both the what and the why in programs, yielding trajectories that are observed and explained. Data-informed analyses are used to improve and inform SDP program strategies and decisions. In SDP programs, the inevitably pursued change can be informed by data that addresses why a particular strategy is preferable. Stewart[34] indicated that, contrary to a data-driven approach, a data-informed approach does not yield a conclusive action to be taken, but rather it informs strategies within the SDP program's context.

Data-inspired analytics is more exploratory and presumes no specific outcomes. Data-inspired analyses use data from multiple sources and seek commonalities. Often data-inspired analyses draws on perception and inference as opposed to concrete statistics. SDP program evaluations based on a wide variety of metrics can employ data-inspired analyses to stimulate innovative SDP ideas. While evidence is commonly used to reveal the past and project probable futures, evaluation less frequently inspires the generation of innovative ideas; yet data-inspired analyses yield innovations. Data-inspired evaluation processes reveal concurrent trends rather than a concrete action based on metrics.

SDP evaluations using data-driven, data-influenced, or data-inspired analyses serve distinct purposes, each with its own risks and limitations yet ultimately contributing to the success of the SDP program. Program evaluation enhances awareness of the successes or failures of a SDP program through a systematized approach of gathering and analyzing information to produce evidentiary metrics related to KPIs.[35] Evaluation in SDP programs involves the collection, review, analysis, and application of SDP data, and analytics is a tool that can be used in SDP program evaluation to yield strategies and guide decisions based on the findings of the process.

Analytics can play a key role in the evaluation of SDP programs. Based on the intended purpose, or mission, each SDP program can determine how analytics can be employed, what analyses can be used, and what stakeholders can be engaged. Each program can delineate what should be measured and how it should be measured. In a properly conducted evaluation, the SDP program establishes how the program will collect data, analyze data, and utilize data. Evaluation is ultimately a systemic process that can incorporate data analytics to influence the decisions to be made, guide the strategies to follow, and reveal the effectiveness of the SDP initiative.

What Is Data Analytics?

The first two decades of the twenty-first century have seen an exponential growth of interest in what is variously termed *data analytics* or *data science* or *artificial intelligence*. Much of the interest has been in big data and the analysis of truly massive datasets, many sourced from social media and providing detailed personal data on the lives of individuals, their likes and dislikes, interests and activities, opinions and beliefs, shopping habits, and so on. The commercial value of such data to marketing departments is obvious. But the growth of big data also raises many ethical issues as witnessed in the controversies around political campaigns that have used big-data analytics to influence the outcome of elections and referendums.

So what is data analytics? The simplest and most succinct definition of data analytics is data analysis for practical purpose. *Data analytics* is the use of statistical analysis and other related techniques to analyze available data to provide an evidential base to support management decision making. As such, data analytics falls within the broad scope of evidence-based management.[36] It can be argued that data analytics should be seen as a branch of operations research. In one of the first comprehensive treatments of the emerging subject field of operations research, Philip Morse and George Kimball offered the following definition of "operations research as a scientific method of providing executive departments with a quantitative basis for decisions regarding the operations under their control."[37] It is a definition that captures the essence of data analytics—quantitative data analysis to support operational decisions.

Data analytics is practice-led, not discipline-led, and, as a consequence, is very different in nature from the data analysis to be found in peer-reviewed academic journals. Discipline-led data analysis is characterized primarily by hypothesis testing in which academic researchers seek empirical evidence to either confirm or contradict theoretical generalizations about observed behavior within their subject field. Discipline-led data analysis is essentially a backward-looking interpretation of systematic patterns in data. Goodness of fit is the key criterion in evaluating a statistical model, with the focus on determining whether the target variables have statistically significant effects. The hypothesis-testing process involves the decontextualization of the data in the sense that individual observations drawn from a sample of unique contexts that differ in the entities observed or the time frame are combined into a homogeneous sample with the specific context of individual observations reduced to a relatively small number of common aspects (e.g., dimensions) that can be measured or categorized.

By contrast, data analytics is practice-led, seeking to provide empirical evidence to support a management decision over the choice of intervention required to resolve a practical problem and improve organizational performance. Hence, by its very nature, data analytics is forward-looking, concerned with supporting management decisions in which a choice must be made between alternative possible courses of action with uncertain future consequences for organizational performance. The feasibility of an intervention and the reliability of the evidential basis for the decision are key criteria for judging the empirical findings of an analytics project. Data analytics does not treat data as a decontextualized, homogeneous sample but rather recognizes the importance of context. Every management decision is unique in its specific context so that effective data analytics must always involve expert evaluation of the applicability in the specific decision context of the empirical generalizations identified by the analysis of the available data.

At the most fundamental level, data analytics differs from academic, discipline-led research in its ontological, epistemological, and methodological presuppositions. Ontology is the study of the nature of reality and being, epistemology is the study of the nature of knowledge, and methodology is the study of the methods for acquiring knowledge. Much of the academic research in the social sciences, as the term *social sciences* suggests, adopts the presuppositions of the natural sciences and seeks to emulate the scientific method. Despite the recognition of the constructivist nature of knowledge, the social sciences remain strongly wedded to hypothesis-testing methods with multivariate statistical methods employed to control the contextual differences between observations so as to parallel the control of context provided by the experimental method in many of the natural sciences. As Tony Lawson[38] argues, this implies a strong ontological presupposition that social reality is a closed system characterized by event regularities. The closed-system approach is combined with the epistemological and methodological presuppositions that statistical methods can be used to detect event regularities empirically, thus providing evidence of causality and an objective standard to test the validity or otherwise of theoretical hypotheses about the nature of the world. Lawson advocates the adoption of an open-systems ontology to understand social phenomena as relationally constituted.[39] A characteristic feature of an open-systems approach is the recognition that, although there is a "deep" structure of causal mechanisms in human behavior, there is no necessity that this deep structure will lead to observable event regularities. In an open system, a myriad of possible influences may be involved in any specific context that fundamentally undermines the ability of multivariate statistical methods to control for contextual differences. In recognizing the importance of context and the inherent limitations of statistical methods, data analytics as a practice-led form of analysis is at least implicitly adopting an open-systems approach in pursuit of reliable knowledge as a basis for action.

How Should Analytics Be Employed?

A data analytics project comprises five stages.

Stage 1: Discovery

The starting point for all analytics projects is the discovery stage. This involves a dialogue between the analyst and decision maker to develop a mutual understanding of the purpose of the project in the sense of what is expected from the project. In particular the analyst needs to be clear on the decisions for which the project is intended to provide an evidential basis to support the management decision making. In addition, the dialogue between the analyst and the decision maker should also clarify the context of the decision as regards what is already known.

Stage 2: Exploration

The exploration stage has three main objectives. First, the quality of the data must be determined, particularly the identification of any missing values and erroneous data. Second, the analyst needs to understand the information structure of the data as regards the distributional properties of the variables (i.e., central tendency, dispersion and shape of the frequency distribution) as well as the degree of association (i.e., collinearity) between the variables. Third, the homogeneity of the dataset must be investigated (i.e., the absence of outliers and structural breaks) to confirm the validity of analyzing the sample data as a single entity. Exploratory data analysis usually involves data visualization of frequency distributions (e.g., histograms) and correlations (e.g., scatterplots) as well as reporting descriptive statistics and the correlation matrix. Data may need to be transformed to make better use of the information at the modeling stage. In particular, many statistical methods assume normally distributed data (i.e., a symmetric, bell-shaped distribution). Skewed (i.e., asymmetrically distributed) data can often be normalized by using the logarithmic transformation to produce log-normal data. Exploration may also involve data reduction when the same information is contained in more than one variable so that it can be possible to combine variables using factor analysis. Similarity between observations may also be explored using cluster analysis. Exploratory techniques such as factor analysis and cluster analysis are often referred to as *unsupervised learning*, a term deriving from machine learning and artificial intelligence and reflecting the exploratory nature of these types of analyses with no predetermined outcome against which to determine the goodness of fit.

Stage 3: Modeling

The modeling stage involves the construction of a simplified, purpose-led, data-based representation of the specific aspect of real-world behavior on which the analytics project is focused. The modeling is purpose-led in that the model design and choice of modeling techniques are driven by the analytical purpose, which is to provide an evidential basis to support a specific decision. The model is a simplified representation because a model necessarily involves abstraction with only relevant, systematic aspects of the real-world situation included and nonsystematic factors treated jointly as a stochastic error process. The model is data-based in the sense that the analyst is searching for a congruent statistical model that best fits the available data and fully captures all of the systematic variation in the dataset. Modeling involves supervised learning in that the outcomes (i.e., dependent variable) to be modeled are known and the model-building process is the search for the best approximation of these known outcomes by combining the predictors (i.e., independent or explanatory variables). Two of the most widely used modeling techniques are linear regression and logistic regression. *Linear regression* is the method for estimating the line of best fit for linear relationships between outcomes measured on a continuous scale and either a single predictor (i.e., simple regression) or multiple predictors (i.e., multiple regression) by minimizing the sum of the squared residuals (i.e., least squares estimation). *Logistic regression* is a classification technique used to model the probabilities of binary categorical outcomes (i.e., maximum likelihood estimation).

Stage 4: Projection

The projection stage involves using the estimated models developed in the modeling stage to answer what-if questions over the possible consequences of alternative interventions under different scenarios. It also involves forecasting future outcomes based on current trends. The projection stage encompasses traditional operations research, applying optimization techniques to identify the best solutions to a variety of operational problems such as inventory management; queuing; location decisions for plants, warehouses, and retail outlets; and route planning (i.e., the traveling salesman problem).

Stage 5: Actionable Insight

The actionable insight stage is the final stage of an analytics project when the analyst presents an evaluation of the alternative possible interventions and makes recommendations to the decision maker.

Who Should Be Involved?

Effective data analytics depends critically on the relationship between the analyst and the decision maker. Without a meaningful and constructive dialogue between the analyst and the decision maker, it is unlikely that the data analytics project will be fit for purpose. The analytics process can be described in essence as *talk*, *analyze*, and *recommend*. The initial step, *talk*, is the dialogue between the analyst and the decision maker in the discovery stage when the analyst must gain a proper understanding of both the purpose and the context of the management decision to be informed by the data analytics project. The analyst is dependent on the decision maker's knowledge and experience, particularly as regards the interests of the various internal and external stakeholders likely to be affected by the decision. Without this understanding of the purpose and context of the decision, the analyst will be unable to effectively translate the decision problem into an analytical problem. And without the effective translation from decision to analysis, it is highly unlikely that the analyst will be able to translate the results of the empirical analysis into actionable insights and recommend a particular course of action. Recommendations will only carry weight with the decision maker if the data analysis generates credible insights that are both explicable and reliable in terms of the expert knowledge and experience of the decision maker.

What Should Be Measured? How Should It Be Measured?

As previously discussed, a model is a simplified, purpose-led, data-based representation of the specific behavior with which the analyst and the decision maker are concerned. The first step in creating a model is to synthesize the current understanding of the situation using the expert knowledge of both academic researchers and practitioners and the experience of the decision makers. This synthesis provides a theoretical model with which to investigate the available data. The theoretical model takes the following general form:

$$(1) \ldots Y_t = f(X_t; C_t)$$

where Y_t represents the outcome at time t, X_t is the set of behavioral actions at time t impacting on the outcome, C_t is the set of other known factors at time t that systematically influence the outcome, and f(.) represents the causal mechanisms linking the performance outcome to the behavioral actions and the systematic contextual influences. In the case of a specific SDP program, the outcome, Y_t, represents the actual performance of the program in a particular period, t, while X_t consists of all of the actions undertaken within that period by those running the program that have impacted on the actual performance. These actions, in turn, may be capable of being broken down into decisions and their implementation. The other known factors, C_t, influencing the outcome represents the systematic aspect of the context in which the program operates.

The next step is to convert the theoretical model into an empirical model capable of being estimated using appropriate statistical techniques. Converting a theoretical model into an empirical model requires three elements: (1) adding a random error term; (2) constructing a measurement system; and (3) sourcing a dataset. The theoretical model needs to be converted from a deterministic model into a stochastic model by adding a random error term, u_t, to capture all the other unknown or non-systematic contextual influences on the outcome.

$$(2) \ldots Y_t = f(X_t; C_t) + u_t$$

These other contextual influences are treated as a random process for the purpose of empirical modeling. The validity of this assumption is checked during the process of diagnostic testing after the model is estimated to ensure that the residual variation (i.e., the variation in the outcome that is unaccounted for by the deterministic factors X_t and C_t) is random.

A measurement system needs to be constructed to obtain appropriate measures of Y_t, X_t, and C_t. Operationalizing the outcome variable is a particularly crucial step in the analytical process since it requires a definition of performance. This can be difficult because performance may be multidimensional and stakeholders may differ in the relative weightings they attach to different aspects of performance. These difficulties are particularly acute when there are trade-offs between different aspects of performance often caused by resource constraints.[40] In the case of multiple performance metrics that cannot be reduced to a single composite metric, the analyst may need to estimate a separate model for each performance metric.

Having decided on the appropriate measures of performance outcomes, behavioral actions, and contextual influences, the analyst needs to source an appropriate dataset. This may consist of time-series data on the current and past performance of the specific entity being studied or cross-sectional data on the performance of other similar entities at a common point in time. The analytical techniques used to estimate the model will depend on the type of data (time-series or cross-sectional), the type of outcome metric (continuous or categorical), and the functional form assumed for the causal mechanism (linear or nonlinear).

How Will Analytics Impact Decisions?

Data analytics impacts decisions by providing an evidential basis to facilitate more informed decision making. Developing an empirical model of performance outcomes allows decision makers to draw on the past performance of their organization or the performance of similar organizations to identify the key drivers of performance and determine their relative importance. The empirical model of performance outcomes can be used to project the likely impact on future performance of alternative interventions as well as projecting the impact on future performance of changes in the contextual influences. Thus the analyst can assist the decision maker in identifying the intervention with the largest or most cost-effective impact on future performance. The empirical model can also be used to undertake contingency planning to adjust the proposed interventions depending on the actual path of future performance. In the case of performance trade-offs, a set of empirical models of the alternative dimensions of performance can help clarify the extent to which improvements in some performance metrics can only be achieved at the expense of a deterioration in other aspects of performance.

How Will Analytics Reflect the Effectiveness of SDP Initiatives?

Data analytics can improve not only the decisions on the choice of SDP initiatives but also the effectiveness of SDP initiatives in the postdecision implementation phase. One of the key outcomes of any SDP analytics project is to determine which performance metrics are most relevant for the decision maker when deciding on a particular SDP initiative. It follows that the performance metrics that have been used to decide on SDP initiatives should become the KPIs with which to track the performance of the SDP program during the implementation phase. These KPIs can be tracked visually using a dashboard to compare the actual levels of the KPIs to their target levels. Tracking the KPIs in the implementation phase will provide a continuous process of performance review. Statistical process control can be used to analyze unexpected negative deviations in the KPIs from their target levels and determine whether the deviations are indicative of a systematic trend toward underperformance or merely a one-off random deviation. If the evidence suggests systematic underperformance, then the remedial actions can be triggered as set out in the contingency planning.

Questions

1. What is data analytics and how is it connected to decision making?
2. What is the difference between formative and summative evaluation?
3. Describe the five stages of analytics.
4. How can data analytics impact SDP initiatives?
5. How does systems thinking relate to the logic model of program evaluation in SDP?
6. Select and research an actual SDP initiative. First, identify the program goals (bottom lines) of the initiative; next, identify the KPIs you would use to measure the effectiveness of that initiative.
7. What is a double bottom line? Describe its importance in SDP initiatives.

Success Strategies

1. Engage a team composed of managerial decision makers and data analysts.
2. Identify and clarify the mission and goals of the SDP initiative to be evaluated.
3. Identify the KPIs of the SDP initiative and determine the appropriate measures for the KPIs.
4. Facilitate translational interaction among the analysts and decision makers by creating appropriate questions, measures, and data dashboards reflecting and sharing relevant results as needed.
5. Use the evidence provided by data analysts to guide decisions.
6. Measure and disseminate results of decisions based on evidentiary metrics to foster continuous learning and support collective systems thinking in an SDP initiative.
7. Utilize the feedback measures to close the loop and begin the process of goal-related evaluation anew.
   Adopted from Frye and Hemmer:[41]
8. SDP programs are fundamentally about change; therefore, program evaluation should be designed to determine whether change has occurred.
9. Program evaluation should analyze for both intended or unintended changes.
10. Program evaluation studies have been strongly influenced by reductionist theory, which attempts to isolate individual program components to determine associations with outcomes.

11. SDP programs are complex, with multiple interactions among participants and the environment, such that system theory or complexity theory may be better suited to informing program evaluation.
12. The association between SDP program elements and outcomes may be nonlinear—small changes in program elements may lead to large changes in outcomes and vice versa; therefore, program assessment must include both process and outcome data.
13. Always keep an open mind—if you believe you can predict the outcome of an SDP program, you may be limiting yourself to an incomplete view of your program.
14. Choose a program evaluation model that allows you to examine for change in the program and one that embraces the complexity of SDP processes and outcomes.

NOTES

1. Roger Levermore, "Evaluating Sport-for-Development Approaches and Critical Issues," *Progress in Development Studies* 11, no. 4 (2011): 339–53.

2. Fred Coalter, "Sport-for-Development: Going beyond the Boundary?" *Sport Society* 13, no. 9 (2010): 1374–91; Bruce Kidd, "A New Social Movement: Sport for Development and Peace," *Sport Society* 11, no. 4 (2008): 370–80, https://doi.org/10.1080/17430430802019268; Levermore, "Evaluating Sport-for-Development Approaches and Critical Issues"; Meredith Whitley, Tanya Forneris, and Bryce Barker, "The Reality of Evaluating Community-Based Sport and Physical Activity Programs to Enhance the Development of Underserved Youth: Challenges and Potential Strategies," *Quest: National Association for Kinesiology in Higher Education* 66, no. 2 (2014): 218–32, https://doi.org/10.1080/00336297.2013.872043.

3. Levermore, "Evaluating Sport-for-Development Approaches and Critical Issues."

4. Robert E. Baker, Pamela H. Baker, Christopher Atwater, and Heather Andrews, "Sport for Development and Peace: A Program Evaluation of a Sport Diplomacy Initiative," *International Journal of Sport Management and Marketing* 16, nos. 1–2 (2016): 52, https://doi.org/10.1504/IJSMM.2015.074932.

5. Kathleen Wilburn and Ralph Wilburn, "The Double Bottom Line: Profit and Social Benefit," *Business Horizons* 57, no. 1 (2014): 11–20, https://doi.org/10.1016/j.bushor.2013.10.001.

6. Robert E. Baker and Craig Esherick, "Sport-Based Initiatives: Playing for Peace," in *Building Cultures of Peace: Transdisciplinary Voices of Hope and Action*, eds. Elavie Ndura-Ouédraogo and Randall Amster (Newcastle upon Tyne, UK: Cambridge Scholars Publishing, 2009), 102–24.

7. Scarvia B. Anderson and Samuel Ball, *The Profession and Practice of Program Evaluation* (San Francisco, CA: Jossey-Bass, 1978).

8. David A. Cook, "Twelve Tips for Evaluating Educational Programs," *Medical Teacher* 32, no. 4 (2010): 296–301, https://doi.org/10.3109/01421590903480121; Steven J. Durning and Paul A. Hemmer, "Program Evaluation," in *ACP Teaching Internal Medicine*, ed. J. Ende (Philadelphia: American College of Physicians, 2010).

9. Judy L. Baker, *Evaluating the Impact of Development Projects on Poverty: A Handbook for Practitioners* (Washington, DC: World Bank Publications, 2000); Lisa Bornstein, "Systems of Accountability, Webs of Deceit? Monitoring and Evaluation in South African NGOs," *Development* 49, no. 2 (2006): 52–61, https://doi.org/10.1057/palgrave.development.1100261; Basil E. Cracknell, *Evaluating Development Aid: Issues, Problems and Solutions* (Newburg Park, CA: Sage, 2000).

10. Levermore, "Evaluating Sport-for-Development Approaches and Critical Issues."

11. Matthew Gitsham, "How Do You Measure the Impact of Corporate Citizenship at the Local Level in a Zone of Conflict?" *The Journal of Corporate Citizenship*, no. 28 (December 1, 2007): 31–42.

12. "Accreditation Council for Graduate Medical Education: Glossary of Terms," ACGME, last modified April 15, 2020.

13. Durning and Hemmer, "Program Evaluation;" Levermore, "Evaluating Sport-for-Development Approaches and Critical Issues."

14. Ann W. Frye and Paul A. Hemmer, "Program Evaluation Models and Related Theories: AMEE Guide No. 67," *Medical Teacher* 34, no. 5 (May 2012): e288–99, https://doi.org/10.3109/0142159X.2012.668637.

15. Frye and Hemmer, "Program Evaluation Models and Related Theories."

16. Stewart Mennin, "Self-organisation, Integration and Curriculum in the Complex World of Medical Education," *Medical Education* 44, no. 1 (January 2010): 20–30.

17. Carol H. Weiss, *Evaluation: Methods for Studying Programs and Policies*, 2nd ed. (Upper Saddle River, NJ: Prentice Hall, 1998), 4.

18. J. Bradley Cousins, Swee C. Goh, Catherine Elliot, Tim Aubry, and Nathalie Gilbert, "Government and Voluntary Sector Differences in Organizational Capacity to Do and Use Evaluation," *Evaluation and Program Planning* 44 (June 2014): 1–13; Pal Ram Prasad, "The Effectiveness of Civil Service Reform Program Implementation and Its Contribution to Social Development: A Case Study of Dilla Town Municipality, Gedeo Zone, Ethiopia," *Quest—The Journal of UGC-HRDC Nainital* [India] 8, no. 3 (2014): 235–43, https://doi.org/10.5958/2249-0035.2014.01089.4.

19. Durning and Hemmer, "Program Evaluation"; Levermore, "Evaluating Sport-for-Development Approaches and Critical Issues."

20. Peter M. Senge, *The Fifth Discipline: The Art and Practice of the Learning*, 2nd ed. (New York: Doubleday, 2006).

21. Frye and Hemmer, "Program Evaluation Models and Related Theories."

22. Lisa W. Knowlton and Cynthia C. Phillips, *The Logic Model Guidebook: Better Strategies for Great Results* (Los Angeles: Sage, 2009).

23. Senge, *The Fifth Discipline*.

24. Michael Q. Patton, *Developmental Evaluation: Applying Complexity Concepts to Enhance Innovation and Use* (New York: Guilford Press, 2011).

25. Sun Tzu, *The Art of War*, China, 5th century BC.

26. Jacqueline M. Stavros and Gina Hinrichs, eds., "SOARing to High and Engaging Performance: An Appreciative Approach to Strategy," *AI Practitioner: International Journal of Appreciative Inquiry* 9, no. 3 (August 2007); Jacqueline M. Stavros and Gina Hinrichs, *The Thin Book of SOAR: Building Strengths-Based Strategy* (Bend, OR: Thin Book Publishers, 2009).

27. Robert E. Baker, Pamela H. Baker, Christopher Atwater, and Craig Esherick, "U.S. Sport Diplomacy in Latin America and the Caribbean: A Programme Evaluation," *Journal of*

Sport for Development 6, no. 10 (2018): 71–85; David M. Fetterman, Shakeh J. Kaftarian, and Abraham Wandersman, *Empowerment Evaluation*, 2nd ed. (London: Sage, 2015).

28. Baker et al., "Sport for Development and Peace."

29. Baker et al., "U.S. Sport Diplomacy in Latin America and the Caribbean: A Programme Evaluation."

30. Fetterman et al., *Empowerment Evaluation*.

31. Kidd, "A New Social Movement"; Levermore, "Evaluating Sport-for-Development Approaches and Critical Issues"; "United Nations Office on Sport for Development and Peace (UNOSDP)," United Nations, last modified 2016, http://www.un.org/wcm/content/site/sport/home/unplayers/unoffice45; United States Department of State, "Bureau of Educational and Cultural Affairs (ECA) Request for Grant Proposals (RFGP): Sports Youth Visitor Program," *Federal Register* 75, no. 198 (2010): 63247–57; Whitley et al., "The Reality of Evaluating Community-Based Sport and Physical Activity Programs."

32. Shayna Stewart, "Are You Data-driven, Data-informed or Data-inspired?" last modified March 21, 2019, https://blog.amplitude.com/data-driven-data-informed-data-inspired.

33. Stewart, "Are You Data-driven, Data-informed or Data-inspired?"

34. Stewart, "Are You Data-driven, Data-informed or Data-inspired?"

35. Durning and Hemmer, "Program Evaluation"; Levermore, "Evaluating Sport-for-Development Approaches and Critical Issues."

36. Jeffrey Pfeffer and Robert I. Sutton, "Evidence-Based Management," Decision Making, *Harvard Business Review*, January 2006, https://hbr.org/2006/01/evidence-based-management.

37. Philip M. Morse and George E. Kimball, *Methods of Operations Research* (London: Chapman and Hall, 1951), 1.

38. Tony Lawson, *The Nature of Social Reality: Issues in Social Ontology* (London: Routledge, 2019).

39. Lawson, *The Nature of Social Reality*.

40. Bill Gerrard, "A Resource-Utilization Model of Organizational Efficiency in Professional Team Sports," *Journal of Sport Management* 19, no. 2 (2005): 143–69.

41. Frye and Hemmer, "Program Evaluation Models and Related Theories."

II
APPLICATIONS OF SPORT FOR DEVELOPMENT AND PEACE

10

Governments and Sport for Development and Peace

Carrie LeCrom and Per G. Svensson

OBJECTIVES

This chapter will:

- Discuss the role and influence of government in the establishment and management of SDP programs.
- Identify some of the countries that have invested in SDP programs.
- Describe the role of the United Nations and other multilateral organizations in the establishment and the promotion of SDP programs.
- Address the three distinct approaches government involvement can take in their SDP policy decisions.

HISTORY OF GOVERNMENT INVOLVEMENT IN SPORT FOR DEVELOPMENT AND PEACE

The use of sport as a mechanism for contributing to development and peacebuilding goals has received significant attention during the past two decades. Sport for development and peace (SDP) is now recognized as a field involving a multitude of stakeholders including nongovernmental organizations (NGOs), funding agencies, national sport federations, private businesses, governments, and intergovernmental agencies.[1] In fact, Richard Giulianotti, Fred Coalter, Holly Collison, and Simon Darnell argued that SDP needs to be viewed as a "strongly institutionalized field of development activity with its own stakeholder networks."[2] A considerable number of academic scholars have also conducted research in the area of SDP; hundreds of published research articles now exist on different facets of SDP.[3] Despite the significant growth of this literature, published research on the role of government in SDP remains largely nonexistent. One of the few exceptions was Arianne Reis, Marcelo Vieira, and Fabiana de Sousa-Mast's analysis of government-led SDP programs in Brazil.[4] The researchers concluded that existing SDP models developed in high-income countries may not necessarily work in low- and middle-income countries. Reis and colleagues also called on SDP researchers to engage in analyzing the different roles of government involvement in SDP.

Most researchers have focused on program outcomes of community-based SDP initiatives[5] or different managerial aspects of the nongovernmental agencies typically responsible for the implementation of SDP programs in local communities around the world.[6] The considerable advances made in our knowledge pertaining to the management of SDP efforts is important considering how many NGOs are actively involved in the SDP field.[7] However, Johann Olav Koss, the founder of Right to Play, one of the oldest and largest SDP NGOs, acknowledges that he

> believe[s] that the future of all children rests with national governments. National policies and programs that incorporate the concept of Sport for Development and Peace, investments in community initiatives, and efforts towards ensuring that sport is accessible to all will ultimately create a healthier and safer world.[8]

An interesting new line of research has emerged during the last few years in scholarship on SDP NGOs pertaining to the growing institutional complexity that these organizations are faced with as a result of the diverse stakeholder groups involved in SDP efforts. For example, because more governments are engaging with SDP, grassroots NGOs are increasingly dealing with multiple institutional logics, which can create significant tensions as a result of different prescriptions for how SDP agencies should function and operate.[9] One area of emphasis in this emerging body of research on organizational hybridity in SDP is the role and influence of governments.

Many SDP NGOs have a relatively long history of interacting with governments in various ways to deliver their programs in local communities. For example, more than a decade ago, Mathare Youth Sports Association, one of the oldest SDP NGOs, already worked with a dozen different government organizations.[10] Others have reported the importance of collaborating with government as a critical strategy for securing the necessary permissions and visas needed for operating SDP events.[11] Ben Sanders, Julie Phillips, and Bart Vanreusel noted that SDP NGOs "cannot, and must not, take over government's service delivery role."[12] Governments have the potential to support and integrate SDP programs into larger regional and national curriculums. However, Bruce Kidd reported evidence of several NGOs expressing hesitation about government involvement since it was seen as competition for their programs.[13] Likewise, Giulianotti reported several SDP practitioners expressing concerns that government partners sought to gain control and power over SDP organizations.[14] In many instances, lack of or at least inadequate provision of services by local governments has often been reported as one of the main reasons for the emergence of SDP NGOs.[15]

It is unfortunate that governments have been perceived as competitors or obstacles for delivering SDP efforts rather than as valuable potential partners and supporters. Governments have the potential to allocate considerable financial and human resources toward SDP through policy strategies and frameworks. Governments can also support the implementation of sport and physical activity programs on a larger scale through national programs and public school systems, which warrants questions about how and when governments have or can engage with SDP.

Although governments are often portrayed to have little involvement in SDP, some governments and intergovernmental agencies have for many decades been at least informally involved in SDP work. For example, several governments have helped subsidize UN agencies operating sport-based programs in refugee camps and other development efforts since the middle of the twentieth century. The governments of a number of high-income countries also increasingly began to support their own SDP-related programs in low- and middle-income countries. As an example, several of the Nordic governments have been actively involved in funding the Open Fun Football Schools program across the Balkans since the middle of the 1990s,[16] while UK governmental organizations and government-funded public bodies have also been engaged to various extents in development work.[17] Similarly, South Africa's government developed a national SDP program titled "Siyadlala" to engage residents in disadvantaged communities in physical activities and sport, as well as a school sport initiative targeting socioeconomic inequalities across the country.[18]

Nevertheless, government involvement and formal policies enacted to support SDP were limited even during the early 2000s.[19] A significant shift was initiated through several key decisions by the United Nations.[20] In 2001, Kofi Annan, the UN Secretary-General, appointed Adolf Ogi as the Special Adviser on SDP[21] and created the UN Office on Sport for Development and Peace. In 2003, members of the United Nations adopted Resolution 58/5, which stipulated that 2005 would be recognized as the International Year of Sport and Physical Education.[22] As part of this mandate, governments around the world were called upon to better support sport-based development projects aimed at the achievement of the eight Millennium Development Goals. The UN-themed year served as a catalyst for the SDP field and fueled the growth of not only more NGOs, but the year also served as a landmark moment for increased SDP involvement by governments from around the world. For example, as a result of the UN-themed year, Germany significantly increased its involvement in SDP activities led through the Ministry of International Affairs, the Ministry of the Interior, the Foreign Office, and the Ministry of Economic Cooperation.[23] Similarly, the government of Ghana developed a new sport policy in 2005 and created a national Sport for Development and Peace Secretariat. This subsequently led to the inclusion of SDP in Ghana's national growth and poverty reduction strategy. As noted by Kidd, Ghana emerged as one of the first low- and middle-income country governments to increasingly advocate for SDP.[24]

A number of other significant events also took place during 2003, including the adoption of the Magglingen Declaration by representatives from more than fifty countries at the International Conference on Sport and Development in Switzerland. Additionally, a Next Step Sport for Development conference was held in Amsterdam, the Netherlands, with a group of international experts and focused on how to mainstream SDP into development policies. Furthermore, the UN Inter-Agency Task Force on Sport for Development and Peace also released its report on the potential role of SDP and concluded with a call for significant increase in the attention and resources provided by governments.[25] Shortly thereafter, in 2004, the UN established the Sport for Development and Peace International Working Group (SDPIWG). Four years later, the working group released a report titled *Harnessing the Power of Sport for Development and Peace: Recommendations to Governments*.[26] The working group report provided the foundation for a number of new government-driven SDP initiatives and SDP policy developments.

In 2013, the members of the UN General Assembly adopted Resolution 67/296, proclaiming April 6 as the "International Day of Sport for Development and Peace," providing another medium for governments to engage with SDP.[27] The eight Millennium Development Goals, which had served an instrumental role for the positioning of many SDP initiatives during the early 2000s, were then replaced in 2015 with the seventeen Sustainable Development Goals (SDGs) outlined in UN Resolution 70/1 titled, "Transforming Our World: The 2030 Agenda for Sustainable Development."[28]

On May 4, 2017, however, UN Secretary-General António Guterres suddenly announced the closing of the UN Office on Sport for Development and Peace.[29] This was initially perceived to leave a clear void in terms of global leadership and advocacy for the SDP field.[30] Although the UN closed its SDP-specific office, it remains involved in SDP under the UN Department of Economic and Social Affairs Division for Inclusive Social Development.

Two other important policy documents for government involvement in SDP—the Declaration of Berlin and the Kazan Action Plan—emerged from two international meetings organized by the United Nations Educational, Scientific and Cultural Organization (UNESCO). The Declaration of Berlin was adopted by 121 member nations of UNESCO in 2013 at the fifth International Conference of Ministers and Senior Officials Responsible for Physical Education and Sport in Berlin, Germany. The Declaration of Berlin specifically identified the potential benefits of increased investments in sport and physical activities and called on governments to develop more inclusive and supportive sport policies.[31]

Another landmark event for government involvement in SDP occurred in 2017 with the adoption of the Kazan Action Plan at the sixth International Conference of Ministers Responsible for Physical Education and Sport in Kazan, Russia. The Kazan Action Plan explicitly called on governments to strengthen the relationship between sport policies and the UN's SDGs.[32] The Commonwealth Secretariat was listed as one of the key potential partners in the Kazan Action Plan for achieving the agreed-upon goals.

Commonwealth Secretariat

The Commonwealth Secretariat is an important agency that has served an instrumental role as a global leader and advocate for SDP policy advancements since the early 2000s. The Commonwealth of Nations, formerly the British Commonwealth, is a voluntary association of 53 nations working together toward shared goals, representing a combined population of around 2.5 billion people. In 2011, the Commonwealth Heads of Government, the highest decision-making body within the Commonwealth of Nations, officially requested that Commonwealth organizations support the growing field of SDP.[33] Specifically, the Commonwealth Heads of Governments called on the Commonwealth Secretariat to engage with SDP. Similar recommendations had previously been made by the Commonwealth Advisory Body on Sport (CABOS).[34]

Subsequently, a framework was developed through in-depth research and consultation with member countries, SDP experts, and CABOS to develop a foundation and structure for the Commonwealth Secretariat's SDP efforts. It is noteworthy that the report developed and embraced the growing body of critically based SDP literature, explicitly noting the dangers of idealistic assumptions about the use of sport as a panacea for social change;[35] the importance of integrating SDP within broader development activities and agendas;[36] and the need for SDP initiatives to be well-planned, structured, managed, and delivered if any desired outcomes are to be achieved.[37] Darnell further called on member countries to enact policies to recognize sport and development within local contexts in order to better promote local agency and avoid misaligned goals between SDP priorities and the local needs of communities where programs are implemented.[38]

The report, titled "The Commonwealth Guide to Advancing Development through Sport," identified key principles for SDP policy development in member countries, including the need for: (1) leveraging existing resources and intentionally developing programs targeting specific development goals; (2) integrating SDP within local, national, and regional development efforts; (3) safeguarding all participants and mandating fully accessible programs; (4) supporting decentralized programs where prospective program participants and local community members engage in the planning process of SDP efforts; and (5) emphasizing research-driven program models and ongoing monitoring and evaluation of SDP for continuous learning. Detailed examples of local programs and their policy contexts from member countries were also provided. Additionally, the Commonwealth Secretariat and CABOS also outlined specific indicators by which member countries could benchmark their efforts to develop effective SDP policy frameworks in areas such as resource mobilization and allocation, SDP capacity-building, the coordination of national SDP networks and forums, and the extent to which SDP is included in nonsport policy strategies.[39] Per Svensson and Jeffrey Levine[40] noted that this report signaled a clear shift in SDP policy documents and identified the Commonwealth Secretariat as the first to portray a discourse in SDP policy that aligned with elements of the Capability Approach by emphasizing a more balanced understanding of the role of sport for social change, the need for local agency, and a decentralized approach compared with prior SDP policy documents.[41]

In 2013, the Commonwealth Secretariat also established the Commonwealth Youth Sport for Development and Peace Working Group to provide an avenue for young practitioners to be part of key dialogues regarding the use of sport for social change around the world.[42] Shortly thereafter, the Commonwealth Secretariat published a series of critically informed papers by leading SDP experts to advance the dialogue on SDP policy and the development of national policies and strategies.[43] In the preface of the report, Bruce Kidd stated,

> Today, there is an urgent need to go beyond the confident platitudes and develop a much more careful understanding of what works and what does not work in SDP. The research makes clear that sport by itself is insufficient to make beneficial change, but that a well co-ordinated multi-sectoral approach is necessary.[44]

Similarly, Oliver Dudfield argued,

> While numerous international and Commonwealth policy declarations and publications have supported the principle of SDP, insufficient support mechanisms, delivery instruments and resourcing currently exist in many member countries to fully scale SDP initiatives. A contributing factor is that in many countries SDP is delegated to sport ministries and sport stakeholders. While many of these actors are highly supportive of SDP, they have to balance elite sport and sport development priorities with investment in SDP drawing from an already over-stretched resource pool.[45]

Giulianotti further identified three distinct types of policy approaches based on an analysis of government involvement in SDP within the Commonwealth. First is the "minimalist approach" where SDP is supported, but government involvement remains limited and fails to contribute to the sustainability of the SDP field. Second is the "active approach" whereby governments actively advocate for SDP and provide significant support for SDP programs and actors. Last, is the "leadership approach," governments not only support SDP but also enact SDP-related policies and actively seek to enhance knowledge among SDP actors.[46]

Following the adoption of the UN SDGs in 2015, the Commonwealth Secretariat commissioned some of the most in-depth consultations to date in the SDP field to analyze and identify how governments can best contribute to the SDGs through SDP.[47] The result was a report that identified SDGs 3, 4, 5, 6, 8, 11, and 16 as the development goals where the SDP field could best contribute. Dudfield and Malcolm Dingwall-Smith also identified specific examples of which targets within each of the SDGs align with SDP. The report was followed by a publication by Iain Lindsey and Tony Chapman that outlined specific evidence-based policy options for how Commonwealth governments could contribute to the prioritized SDGs.[48]

Specifically, Lindsey and Chapman identified four overarching policy pathways: (1) government-led implementation of SDP efforts; (2) structured implementation partnerships; (3) complementary implementation; and (4) autonomous implementation. The four approaches were identified to provide flexible options given the different contexts and needs across members of the Commonwealth of Nations. Furthermore, Lindsey and Chapman[49] noted the significant role governments can play in the SDP field by marshaling much-needed financial resources and operational support to already established SDP NGOs that tend to be characterized by significant capacity constraints.[50]

A key theme throughout the Commonwealth Secretariat's policy reports and consultations has been the conclusion that multisectorial collaborations are critical for effective SDP efforts to be developed since the complexity of the underlying issues are manifold and transcend the boundaries of what any single agency can achieve on its own. This position aligns with key tenets of other landmark policy documents, including the Kazan Action Plan, which explicitly identified that the contribution of sport to the SDGs cannot be fully realized without collaborative solutions and coordinated efforts across different policy areas.[51] However, there remain significant opportunities for improved support and involvement by governments in SDP if more transformative outcomes are to be achieved. For example, Svensson and Richard Loat utilized the concept of bridge-building to highlight the potential ways that governments (and other stakeholder groups) can develop more meaningful and sustainable SDP collaborations.[52] As a result of the cross-cutting nature of SDP, the Commonwealth Secretariat has now published a toolkit and self-evaluation checklist for how member governments can improve their SDP-related policy coherence.[53]

GOVERNMENTS SUPPORTING SPORT FOR DEVELOPMENT AND PEACE

In conceptualizing concrete ways governments can better engage in SDP, looking at what others are already doing can be beneficial. The Governments in Action report, produced by the International Working Group on Sport for Development and Peace, identifies four broad categories under which the relationship between governments and SDP exist: (1) mobilizing support and action for SDP; (2) developing SDP policies and programs; (3) implementing SDP policies and programs; and (4) mobilizing resources to support SDP.[54] Most governments that are highly involved in SDP are doing all of these things on some level, but examples of each from different countries around the globe will be highlighted to demonstrate the depth of ways governments can engage with SDP meaningfully.

Mobilizing Government Support and Action for SDP

Mobilizing government support and action for SDP is an important first step and it comes about in several different ways. The influence that the United Nations had internationally in the early 2000s cannot be overlooked as having influenced

Figure 10.1. US Ambassador Tim Roemer speaking to a group at a basketball clinic in New Delhi, India. *Credit*: J. D. Walsh

government SDP mobilization efforts. Beyond that, some countries conducted self-research on social issues and needs within their countries, positioning sport as a leading strategy in attacking the issues.[55] Over the last several decades, sport has emerged as a strategic tool in development efforts, and mobilization for SDP at the government level has grown.[56]

In addition, mobilization of government support and action in regard to SDP has been influenced by cross-country collaboration. Many government officials attend international sport-based conferences and network with their counterparts in other countries' ministries to discuss strategies. These meetings have ranged from SDP-centered gatherings such as the 2003 and 2005 Sport and Development Conference in Magglingen, Switzerland, to larger sport-based conferences including the International Working Group on Women and Sport World Conference, as well as UNESCO's International Conference of Ministers and Senior Officials Responsible for Physical Education and Sport. Additionally, mobilization of government support for SDP has also evolved from officials' attendance at broader international meetings organized by intergovernmental bodies such as the Commonwealth Secretariat and the European Commission, through this, sport is often discussed as an important tool. For instance, "[i]n Canada, involvement in the Commonwealth Committee on Development through Sport was credited with increasing government interest in

Sport for Development and Peace. In the Netherlands, government participation in forums organized by the International Olympic Committee had similar results."[57]

As an example of mobilizing support for SDP, the government of Zambia utilized a strategy of interdepartmental collaboration. Each ministry within the government identified a representative to focus on SDP, forming a collaborative committee that represented all parts of Zambian government.[58] Building on this over time, the government came to see the impact sport could have on young people in the country and has further mobilized support for SDP with each iteration of policy.[59] In speaking on its 2016 revised policy, Bessie Malilwe Chelemu, director of Sport Ministry for Youth, Sport and Child Development, noted:

> Young people below the age of 25 make up 82 percent of the Zambian population. This kind of population distribution presents challenges for promoting social and economic development, particularly for meeting the needs of young people. Sport can play a role in addressing these issues if supported by the implementation of appropriate development-orientated sport policy.[60]

This collaborative mobilization effort resulted in a revised national policy that uses sport to address economic diversification, job creation, human capital, and a supportive government environment in Zambia's Vision 2030.[61] This example paints a picture of how a country's government can move from mobilizing support for SDP to developing national-level policies and programs.

Developing SDP Policies and Programs

Following the mobilization of government support for SDP, the next critical step is often the development, discussion, revision, and implementation of national policies. The integration of sport into national policies and strategies comes in many forms across the globe. At the highest level, some national governments have embraced sport so far as to integrate it into their constitutions or introduce legislation deeming it a right to all citizens. Others, recognizing sport as a tool in achieving their development goals, have established National Sport Policies noting specifically how sport will be used within each nation.

For example, the government of Sierra Leone, led by its Ministry of Sports, created a national sports policy in 2015, citing the ways sport could be used specifically to support development and peace efforts. The country's *National Sport for Development and Peace (SDP) Strategy and Action Plan* identifies ways sport can take a leading role in many strategic initiatives for the country and discusses cross-departmental collaborations that will be necessary for success. Additionally, as part of the policy implementation, Sierra Leone's National Sport for All Commission is tasked with taking a leading role in the country's health objectives. This comprehensive policy lays out not only ideas but also strategies that are starting to be implemented and already having early success.[62]

Meanwhile, Argentina's National Sport Policy resulted in the creation of Ente Nacional e Alto Rendimiento Deportivo (ENARD), a nonprofit, nonstate organization run by the National Olympic Committee and the Argentina Secretariat for Sport (the social development branch of Argentina's government). This organization is supported through taxes (approximately $35 million annually), and its focus is on community integration and social development through sport and coaching education.[63] Similarly, the government of Tonga, led by Tonga's Ministries of Internal Affairs and Health, developed a netball-based SDP program through collaborations with the Australian Government and the national governing bodies of netball in Tonga and Australia.[64] The program was developed to improve accessibility and challenge cultural norms regarding physical activity for girls and women in efforts to decrease the nation's high rates of noncommunicable diseases.[65] These are just a few concrete examples of government-developed SDP programs and policies.

Other governments have chosen to integrate sport into existing national priorities, reports, or policies. For example, in Mozambique sport has been integrated into several national policies, including the Strategic Plan of the Ministry of Youth and Sport, the Government Five-Year Plan, the Social Economic Plan, and the Sports Law (sport for all).[66] Through this combination, sport cuts across several government platforms, addressing various social issues in the country. This has especially been seen in nations incorporating sport into their national poverty reduction strategy documents. For instance, Canada's "Opportunity for All" poverty reduction strategy calls out sport as a tool to reduce poverty across the country. Specifically, the country's Sport for Social Development in Indigenous Communities program utilizes the Right to Play model, instilling the importance of education and self-concept into participants in its more than three hundred Indigenous communities.[67] Over five years, beginning in 2018 and 2019, more than $47.5 million will be invested in this sport-specific program to channel the use of sport for social development in terms of poverty reduction.

Government strategies and integration typically include working with sport-based organizations, ministries, and NGOs across the country to collectively plot a direction. As an example, the Government of Brazil developed its policy "through a national engagement process involving 80,000 Brazilians at a five-day sport conference attended by delegates from each of Brazil's 26 states."[68] Their sport policies, therefore, have broad appeal and buy-in straightaway, giving them a better chance for success and true impact. Similarly, the government of India supports the Maidan Network, a platform for information sharing across SDP within the country. Over the years, it has organized several Maidan Summits (led by NGO Magic Bus); provided support; discussed strategies and best practices; explored debates in the space; and overall created a network of governments, NGOs, academics, and corporations supporting SDP efforts in India.[69]

Implementing SDP Policies and Programs

The implementation of SDP policies and programs, once developed, must fall to those both inside and outside the government itself. Lindsey and Chapman's framework provides a useful guide to different approaches for governments to implement SDP efforts.[70] First, governments can independently enact SDP efforts such as the provision of SDP programming in public schools or regulatory policymaking for existing sport organizations through a *government-led implementation* of SDP efforts. Second, governments may partner with existing NGOs such as national sport federations and grassroots SDP agencies to deliver SDP initiatives and work toward agreed-upon objectives through *structured implementation partnerships*. Third, governments may coordinate efforts with SDP actors from other sectors through a strength-based approach to achieve shared goals through *complementary implementation* of SDP efforts. Last, governments may decide to let SDP actors from other sectors independently implement programming to achieve SDP policy goals through so-called autonomous implementation.

Figure 10.2. Partnership among local and government leaders can fuel community engagement in SDP. *Credit*: J. D. Walsh

Many national governments report working with external groups to most effectively implement SDP programming in some way or form. For some countries, committees are developed that create mechanisms and support for implementation. These are typically committees made up of government officials, sport-based organizations, NGOs, and others doing the work of SDP on the ground. Still, some governments work more closely with a small number of key partners to ensure programming is being implemented effectively. Educational systems, schools, local commissions, and sport federations are a few of these. Depending on the social goal, certain partners may be better equipped to play a role in program implementation.

In India, as an example, the government has developed a partnership over time with an international NGO called Magic Bus. Magic Bus has an overarching goal of moving children out of poverty into a livelihood over their life span, specifically doing this through a sport-based curriculum in schools. Much of their work focuses on education, health, and gender equity, all major topics the government of India is tackling daily. Magic Bus and the government of India have a memorandum of understanding, tagging Magic Bus as a "knowledge and technical partner" in their rural sports initiative (Panchayati Yuva Khel Evam Krida Abhiyan), training coaches and teachers across the country, and serving in an advisory capacity to advocate for children's rights. Magic Bus works with India's central government to develop institutional support for SDP on a national level. At the same time, Magic Bus is also connected with several state governments in India including the governments of Andhra Pradesh, Delhi, Maharashtra, and Mizoram.[71]

Still other governments rely on collaboration with key partners such as the UN, UNESCO, UNICEF (formerly United Nations International Children's Emergency Fund), or groups doing significant SDP work in multiple countries. This allows them to build on best practices and learn from other governments so they are implementing the most effective SDP programming. In the Netherlands, in establishing collaborations both nationally and internationally, the Ministries of Foreign Affairs and Health, Welfare and Sports commissioned a symposium on the subject of SDP in 1998. Through this, a memorandum was established that put most of the work of SDP in the hands of a government subsidized program run by NCDO, an independent administrative body.[72] This organization has continued to play a leading role in the SDP across the country and other developing nations, centralizing expertise and knowledge for effective government implementation of SDP.

Mobilizing Resources to Support SDP

A final key step to governments fully engaging with and embracing SDP as part of their national policies and practices is mobilizing resources. So much of SDP is contingent on funding, equipment, and other resources, and governments involved in the work are not immune to this need. In terms of nonfinancial resources that governments have capitalized on in regard to SDP, many have partnered with or even organized or hosted major sporting events in the countries, utilizing that platform to spread their social messages (e.g., health, disability, race). Sport's popularity is often conducive to this method of mass knowledge transfer. For example, Norway's government has developed a strategy of culture and sport cooperation with a number of low- and middle-income countries.[73] With a strong governmental focus on peace, democratic values, and sustainable living, Norway's Ministry of Foreign Affairs has recognized sport's role in promoting these values within and outside the country through several sport-based initiatives. The Norway Cup is a week-long youth soccer tournament that sponsors visitors from abroad, typically having more than fifty different countries represented in the event. The aim of the tournament, as communicated by the Norwegian Minister of Foreign Affairs, is to "win friends for Norway through sport. . . . The project plays a role in supporting internationalization and co-operation between Norway and, for example, Brazil, Kenya, and Palestine."[74] Norway also has a long history of supporting SDP efforts through the Norwegian Confederation of Sport (NIF) and the Norwegian Development Cooperation Agency (NORAD) in countries such as Tanzania, Namibia, South Africa, Zambia, and Zimbabwe.[75] The nature of these initiatives has evolved over time.[76] Norway continues to mobilize resources (funding, equipment, etc.) for numerous local SDP organizations such as Edusport in Zambia. Norway also serves as a long-time steering group member and supporter of the International Platform for Sport and Development (sportanddev.org).

One of the leading nations in mobilizing resources to support SDP is Australia; its influence is felt across the Indo-Pacific region. Australia's government has been actively engaged in supporting sport for social change for decades. In 2019, the Minister for Foreign Affairs and Minister for Sport co-released *Sport 2030*, the country's second iteration of a sport diplomacy policy.[77] The policy acknowledges sport as an economic driver, a diplomatic tool, and a means for contributing to the achievement of numerous development goals across the region and lays out strategies and initiatives aimed at harnessing sport's power to promote social change. Since 2006, Australia has operated the Australian Sports Outreach Program (ASOP), which is anchored around building the capacity of local partners to develop, implement, and manage SDP programs focused on locally identified development goals.[78] As an example, its current flagship ASOP SDP initiative, Pacific Sports Partnerships (PSP), established in 2009, has awarded more than $39 million AUD in funding to support local organizations implementing SDP initiatives across the Pacific islands. The PSP programs focus predominantly on noncommunicable diseases; physical inactivity; and inequalities experienced by women, girls, and people living with disabilities.[79] Because of its long history of investment in SDP, Australia continues to be an example for other governments. In numerous countries across the globe, national governments take on the role of providing low-cost equipment to sports programs that are engaged in SDP. They are additionally utilizing their own national pools of funding to support SDP. To raise funding for this type of programming, governments are implementing lotteries, taxation programs, or even seeking sponsorships from the private sector. This funding can then be granted or gifted to SDP initiatives to support their implementation and growth.

As another example of mobilizing financial resources for SDP, the US Department of State offers annual grants to fund public, private, and nonprofit organizations implementing cross-cultural exchanges for shared learning of how sport can be leveraged as a catalyst for change in local communities. Focusing on a broad range of social issues (health, disability, gender, the environment), the overall goal of the program is to utilize sport for diplomatic purposes.[80] The US government supports these programs financially, but it also provides other resources and technical support while monitoring them in terms of being in line with national priorities. The support of the Sports Diplomacy program since 2002, even in times of budget cuts and difficult financial challenges in the United States, demonstrates the government's commitment to mobilize resources and support for SDP.

Still other governments are supplementing financial support with more creative resources and technical support for SDP. Botswana, for example, with a focus on preventing noncommunicable diseases, has incentivized sport participation and physical activity through its National Sport and Recreation Policy and the Botswana National Fitness Policy. As a piece of this, businesses have been encouraged to release employees for two hours of business time the last Friday of the month for physical activities.

> Under this programme, all employees of the public sector (who represent the majority of the labour force in Botswana) are released to participate in workplace-organised sport or physical activity without any loss of income or adverse consequences. Government departments and agencies also have the flexibility to choose the day or week of the month in which they wish to dedicate time to this activity.[81]

The government is offering wellness officers and opening up stadiums, gyms, and halls free of charge during this time to support the initiative.

Additionally, many governments engage elite athletes as ambassadors of SDP and role models across their countries and abroad, which has wide appeal to youth.[82] For example, the US Department of State deploys sports envoys in an effort to improve cultural relations between the United States and other countries. They do this by sending professional and elite US athletes and coaches to foreign countries as ambassadors.

> Partnering with the US Olympic Committee, US sports federations and professional leagues in the US, the envoy program identifies successful American athletes and former athletes who represent the country on foreign soil. Developed through US embassies and consulates, delegates run sport camps and clinics, engaging with young athletes in important conversations surrounding the power of sport, leadership, and diversity.[83]

Similarly, soccer star Didier Drogba championed this strategy using his celebrity status to promote peace and stability in his home country of Côte d'Ivoire. He used the 2007 Africa Cup of Nations qualifier as an opportunity to bring together the government and rebel forces in peace talks, clearly demonstrating the strength of sport for development and peace.[84]

CONCLUSION

As the legitimacy and support for SDP as a change maker has grown over the last several decades, it is difficult for governments to overlook the opportunities sport provides. As outlined in this chapter, there are several pathways to success for governments embracing sport as a strategic tool in their development efforts. Governments across the globe and across the political and financial spectrum have found creative ways to utilize sport in supporting their goals. Whether sport is integrated into governments' constitutions or policies directly, or whether it is a support mechanism within government-sponsored initiatives, the partnerships and collaborations sport has provided to government entities allow them to advance their social strategies in a different way. While there is no one blueprint for success, the various ways governments have engaged with sport show the variety, creativity, and flexibility of options. As monitoring and evaluation of programming continues, policies and programs are likely to mature and evolve as well, but sport for development is likely to continue to play a role in governments into the foreseeable future.

Questions

1. What are some of the goals of these governmental SDP programs?
2. How are SDP programs implemented by government?
3. Differentiate between sport for development and sport diplomacy.
4. What government ministries have engaged in SDP programs?
5. Which UN Secretary-General closed the UN Office on Sport for Development and Peace? Why do you think this decision was made?

Learning Activities

1. Study the website for the SDP organization Magic Bus discussed on page 192.
2. Find the website for one of the SDP conferences discussed in this chapter (e.g., the International Working Group on Women and Sport World Conference or the sixth International Conference of Ministers Responsible for Physical Education and Sport in Kazan, Russia). Identify details of the program. Who attended? Who were the major sponsors or conveners?

Strategies for Success

1. Government resources can provide SDP organizations with the means to create valuable programs for citizens.
2. National government partnerships with local businesses, state governments, public schools, sports federations, leagues, and recreation departments can be leveraged by SDP NGOs to reach a larger group of people.

3. Partnering with elite athletes for targeted SDP programs has a wide appeal to young people.
4. Government monitoring and the regular evaluation of programs funded by the taxpayer are essential.

NOTES

1. Richard Giulianotti, Hans Hognestad, and Ramón Spaaij, "Sport for Development and Peace: Power, Politics, and Patronage," *Journal of Global Sport Management* 1, nos. 3–4 (2016): 129–41; Per G. Svensson and Marion E. Hambrick, "Exploring How External Stakeholders Shape Social Innovation in Sport for Development and Peace," *Sport Management Review* 22, no. 4 (August 2019): 540–52.

2. Richard Giulianotti, Fred Coalter, Holly Collison, and Simon C. Darnell, "Rethinking Sportland: A New Research Agenda for the Sport for Development and Peace Sector," *Journal of Sport and Social Issues* 43, no. 6 (2019): 411–37. https://doi./10.1177%2F0193723519867590.

3. Gareth J. Jones, Michael B. Edwards, Jason N. Bocarro, Kyle S. Bunds, and Jordan W. Smith, "An Integrative Review of Sport-Based Youth Development Literature," *Sport in Society* 20, no. 1 (2017): 161–79; Nico Schulenkorf, Emma Sherry, and Katie Rowe, "Sport for Development: An Integrated Literature Review," *Journal of Sport Management* 30, no. 1 (2016): 22–39; Meredith A. Whitley, William V. Massey, Martin Camiré, Mish Boutet, and Amanda Borbee, "Sport-Based Youth Development Interventions in the United States: A Systematic Review," *BMC Public Health* 19, no. 1 (2019): article 89.

4. Arianne C. Reis, Marcelo Carvalho Vieira, and Fabiana Rodrigues de Sousa-Mast, "'Sport for Development' in Developing Countries: The Case of the Vilas Olímpicas do Rio de Janeiro," *Sport Management Review* 19, vol. 2 (April 2016): 107–19.

5. Meredith A. Whitley et al., "A Systematic Review of Sport for Development Interventions across Six Global Cities," *Sport Management Review* 22, no. 2 (April 2019): 181–93.

6. Nico Schulenkorf, "Managing Sport-for-Development: Reflections and Outlook," *Sport Management Review* 20, no. 3 (June 2017): 243–51.

7. Per G. Svensson and Hilary Woods, "A Systematic Overview of Sport for Development and Peace Organisations," *Journal of Sport for Development* 5, no. 9 (2017): 36–48.

8. Sport for Development and Peace International Working Group (SDPIWG), *Harnessing the Power of Sport for Development and Peace: Recommendations to Governments* (Toronto, ON: Right to Play, 2008).

9. Marlene A. Dixon and Per G. Svensson, "A Nascent Sport for Development and Peace Organization's Response to Institutional Complexity: The Emergence of a Hybrid Agency in Kenya," *Journal of Sport Management* 33, no. 5 (August 2019), https://doi.org/10.1123/jsm.2019-0065; Katherine Raw, Emma Sherry, and Katie Rowe, "Sport-for-Development Organizational Hybridity: From Differentiated to Dysfunctional," *Journal of Sport Management* 33, no. 5 (2019): 467–80, https://doi.org/10.1123/jsm.2018-0273; Per G. Svensson, "Organizational Hybridity: A Conceptualization of How Sport for Development and Peace Organizations Respond to Divergent Institutional Demands," *Sport Management Review* 20, no. 5 (November 2017): 443–54; Per G. Svensson and Chad S. Seifried, "Navigating Plurality

in Hybrid Organizing: The Case of Sport for Development and Peace Entrepreneurs," *Journal of Sport Management* 31, no. 2 (2017): 176–90.

10. Roger Levermore, "Sport in International Development: Time to Treat It Seriously?" *The Brown Journal of World Affairs* 14, no. 2 (2008): 55–66.

11. Nico Schulenkorf and Deborah Edwards, "Maximizing Positive Social Impacts: Strategies for Sustaining and Leveraging the Benefits of Intercommunity Sport Events in Divided Societies," *Journal of Sport Management* 26, no. 5 (2012): 376–90.

12. Ben Sanders, Julie Phillips, and Bart Vanreusel, "Opportunities and Challenges Facing NGOs Using Sport as a Vehicle for Development in Post-Apartheid South Africa," *Sport, Education and Society* 19, no. 6 (2014): 799.

13. Bruce Kidd, "A New Social Movement: Sport for Development and Peace," *Sport in Society* 11, no. 4 (July 2008): 370–80.

14. Richard Giulianotti, "Sport, Transnational Peacemaking, and Global Civil Society: Exploring the Reflective Discourses of 'Sport, Development, and Peace' Project Officials," *Journal of Sport and Social Issues* 35, no. 1 (2011): 50–71.

15. Iain Lindsey, "Community Collaboration in Development Work with Young People: Perspectives from Zambian Communities," *Development in Practice* 23, no. 4 (2013): 481–95.

16. Patrick K. Gasser and Anders Levinsen, "Breaking Post-War Ice: Open Fun Football Schools in Bosnia and Herzegovina," *Sport in Society* 7, no. 3 (Autumn 2004): 457–72.

17. Aaron Beacom, "A Question of Motives: Reciprocity, Sport and Development Assistance," *European Sport Management Quarterly* 7, no. 1 (2007): 81–107; David R. Black, "The Ambiguities of Development: Implications for 'Development through Sport,'" *Sport in Society* 13, no. 1 (January 2010): 121–29.

18. Cora Burnett, "Engaging Sport-for-Development for Social Impact in the South African Context," *Sport in Society* 12, no. 9 (November 2009): 1192–295; Cora Burnett, "The Impact of a Sport-for-Education Programme in the South African Context of Poverty," *Sport in Society* 17, no. 6 (2014): 722–35.

19. Kidd, "A New Social Movement: Sport for Development and Peace," 370–80.

20. Ingrid Beutler, "Sport Serving Development and Peace: Achieving the Goals of the United Nations through Sport," *Sport in Society* 11, no. 4 (July 2008): 359–69.

21. United Nations, "Special Adviser on Sport for Development and Peace (SG/A/768)," accessed February 24, 2020, https://www.un.org/press/en/2001/sga768.doc.htm.

22. United Nations, *Sport as a Tool for Development and Peace: Towards Achieving the United Nations Millennium Development Goals* (New York: United Nations, 2003).

23. Sport for Development and Peace International Working Group (SDPIWG), *Harnessing the Power of Sport for Development and Peace*.

24. Bruce Kidd, "Cautions, Questions and Opportunities in Sport for Development and Peace," *Third World Quarterly* 32, no. 3 (2011): 603–9.

25. United Nations, *Sport as a Tool for Development and Peace*.

26. SDPIWG, *Harnessing the Power of Sport for Development and Peace*.

27. United Nations, "International Day of Sport for Development and Peace (A/RES/67/296)," 2013.

28. United Nations, "Transforming Our World: The 2030 Agenda for Sustainable Development (A/RES/70/1)," accessed February 24, 2020, https://undocs.org/A/RES/70/1.

29. United Nations, "Daily Press Briefing by the Office of the Spokesperson for the Secretary-General," May 4, 2017, https://www.un.org/press/en/2017/db170504.doc.htm.

30. Marc Probst and Paul Hunt, "The Quiet Demise of the UNOSDP: Where Do We Go from Here?" May 15, 2017, https://www.sportanddev.org/en/article/news/quiet-demise-unosdp-where-do-we-go-here.

31. UNESCO, "Declaration of Berlin," accessed February 24, 2020, http://www.unesco.org/new/en/social-and-human-sciences/themes/physical-education-and-sport/mineps-2013/declaration/.

32. UNESCO, "Kazan Action Plan," accessed February 24, 2020, https://en.unesco.org/mineps6/kazan-action-plan.

33. Oliver Dudfield, ed., *Strengthening Sport for Development and Peace: National Policies and Strategies* (London: Commonwealth Secretariat, 2014).

34. Dudfield, *Strengthening Sport for Development and Peace*.

35. Black, "The Ambiguities of Development"; Douglas Hartmann and Christina Kwauk, "Sport and Development: An Overview, Critique, and Reconstruction," *Journal of Sport and Social Issues* 35, no. 3 (2011): 284–305; John Sugden, "Critical Left-Realism and Sport Interventions in Divided Societies," *International Review for the Sociology of Sport* 45, no. 3 (2010): 258–72.

36. Simon C. Darnell and David R. Black, "Mainstreaming Sport into International Development Studies," *Third World Quarterly* 32, no. 3 (2011): 367–78.

37. Sugden, "Critical Left-Realism and Sport Interventions in Divided Societies."

38. Simon Darnell, "Critical Considerations for Sport for Development and Peace Policy Development," in *Strengthening Sport for Development and Peace: National Policies and Strategies*, ed. Oliver Dudfield (London: Commonwealth Secretariat, 2014), 25–29.

39. Tess Kay and Oliver Dudfield, *The Commonwealth Guide to Advancing Development through Sport* (London: Commonwealth Secretariat, 2013).

40. Per G. Svensson and Jeffrey Levine, "Rethinking Sport for Development and Peace: The Capability Approach," *Sport in Society* 20, no. 7 (2017): 905–23.

41. Fred Coalter, "The Politics of Sport-for-Development: Limited Focus Programmes and Broad Gauge Problems?" *International Review for the Sociology of Sport* 45, no. 3 (2010): 295–314; Lyndsay M. C. Hayhurst, "The Power to Shape Policy: Charting Sport for Development and Peace Policy Discourses," *International Journal of Sport Policy* 1, no. 2 (July 2009): 203–27.

42. The Commonwealth Youth Sport for Development and Peace Working Group, "The Commonwealth Youth Sport for Development and Peace Working Group," accessed February 24, 2020, http://thecommonwealth.org/commonwealth-youth-sport-development-and-peace-working-group.

43. Dudfield, *Strengthening Sport for Development and Peace*.

44. Dudfield, *Strengthening Sport for Development and Peace*, iv.

45. Dudfield, *Strengthening Sport for Development and Peace*, 6.

46. Richard Giulianotti, "Sport for Development and Peace Policy Options in the Commonwealth," in *Strengthening Sport for Development and Peace: National Policies and Strategies*, ed. Oliver Dudfield (London: Commonwealth Secretariat, 2014), 13–24.

47. Oliver Dudfield and Malcolm Dingwall-Smith, *Sport for Development and Peace and the 2030 Agenda for Sustainable Development* (London: Commonwealth Secretariat, 2015).

48. Iain Lindsey and Tony Chapman, *Enhancing the Contribution of Sport to the Sustainable Development Goals* (London: Commonwealth Secretariat, 2017).

49. Lindsay and Chapman, *Enhancing the Contribution of Sport to the Sustainable Development Goals*.

50. Ryan Clutterbuck and Alison Doherty, "Organizational Capacity for Domestic Sport for Development," *Journal of Sport for Development* 7, no. 12 (August 2019): 16–32; Per G. Svensson, Fredrik O. Andersson, and Lewis Faulk, "A Quantitative Assessment of Organizational Capacity and Organizational Life Stages in Sport for Development and Peace," *Journal of Sport Management* 32, no. 3 (2018): 295–313.

51. UNESCO, "Kazan Action Plan."

52. Per G. Svensson and Richard Loat, "Bridge-Building for Social Transformation in Sport for Development and Peace," *Journal of Sport Management* 33, no. 5 (2019): 426–39, https://doi.org/10.1123/jsm.2018-0258.

53. Iain Lindsey, *Strengthening Sport-Related Policy Coherence: Commonwealth Toolkit and Self-Evaluation* (London: Commonwealth Secretariat, 2018).

54. Sport for Development and Peace International Working Group (SDPIWG), *Sport for Development and Peace: Governments in Action* (Toronto, ON: Right to Play, 2007).

55. SDPIWG, *Sport for Development and Peace*.

56. Dudfield and Dingwall-Smith, *Sport for Development and Peace and the 2030 Agenda for Sustainable Development*.

57. SDPIWG, *Sport for Development and Peace*, 8.

58. SDPIWG, *Sport for Development and Peace*.

59. Davies Banda and Hikabwa Chipande, "Zambia: The SDP Ideal?" in *Routledge Handbook of Sport for Development and Peace*, ed. Holly Collison, Simon C. Darnell, Richard Giulianotti, and P. David Howe (New York: Routledge, 2019), 517–27.

60. Lindsey and Chapman, *Enhancing the Contribution of Sport to the Sustainable Development Goals*, 20.

61. Zambia Case Study, "Sport for Development and Peace," *Commonwealth Secretariat*, accessed February 24, 2020, http://thecommonwealth.org/sites/default/files/inline/Zambia%20Fact%20Sheet.pdf.

62. Lindsey and Chapman, *Enhancing the Contribution of Sport to the Sustainable Development Goals*.

63. Parliamentary Monitoring Group [South Africa], "ENARD High Level Performance in Sport: Argentinian Ambassador's Briefing," June 12, 2012, https://pmg.org.za/committee-meeting/14547/.

64. Dudfield and Dingwall-Smith, *Sport for Development and Peace and the 2030 Agenda for Sustainable Development*.

65. Australian Government, "The Impact of Development through Sport: Results of Research Conducted on the Australian Sports Outreach Program in Tonga," accessed February 23, 2020, https://www.sportanddev.org/sites/default/files/downloads/tonga.pdf.

66. Marion Keim and Christo de Coning, eds., *Sport and Development Policy in Africa: Results of a Collaborative Study of Selected Country Cases* (Stellenbosch, South Africa: Sun Press, 2014).

67. "Opportunity for All: Canada's First Poverty Reduction Strategy," *Employment and Social Development Canada* (Ottawa: Her Majesty the Queen in Right of Canada, Government of Canada 2018), accessed February 24, 2020, https://www.canada.ca/en/employment-social-development/programs/poverty-reduction/reports/strategy.html.

68. SDPIWG, *Sport for Development and Peace*, 11.

69. Maidan, "Maidan Summit," accessed February 24, 2020, https://www.maidan.in/index.htm.

70. Lindsey and Chapman, *Enhancing the Contribution of Sport to the Sustainable Development Goals*.

71. Magic Bus USA, "Frequently Asked Questions," accessed February 24, 2020, https://www.magicbususa.org/faqs.

72. Frank Van Eekeren, "Sport and Development: Challenges in a New Arena," in *Sport and Development*, ed. Yves Vanden Auweele, Charles Malcolm, and Bert Meulders (Leuven, Belgium: Lannoo Campus, 2006), 19–34.

73. Hans Hognestad, "Norway: Charity or Development?" in *Routledge Handbook of Sport for Development and Peace*, ed. Holly Collison et al. (New York: Routledge, 2019), 484–94.

74. Michał Kobierecki, "Sports Diplomacy of Norway," *International Studies Interdisciplinary Political and Cultural Journal* 20, no. 1 (2017): 131–46, https://doi.org/10.1515/ipcj-2017-0021.

75. Hognestad, "Norway: Charity or Development?"

76. Anders Hasselgård and Solveig Straume, "Sport for Development and Peace Policy Discourse and Local Practice: Norwegian Sport for Development and Peace to Zimbabwe," *International Journal of Sport Policy and Politics* 7, no. 1 (2015): 87–103; Hognestad, "Norway: Charity or Development?"; Solveig Straume, "Norwegian Naivety Meets Tanzanian Reality: The Case of the Norwegian Sports Development Aid Programme, Sport for All, in Dar es Salaam in the 1980s," *The International Journal of the History of Sport* 29, no. 11 (August 2012): 1577–99.

77. *Sports Diplomacy 2030*, Commonwealth of Australia's Department of Health, publication number 12405, 2019, https://dfat.gov.au/about-us/publications/Documents/sports-diplomacy-2030.pdf.

78. Allison Simmons, "Evaluating the Contribution Sport Makes to Development Objectives in the Pacific," in *Strengthening Sport for Development and Peace: National Policies and Strategies*, ed. Oliver Dudfield (London: Commonwealth Secretariat, 2014), 76–83.

79. Australian Government, "Sport for Development in the Pacific," accessed February 23, 2020, https://dfat.gov.au/people-to-people/sport/sport-for-development/pacific/pages/sport-for-development-pacific.aspx.

80. Carrie W. LeCrom and Melissa Ferry, "The United States Government's Role in Sport Diplomacy," in *Case Studies in Sport Diplomacy*, ed. Craig Esherick, Robert E. Baker, Steven Jackson, and Michael Sam (Morgantown, WV: FIT Publishing, 2017).

81. Lindsey and Chapman, *Enhancing the Contribution of Sport to the Sustainable Development Goals*, 58.

82. SDPIWG, *Sport for Development and Peace*.

83. LeCrom and Ferry, "The United States Government's Role in Sport Diplomacy," 24.

84. Dudfield and Dingwall-Smith, *Sport for Development and Peace and the 2030 Agenda for Sustainable Development*.

11

Discoveries from an Intimate View into Sport Programs as a Catalyst for Change

Soolmaz Abooali

OBJECTIVES

This chapter will:

- Discuss how sport can be used for development, change, and peacebuilding.
- Address the roles of the Designer and the Implementer in sport for development and peace programs.
- Describe the skills necessary to conduct effective sport for development and peace programs.
- Leverage the role of observation in the analysis of sport for development and peace programs.
- Understand the importance of communication between Implementers and Designers for effective sport for development and peace programs.

Those of us who have experienced sport on some level can attest to the power of sport. We see this manifest in the examples of the athlete turned coach, announcer, or commentator; in the sport-minded parents who harbor hopes for their children to become the next star athlete; and in the individuals who express a sense of awe and accomplishment when meeting an active or former athlete. The unique effect of sport is also evident in the athlete or sportsperson who passionately believes that experiences gained through sport have a sort of magical and powerful ability to develop responsible, conscientious individuals of tomorrow who are not only capable of overcoming conflict but are also able to forge positive change in society.

Recognizing the vast potential of sport, nongovernmental organizations (NGOs) have formed a plethora of sport for change (SfC) programs in the United States and abroad over the past two decades.[1] These programs claim that micro-level changes that result from engaging in sport (i.e., individual level) will lead to macro-level changes.[2] For example, current research on sport-based programs indicate a significant focus on addressing social and structural conflict through cultivating individual outcomes, from cognitive and social life skills[3] and general life skills[4] to positive youth development outcomes in personal, social, and physical domains.[5]

While some prefer to identify such programs as SfC initiatives, these programs are more commonly known as sport for development and peace (SDP) initiatives. In the original study that is the basis for this chapter, the more broad-based term of *SfC* was used; however, for this discussion the more explicit SDP terminology has been infused. Scholars interested in the sport-based approaches to creating positive change discussed in this chapter sometimes have labeled such claims as unproven and overly ambitious.[6] To better understand what transpires at SDP programs, I[7] conducted an in-depth study using a different approach from the more commonly used monitoring and evaluation lens that examines the accuracy of SDP claims. Instead, this study sought to better understand why, despite the critiques, such micro- to macro-level claims continue to be made by SDP actors, identified as those who design (Designers) and those who implement programs in real-time (Implementers). Through an iterative, multilayered methodology, the researchers used interviews-observations-interviews with Designers and Implementers at NGOs in underserved communities in the United States. The study discovered pointed insights into how sport is believed, as well as utilized, to address conflict and foster positive change. Among other findings, the research unearthed the logical underpinnings or pathways of change (also referred to as *theory of change*) used in SDP programs, thereby addressing scholars' call for increased theoretical understanding in the SDP field.[8]

The study also adopted a conflict resolution lens, as opposed to the more widely used sociological lens, to explore "the assumptions which not only drive people and their world, but also into the assumptions surrounding the root causes of conflict as perceived by those affected."[9] This approach ultimately enables SDP actors to "enhance program design and evaluation by focusing on a more preliminary yet foundational level: pathways of change, assumptions, and underlying elements of sport and conflict, separately and collectively."[10] Using such knowledge, SDP programs can continue to be evaluated for their claims, although with the benefit of having more informed data.

The following sections of this chapter share a select set of findings from the study, gained through an intimate vantage point into comparing what is believed to happen and what actually transpires in SDP programs.

ASSUMPTIONS AND CONCEPTUALIZATIONS OF SPORT AND CONFLICT

Interviews with Designers and Implementers revealed that sport is primarily defined in terms of what it can do, as opposed to what it is. Specifically, sport was identified

Figure 11.1. Celebrating new friendships among basketball players from the Democratic Republic of the Congo and the United States. *Credit*: Center for Sport Management at George Mason University

as having the ability to: (1) connect people; (2) include competition; (3) develop identity; (4) attract people; (5) involve teaching; and (6) act as a space where social-emotional skills and life skills can be exercised.[11] Such abilities align with those that SDP actors reported experiencing during their time as athletes, which became an influential part of their personal development (e.g., trust, communication, relationship-building, community-building) and career choices. Given that sport acted as a positive and empowering theme in SDP actors' lives, albeit in slightly different ways, the experiences it lent them as individuals became the dominant lens through which the world—including its conflicts and its resolutions—was viewed.

Through exploring what sport means to SDP actors, three key assumptions emerged. The first is that SDP actors believe that what sport can do—the aforementioned six elements—is replicable for others who engage in sport. The second assumption is that the physicality of sport is believed to be the fundamental piece that allows for freedom of expression through which individuals are able to *exercise agency*—one's capacity to control his or her own choices despite any existing conflict. These two assumptions connect to a third, which is that the abilities of sport can indeed be used by individuals to address conflict and create positive change. In other words, individuals have the power to be agents of change in society.

The focus on the individual level emerged as a factor that linked to SDP actors' conceptualization of conflict. Indeed, interviewees could not discuss their SDP programs without discussing conflict in one way or another. Both Designers and Implementers included in the study perceived conflict in three ways:

1. As an internal phenomenon within and between individuals that can manifest as a form of harm (lack of belief in self)
2. As an opportunity for individual growth
3. As a structural phenomenon that translates as a lack of access to resources and opportunities and which prevents the fulfillment of basic human needs

A fourth conceptualization of conflict emerged through a discussion with an Implementer, who defined conflict as a lack of motivation to create change beyond the level of self, such as socioeconomic change. Although there was a recognition of structural factors, conflict was once again predominantly understood as a phenomenon that circles back to the individual.

The strong focus on the individual level from SDP actors was logical and expected. Those in this study shared that they experienced positive change through sport, specifically by gaining self-confidence, the sense of belonging and safety, and connecting with others. The absence of these fundamental basic human needs had come to represent, for some SDP actors, the root causes of conflict. For example, even with the recognition that lack of access to resources and opportunities is created by structural violence (poverty, unequal distribution of resources), SDP actors continued to perceive such a lack of access in terms of prevention of human needs—needs that for them were fulfilled through the vehicle of sport and that enabled them to thrive in other areas of life despite any obstacles. Accordingly, SDP programs focus heavily on individuals' development through satisfying basic human needs so as to help its participants overcome conflict.

In this sense, many SDP actors have subconsciously adopted a Burtonian[12] lens to conflict, where basic human needs such as identity, recognition, security, and personal development cannot be negotiated away in the process of resolution. They are, as conflict scholar John Burton argues, primordial, and their fulfillment is necessary in order to prevent or resolve conflict.[13] This finding provides a counterargument to sociologist Fred Coalter's critique that "micro-level effects are, wrongly, generalized to the macro-level";[14] the critique is misplaced because it discredits SDP actors' experiences and resulting perceptions at the micro-level (of what sport has done for them) in relation to how they perceive conflict at the macro-level (as fulfilling basic human needs that have enabled them to successfully gain access to resources and opportunities). This study's exploration into how and why SDP actors and programs use sport to address conflict helps to highlight that scholars and practitioners are essentially having two related, yet different, conversations. SDP actors' assumptions are based on their personal experiences that define what conflict is; they do not conceptualize, nor do they operate purely from how macro-level conflict is understood in scholarship.

More so to this point, a closer examination of SDP curricula shows that they are predominantly grounded in scholarship from clinical and education psychology, childhood development, and organizational leadership. The vast majority of curricula included in this study used limited or random resources on macro-level conflict, conflict resolution, and peace concepts and frameworks.

WHAT TRANSPIRES IN SPORT FOR DEVELOPMENT AND PEACE PROGRAMS

SDP programs are designed to address conflict and create positive change primarily by improving access to services and opportunities in addition to offering sport and nonsport components such as mental health services, academic support, and mentoring opportunities. A popular strategy used in these programs is to translate nonsport concepts into sport-based activities where the goal is to help participants learn, reinforce, and apply certain skills that enable them to overcome conflict. Toward this aim, my findings revealed that SDP programs seek to achieve three specific goals:

1. Create safe spaces that foster a sense of openness.
2. Fulfill basic human needs (to feel safe, to connect, to belong).
3. Encourage individuals to reimagine their existing ideas of what is possible.[15]

In other words, SDP programs strive to create spaces where participants can feel open, safe, and connected in mind and in spirit so that they are able to experience the possibility of a different reality (and future). So how exactly is this believed to happen? The concept of *shifts in perception* is significant to the answer.

The Concept of Shifts

The concept of encouraging shifts in perception emerged as a key element in what SDP programs seek to accomplish in their work. First, shifts are understood as reimagining existing ways of thinking, feeling, and being—the expansion of boundaries that dictate what is possible. Such reimagination is dependent on the development of skills and abilities that are believed to promote positive changes within individuals (an awareness of self) and between individuals (relationship building). They are:

- Communication (listening)
- Awareness of others
- Identifying and processing emotions
- Taking ownership of what transpires in one's immediate environment

- Embracing the challenges of conflict
- Focusing on lifelong learning[16]

Cultivating skills that prioritize learning of self and others in various kinds of situations—such as in emotionally tense situations—is further believed to enable individuals to create change at other levels of society as agents of change.

Secondly, through an examination of SDP curricula as well as observations incorporated into the methodology of the study, shifts are believed to transpire at two loci of change:

1. Spaces between existing reality and reimagined reality
2. Spaces within frozen reality[17]

For the first approach, the idea is that somewhere between one's existing reality and the moment when they reimagine a new reality, a positive shift will occur. Throughout the sport and nonsport components of a program, SDP actors teach and reinforce preset desired outcomes to their participants so as to facilitate shifts. The second approach, spaces within frozen reality, relies heavily (and solely in some cases) on simulated play activities (paired with dialogue sessions) that mimic challenges, and where participants must embrace the conflict at hand to complete the activities. In this approach, other kinds of nonsport components such as mentoring or academic services are not included in the program to teach and reinforce preset lessons or outcomes; instead, the activities and dialogue sessions are almost purely driven by the participants themselves while Implementers follow suit and facilitate.

The latter finding, spaces within frozen reality, served to provide deeper insights into what actually happens through the use of sport. The process involves *freezing* the challenges that contribute to a particular conflict using sport and play activities. Participants explore different ways to resolve the challenge as a way to tap into what is believed to be their innate capacity to address conflict. The freezing concept is akin to social psychologist Kurt Lewin's three-step interpretation of the process of change in individuals.[18] Lewin argues that the first step involves *unfreezing*, or developing an openness toward something different than the existing condition.[19] Employing strategies that increase motivation is one example of helping to create openness—in SDP curricula, sport is the vehicle that creates a sense of motivation and openness within individuals to share and explore experiences (as specified by SDP actors). Once openness is realized, action is required to generate movement to a new level, or *change*. Action, in this case, can be translated as the physicality and live action of sport, identified by SDP actors as a fundamental piece that allows for freedom of expression through which individuals are able to exercise agency. The third and final step in the process of creating change in individuals is *refreezing*, which involves establishing actions or processes that support a new level of behavior. New processes or standards are developed at this stage to ensure that new behaviors stick.[20]

The power of sport in this respect, and as found through observations undertaken in the study, lies in its ability to act as a culture-creating vehicle that establishes new ways and norms of being that are different from those of one's existing reality. This finding helps to frame sport as having the ability to create a *third culture*, a concept described by communication scholar Benjamin Broome.[21] Third culture "can only develop through interaction in which participants are willing to open themselves to new meanings, to engage in genuine dialogue, and to constantly respond to the new demands emanating from the situation."[22] Third culture is further believed to foster relational empathy, an ability that is "essential for successful conflict resolution"[23] and which aligns with SDP goals to strengthen one's relationship-building skills.

Regardless of which of the two approaches (spaces between existing reality and reimagined reality or spaces within frozen reality) are used to foster change, SDP curricula use sport (and play) as the vehicle to address conflict as perceived by SDP actors. This includes conflict as (1) an internal phenomenon (emotions and thoughts); (2) an opportunity for growth (awareness of self and others); (3) a form of harm (toward self and others); and (4) a lack of access to services and opportunities (academic support, mental health services, professional development). Indeed, the pathway of change in SDP programs is premised on the assumption that individuals, having the necessary abilities, skills, and innate agency, are the nucleus of change.

THE ART OF IMPLEMENTERS: RELYING ON WHAT IMPLEMENTERS KNOW AND DO

To facilitate a pathway of change that starts with individuals themselves, Designers rely heavily on Implementers; Implementers are those who work directly with program participants to use sport as an effective process-inducing vehicle (i.e., the process of facilitating shifts). Efforts are made to ensure communication between Designers and Implementers, which takes place in two primary ways. First, trainings and workshops are offered to inform Implementers about relevant knowledge with which they can effectively teach, connect with kids, and reflect on their behaviors in the process. Second, communication between Designers and Implementers is encouraged through feedback systems (face-to-face, phone, virtual meetings) that enable information sharing about curricula and how it relates to target audiences.

What Implementers know—and its perceived value—was found to be a critical piece to ensuring the effectiveness of SDP programs. By virtue of working directly with participants, Designers believed that Implementers gained knowledge from the context and specific needs (cultural awareness) of the communities in which curricula are applied. Such knowledge is generally collected to ensure that SDP curricula is context specific and flexible enough to be adjusted based on specific and changing needs of communities. Given Implementers' insights, they have agency to co-design and apply curricula as they believe necessary to effectively meet the needs of program participants.

Designers also believed that Implementers' firsthand, contextual knowledge gave them the ability to recognize teachable moments where participants were more receptive to listen to lessons being taught. Creating a supportive environment based on inclusion, tolerance, and respect are elements that Designers believed would help Implementers to leverage teachable moments, thereby increasing opportunities that foster connections with kids in meaningful ways—connections that promote individual and relational skills necessary for overcoming conflict and creating change beyond the self (macro-level).

FROM THE GROUND UP: THE SIGNIFICANCE OF EXPLORING PRACTICE

While interviews and theoretical assessments have their own value, there is no replacement for observing what actually transpires on the ground in SDP programs and learning directly from those engaged in practice—those who implement programs. Observations of and postobservation interviews with Implementers helped to unearth what they do, what they know, and how they teach what they know. Moreover, observations provided specifics that Designers did not articulate such as what composes safe spaces and shifts in perception of self and others, how to make explicit the connections between sport and nonsport contexts for participants (i.e., transferring lessons learned through sport into other areas of life), and what exactly teachable moments entail. Additionally, Implementers helped to reveal a fourth conceptualization of conflict as the lack of motivation to create change beyond the individual level (i.e., socioeconomic). The art of Implementers is therefore a significant piece of understanding what transpires in SDP programs.

More specifically, observations revealed that Implementers created safe spaces that

- were comfortable for participants
- fostered openness, familiarity, and trust
- satisfied a sense of belonging[24]

To do so, they cultivated an atmosphere that emphasized belonging (family) as well as participants' physical comfort in the space. Designers expressed that shifts in perception of self and others transpired through encouraging individuals to reimagine new ways of being, thinking, and feeling. In application, however, this concept was much more explicit through observing the interactions between Implementers and participants. Shifts, therefore, take place in three specific ways in SDP programs:

1. Helping individuals to exercise agency over their perception-making abilities
2. Creating a new culture among other cultures using sport as the common language

3. Manipulating or activating biological senses (feeling, touching, hearing, seeing) through play activities that are designed to simulate challenges of conflict[25]

The element of physicality and live action enabled through sport and play activities were further observed and identified by Implementers as key to these processes because they tap into another layer of learning beyond what the mind can grasp. As a specific example, biological senses such as sight were manipulated by Implementers so as to facilitate a process that enables participants to feel through conflict and its challenges at a more intimate (physical) level of understanding. Implementers then facilitated discussion sessions where they asked open-ended, probing questions that encouraged participants to reflect on potential connections between learning derived from their physical experiences and conditions in sport with their learning derived from the mind.

Indeed, a strong correlation exists between the body and the mind.[26] For example, the individuals who live in poverty and starvation, who are victims of domestic violence, or have been physically harassed and discriminated against seemed to understand structural violence on a different level than those who read about such situations. Experiences gained through somatic means (one's biological senses) are profoundly influential to informing individuals' worldviews and their responses to conflict; the more the senses are engaged, the greater is the influence on learning and memory. Along with learning invoked at the cognitive level, somatically induced experiences are what constitute an individual's complete reality.

However, this study found that it was not simply about making connections between the lessons gained through sport and nonsport components to be explicit, as Designers had expressed, but rather about connecting participants' behaviors (physical expressions) to their thinking (perceptions), ideally immediately after somatic experiences to leverage the ripeness of learning from the body and translating it to learning at the cognitive level (and vice versa). Observations revealed that to do so, Implementers exercised several important abilities:

- Being a clear communicator
- Multitasking and thinking quickly
- Managing silent moments as opportunities to invoke reflection
- Alternating between the role of an Implementer and participant[27]

Such abilities helped Implementers to recognize and leverage teachable moments, which they defined more explicitly than Designers as watching participants' reactions for moments or incidences of (1) silence; (2) level of physical engagement; (3) sharing of personal information; (4) development of new relationships; and (5) exercising control or lack thereof over emotions and environment.

These reactions are believed to serve as indicators for openings through which participants can explore (or be taught) skills and new ideas that alter their existing realities of what is possible—essentially shifts in perceptions. Berenike Carstarphen[28] identifies that shifts can be understood through indicators at different levels of analysis such as affective, cognitive, nonverbal, and verbal. Carstarphen argues that the more sudden and dramatic the indicators (or reactions), the more likely the indicator and shift can be observed.[29] Herein lies the uniqueness of sport because through its physicality and live action, a range of indicators take place rapidly and suddenly, suggesting a higher chance that shifts can be identified and facilitated by Implementers.

Figure 11.2 illustrates an overall representation of findings from the study, where the light-colored shapes highlight key concepts offered by Designers about how and why sport was used to address conflict and create positive change. The dark-colored shapes, on the other hand, highlight the areas in which Implementers were able to operationalize key concepts.

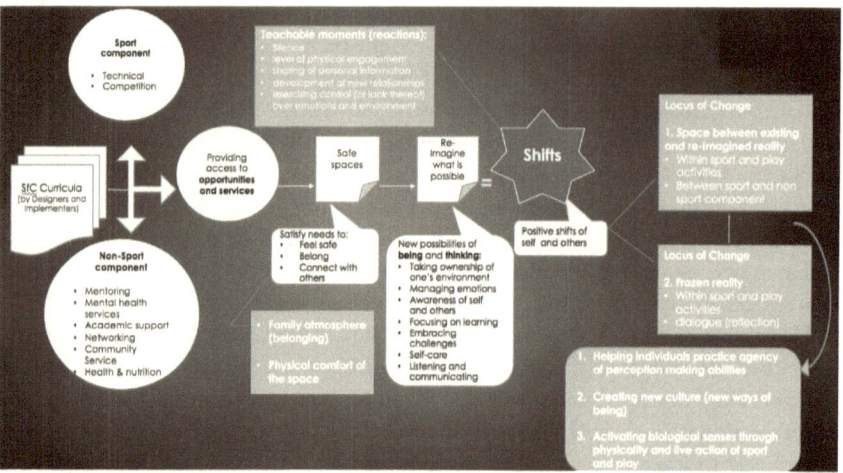

Figure 11.2. Representation of Designers' and Implementers' key areas of knowledge about how and why sport is used to address conflict and create positive change.

WHAT'S IN A DISCUSSION? CONNECTING BEHAVIOR AND PERCEPTION

Designers and Implementers expressed a heavy emphasis on discussion sessions that were constructed to make explicit the connection between lessons learned in sport to life contexts. Toward this aim, Implementers posed questions that encouraged participants to explore meanings behind the lessons and skills taught (e.g., to celebrate, to not give up), to discover solutions to challenges that allow conflict to ensue, and to encourage participants to feel open enough to share sensitive information about the conflicts they faced. In their framing of questions, Implementers emphasized participants' learning derived from physical expressions (behavior) in sport and play with learning derived from the mind (perception).

Making the behavior-perception connections explicit is an important feature in conflict-based frameworks, such as in Johan Galtung's ABC Triangle. This framework depicts that "[t]he formation of a situation of goal incompatibility (a conflict situation) gives rise to adversaries' conflict behavior in order to achieve their (apparently incompatible) goals, plus a related set of perceptions and attitudes about themselves, the Other(s) and 'third' parties affected or affecting the relationship of conflict."[30] Additionally, John Mezirow[31] discussed shifts as *frames of reference*[30] that are "structures of assumptions through which we understand our experiences. They selectively shape and delimit expectations, perception, cognition, and feelings. They set our 'line of action.'"[32] To this concept, Richard Kiely's[33] work added that in dialogue and situations where individuals are confronted with perspectives or experiences that do not match their frame of reference, they experience a cognitive dissonance. The locus of change happens at the level of intensity of the dissonance. For example, low-intensity encounters can be more easily integrated into existing frames of reference, while high-intensity encounters, which often involve emotional reactions, lead to transformational change at the level of questioning and reflecting on assumptions because they differ so intensely with existing frames of reference.

With respect to SDP programs, findings from this study demonstrated that sport can be used to simulate elements of conflict in sport and play-based activities. This approach enables individuals to explore their perceptions and behaviors and then later discuss what took place within the conflict-related context. More specifically, including dialogue before, during, or after sport and play activities leverages immediate experiences gained at the somatic level and connects them to learning at the mind level. The timeliness of making such connections adds another element to the level of intensity in any cognitive dissonance experienced by participants during sport. Additionally, given that the physicality and live action of sport elicits a range of reactions across affective, cognitive, nonverbal, and verbal levels, there is greater chance for high-intensity encounters that create cognitive dissonance. Through skilled Implementers who facilitate the process, such cognitive dissonance can lead to participants engaging in questioning and reflecting on assumptions of existing frames of reference or existing realities. In this sense, sport can act as an effective vehicle that fosters shifts in perception and transforms individuals' behavior.

Interventions focused on the mind-body package through sport can enable interveners to help individuals become more mindful of aligning their perceptions and behaviors toward positive change (of self and with others), thereby increasing the chance that what one thinks and does matches. Herein lies the power of sport—in its perceived ability to merge disconnects between the mind (perceptions) and body (behaviors) so as to engage the whole person and the whole reality of individuals in the aim to move toward positive change. Essentially, this is the logic through which SDP programs seek to create agents of change who are capable of going from micro- to macro-level change.

THEORY OF CHANGE IN SDP PROGRAMS

Two over-arching categories emerged from this study as capturing the central processes or drivers by which change, such as a shift in perception, is believed to come about for individuals in relation to fostering micro-level change:

1. Teaching skills that are believed to enable individuals to lead and support social and structural policies that create equitable access to resources and opportunities
2. Helping individuals tap into their innate capacity to work within social and structural systems so as to create equitable access to resources and opportunities[34]

Whether the primary strategy is to teach specific skills or to enable individuals to tap into their innate capacity to resolve conflict, at the core of SDP programs lies the theory that if sport is used as a vehicle to foster positive changes within and among individuals, then the groundwork for supporting positive change at social and structural levels has been established. Such an approach connects with the conflict and peace theory "Inside-Out Peacebuilding," which states that when individuals (or enough individuals) experience inner transformation, "they can influence societal patterns, identity groups, institutional performance, and other key actors toward constructive conflict engagement."[35] Specifically, the theory of change of this theory is that

> if key actors and/or enough individuals undergo constructive shifts in their consciousness, such as developing more universal identities or awareness of identity formation, then their commitment and capacity for the peaceful resolution of conflicts, and for resisting mobilization of conflictual identities, will increase and can influence social change in that area.[36]

More pointedly, the concept of shifts in perception or *shifts in consciousness* emerged as a key component in SDP programs and fell within the Inside-Out Peacebuilding theory. Shifts in consciousness argues that transformations in individuals' consciousness through reflection, cognitive dissonance, and other experiences can lead them to develop new ways of thinking about ways to cultivate peace; the premise is also that large quantities of transformed individuals will lead to social change.[37]

Given the connection of these theories to SDP programs' assumptions, efforts, and goals, exploring indicators of this conflict theory would help SDP actors to dissect how "internal awareness of biases, attitudes, motivations" may lead to "agency (behavior), feelings of empowerment, awareness of choices, commitment, ability to engage constructively, respect, [and] choices."[38] Such an exploration would not only inform SDP actors and thereby their curricula about ways they can capture positive change with respect to addressing conflict, but it can also foster reflective practices at the level of assumptions among Designers and Implementers. Additionally, the process of developing indicators provides a specific framework that can encourage

SDP actors to better articulate what change means at the level of assumptions, how change happens, and at what levels change takes place.

LOOKING TO THE FUTURE

Through the approach of exploring theory of change, the assumptions and conceptualizations of sport, conflict, and change, the hope is that SDP actors will find use for and be encouraged to incorporate such knowledge into how they design, apply, research, and assess existing and future SDP interventions. As a start, opportunities between scholars and practitioners in the SDP field should be created to discuss and reach consensus on what terms such as *conflict* and *change* entail so that future claims and critiques are made using baseline understandings grounded in a clarity of assumptions. Such discussions should include the personal experiences of SDP actors who design and apply curricula, given that findings in this study demonstrated a strong connection between personal experiences with how and what sport is believed to do.

Workshop and training opportunities for SDP actors should be created to expand the SDP field's currently limited (and often randomly selected) pool of conflict and peace theories, concepts, and frameworks. This work can inform and enhance SDP curricula in not only the kinds of skills taught (i.e., conflict resolution skills), but in how they relate to specific structural factors, which are relevant to the broader context of the communities in which programs operate.

It is also important to explore conflict and peace theories that emphasize the concept of paradigm shifts, particularly in relation to key indicators. This approach will help SDP actors to better articulate causal pathways of change and to identify and tangibly capture kinds of change that transpire as well as how each kind of change relates to another. Such an approach can help SDP actors to develop theories of change in a comprehensive, theoretically grounded manner that can enhance (and focus) monitoring and evaluation efforts that assess the accuracy of program claims.

Future research should explore the somatic element to better understand the ways in which conflict intervention efforts can incorporate a mind-body approach. Methods examining the role of physicality, live action, and manipulation of biological senses to foster shifts in perceptions within and among individuals are essential, particularly as they relate to altering one's existing realities (ways of being, thinking, feeling).

Sport does indeed have power. Often, this power feels and looks like magic that emanates across different areas of an individual's life. Sport is an embodied experience that engages the mind-body of each individual who plays, where each individual has a similar yet unique set of experiences. Until researchers and practitioners begin to explore sport at the most basic level of assumptions (of self, others, and one's environment) with those who design and conduct sport-based programs, our understanding of what actually transpires and how effective sport can be will remain at odds, as will our discussions on SDP.

Questions

1. What are some of the drivers of change in SDP programs?
2. Why is communication important in the implementation and planning process of effective SDP programs?
3. What are some valuable skills when SDP managers are looking for effective Implementers for their programs?
4. After reading this chapter, how would you define "sport" as it applies to SDP programs?

Case Study

You are the program manager of an NGO and have been approached by an angel donor who cares deeply about the high crime rates in an underserved community in Washington, DC. The donor would like you to create a long-term program that provides engaging options for young kids (eight to twelve years old) to deter them from becoming involved in violent activities, particularly as they enter adolescence. As a lifelong athlete, you have experienced many personal benefits through sport and believe that it can be the appropriate vehicle for creating the engaging and effective program required by the donor.

Among your objectives to offer competitive and recreational sport opportunities as well as academic mentorship that provide alternate life paths, a key objective of your program is to develop the youth's self-confidence. By providing a multipronged yet largely sport-based opportunity where none currently exists, you hope to foster positive change in the community—starting with empowering one child at a time.

As you create your organization's curriculum using the information learned throughout this chapter, consider the following questions:

- Why are you using sport in the first place? Which sport and how?
- What kind of components will your curriculum include (i.e., sport and non-sport components)?
- What are specific objectives you will aim to achieve to change or shift the youth's perceptions? What will a change in perception entail (of whom, of what, etc.)?
- What is the logic (scholarly and personal) that grounds your thinking about how and why your sport-based program will foster an increase in self-confidence?
- What, if any, assumptions are you, as the program manager, making as you create the curriculum?
- What skills are essential for coaches (those who will implement the curriculum) to demonstrate?

Strategies for Success

1. The importance of communication cannot be overemphasized.
2. Managers of SDP programs should be looking for specific skills when hiring Implementers for their programs.

3. Training is important for SDP program actors.
4. SDP programs should utilize conflict resolution concepts in the design and the implementation in order to be effective.

NOTES

1. Roger Levermore, "Sport: A New Engine of Development?" *Progress in Development Studies* 8, no. 2 (2008): 183–90; Meredith Whitley, Kelly Farrell, Eli Wolff, and Sarah J. Hillyer, "Sport for Development and Peace: Surveying Actors in the Field," *Journal of Sport for Development* 7, no. 12 (2019): 1–15.

2. Jay Coakley, "Youth Sports: What Counts as 'Positive Development'?" *Journal of Sport and Social Issues* 35, no. 3 (2011): 306–24; Fred Coalter, *Sport for Development: What Game Are We Playing?* (New York: Routledge, 2013).

3. Niels Hermens, Sabina Super, Kirsten Verkooijen, and Maria Koelen, "A Systematic Review of Life Skill Development through Sports Programs Serving Socially Vulnerable Youth," *Research Quarterly for Exercise and Sport* 88, no. 4 (2017): 408–24.

4. Laurenz Langer, "Sport for Development: A Systematic Map of Evidence from Africa," *South African Review of Sociology* 46, no. 1 (2015): 66–86; Simon C. Darnell, "Power, Politics and 'Sport for Development and Peace': Investigating the Utility of Sport for International Development," *Sociology of Sport Journal* 27, no. 1 (2010): 54–75; Tess Kay and Steven Bradbury, "Youth Sport Volunteering: Developing Social Capital?" *Sport, Education and Society* 14, no. 1 (2009): 121–40.

5. Nicholas Holt, Colin Deal, and Christine Smyth, "Future Directions for Positive Youth Development through Sport," in *Positive Youth Development through Sport*, 2nd ed., Nicholas L. Holt (Abingdon, UK: Routledge, 2016), 231–40.

6. Fred Coalter, "The Politics of Sport for-Development: Limited Focus Programmes and Broad Gauge Problems?" *International Review for the Sociology of Sport* 45, no. 3 (2010): 295–314; William Massey, Meredith Whitley, Lindsey Blom, and Lawrence Gerstein, "Sport for Development and Peace: A Systems Theory Perspective on Promoting Sustainable Change," *International Journal of Sport Management and Marketing* 16, nos. 1–2 (2015): 18–35.

7. Soolmaz Abooali, "Sport for Change: An Exploration into Theory and Practice" (PhD diss., George Mason University, 2019).

8. Abooli, "Sport for Change"; Whitley et al., "Sport for Development and Peace"; Coalter, *Sport for Development*.

9. Abooali, "Sport for Change," 14.

10. Abooali, "Sport for Change," 94.

11. Abooali, "Sport for Change."

12. John Burton, *Conflict: Basic Human Needs* (New York: St. Martin's Press, 1990). Conflict scholar John Burton argued that universal needs of human beings must be fulfilled to prevent or resolve conflicts. These are needs for consistency of response, stimulation, security, recognition, justice, rationality, and control. Burton identified that the most salient need to understand a social conflict is identity, recognition, security, and personal development, none of which could be negotiated away.

13. Burton, *Conflict*.

14. Coalter, "The Politics of Sport for Development," 205.

15. Abooali, "Sport for Change."

16. Abooali, "Sport for Change."
17. Abooali, "Sport for Change."
18. Kurt Lewin, "Group Decision and Social Change," in *Readings in Social Psychology*, ed. Eleanor Maccoby, Theodore Newcomb, and Eugene Hartley (New York: Holt, Reinhart and Winston, 1974), 197–211.
19. Lewin, "Group Decision and Social Change."
20. Eric Marcus, "Change and Conflict: Motivation, Resistance, and Commitment," in *The Handbook of Conflict Resolution: Theory and Practice*, ed. Morton Deutsch, Peter T. Coleman, and Eric C. Marcus (San Francisco, CA: Jossey-Bass, 2006), 440.
21. Benjamin Broome, "Building Shared Meaning: Implications of a Relational Approach to Empathy for Teaching Intercultural Communication," *Communication Education* 40, no. 3 (1991): 235–49.
22. Benjamin J. Broome, "Managing Differences in Conflict Resolution: The Role of Relational Empathy," in *Conflict Resolution Theory and Practice: Integration and Application*, ed. Dennis J. D. Sandole and Hugo van der Merwe (Manchester, UK: Manchester University Press, 1993), 97–111.
23. Broome, "Managing Differences in Conflict Resolution," 104.
24. Abooali, "Sport for Change."
25. Abooali, "Sport for Change."
26. Michael Soth, "What Therapeutic Hope for a Subjective Mind in an Objectified Body?" *Body, Movement and Dance in Psychotherapy* 1, no. 1 (2006): 43–56; Catherine Athanasiadou and Andrea Halewood, "A Grounded Theory Exploration of Therapists' Experiences of Somatic Phenomena in the Countertransference," *European Journal of Psychotherapy and Counselling* 13, no. 3 (2011): 247–62.
27. Abooali, "Sport for Change."
28. Berenike Carstarphen, "Shift Happens: Transformations during Small Group Interventions in Protracted Social Conflicts" (PhD diss., George Mason University, 2003).
29. Carstarphen, "Shift Happens."
30. Christopher Mitchell, "Conflict, Social Change and Conflict Resolution," accessed March 1, 2019, https://www.berghoffoundation.org/fileadmin/redaktion/Publications/Handbook/Dialogue_Chapters/dialogue5_mitchell_lead-1.pdf, page 5.
31. John Mezirow, "Transformative Learning: Theory to Practice," *New Directions for Adult and Continuing Education* 74 (1997): 5–12.
32. Mezirow, "Transformative Learning," 5.
33. Richard Kiely, "A Transformative Learning Model for Service-Learning: A Longitudinal Case Study," *Michigan Journal of Community Service Learning* 12 (Fall 2005): 5–22.
34. Abooali, "Sport for Change."
35. Susan Allen Nan, "Theories of Change and Indicator Development in Conflict Management and Mitigation," accessed February 10, 2019, http://pdf.usaid.gov/pdf_docs/PNADS460.pdf, page 15.
36. Nan, "Theories of Change and Indicator Development in Conflict Management and Mitigation," 72.
37. Susan Allen Nan, "Consciousness in Culture-Based Conflict and Conflict Resolution," *Conflict Resolution Quarterly* 28, no. 3 (2011): 239–62.
38. Nan, "Theories of Change and Indicator Development in Conflict Management and Mitigation," 3.

12

For-profit Involvement in Sport for Development and Peace

Craig Esherick

OBJECTIVES

This chapter will:

- Assess the direct and indirect activity of the for-profit sector in efforts to use sport for development and community engagement and to bring groups closer together.
- Analyze how for-profit organizations collaborate with sport development nongovernmental organizations.
- Discuss the for-profit organizations that work in the sport for development and sport for development and peace space.

In the world of sport for development and peace (SDP), the landscape has been dominated by nongovernmental organizations that operate on a not-for-profit model. In chapter 13, Jon Welty Peachey and Nico Schulenkorf note that there are a thousand organizations engaged in some aspect of SDP work around the globe. Organizations such as Girls Empowerment through Sport, Street Soccer USA, and Kids Play International all rely on grants and donations to sustain their organizations. The aforementioned organizations operate on the nonprofit model, as do many others. There are some governmental (taxpayer financed) organizations that engage in sport for development (Ghana and the Sport for Development and Peace Secretariat), sport for community building (Argentina's Ente Nacional e Alto Rendimiento Deportivo) and sport diplomacy programs (United States and the Sports United division of the Department of State). Carrie LeCrom and Per Svensson covered this model (public and taxpayer financed) of SDP in chapter 10 and Stuart Murray and Shinae Haidley's discussion of sport diplomacy can be found in chapter 5. One other type of sport organization business is involved, both directly and indirectly, in the delivery of SDP programs. The role of *for-profit* businesses is underappreciated in this conversation. For-profit organizations represent a small percentage of businesses that manage programs directly, but the contributions of these businesses are substantial. Businesses that operate for profit and those businesses (the International Olympic Committee [IOC] and Federacion Internationale Futbol Association [FIFA], for example) that generate revenue from the for-profit sector through their ownership of valuable TV and marketing rights are major players in the sport for development arena. This chapter outlines the involvement of the for-profit sector and discusses how it fits within the sport for development and peace conversation.

THE FIRST TEE

The First Tee organization operates programs in all fifty of the US states and in six international locations. The organization was formed to educate young people, help them develop life skills, and, not coincidentally, increase the popularity of the sport of golf in targeted areas (locations and demographic groups) where golf has historically not been very popular.[1] Young people can find these "sport development" organizations at local golf courses, schools, and youth centers. The First Tee receives substantial support from many of the major golf organizations in the United States: the Professional Golf Association (PGA), the Masters (one of the four major annual professional golf tournaments for men), the United States Golf Association, the PGA Tour, and the Ladies Professional Golf Association.[2] Each of these *sport associations* earns substantial revenue from the sale of marketing and television rights to golf tournaments they own. They also generate revenue from the sale of golf-related merchandise.

The First Tee has been the beneficiary of a sizable amount of sponsorship support from golf businesses. *Golf Digest* (a magazine and website), the Calloway Company (a golf manufacturer), American Golf, Century Golf Partners, Tournament Players Clubs, CBS (PGA Tour broadcaster), NBC (owns the Golf Channel), PGA Tour Superstores (golf retail business), and Dick's Sporting Goods (golf-related equipment, shoes, and apparel) are all First Tee sponsors. An increase or a decrease in the number of golfers or golf fans influences the bottom line for all of these businesses in any given year. A contribution to First Tee for these organizations serves two purposes: they can trumpet their corporate social responsibility (CSR) and help to grow the game of golf. Nongolf businesses like Coca-Cola, AT&T, Chevron, Hertz, Exelon, Wells Fargo, and Altrea also have sponsorship agreements with First Tee.[3] First Tee teaches young people the rules of golf while developing their interest in the game and improving their golf skills. Golf is used as an enticement to also offer character development programs, life skills programs, and career guidance, all of which are clearly "sport for development" programs. Joe Louis Barrow, Jr., the son of the great boxer Joe Louis and the former CEO of The First Tee, was interviewed by the *New York*

Times and was asked to describe the impact of the organization. He acknowledged the organization's ability to grow the game, but he thought that the greatest impact of First Tee, by locating many of their centers in disadvantaged communities, was as a youth development organization.[4]

First Tee businesses provide economic development in all of the communities where they operate, including employment for their full-time and part-time employees. First Tee hires golf instructors at all of their locations, but there are many education professionals who work hand in hand with these sport instructors and coaches. They try to develop well-rounded young people who also learn to appreciate the sport of golf as program participants. The willing involvement of the many for-profit businesses has made this organization much more sustainable. Many scholars who have written about sport for development and peace note the issues that some nonprofits face with both fundraising and sustaining their activities for the long term.[5]

PLAY BALL

Play Ball is a sport development program created by USA Baseball, USA Softball, Major League Baseball (MLB), Little League, and Minor League Baseball (MiLB). Like the First Tee organization, Play Ball mixes a positive youth development program with a sport instruction curriculum to increase the interest in diamond sports for athletes and baseball fans. Partners in the funding and the offering of Play Ball are organizations such as Nathan's, Chevrolet, Scotts, and the Boys & Girls Clubs of America.[6] Several of the founding organizations (MLB and MiLB) earn substantial revenue from profit-making activities like the sale of television rights, marketing rights, baseball team–related merchandise, and tickets to professional baseball games. Little League, another Play Ball sponsor, operates a youth baseball organization, but they also have a lucrative television contract with ESPN for their August baseball championship (Little League World Series). The Play Ball umbrella has been used to set up many programs: RBI, Fun at Bat, Hit and Run, MLB Hit and Run, Pitch Smart, and MLB Youth Academies were all created to grow the game of baseball.[7] All of these *sport development* and *sport for development* programs receive substantial support from for-profit businesses.

The MLB Youth Academies are located in seven cities where MLB franchises are found: LA (Compton); Houston; Washington, DC; Cincinnati; Philadelphia; Kansas City, Missouri; and Dallas. Academies are set to open in New York (The Bronx); Chicago, and San Francisco.[8] An eleventh MLB Academy is located in the city of New Orleans, which does not have an MLB team but has had several different minor league franchises over the span of more than one hundred years, including the Pelicans, Baby Cakes, and Zephyrs. The MLB academies are an interesting combination of sport development and youth educational organizations funded primarily by MLB and many of their franchises. This investment in the local community also falls under the category of corporate social responsibility (CSR) programming (see chapter 7) by each of these for-profit businesses, but the hook for many who participate in MLB academy programming are the diamond sports of softball and baseball, as well as the prominence of a local MLB franchise. Each of the franchises wants to give back (CSR) while they grow the games of softball and baseball in their communities (sport development).

FEDERACION INTERNATIONALE FUTBOL ASSOCIATION

FIFA is the international soccer federation that owns the television and marketing rights to the Men's and Women's World Cup. These two events occur every four years and bring in substantial revenue for FIFA and their member organizations (national soccer federations). FIFA spends some of this windfall on programs to promote the game of soccer (sport development) in member nations, as well as on developing a soccer infrastructure where needed in selected economically underdeveloped locations. In a goal statement that can be found on their website, the organization says it is committed to growing the game to the point where more than 60 percent of the world's population participates as a player, fan, referee, or coach.[9] As a result, they are committed to spending $4 billion toward this effort.[10] FIFA Forward is the program that provides money for the training of coaches, the development of soccer officials, new soccer fields, support for youth leagues, and the funding of tournaments and other soccer competitions in member countries.[11] The national soccer federations that receive the FIFA funds can use the money for the purchase of uniforms, balls, and other equipment that is necessary to play and teach the game of soccer. The target organizations for FIFA Forward are youth soccer programs, beach soccer leagues, female soccer teams, and futsal programs.[12] The overarching themes for FIFA are to develop the skills of soccer-playing young people around the world; to increase the competency of the coaching; and to encourage more females to play, coach, and officiate the sport of soccer.[13] These "sport development" programs are made possible by the massive revenue produced from the marketing and televising of the Men's and Women's World Cup.

FIFA established the Foundation Community Program to operate like a typical SDP nonprofit; FIFA invites applications from well-established nonprofit organizations that use soccer for social change.[14] Typical programs address such social issues as health promotion, peacebuilding, youth leadership development, gender equality, and refugees.

Other FIFA-funded programs with SDP components are the Financial Assistance Program, the Goal Program, Guardians, Football for Schools and Recovery Programme, and Football for Hope.[15]

NATIONAL BASKETBALL ASSOCIATION

The National Basketball Association (NBA) is the premier professional men's basketball league in the world. The league has thirty franchises, including one franchise in Canada (Toronto), the 2020 NBA Champion Raptors. The NBA is truly a global league with offices worldwide. NBA games are televised or streamed over the internet on every continent except Antarctica, and the league is composed of basketball players from countries all over the world. The sport of basketball has become one of the most popular in the world, and the stars of the NBA have become household names to basketball fans everywhere. The league would like to make the sport even more popular (and profitable).

The NBA has instituted a global strategy to grow league revenue while also growing the game of basketball. One of the programs developed to grow the game began right after the beginning of a new millennium (2001). The first Basketball without Borders (BWB) program was held in Trieste, Italy, and the young basketball players invited to this first camp were from regions of the former Yugoslavia: Serbs, Croats, Macedonians, Bosnians, Montenegrins, and Slovenians participated.[16] Developing the sport of basketball was but one of the goals of this first BWB program. Vlade Divac, the Sacramento Kings general manager and the former Yugoslavian national team captain, suggested to the NBA office that a camp like this could help build community in a Balkan region torn apart by civil war (SDP). The NBA partnered with for-profit businesses like Benetton, Nike, blu (a mobile phone business), and Champion to support the inaugural BWB program.[17] FIBA (International Basketball Federation) and the United Nations provided support in the planning and organizing stages of the inaugural BWB program. Organizers chose ten players between the ages of twelve and fourteen from each of the regions of the former Yugoslavia. They participated in basketball clinics over a number of days and played games on teams composed of a mix of players from each of these regions. Former and current NBA players from the region, along with Divac, participated as coaches and clinicians. Basketball is unique in this sport for development opportunity because the players are so physically close to each other; Gordon Allport[18] developed the *contact theory* of peacebuilding, and it could be argued that the NBA put this method to good use in their first BWB program. The NBA was happy with the results and thus BWB as a sport development (and SDP) program was born.[19]

In concert with the BWB initiative, the NBA has established academies in India, China, Australia, and Senegal.[20] These academies are opportunities to grow the game like the academies managed and established by MLB and their franchises mentioned earlier in this chapter. There is a sport for development component to this investment; however, like their baseball counterparts (MLB academies), they combine programs that are clearly sport development. They provide a measure of economic development for the local area where they are situated. There is a heavy dose of basketball training at these academies, but the NBA is also looking to raise the level of basketball coaching, sport science, basketball officiating, and sport management skills of all locals who participate in these academy activities. The players who participate in the academies develop pathways to professional basketball leagues in Europe, Australia, and Asia. Some are interested in the NBA Developmental League (G League). Some academy players want to attend college in the United States and play Division I basketball, and the most talented of the academy players will be drafted by the NBA. Like the BWB initiative, the academies are a chance for all of the local participants to develop networks with NBA players, coaches, referees, and sport managers. This development of a network is a way for participants to acquire social capital and is part and parcel of all three of the NBA programs discussed in this chapter.

One of the academies in China has come under fire and was closed by the NBA in 2020. This has brought some pressure upon the NBA to examine not only the other academies operating in China but the business relationship with the Chinese government.[21]

The third leg of this sport (basketball) development stool is a new program centered on youth basketball: the Jr. NBA. This initiative combines development clinics and leagues all over the world with an annual international championship in Orlando, Florida, in August. Competition and the development of basketball skills are an important part of the Jr. NBA, but the program combines sport for development goals at each stage. An award ceremony is held at the site of the international championship and players are recognized for exhibiting valuable character traits like determination, respect, teamwork, and community building and leadership ability. Youth basketball players from all over the world interact with their peers and so do the coaches from all of the Jr. NBA teams.

REAL MADRID

An interesting SDP program sponsored by the iconic football club Real Madrid is a partnership with the Arlington Soccer Association and Arlington Public Schools in Arlington, Virginia. The program is, first and foremost, a soccer instructional and development program, but it falls very much in line with SDP programs managed by many nonprofit organizations around the world. The program delivers not only instruction in the sport but also a character-building series of components in an after-school setting. The program is aimed at a target population of young people who attend nine different public schools in Arlington. The program was developed by Real Madrid and their soccer coaches. It includes soccer drills and other components used to develop self-discipline and teamwork. Students are selected from a population of kids who receive 50 to 90 percent of their lunch subsidized; the administrators also look for kids who might need help with academics and those with behavioral or family-related issues.[22] Soccer is used as the hook to improve performance in the classroom and develop better citizens. Real Madrid Foundation has also developed a partnership with Kaptiva Sports; this partnership helps Real deliver soccer clinics in multiple cities in the United States. There is a business component to this program in that Real is able to widen their fan base across the United States, but this initiative has components of both sport development and sport for development in the planning and delivery of the soccer clinics.

Chapter 12 223

NIKE

Figure 12.1. Former Secretary of State John Kerry looks on as a young girl in Algiers scores a goal at a Nike facility. *Credit*: Sports Diplomacy Division, US Department of State

Nike is the largest sporting goods manufacturer in the world. The company was founded by Phil Knight in the early 1970s. In 2019, the company reported sales revenue of $39.1 billion and its market value was almost $160 billion.[23] Nike is active in the sport for development space all over the world. They have extended their reach by partnering with organizations that engage in sport for development work and they also make substantial contributions to programs that would be characterized as CSR initiatives (see chapter 7). Nike is active in Oregon, where their headquarters is located. The Nike School Innovation Fund is the organization that distributes these funds to schools in the state; they also have partnered with an organization that supports mentoring for young people.[24]

Some of the sport for development partners are organizations that have been active sport for development players for quite some time. Nike provides support for organizations like the Boys & Girls Clubs, Coaches across Continents, and Peace Players International.[25]

Peace Players originally worked as a sport for peace organization in locations like Belfast, Northern Ireland; Israel; Palestine; and Cyprus. These four locations were fraught with conflict and years of violence. The organization worked with Protestants and Catholics, Jews and Arabs, Greeks and Turks; basketball was used as the hook to develop better relationships between these groups from the grassroots up. The organization has recently developed leadership programs in underserved communities in the United States. Sport is the development tool in these programs too. The goals are to build community, use sport to create positive values, develop leaders in the community, and, lastly, improve the sports skills of the participants. This is *not* an elite athlete development organization.

Figure 12.2. Collaboration among key players supports effective implementation of SDP initiatives. *Credit*: Sports Diplomacy Division, US Department of State

Two organizations sponsored by Nike in Los Angeles are organized along similar sport for development purposes, but they also have a sport development agenda. Women Coach LA and the Mamba League (also supported by the late Kobe Bryant) want to create more female coaches and athletes. Nike also sponsors an organization in China called Mini Basketball. The company donates child-sized equipment to schools and supports physical education training for teachers.[26] The business objective is not only to enhance the interest in basketball in China but also to develop a greater appreciation for physical fitness at a young age.

ADIDAS

Adidas is a sporting goods company that manufactures apparel, footwear, and equipment. The company is based in Germany and was the brainchild of Adolph Dassler. Adidas has been in this business since the 1930s and it is the second largest company in the sporting-goods world, following Nike.

Adidas supports a large number of sport for development organizations around the world under the Adidas Fund umbrella. Run for Love (Japan and China), Right to Play (China), Open Sunday (Switzerland), Promo Jeune Basket (Congo), Score (South Africa), and Tiempo de Juego are just some of these organizations. One example of the organizations that Adidas supports is Moving the Goalposts, based in Kenya; the organization focuses on girls and women and uses the sport of soccer to develop life skills and leadership skills. The NGO provides sports administration, coaching education, and sports-based first aid training. They also manage soccer leagues, games, and tournaments. Adidas Brazil supports an organization based in Brazil called Gol de Litra. They run after-school programs that are sport based but also teach life skills and community building social values. In 2015, Adidas partnered with the Chinese Minister of Education to develop a soccer training program and a physical education program in Chinese schools, similar to the Nike program mentioned previously.[27] They also supported a national summer camp initiative.

SKATEISTAN

Skateistan is an award-winning sport for development organization that uses the sport of skateboarding to hook young people to participate in many of their programs. Skateistan was the brainchild of Oliver Percovich, an Australian skateboarder and researcher. The idea was hatched in, of all places, Kabul, Afghanistan. Percovich moved to Afghanistan and brought three skateboards. He developed a following of young people who were intrigued by this activity and Percovich gradually built a large following of young people who were fascinated by skateboarding. Percovich came up with the idea of developing educational programming around this activity. This led to the formation of an organization and a fundraising effort that continues to this day. He received early support from skateboarding equipment manufacturers who donated boards and other safety gear. Eventually, the organization expanded to Cambodia and South Africa. Percovich moved the headquarters of the organization to Germany; Skateistan now has more than fifty employees on three continents.[28]

Percovich has a cross-section of organizations providing funding for its programs and activities.[29] Many governments have donated to the program and the Afghanistan National Olympic Committee donated the land for the first Skateistan School and skateboard facility. A German company designed the building; the governments of Denmark and Finland provided funding.[30] Several foundations provided funding and Google is one of the for-profit businesses that supports Skateistan now. Skateistan has developed partnerships with some of the skateboarding companies, using the Skateistan name and logo to sell merchandise and produce revenue to supplement their other fundraising efforts.[31] This strategy is unusual for an SDP organization and is one that others might want to try to replicate to provide a more sustainable financial foundation.

THE INTERNATIONAL OLYMPIC COMMITTEE AND SPORT FOR HOPE

The IOC devised the Sport for Hope program to create educational, sport, and social development opportunities for underdeveloped communities in two member countries of the organization: Zambia and Haiti. The IOC, along with many partners, built training centers in Lusaka, Zambia, and Port au Prince, Haiti. The intent for these multisport facilities was to use them primarily for sport but also for other education-related, community-based projects.[32] The Samsung Corporation and Merifin Capital were two for-profit businesses that participated in this IOC managed program. International and national sport federations, the Inter-America Development Bank, the Confederation of Southern African National Olympic Committees, the United States Olympic Committee, UK Sports, and the Japanese Olympic Committee all contributed to one of these projects.[33] The major funding source for much of the support from the national and international sports organizations was the massive television and marketing rights that these organizations share in as members of the International Olympic Committee.[34] The IOC selected Zambia and Haiti for two reasons: their relative need for sports infrastructure help and the state of their national economies.[35]

The IOC set ambitious development goals for these two sports centers; they were to be used by the national sport federations as training sites for elite athletes.[36] These activities would help to promote community sport and provide physical fitness outlets for the greater population.[37] The centers would also be a place where local organizations could provide educational programs and social development programs and be a source of rental revenue for local organizations that were able to pay a fee to use the space for a variety of activities. The Lusaka facility offered programs on gender equality and health education. The managers of the facility in Haiti developed a sustainability project involving two objectives: the cultivation of a local garden that could provide food for the center and the planting of trees in the surrounding area of the athletic fields and indoor training facility.

The IOC plan for these two centers for hope was to have the local government and sports organizations eventually take ownership of these facilities. This plan has been criticized by commentators as just another example of wealthy countries and powerful sports organizations exploiting others for their own gain.[38] In effect, the argument is that this was a photo-op for the IOC, the Global North, the United States, and the United Nations. The investment made was not sustainable and there were accusations of corruption in the implementation of the construction projects.[39]

Questions

1. How do for-profit organizations collaborate with sport development NGOs?
2. Discuss specific examples of for-profit organizations that work in the sport for development and sport for development and peace space. Compare and contrast their approaches to making a sustainable impact.

Learning Activity

1. Select three for-profit organizations that support sport for development initiatives. Assess both the direct and indirect activities they use to support community engagement and bring groups closer together.

NOTES

1. "About," First Tee, accessed January 14, 2021, https://firsttee.org/about/.
2. "Partners," First Tee, accessed January 14, 2021, https://firsttee.org/partners/.
3. "Partners."
4. Gary Santaniello, "A Lasting Influence in Golf Descends from a Boxing Legend," *New York Times*, September 29, 2017, https://www.nytimes.com/2017/09/29/sports/golf/joe-barrow-first-tee.html.
5. Fred Coalter, *Sport for Development: What Game Are We Playing?* (New York: Routledge, 2013); Per G. Svensson and Marion E. Hambrick, "'Pick and Choose Our Battles': Understanding Organizational Capacity in a Sport for Development and Peace Organization," *Sport Management Review* 19, no. 2 (2015): 120–13; Jon Welty Peachey and Adam Cohen, "Research Partnerships in Sport for Development and Peace: Challenges, Barriers, Strategies," *Journal of Sport Management* 30, no. 3 (2016): 282–97.
6. "Partners," Play Ball, accessed January 14, 2021, https://playball.org/partners/.
7. "Ways to Play," Play Ball, accessed January 14, 2021, https://playball.org/ways-to-play/.
8. "Academies," MLB, accessed August 17, 2021, https://mlb.com/mlb-youth-academy/.
9. "About FIFA," FIFA, accessed January 14, 2021, https://www.fifa.com/about-fifa/who-we-are/.
10. FIFA, "About FIFA."
11. "FIFA Forward," FIFA, accessed January 14, 2021, https://www.fifa.com/what-we-do/fifa-forward/.
12. FIFA, "FIFA Forward."
13. FIFA, "About FIFA."
14. "FIFA Foundation," FIFA, accessed January 14, 2021, https://www.fifa.com/what-we-do/fifa-foundation/.
15. FIFA, "About FIFA."
16. "'Basketball without Borders': National Basketball Association Stars to Conduct Camp for Children from Former Yugoslavia," United Nations, published March 26, 2001, https://www.un.org/press/en/2001/socnar823.doc.htm.
17. United Nations, "'Basketball without Borders': National Basketball Association Stars to Conduct Camp for Children from Former Yugoslavia."
18. Gordon W. Allport, *The Nature of Prejudice* (Cambridge, MA: Addison-Wesley, 1954).
19. "Basketball without Borders," NBA, accessed January 14, 2021, http://global.nba.com/basketball-without-borders/.
20. "NBA Academy," NBA, accessed January 14, 2021, https://nbaacademy.nba.com/.
21. Steve Fainaru and Mark Fainaru-Wade, "ESPN Investigation Finds Coaches at NBA China Academies Complained of Player Abuse, Lack of Schooling," ESPN, July 29,

2020, https://www.espn.com/nba/story/_/id/29553829/espn-investigation-finds-coaches-nba-china-academies-complained-player-abuse-lack-schooling.

22. "Real Madrid Social-Sport Academy After-School Program," Arlington Soccer Association, accessed January 14, 2021, http://arlingtonsoccer.com/programs/other-programs/real-madrid-program.

23. "Nike Inc. Reports Fiscal Fourth Quarter 2019 and Full Year Results," *Nike News*, published June 27, 2019, https://news.nike.com/news/nike-inc-reports-fiscal-2019-fourth-quarter-and-full-year-results.

24. Nike, "Our Approach to Community Impact," accessed January 14, 2021, https://purpose.nike.com/community-impact.

25. Nike, "Our Approach to Community Impact."

26. Nike, "Our Approach to Community Impact."

27. "Adidas Fund Projects," Adidas, accessed January 14, 2021, https://www.adidas-group.com/media/filer_public/2013/11/15/adidas_fund_projects_en.pdf.

28. Jim Murphy, "Skateistan: International Skateboarding Schools, Skateparks and Advocacy," *Juice*, July 15, 2017, https://juicemagazine.com/home/skateistan-international-skateboarding-schools-skateparks-and-advocacy/.

29. Holly Thorpe, "Maximizing Action Sports for Development," in *Strengthening Sport for Development and Peace: National Policies and Strategies*, ed. Oliver Dudfield (London: Commonwealth Secretariat, 2014), 40–57; Murphy, "Skateistan: International Skateboarding Schools, Skateparks and Advocacy."

30. Murphy, "Skateistan: International Skateboarding Schools, Skateparks and Advocacy."

31. Thorpe, "Maximizing Action Sports for Development."

32. Nick Butler, "Sport for Hope Centre in Haiti Opened by IOC President in Latest Example of Sport Boosting Wider Development," Inside the Games, July 15, 2014, https://www.insidethegames.biz/articles/1021320/sport-for-hope-centre-in-haiti-opened-by-ioc-president-in-latest-example-of-sport-boosting-wider-development.

33. Karen Rosen, "Sport for Hope Inaugurated in Zambia," *Around the Rings*, May 11, 2010, http://aroundtherings.com/site/A__34753/Title__Sports-For-Hope-Inaugurated-in-Zambia/292/Articles.

34. International Olympic Committee, "IOC Brings Hope to Haiti with Opening of New Sport Centre," published July 15, 2014, https://www.olympic.org/news/ioc-brings-hope-to-haiti-with-opening-of-new-sport-centre-1.

35. AIBA (International Boxing Association), "AIBA Becomes Official Supporter of Haiti Sport for Hope Project," January 5, 2014, https://www.eubcboxing.org/news/aiba-becomes-official-supporter-of-the-haiti-sport-for-hope-project/.

36. AIBA, "AIBA Becomes Official Supporter of Haiti Sport for Hope Project."

37. Butler, "Sport for Hope Centre in Haiti Opened by IOC President in Latest Example of Sport Boosting Wider Development"; International Olympic Committee, "IOC Brings Hope to Haiti with Opening of New Sport Centre."

38. Scott Jedlicka, "Sport for Hope in Haiti: Disaster Diplomacy or Disaster Capitalism?" in *Case Studies in Sport Diplomacy*, eds. Craig Esherick, Robert E. Baker, Steven Jackson, and Michael Sam (Morgantown, WV: FiT, 2017), 69–86.

39. Jedlicka, "Sport for Hope in Haiti: Disaster Diplomacy or Disaster Capitalism?"

13

Current Trends and Future Directions in Sport for Development and Peace

Jon Welty Peachey and Nico Schulenkorf

OBJECTIVES

This chapter will:

- Assess the current status of the SDP landscape.
- Describe theory building in SDP.
- Address the ongoing global proliferation of SDP programs.
- Discuss the need to reduce the sport evangelism and neocolonialism on which SDP was grounded.
- Explain prospects for Indigenous-oriented academic-practitioner partnerships.
- Describe the role of gender in SDP through women's empowerment.

From a relative backwater in the sport industry, the field of sport for development and peace (SDP) has grown exponentially over the past two decades to where it is now an in-vogue, and much-published, area of research across multiple disciplinary traditions and journals such as sport management, sport sociology, political science, international relations, development studies, and youth development, among others. A journal devoted to publishing the latest research in SDP has emerged: the *Journal of Sport for Development*. SDP has come a long way from its roots in programs for wounded veterans returning from World War I,[1] and even further back in history when wars were halted and temporary truces established during the ancient Olympic Games.[2] Approximately one thousand organizations across the globe now work in some aspect of SDP, from small nonprofits to larger groups and nongovernmental organizations such as the Laureus Foundation and Right to Play.[3] The United Nations even embraced the potential of sport to contribute to development agendas by

Figure 13.1. SDP can be a vehicle for attaining and sustaining goals. *Credit*: **Sports Diplomacy Division, US Department of State**

establishing the Office on Sport for Development and Peace, although this office closed in 2017. Nevertheless, SDP is continuing to grow in practice and scholarship.

Admittedly, much of the early scholarship and practice in SDP was highly evangelical about the "power of sport" to achieve development aims, without necessarily having evidence to back up these claims.[4] SDP organizations also tended to approach their development work through a neocolonial lens, designing programs in the Global North or high-income countries (HIC) and then importing them to local communities and contexts in the Global South or low- to middle-income countries (LMIC) with little input by local stakeholders.[5] This all sparked criticism by many scholars about sport's potential role in development and its unique contribution.[6] Fortunately, today, scholars and SDP organizations alike are less evangelical or neocolonial in their approach although this has not totally dissipated.[7] Overall, SDP scholarship is showing that, if designed and managed well, sport has the potential to help achieve myriad development outcomes, although certainly not in all cases or contexts.[8] For instance, research has shown that sport can help develop social capital, expand networks, and improve life situations of participants;[9] reduce prejudice among youth from different cultures and backgrounds;[10] improve cross-cultural relations among disparate and politically opposed community groups;[11] and serve as a vehicle through which to address issues of women and girls' empowerment;[12] among many others.

All of this development in scholarship and practice in SDP warrants reflection on where the field is going in the next decades. This brings us to the purpose of this chapter, which is to provide an overview of the current trends in SDP research and practice, and then, importantly, to share our thoughts on future directions for the field. To ground our reflections on SDP, we embrace the broad definition of the field offered by Alexis Lyras and Jon Welty Peachey. SDP is:

> The use of sport to exert a positive influence on public health, the socialization of children, youth and adults, the social inclusion of the disadvantaged, the economic development of regions and states, and on fostering intercultural exchange and conflict resolution.[13]

The authors have a combined thirty-seven years in SDP-related pursuits as practitioners and academics. We offer our thoughts on current trends in research and practice in SDP, followed by our collective thinking on the future of the field. We do not wish to claim that our reflections here are all-encompassing nor that we have captured all of the directions scholarship and practice may move in the near future; many excellent scholars and practitioners in the SDP space could certainly add to and enhance our agenda. However, we hope that what follows can in some small way motivate students, scholars, and practitioners to think about and activate potential directions for their own work within the field.

CURRENT TRENDS IN SPORT FOR DEVELOPMENT AND PEACE

As scholarship and practice in SDP continue to expand, a number of trends in theorizing, research, and practice have emerged. This section reviews several salient trends: (1) theory building from a theory to practice/practice to theory standpoint; (2) proliferation of programs; (3) decrease in sport evangelism and neocolonialism; (4) more sophisticated academic-practitioner partnerships; and (5) gender issues in SDP.

Theory to Practice/Practice to Theory

Scholars have been wrestling with the prospect of theory building in SDP for some time. While there are some notable examples of theories and conceptual frameworks that have emerged in the SDP space since 2010,[14] many scholars have continued to borrow theories from other disciplines to frame their work, such as social capital theory and intergroup contact theory.[15] Scholars have also questioned whether or not there can be grand theories in SDP because of the complexities of cultures, contexts, and populations served.[16] Given this backdrop, there has been emerging inquiry into exploring the theory to practice and practice to theory connection in sport for social change, which includes SDP. Prominently, a recent special issue in the *Journal of Sport Management* (Sport for Social Change: Bridging the Theory-Practice Divide, published in September 2019) features a number of scholars conceptualizing how theory can drive and support SDP program development and also how theory can be grounded in practice, with practice driving theory development. This connection between theory and practice is an important consideration, as there has often been a divide between theory and practice in the SDP space.[17] Going forward, practitioners need to base their program logic models on sound theoretical frameworks, and conversely, scholars should also utilize SDP practice to inform theory development, all of which helps answer the compelling question of "why sport?"

Proliferation of Programs

With approximately one thousand organizations now operating across continents, countries, and cultures, the SDP space has expanded rapidly over the past decade. Not all of this growth and expansion is necessarily positive, as the profusion of SDP organizations means that there is now more competition for funding dollars and program participants in many geographic areas. According to Per Svensson and Hilary Woods, who conducted a survey of SDP organizations operating around the world, most SDP programs are geographically focused on Africa for their programming, but organizations are headquartered across Asia, Europe, Latin America, and North America.[18] Importantly, many organizations appear to have their headquarters in the geographic region in which they are delivering programming, an encouraging sign to help further distance SDP from its neocolonial roots. While SDP organizations focus on many social issues, livelihoods and health are the most common focal areas. Organizations are employing myriad types of sports in their programming, from cricket and rugby to soccer (football), which is utilized by about one-third of all organizations. Some program logic models embrace a sport plus emphasis, where sport is modified and augmented with other forms of nonsport programming to achieve targeted outcomes, while others follow more of a plus sport model, where sport is the hook to attract individuals to the program, and then they are connected with other social services. Still others employ a hybrid of these two approaches.[19]

While it has become common for SDP organizations to want to scale up their programming efforts to reach more individuals and expand geographically, this is not always desirable. For instance, recent work by Welty Peachey, Adam Cohen, and Nari Shin found that scaling up programming and operations comes with a host of challenges and can shift the SDP organization away from its core competencies and lead to potential mission drift.[20] As an organization grows and takes on new organizational forms, there may not always be skilled managers and leaders in place to effectively help an organization navigate forward. Thus it is advised that SDP organizations carefully consider the best way for them to achieve sustained impact, with depth rather than breadth of programming perhaps being more advisable in some instances.

Decrease in Sport Evangelism and Neocolonialism

As mentioned, while SDP scholars and practitioners early on embraced a problematic sport evangelism and neocolonial approach to much of their work, today, scholars and practitioners have a more informed and considered understanding of the role of sport in development and on the critical need to involve local communities in design and development of programming.[21] Of course, there are still agencies, organizations, scholars, and practitioners who trumpet the power of sport as the cure all to social ills and who design programs with little to no input from local stakeholders.[22] Nevertheless, these ill-informed approaches do appear to be decreasing, perhaps because of continued admonitions and calls from critical scholars to eschew SDP's neocolonial and evangelical roots.[23] It is encouraging that SDP stakeholders are now realizing the vital need to temper claims about sport's impact and role and to embrace the need for robust evaluation mechanisms to provide evidence of programmatic effects. There are still many evaluation challenges in the SDP space that inhibit some organizations from engaging in rigorous evaluation, such as lack of time and knowledge,[24] but many are now realizing that concrete evidence is necessary to acquire funding and to enable program sustainability. Linked to this is a greater focus on sustainability in the SDP space, and the recognition that local stakeholders and communities must be involved in all facets of program design and delivery for this sustainability to be achieved.[25] These are all encouraging signs that SDP will continue to have a seat at the table in development circles in the next decades.

More Sophisticated Academic-Practitioner Partnerships

For many years, those in the academic space and SDP practitioners have been partnering together primarily for programmatic evaluation purposes and for consultation related to program design and implementation. These partnerships have grown in number and sophistication over the years, and this trend will likely continue. Many SDP practitioners realize they may not have the necessary capacity in-house to design and administer robust evaluation schemes and often reach out to academics for assistance in providing these services. For instance, Tracy Evans, a three-time Olympian in freestyle skiing and founder of the SDP organization Kids Play International, which aims to promote gender equity and the Olympic values by introducing less-familiar sports to children in postgenocide-affected countries like Rwanda and Cambodia, recently provided a keynote address at the annual conference of the North American Society for Sport Management.[26] During her address, she shared that her organization did not have the knowledge or capacity to conduct a robust, long-term evaluation of her programs, so she partnered with researchers at Virginia Tech University to design and administer the evaluation scheme. This practice is quite common in the SDP space and helps to bridge the academic-practitioner divide.

When these types of research partnerships first began, it was common practice for academics to approach SDP organizations with ideas about what they wished to study and outcomes they wished to measure and to administer an evaluation scheme with endorsement from the SDP organization but without much of its input into the evaluation process and outcomes to focus on.[27] Today, however, these research partnerships have evolved and are more sophisticated in their approach, with academics and practitioners working together to design a comprehensive and robust evaluation scheme from the outset that measures outcomes on which the organization truly wishes to capture data. For example, when the first author initially began working with Street Soccer USA (SSUSA)—a nonprofit SDP organization founded on the premise of helping individuals suffering from homelessness improve their life situations through the sport of soccer—he approached the organization with an idea for a research project to investigate social capital development in program participants and volunteers. While the organization had input into the project, it was not involved from the outset in determining design and outcomes to investigate. Over the past ten years, as Welty Peachey has continued to work with SSUSA, the partnership has evolved to one where the organization often initiates the idea for the research to capture data on outcomes of importance to it, rather than being researcher-driven. Most recently, this has entailed launching a new research project focused on how followers develop into leaders within their organization, particularly into servant leaders.

This example highlights the trend for scholars to become more reflexive in their approach to conducting research in the SDP space.[28] It is important for contemporary SDP researchers to be flexible and innovative in their research approaches and to engage from the outset with practitioners to design locally relevant projects that will add value to the organization and its mission. These reflexive and inclusive participatory research approaches should be the norm going forward to create meaningful change and provide information that is relevant and useful to the organization.[29]

However, academic-practitioner partnerships in the SDP space are not without their challenges. Many times, scholars have provided deliverables to SDP organizations that are written in academic jargon and generally unhelpful to the organization or, unfortunately, have not provided deliverables to the organization as promised.[30] The latter point is concerning, as it furthers the academic-practitioner divide and cautions SDP organizations against seeking out academic partnerships in the future. Some academics have been prone to gathering the data they need to publish in peer-reviewed journals to satisfy the demands for promotion and tenure at their institutions and then not following up with or providing helpful information to the organization under study. This illustrates the differing goals that academics and SDP organizations may have with regard to the outputs of the research study.[31] However, by being more reflexive and participatory in their research approach, and by fostering integrative cultural experiences with a focus on program sustainability,[32] academics can continue to be a vital support to SDP organizations in the achievement of their missions.

Gender Issues in SDP

Finally, recent conversations in the SDP space have also revolved around the increasing presence and participation of women and girls in SDP, examining the lived realities of program participants, volunteers, and staff.[33] This is an area within SDP that has been noticeably lacking from conversations and scholarship.[34] Fortunately, recent work and conversations have emerged around how girls can be new agents of social change and contribute uniquely to development agendas,[35] highlighted by a special issue in the *Sport in Society* journal in 2015 devoted to girls, international development, and the politics of sport. All of this work points to the fact that, with the increased presence of women and girls in the SDP space, a more nuanced and considered examination is warranted of how development projects are managed and operated, how participants feel about their experiences, and how evidence of outcomes is generated.[36]

This "Girl Effect" movement[37] revolves around the notion that girls can be an answer to the development problems in contemporary society and be change agents and catalysts in their communities. Programs emphasizing girls' empowerment have been referred to as sport, gender, and development programs. Much of the recent research

Figure 13.2. This group in Mauritania shows us that every voice matters when building SDP programs. *Credit*: Sports Diplomacy Division, US Department of State

in this area has explored the concept from postcolonial feminist perspectives,[38] often critiquing existing SDP interventions for their neoliberal political and ideological agendas.[39] Megan Chawansky, for instance, has challenged scholars and practitioners to reconsider how gender is constructed and understood in the SDP space.[40]

To illustrate, in their participatory action research project with the Girls' Empowerment through Sport (GET) Cricket Program in Papua New Guinea aimed at "empowering young women and increasing their critical awareness of sociocultural issues related to health, gender inequality, and domestic violence," Emma Seal and Emma Sherry revealed that the initiative did help to address various sociocultural issues related to gender in society.[41] Specifically, they found that the GET program acted as a viable resistance site for girls to confront traditional gendered relations embedded in societal perceptions, in addition to improving the overall well-being, motivation, and self-efficacy of the girls involved in the program. On the whole, the program is providing women and girls with the belief that they can enact change in their society and its structures and systems that may inhibit gender equality. This is just one example of myriad programs around the world targeting girls' empowerment through sport, a focus in SDP we only expect to continue to expand in the coming years, as gender issues and challenges are a critical concern in many cultures and contexts.

FUTURE DIRECTIONS IN SDP

Following on from the previous discussion of current trends in SDP, we now turn toward providing future opportunities in SDP research. In doing so, we build on recent SDP reflections[42] and our latest considerations of some of the areas that have not yet received sufficient focus in the literature. Again, we believe that our suggestions here are relevant and meaningful opportunities to move the SDP field forward, without claiming that they capture all possible future directions. These include (1) novel approaches to leadership; (2) social entrepreneurship; (3) design thinking; and (4) Indigenous approaches and voices.

Novel Approaches to Leadership

While leadership is arguably one of the most researched topics in the field of business studies, the concept still needs to be fully understood in different social and managerial contexts.[43] As such, leadership presents a truly complex and culturally influenced phenomenon,[44] and we suggest that SDP research around leadership development, management, and succession planning presents exciting opportunities for further theoretical and empirical debate. This is particularly relevant given that SDP projects often rely on individual "cause champions" or change agents to generate and maintain momentum.[45] In other words, the strategic planning for leadership development is of particular importance for the effectiveness and sustainability of programs.

Despite the growing significance of leadership knowledge in the SDP field, there has been limited research conducted on leadership development and succession planning from a sport management perspective (for a notable exception, see Andy Wright and Jean Côté, 2003).[46] As such, scholars have ample opportunity to contribute to this field of scholarship. Nico Schulenkorf has suggested that researchers could, for example, engage in comparative multicase studies to investigate the strategies and processes employed by different SDP programs with the intent of providing theoretical frameworks or practical recommendations for best practice.[47] At the same time, the particular challenges of leadership in the SDP sector could be explored in more detail, and new conceptualizations such as cross-border leadership[48] could be considered and applied.

Social Entrepreneurship

The business concept of entrepreneurship promises to play an increasingly important role in SDP practice and research, especially given the challenge of many SDP programs to sustain themselves beyond the time of external funding. As a recent SDP review has found, to date there are unfortunately only a limited number of studies conducted in this space and in fact on the wider topic of building and improving livelihoods through sport overall.[49] However, in practice, different SDP organizations have turned toward new and innovative business models—including social entrepreneurship—to achieve financial growth and independence. For instance, the Kick4Life program in Lesotho has taken an innovative entrepreneurial approach toward community development by combining its charitable SDP initiatives with professional sport programs that are able to generate financial gains from high-profile matches played on a regular basis.[50] In addition, Kick4Life has created a sport tourism and hospitality venture around its SDP programs, which shows the organization's entrepreneurial thinking and ability to move beyond a complete dependency model of traditional aid and social service provision.

Given this practical example—and similar ventures in other SDP settings around the world—scholars can and should use the opportunity to cooperate with organizations to make a stronger contribution to the SDP entrepreneurship literature. They would add to a currently small canon of work that has approached entrepreneurship in the context of SDP. In fact, Cohen and Welty Peachey's investigation into the motivations and experiences of a former female SDP participant who developed into a social entrepreneur presents one of the few SDP entrepreneurship study completed thus far.[51] In the future, studies could be conducted on how the different types of entrepreneurs—including social and for-profit—will coexist in the SDP arena. On a micro-level, it may also be timely to conduct a longer-term study on post SDP involvement and employment in an attempt to investigate if and how former SDP participants return to the SDP work arena—as entrepreneurs or otherwise. Here, Michael Hoekman and colleagues have made a start by investigating what they have labeled "re-engaged youth" in SDP; an interesting phenomenon deserving much more engagement by researchers in the future.[52]

Design Thinking

To remain innovative and "hip," the fields of business and management on a regular basis focus on new and creative ideas, concepts, and terms. Some of these seem to be more relevant and meaningful than others. For example, for a number of years the sporting world has placed increasing attention on issues related to "sustainability," and in a sport-event context, no manager could do without plans for "legacy." These are great concepts in principle but, as many SDP projects have shown, they have remained part of the managerial tick-list rather than become a serious managerial focus. Other examples include business buzzwords such as *ideation*, *disruption*, *radical transparency*, and *the Future*, which promise significant positive change or advancement but have often remained nothing but lip service.

Similar accusations can be related to the concept of "Design Thinking." However, in recent years, management scholars and entrepreneurs from around the world have started to investigate and apply this allegedly lofty business concept in more detail.[53] In a nutshell, Design Thinking is concerned with generating additional value and benefits to people, communities, and organizations through imagining and experimenting; in other words, in an active pursuit of novelty, people aim to think big and achieve something better.

Design Thinking has slowly been making its way into the sport management and SDP domains. As such, a recent scoping study by Greg Joachim, Schulenkorf, Katie Schlenker, and Stephen Frawley not only determined the extent to which Design Thinking mentalities and approaches already exist within SDP research and practice but also the various ways in which they manifest.[54] The findings allowed for the provision of specific recommendations for SDP organizations, particularly those with limited organizational capacity regarding logical points of entry for employing Design Thinking in the pursuit of organizational innovation. For instance, Joachim and colleagues suggested that to achieve deep user understanding and a true diversity of perspectives—key themes in Design Thinking practice—SDP organizations should include "disconnected (or subjugated) local voices in the design of programs, thus closing the gap between those who deliver SFD [sport-for-development] programs and those who stand to benefit from them."[55] Techniques for achieving such deep user understanding focus on keeping the users at the center of all practice, including informal conversations with users, the collaborative development of empathy maps, role-play exercises, and ethnographic research.[56] Moreover, with a multidimensional concern for diversity in mind, users should ideally represent a complementary set of skills, personalities, and even hierarchal positions to maximize innovation.

Overall, while more conceptual research and empirical testing is needed in the Design Thinking space to truly understand the relationship between innovation and aspects of social and economic productivity and effectiveness, it seems that SDP scholars have made an important first step toward demystifying the concept and preparing for a more creative and human-centered future.

Indigenous Voices and Approaches

As alluded to in the introduction of this chapter, early scholarship and practice in SDP was highly evangelical about the "power of sport" to achieve development aims without necessarily providing evidence to back up these claims.[57] Fortunately, over the past decade, SDP organizations and researchers have started to conduct different research projects and monitoring and evaluation exercises to generate SDP-specific, evidence-based research outcomes. Unfortunately, research has often been carried out by academics from HICs with little input by scholars from an LMIC context.[58] In fact, a recent review of SDP literature shows that although the majority of SDP programs are carried out in Africa, Asia, and Latin America, 90 percent of SDP authors are based in North America, Europe, and Australia.[59] Lamentably, only 8 percent of SDP studies have contributors from the countries in which the programs are delivered. As such, it seems that SDP research has thus far failed to fully engage with the wealth and diversity of local and Indigenous voices, knowledge, experiences, and expertise.

Overall, there is an urgent need to engage better with LMIC scholars and to conduct collaborative, participatory SDP research in the future. Participatory research is differentiated from conventional research methodologies "not in methods but in the attitudes of researchers, which in turn determine how, by and for whom research is conceptualized and conducted."[60] In the context of SDP programs, Holly Collison, Richard Giulianotti, P. David Howe, and Simon Darnell have highlighted "the importance of building strong relationships with skilled, experienced and informed locals in order to collect accurate and valuable data in unfamiliar locations."[61] However, true participatory research even goes beyond this statement as it aims to align power and control within the research process. As Andrea Cornwall and Rachel Jewkes note, the most striking difference between participatory and conventional methodologies lies in "who defines research problems and who generates, analyzes, represents, owns and acts on the information which is sought."[62] Importantly, these issues affect all phases of the research process from the development of research questions through the communication of the results for action.[63] Participatory research thus positions local people as the most knowledgeable actors in the research process.

With this in mind, there is a lot to learn from Indigenous approaches to conducting research in regard to methodology, approach, techniques, and customs. While important contributions have started to be made, the SDP community is in a position to embrace this space much more aggressively. A good example of integrating Indigenous voices into SDP discourses is provided by Oscar Mwaanga and Kabanda Mwansa, who exemplify the use of Ubuntu philosophy in designing and managing an international SDP program in Zambia.[64] Their study provides some evidence of research hybridity where the particular SDP program was influenced by both Ubuntu and Christian philosophies. This suggests that there may be space for more intercultural and even interfaith engagements in certain SDP settings, which would open up new opportunities for SDP planning, management, and evaluation.

Another good example of an approach that allows for a marriage of Western and Indigenous research is Talanoa. In fact, Rochelle Stewart-Withers, Koli Sewabu, and Sam Richardson highlight Talanoa as an appropriate and meaningful approach toward working *with* Pacific people and decentering conventional Western approaches to qualitative research.[65] In an SDP research setting, Jack Thomas Sugden, Schulenkorf, Daryl Adair, and Frawley have provided a study where Talanoa made an important contribution as a culturally appropriate approach for international scholars to employ.[66] In particular, when aiming to understand local culture and context—in their case the role of sport in reflecting and shaping group dynamics between Indigenous and Indian Fijians—Talanoa offered a much deeper engagement opportunity than traditional research methods could have provided. In fact, under a short-term ethnography paradigm, the Talanoa approach required detailed planning, willingness to engage, and the maximizing of local opportunities but also allowed for traditional research techniques to accompany Indigenous methods.[67] Hence, we suggest that the debate around local versus international research is really not a question of either-or; in fact, as the examples here have alluded to, there is ample opportunity to achieve reciprocal engagement and benefit through meaningful collaboration.

CONCLUSION

In this chapter, we set out to review some of the current trends in the SDP field along with outlining several future directions for research. While the field has experienced significant growth over the past twenty years and is moving away from its evangelical and neocolonial roots, there is still much opportunity for continued growth and development in scholarship, practice, and in bridging the theory-practice divide. We are encouraged and excited that scholars and practitioners seem to be taking a more nuanced and realistic approach to design, implementation, evaluation, and research within the SDP space. We are also encouraged that more attention and understanding have been given to the importance of locally driven research and involvement in SDP, although there is much more that can be done here to involve local and Indigenous voices in all phases of SDP program design and implementation, as well as to invite and collaborate with Indigenous scholars. With more SDP organizations emerging across the globe, increased integration of sport into government policy agendas, and burgeoning empirical and conceptual interest from scholars, the SDP field has great potential to contribute to the betterment of a global society. It is our hope that this chapter has stimulated those involved in SDP to consider new ways they can actively contribute to the field in the coming years.

Questions

1. Develop a hypothetical SDP program proposal, addressing the following:

a. The purpose of the SDP program and its explicit goals
b. The incorporation of Indigenous input in the planning, implementation, and evaluation of the SDP program
c. The inclusion of an academic-practitioner partnership
d. The incorporation of entrepreneurial strategies to sustain and extend the program
e. The incorporation of an evaluation system that provides evidence of the SDP program's effectiveness relative to its purpose
2. Describe how past SDP programs have reflected sport evangelism and neocolonial perspectives.
3. Identify an existing SDP program. Research it and assess it in the following areas:
a. What is the theory on which it is grounded?
b. How is it funded? Is it entrepreneurial?
c. Does it incorporate Indigenous input?
d. Does it include academic-practitioner partnerships?
e. Does it address gender issues and women's empowerment?

Strategies for Success

1. Form an academic-practitioner partnership with explicit SDP program purpose.
2. Along with local partners, determine the current unique circumstances and subsequent SDP program goals.
3. Engage a diverse perspective inclusive of Indigenous involvement to ensure local intentions are addressed.
4. Frame the SDP research and program evaluation in appropriate theory to provide evidence of outcomes.
5. Limit neocolonial and evangelical perspectives by soliciting Indigenous cooperation in the planning, execution, and evaluation of the SDP program.

NOTES

1. Cora Burnett, "Social Impact Assessment and Sport Development," *International Review for the Sociology of Sport* 36, no. 1 (March 2001): 46–52.
2. Jon Welty Peachey and Adam Cohen, "Sport for Social Change and Development," in *Sociology of Sport and Physical Activity*, ed. George B. Cunningham and John N. Singer (College Station, TX: Center for Sport Management Research and Education, 2012).
3. Per G. Svensson and Hilary Woods, "A Systematic Overview of Sport for Development and Peace Organisations," *Journal of Sport for Development* 5, no. 9 (2017): 36–48.
4. Fred Coalter, *Sport for Development: What Game Are We Playing?* (London: Routledge, 2013).
5. Simon C. Darnell and Lyndsay Hayhurst, "Sport for Decolonization: Exploring a New Praxis of Sport for Development," *Progress in Development Studies* 11, no. 3 (2011): 183–96.

6. Simon C. Darnell, *Sport for Development and Peace: A Critical Sociology* (London: Bloomsbury Academic, 2012); Lyndsay M. C. Hayhurst, Tess Kay, and Megan Chawansky, eds. *Beyond Sport for Development and Peace: Transnational Perspectives on Theory, Policy and Practice* (New York: Routledge, 2015); Kevin Harris and Andrew Adams, "Power and Discourse in the Politics of Evidence in Sport for Development," *Sport Management Review* 19 no. 2 (2016): 97–106.

7. Jon Welty Peachey, Allison Musser, Nari Shin, and Adam Cohen, "Interrogating the Motivations of Sport for Development and Peace Practitioners," *International Review for the Sociology of Sport* 53, no. 7 (2018): 767–87.

8. Nico Schulenkorf, "Managing Sport-for-Development: Reflections and Outlook," *Sport Management Review* 20, no. 3 (2017): 243–51; Nico Schulenkorf, Emma Sherry, and Katie Rowe, "Sport for Development: An Integrated Literature Review," *Journal of Sport Management* 30, no. 1 (2016): 22–39.

9. Ramón Spaaij, "Sport as a Vehicle for Social Mobility and Regulation of Disadvantaged Urban Youth," *International Review for the Sociology of Sport* 44, nos. 2–3 (2009): 247–64; Andrew Adams, Kevin Harris, and Iain Lindsey, "Examining the Capacity of a Sport for Development Programme to Create Social Capital," *Sport in Society* 21, no. 3 (2018): 558–73; Ran Zhou and Kyriaki Kaplanidou, "Building Social Capital from Sport Event Participation: An Exploration of the Social Impacts of Participatory Sport Events on the Community," *Sport Management Review* 21, no. 5 (2018): 491–503.

10. Jon Welty Peachey, George B. Cunningham, Alexis Lyras, Adam Cohen, and Jennifer Bruening, "The Influence of a Sport-for-Peace Event on Prejudice and Change Agent Self-Efficacy," *Journal of Sport Management* 29, no. 3 (2015): 229–44.

11. John Sugden, "Teaching and Playing Sport for Conflict Resolution and Co-Existence in Israel," *International Review for the Sociology of Sport* 41, no. 2 (2006): 221–40; Nico Schulenkorf and Deborah Edwards, "Maximizing Positive Social Impacts: Strategies for Sustaining and Leveraging the Benefits of Intercommunity Sport Events in Divided Societies," *Journal of Sport Management* 26, no. 5 (2012): 376–90.

12. Lyndsay Hayhurst, "Girls as the 'New' Agents of Social Change? Exploring the Girl Effect through Sport, Gender, and Development Programs in Uganda," *Sociological Research Online* 18, no. 2 (2013): 1–12; Emma Seal and Emma Sherry, "Exploring Empowerment and Gender Relations in a Sport for Development Program in Papua New Guinea," *Sociology of Sport Journal* 35, no. 3 (2018): 247–57.

13. Alexis Lyras and Jon Welty Peachey, "Integrating Sport-for-Development Theory and Praxis," *Sport Management Review* 14, no. 4 (2011): 311–26.

14. See for example Coalter, *Sport for Development: What Game Are We Playing?*; Lyras and Welty Peachey, "Integrating Sport-for-Development Theory and Praxis," 311–26; Nico Schulenkorf and Katja Siefken, "Managing Sport-for-Development and Healthy Lifestyles: The Sport-for-Health Model," *Sport Management Review* 22, no. 1 (2019): 96–107.

15. Schulenkorf, Sherry, and Rowe, "Sport for Development: An Integrated Literature Review," 22–39.

16. Nico Schulenkorf and Ramón Spaaij, "Commentary: Reflections on Theory Building in Sport for Development and Peace," *International Journal of Sport Management and Marketing* 16, nos. 1–2 (2015): 71–77; Jon Welty Peachey, "Sport for Development Theory Building and Program Design: Introduction to the Special Issue," *International Journal of Sport Management and Marketing* 16, nos. 1–2 (2015): 1–4.

17. Jon Welty Peachey and Adam Cohen, "Research Partnerships in Sport for Development and Peace: Challenges, Barriers, Strategies," *Journal of Sport Management* 30, no. 3 (2016): 282–97.

18. Svensson and Woods, "A Systematic Overview of Sport for Development and Peace Organisations," 36–48.

19. Coalter, *Sport for Development: What Game Are We Playing?*

20. Jon Welty Peachey, Adam Cohen, and Nari Shin, "Constraints and Strategies to Scaling Up in Sport for Development and Peace Organizations: Evidence from the Field," *Nonprofit and Voluntary Sector Quarterly* 9, no. 3 (2020): 611–30.

21. Schulenkorf, "Managing Sport-for-Development: Reflections and Outlook," 243–51.

22. Welty Peachy et al., "Interrogating the Motivations of Sport for Development and Peace Practitioners."

23. Simon C. Darnell, Megan Chawansky, David Marchesseault, Matthew Holmes, and Lyndsay Hayhurst, "The State of Play: Critical Sociological Insights into Recent 'Sport for Development and Peace' Research," *International Review for the Sociology of Sport* 53, no. 2 (2018): 133–51.

24. Welty Peachy and Cohen, "Research Partnerships in Sport for Development and Peace: Challenges, Barriers, Strategies," 282–97.

25. Coalter, *Sport for Development: What Game Are We Playing?*; Schulenkorf, "Managing Sport-for-Development: Reflections and Outlook," 243–51.

26. Tracy Evans, "Kids Play International" (keynote address, North American Society for Sport Management annual conference, New Orleans, May 2019).

27. Welty Peachey and Cohen, "Research Partnerships in Sport for Development and Peace: Challenges, Barriers, Strategies," 282–97.

28. Emma Sherry, Nico Schulenkorf, Emma Seal, Matthew Nicholson, and Russell Hoye, "Sport-for-Development: Inclusive, Reflexive, and Meaningful Research in Low- and Middle-Income Settings," *Sport Management Review* 20, no. 1 (2017): 69–80; Ramón Spaaij, Nico Schulenkorf, Ruth Jeanes, and Sarah Oxford "Participatory Research in Sport-for-Development: Complexities, Experiences and (Missed) Opportunities," *Sport Management Review* 21, no. 1 (2018): 25–37.

29. Sherry et al., "Sport-for-Development: Inclusive, Reflexive, and Meaningful Research in Low- and Middle-Income Settings," 69–80.

30. Welty Peachey and Cohen, "Research Partnerships in Sport for Development and Peace: Challenges, Barriers, Strategies," 282–97.

31. Jon Welty Peachey and Adam Cohen, "Reflections from Sport-for-Development Scholars: Challenges, Barriers, and Strategies of the Field," *Journal of Sport for Development* 3, no. 4 (2015): 16–27.

32. Carrie LeCrom and Brendan Dwyer, "From Evaluator to Insider: An Academic's Guide to Managing Sport-for-Development Programs," *Sport in Society* 18, no. 6 (2015): 652–58.

33. Seal and Sherry, "Exploring Empowerment and Gender Relations in a Sport for Development Program in Papua New Guinea," 247–57.

34. Lyndsay Hayhurst, "Girls as the 'New' Agents of Social Change? Exploring the Girl Effect through Sport, Gender, and Development Programs in Uganda."

35. Megan Chawansky and Lyndsay Hayhurst, "Girls, International Development and the Politics of Sport: Introduction," *Sport in Society: Cultures, Commerce, Media, Politics* 18, no. 8 (2015): 877–81.

36. Seal and Sherry, "Exploring Empowerment and Gender Relations in a Sport for Development Program in Papua New Guinea," 247–57.

37. Lyndsay Hayhurst, "The Corporatization of Sport, Gender and Development: Postcolonial IR Feminisms, Transnational Private Governance and Global Corporate Social Engagement," *Third World Quarterly* 32, no. 3 (2011): 531–49; Hayhurst, "Girls as the 'New' Agents of Social Change? Exploring the Girl Effect through Sport, Gender, and Development Programs in Uganda," 1–12.

38. Shawn D. Forde and Wendy Frisby, "Just Be Empowered: How Girls Are Represented in a Sport for Development and Peace HIV/AIDS Prevention Manual," *Sport in Society* 18, no. 3 (2015): 882–94; Lyndsay Hayhurst, Audrey Giles, and Jan Wright, "Biopedagogies and Indigenous Knowledge: Examining Sport for Development and Peace for Urban Indigenous Young Women in Canada and Australia," *Sport, Education and Society* 21, no. 4 (2016): 549–69.

39. Seal and Sherry, "Exploring Empowerment and Gender Relations in a Sport for Development Program in Papua New Guinea."

40. Megan Chawansky, "New Social Movements, Old Gender Games? Locating Girls in the Sport for Development and Peace Movement," in *Critical Aspects of Gender in Conflict Resolution, Peacebuilding, and Social Movements*, ed. Anna Snyder and Stephanie Stobbe (London: Emerald, 2011), 121–34.

41. Seal and Sherry, "Exploring Empowerment and Gender Relations in a Sport for Development Program in Papua New Guinea," 247.

42. Schulenkorf, "Managing Sport-for-Development: Reflections and Outlook," 243–51.

43. Stephen Frawley, Laura Misener, Daniel Lock, and Nico Schulenkorf, *Global Sport Leadership* (London: Routledge, 2019).

44. Morgan W. McCall, "Recasting Leadership Development," *Industrial and Organizational Psychology* 3, no. 1 (2010): 3–19.

45. Michael B. Edwards, "The Role of Sport in Community Capacity Building: An Examination of Sport for Development Research and Practice," *Sport Management Review* 18, no. 1 (2015): 6–19; Nico Schulenkorf, "The Roles and Responsibilities of a Change Agent in Sport Event Development Projects," *Sport Management Review* 13, no. 2 (May 2010): 118–28.

46. Andy Wright and Jean Côté, "A Retrospective Analysis of Leadership Development through Sport," *Sport Psychologist* 17, no. 3 (2003): 268–91.

47. Schulenkorf, "Managing Sport-for-Development: Reflections and Outlook," 243–51.

48. Frawley et al., *Global Sport Leadership*.

49. Schulenkorf, Sherry, and Rowe, "Sport for Development: An Integrated Literature Review," 22–39.

50. Kick4Life, "How Kick4Life FC Works," accessed 2019, http://www.kick4life.org/about/about-k4l/.

51. Adam Cohen and Jon Welty Peachey, "The Making of a Social Entrepreneur: From Participant to Cause Champion within a Sport-for-Development Context," *Sport Management Review* 18, no. 1 (2015): 111–25.

52. Michael J. Hoekman and Nico Schulenkorf, "Sustainable Management of Sport-for-Development through Youth Re-Engagement: The FREYCA Framework," in *Beyond Sport for Development and Peace*, ed. Lyndsay M. C. Hayhurst, Tess Kay, and Megan Chawansky (New York: Routledge, 2015); Michael J. Hoekman, Nico Schulenkorf, and Jon Welty Peachey, "Re-Engaging Local Youth for Sustainable Sport-for-Development," *Sport Management Review* 22, no. 5 (2019): 613–25, https://doi.org/10.1016/j.smr.2018.09.001.

53. Tim Brown, "Design Thinking," *Harvard Business Review* 86, no. 6 (2008): 84; Jeanne Liedtka and Tim Olgilvie, *Designing for Growth: A Design Thinking Toolkit for Managers* (New York: Columbia University Press, 2011); Antonia Ward, Ellie Runcie, and Lesley Morris, "Embedding Innovation: Design Thinking for Small Enterprises," *Journal of Business Strategy* 30, nos. 2–3 (2009): 78–84.

54. Greg Joachim, Nico Schulenkorf, Katie Schlenker, and Stephen Frawley, "Design Thinking and Sport for Development: Enhancing Organizational Innovation," *Managing Sport and Leisure* 25, no. 3 (May 2020): 175–202, https://doi.org/10.1080/23750472.2019.1611471.

55. Joachim et al., "Design Thinking and Sport for Development: Enhancing Organizational Innovation."

56. Lisa Carlgren, Ingo Rauth, and Maria Elmquist, "Framing Design Thinking: The Concept in Idea and Enactment," *Creativity and Innovation Management* 25, no. 1 (March 2016): 38–57.

57. Coalter, *Sport for Development: What Game Are We Playing?*

58. Tony Rossi and Ruth Jeanes, "Education, Pedagogy and Sport for Development: Addressing Seldom Asked Questions," *Sport, Education and Society* 21, no. 4 (2016): 483–94.

59. Schulenkorf, Sherry, and Rowe, "Sport for Development: An Integrated Literature Review," 22–39.

60. Andrea Cornwall and Rachel Jewkes, "What Is Participatory Research?" *Social Science and Medicine* 41, no. 12 (December 1995): 1667–76.

61. Holly Collison, Simon Darnell, Richard Giulianotti, and P. David Howe, "Sport for Social Change and Development: Sustaining Transnational Partnerships and Adapting International Curriculums to Local Contexts in Rwanda," *The International Journal of the History of Sport* 33, no. 15 (2016): 1685–99.

62. Andrea Cornwall and Rachel Jewkes, "What Is Participatory Research?"

63. Wendy Frisby, Colleen Reid, Sydney Millar, and Larena Hoebner, "Putting 'Participatory' into Participatory Forms of Action Research," *Journal of Sport Management* 19, no. 4 (2005): 367–86.

64. Oscar Mwaanga and Kabanda Mwansa, "Indigenous Discourses in Sport for Development and Peace: A Case Study of the Ubuntu Cultural Philosophy in EduSport Foundation, Zambia," in *Global Sport-for-Development: Critical Perspectives*, ed. Nico Schulenkorf and Daryl Adair (London: Palgrave Macmillan, 2013): 115–33.

65. Rochelle Stewart-Withers, Koli Sewabu, and Sam Richardson, "Talanoa: A Contemporary Qualitative Methodology for Sport Management," *Sport Management Review* 20, no. 1 (2017): 55–68.

66. Jack Thomas Sugden, Nico Schulenkorf, Daryl Adair, and Stephen Frawley, "The Role of Sport in Reflecting and Shaping Group Dynamics: The 'Intergroup Relations Continuum' and Its Application to Fijian Rugby and Soccer," *Sport Management Review* 23, no. 2 (2020): 271–83.

67. Jack Thomas Sugden, Daryl Adair, Nico Schulenkorf, and Stephen Frawley, "Exploring Sport and Intergroup Relations in Fiji: Guidance for Researchers Undertaking Short-Term Ethnography," *Sociology of Sport Journal* 36, no. 4 (2019): 1–12, doi: https://doi.org/10.1123/ssj.2018-0165.

Selected Bibliography

Agha, Nola, and Marijke Taks. "A Theoretical Comparison of the Economic Impact of Large and Small Events." *International Journal of Sport Finance* 10, no. 3 (2015): 199–216.
Anderson, James, and Marijke Taks. "Urban Governance of Non-Mega Sport Events: A Socio-Political Discourse Analysis." In *Research Handbook on Sports Governance*, edited by Mathieu Winand and Christos Anagnostopoulos. Cheltenham, UK: Edward Elgar Publishing, 2019.
Babiak, Kathy, and Richard Wolfe. "More Than Just a Game? Corporate Social Responsibility and Super Bowl XL." *Sport Marketing Quarterly* 15, no. 4 (2006): 214.
———. "Perspectives on Social Responsibility in Sport." In *Handbook of Sport and Corporate Social Responsibility*, edited by Juan Luis Paramio Salcines, Kathy Babiak, and Geoff Walters, 17–34. London: Routledge, 2013.
Babiak, Kathy, and Daniel Yang. "Toward Developing Strategic Partnerships between SDP and Corporate Organizations: Elements of Effective Partnership Interactions." In *Partnerships and Alliances in Sport for Development and Peace*, edited by Jon Welty Peachey, B. Christine Green, and Laurence Chalip, 189–216. Urbana, IL: Sagamore–Venture, 2020.
Baker, Robert E., Pamela H. Baker, Christopher Atwater, and Heather Andrews. "Sport for Development and Peace: A Program Evaluation of a Sport Diplomacy Initiative." *International Journal of Sport Management and Marketing* 16, nos.1–2 (2015): 52–70. https:/doi.org/10.1504/IJSMM.2015.074932.
Baker, Robert E., Pamela H. Baker, Christopher Atwater, and Craig Esherick. "U.S. Sport Diplomacy in Latin America and the Caribbean: A Programme Evaluation." *Journal of Sport for Development* 6, no. 10 (2018): 71–85.
Baker, Robert E., Pamela Hudson Baker, Anya Evmenova, and Laura Hayes-Harris. "Perceptions of International Sport Exchange Participants Regarding Inclusive Sport." *International Journal of Sport Management* 16, no. 3 (July 2015): 417–36.
Baker, Robert E., and Craig Esherick. "Sport-Based Peace Initiatives: Playing for Peace." In *Building Cultures of Peace: Transdisciplinary Voices of Hope and Action*, edited by Elavie

Ndura-Ouédraogo and Randall Amster, 102–24. Newcastle upon Tyne, UK: Cambridge Scholars Publishing, 2009.

Chalip, Laurence. "Beyond Impact: A General Model for Sport Event Leverage." In *Sport Tourism: Interrelationships, Impacts and Issues*, edited by Brent W. Ritchie and Daryl Adair, 226–52. Clevedon, UK: Channel View, 2004.

———. "From Legacies to Leverage." In *Leveraging Legacies from Sports Mega-Events: Concepts and Cases*, edited by Jonathan Grix, 2–12. Basingstoke, UK: Palgrave Macmillan, 2014.

———. "Marketing, Media, and Place Promotion." In *Sport Tourism Destinations: Issues, Opportunities and Analysis*, edited by James Higham, 162–76. Oxford: Butterworth-Heinemann, 2005.

———. "Toward a Distinctive Sport Management Discipline." *Journal of Sport Management* 20, no. 1 (2006): 1–21.

———. "Trading Legacy for Leverage." In *Legacies and Mega Events: Fact or Fairy Tales?* edited by Ian Brittain, Jason Bocarro, Terri Byers, and Kamilla Swart, 25–42. Abingdon, UK: Routledge, 2017.

Chalip, Laurence, and Carla A. Costa. "Sport Event Tourism and the Destination Brand: Towards a General Theory." *Sport in Society* 8, no. 2 (2005): 218–37.

Chalip, Laurence, and B. Christine Green. "Establishing and Maintaining a Modified Youth Sport Program: Lessons from Hotelling's Location Game." *Sociology of Sport Journal* 15, no. 4 (1998): 326–42.

Chalip, Laurence, B. Christine Green, Marijke Taks, and Laura Misener. "Creating Sport Participation from Sport Events: Making It Happen." *International Journal of Sport Policy and Politics* 9, no. 2 (2017): 257–76.

Chalip, Laurence, Keri Schwab, and Daniel Dustin. "Bridging the Sport and Recreation Divide." *Schole* 25, no. 1 (2010): 1–10.

Chalip, Laurence, and E. Philip Scott. "Centrifugal Social Forces in a Youth Sport League." *Sport Management Review* 8, no. 1 (May 2005): 43–67.

Cohen, Adam, and Jon Welty Peachey. "The Making of a Social Entrepreneur: From Participant to Cause Champion within a Sport-for-Development Context." *Sport Management Review* 18, no. 1 (2015): 111–25.

Dixon, Marlene A., Arden J. Anderson, Robert E. Baker, Pamela H. Baker, and Craig Esherick. "Management in Sport for Development: Examining the Structure and Processes of a Sport Diplomacy Initiative." *International Journal of Sport Management and Marketing* 19, nos. 3–4 (2019): 268–92.

Dixon, Marlene A., and Per G. Svensson. "A Nascent Sport for Development and Peace Organization's Response to Institutional Complexity: The Emergence of a Hybrid Agency in Kenya." *Journal of Sport Management* 33, no. 5 (August 2019). https://doi.org/10.1123/jsm.2019-0065.

Frawley, Stephen, Laura Misener, Daniel Lock, and Nico Schulenkorf. *Global Sport Leadership*. London: Routledge, 2019.

Gerrard, Bill. "A Resource-Utilization Model of Organizational Efficiency in Professional Team Sports." *Journal of Sport Management* 19, no. 2 (2005): 143–69.

Green, B. Christine. "Action Research in Youth Soccer: Assessing the Acceptability of an Alternative Program." *Journal of Sport Management* 11, no. 1 (1997): 29–44.

———. "Building Sport Programs to Optimize Athlete Recruitment, Retention, and Transition: Toward a Normative Theory of Sport Development." *Journal of Sport Management* 19, no. 3 (2005): 233–53.

———. "Sport as an Agent for Social and Personal Change." In *Management of Sport Development*, edited by Vassil Girginov, 129–46. Oxford: Elsevier, 2008.

Green, B. Christine, and Laurence Chalip. "The Influence of Club/Travel Teams on Youth Sport." In *Youth Sports in America: The Most Important Issues in Youth Sports Today*, edited by Skye G. Arthur-Banning, Mary Sara Wells, and P. Brian Greenwood. Santa Barbara, CA: ABC-CLIO/Greenwood, 2018.

———. "Sport Tourism as the Celebration of Subculture." *Annals of Tourism Research* 25, no. 2 (April 1998): 275–91.

Hill, Brad, and B. Christine Green. "Give the Bench the Boot! Using Manning Theory to Design Youth-Sport Programs." *Journal of Sport Management* 22, no. 2 (2008): 184–204.

Hoekman, Michael J., and Nico Schulenkorf. "Sustainable Management of Sport-for-Development through Youth Re-Engagement: The FREYCA Framework." In *Beyond Sport for Development and Peace*, edited by Lyndsay M. C. Hayhurst, Tess Kay, and Megan Chawansky. New York: Routledge, 2015.

Hoekman, Michael J., Nico Schulenkorf, and Jon Welty Peachey. "Re-Engaging Local Youth for Sustainable Sport-for-Development." *Sport Management Review* 22, no. 5 (2019): 613–25. https://doi.org/10.1016/j.smr.2018.09.001.

Horne, Edward, and Matthew Brown. "The Retention of Adult Sport Participants: The Challenge of Player Ratings." *Journal of Applied Sport Management* 11, no. 1 (2019): 24–35.

Jedlicka, Scott. "Sport for Hope in Haiti: Disaster Diplomacy or Disaster Capitalism?" In *Case Studies in Sport Diplomacy*, edited by Craig Esherick, Robert E. Baker, Steven Jackson, and Michael Sam, 69–86. Morgantown, WV: FiT, 2017.

Joachim, Greg, Nico Schulenkorf, Katie Schlenker, and Stephen Frawley. "Design Thinking and Sport for Development: Enhancing Organizational Innovation." *Managing Sport and Leisure* 25, no. 3 (2020): 175–202. https://doi.org/10.1080/23750472.2019.1611471.

LeCrom, Carrie, and Brendan Dwyer. "From Evaluator to Insider: An Academic's Guide to Managing Sport-for-Development Programs." *Sport in Society* 18, no. 6 (2015): 652–58.

LeCrom, Carrie W., and Melissa Ferry. "The United States Government's Role in Sport Diplomacy." In *Case Studies in Sport Diplomacy*, edited by Craig Esherick, Robert E. Baker, Steven Jackson, and Michael Sam, 19–38. Morgantown, WV: FiT, 2017.

Lyras, Alexis, and Jon Welty Peachey. "Integrating Sport-for-Development Theory and Praxis." *Sport Management Review* 14, no. 4 (November 2011): 311–26.

McCann, K. David, B. Christine Green, and Laurence Chalip. "Recruit and Retain Study." *Report to USA Rugby and World Rugby*. Boulder, CO: Sport Development Concepts, 2015.

Misener, Laura, Marijke Taks, Laurence Chalip, and B. Christine Green. "The Elusive 'Trickle-Down Effect' of Sport Events: Assumptions and Missed Opportunities." *Managing Sport and Leisure* 20, no. 2 (2015): 135–56.

Murray, Stuart. "Sports Diplomacy in the Australian Context: Theory into Strategy." *Politics and Policy* 45, no. 5 (2017): 845.

———. "The Two Halves of Sports Diplomacy." *Diplomacy and Statecraft* 23, no. 3 (2012): 576–92.

Murray, Stuart, and Geoffrey Allen Pigman. "Mapping the Relationship between International Sport and Diplomacy." *Sport in Society* 17, no. 9 (2014): 1102.

Murray, Stuart, Paul Sharp, Geoffrey Wiseman, David Criekemans, and Jan Melissen. "The Present and Future of Diplomacy and Diplomatic Studies." *International Studies Review* 13, no. 4 (December 2011): 709–28.

Schulenkorf, Nico. "Managing Sport-for-Development: Reflections and Outlook." *Sport Management Review* 20, no. 3 (June 2017): 243–51.

———. "The Roles and Responsibilities of a Change Agent in Sport Event Development Projects." *Sport Management Review* 13, no. 2 (May 2010): 118–28.

Schulenkorf, Nico, and Daryl Adair. "Sport-for-Development: The Emergence and Growth of a New Genre." In *Global Sport-for-Development: Critical Perspectives*, edited by Nico Schulenkorf and Daryl Adair, 3–14. London: Palgrave Macmillan, 2013.

Schulenkorf, Nico, and Deborah Edwards. "Maximizing Positive Social Impacts: Strategies for Sustaining and Leveraging the Benefits of Intercommunity Sport Events in Divided Societies." *Journal of Sport Management* 26, no. 5 (2012): 376–90.

Schulenkorf, Nico, Emma Sherry, and Katie Rowe. "Sport for Development: An Integrated Literature Review." *Journal of Sport Management* 30, no. 1 (2016): 22–39.

Schulenkorf, Nico, and Katja Siefken. "Managing Sport-for-Development and Healthy Lifestyles: The Sport-for-Health Model." *Sport Management Review* 22, no. 1 (2019): 96–107.

Schulenkorf, Nico, and Ramón Spaaij. "Commentary: Reflections on Theory Building in Sport for Development and Peace." *International Journal of Sport Management and Marketing* 16, nos. 1–2 (2015): 71–77.

Schulenkorf, Nico, John Sugden, and Jack Sugden. "Sport for Conflict Resolution and Peace Building." In *Managing Sport Development: An International Approach*, edited by Emma Sherry, Nico Schulenkorf, and Pamm Phillips. New York: Routledge, 2016.

Sherry, Emma, Nico Schulenkorf, Emma Seal, Matthew Nicholson, and Russell Hoye. "Sport-for-Development: Inclusive, Reflexive, and Meaningful Research in Low- and Middle-Income Settings." *Sport Management Review* 20, no. 1 (2017): 69–80.

Smith, Natalie L., and B. Christine Green. "Positive Socialization in Sport." In *Understanding the Value of Sport Management: An Introduction to the Field*, edited by Matthew Bowers and Marlene A. Dixon, 39–60. Champaign, IL: Sagamore, 2015.

Sparvero, Emily, Laurence Chalip, and B. Christine Green. "Laissez Faire Sport Development: Building Elite Athletes in the United States." In *Comparative Elite Sport Development*, edited by Barrie Houlihan and Mick Green, 242–10. Oxford: Butterworth-Heinemann, 2008.

Sugden, Jack Thomas, Daryl Adair, Nico Schulenkorf, and Stephen Frawley. "Exploring Sport and Intergroup Relations in Fiji: Guidance for Researchers Undertaking Short-Term Ethnography." *Sociology of Sport Journal* 36, no. 4 (2019): 1–12. https://doi.org/10.1123/ssj.2018-0165.

Sugden, Jack Thomas, Nico Schulenkorf, Daryl Adair, and Stephen Frawley. "The Role of Sport in Reflecting and Shaping Group Dynamics: The 'Intergroup Relations Continuum' and Its Application to Fijian Rugby and Soccer." *Sport Management Review* 23, no. 2 (2020): 271–83. https://doi.org/10.1016/j.smr.2019.02.001.

Svensson, Per G. "Organizational Hybridity: A Conceptualization of How Sport for Development and Peace Organizations Respond to Divergent Institutional Demands." *Sport Management Review* 20, no. 5 (November 2017): 443–54.

Svensson, Per G., Fredrik O. Andersson, and Lewis Faulk. "A Quantitative Assessment of Organizational Capacity and Organizational Life Stages in Sport for Development and Peace." *Journal of Sport Management* 32, no. 3 (2018): 295–313.

Svensson, Per G., and Marion E. Hambrick. "Exploring How External Stakeholders Shape Social Innovation in Sport for Development and Peace." *Sport Management Review* 22, no. 4 (August 2019): 540–52.

———. "'Pick and Choose Our Battles': Understanding Organizational Capacity in a Sport for Development and Peace Organization." *Sport Management Review* 19, no. 2 (2015): 120–13.

Svensson, Per G., and Jeffrey Levine. "Rethinking Sport for Development and Peace: The Capability Approach." *Sport in Society* 20, no. 7 (2017): 905–23.

Svensson, Per G., and Richard Loat. "Bridge-Building for Social Transformation in Sport for Development and Peace." *Journal of Sport Management* 33, no. 5 (2019): 426–39. https://doi.org/10.1123/jsm.2018-0258.

Svensson, Per G., Tara S. Mahoney, and Marion E. Hambrick. "Twitter as a Communication Tool for Nonprofits: A Study of Sport-for-Development Organizations." *Nonprofit and Voluntary Sector Quarterly* 44, no. 6 (2015): 1086–106.

Svensson, Per G. and Chad S. Seifried. "Navigating Plurality in Hybrid Organizing: The Case of Sport for Development and Peace Entrepreneurs." *Journal of Sport Management* 31, no. 2 (2017): 176–90.

Svensson, Per G., and Hilary Woods. "A Systematic Overview of Sport for Development and Peace Organisations." *Journal of Sport for Development* 5, no. 9 (September 2017): 36–48.

Taks, Marijke. "The Rise and Fall of Mega Sport Events: The Future Is on Non-Mega Sport Events." In *Ethics and Governance in Sport: The Future of Sport Imagined*, edited by Yves Vanden Auweele, Elaine Cook, and Jim Parry, 84–93. London: Routledge, 2016.

———. "Social Sustainability of Non-Mega Sport Events in a Global World." *European Journal for Sport and Society* 10, no. 2 (2013): 121–41.

Taks, Marijke, Laurence Chalip, and B. Christine Green. "Impacts and Strategic Outcomes from Non-Mega Sport Events for Local Communities." *European Sport Management Quarterly* 15, no. 1 (2015): 1–6.

Taks, Marijke, Laurence Chalip, B. Christine Green, Stefan Kesenne, and Scott Martyn. "Factors Affecting Repeat Visitation and Flow-on Tourism as Sources of Event Strategy Sustainability." *Journal of Sport and Tourism* 14, nos. 2–3 (2009): 121–42.

Taks, Marijke, B. Christine Green, Laura Misener, and Laurence Chalip. "Evaluating Sport Development Outcomes: The Case of a Medium-Sized International Sport Event." *European Sport Management Quarterly* 14, no. 3 (2014): 213–37.

———. "Sport Participation from Sport Events: Why It Doesn't Happen?" *Marketing Intelligence & Planning* 36, no. 2 (2018): 185–98.

Taks, Marijke, Stefan Kesenne, Laurence Chalip, and B. Christine Green. "Economic Impact Analysis versus Cost Benefit Analysis: The Case of a Medium-Sized Sport Event." *International Journal of Sport Finance* 6, no. 3 (2011): 187–203.

Taks, Marijke, Meagan Littlejohn, Ryan Snelgrove, and Laura Wood. "Sport Events and Residential Happiness: The Case of Two Non-Mega Sport Events." *Journal of Global Sport Management* 1, nos. 3–4 (2016): 90–109.

Welty Peachey, Jon. "Sport for Development Theory Building and Program Design: Introduction to the Special Issue." *International Journal of Sport Management and Marketing* 16, nos. 1–2 (2015): 1–4.

Welty Peachey, Jon, and Adam Cohen. "Reflections from Sport-for-Development Scholars: Challenges, Barriers, and Strategies of the Field." *Journal of Sport for Development* 3, no. 4 (2015): 16–27.

———. "Research Partnerships in Sport for Development and Peace: Challenges, Barriers, Strategies." *Journal of Sport Management* 30, no. 3 (2016): 282–97.

———. "Sport for Social Change and Development." In *Sociology of Sport and Physical Activity*, edited by George B. Cunningham and John N. Singer. College Station, TX: Center for Sport Management Research and Education, 2012.

Welty Peachey, Jon, Adam Cohen, John Borland, and Alexis Lyras. "Building Social Capital: Examining the Impact of Street Soccer USA on its Volunteers." *International Review for the Sociology of Sport* 48, no. 1 (February 2013): 20–37.

Welty Peachey, Jon, Adam Cohen, and Nari Shin. "Constraints and Strategies to Scaling Up in Sport for Development and Peace Organizations: Evidence from the Field." *Nonprofit and Voluntary Sector Quarterly* 49, no. 3 (2019): 611–30.

Welty Peachey, Jon, George B. Cunningham, Alexis Lyras, Adam Cohen, and Jennifer Bruening. "The Influence of a Sport-for-Peace Event on Prejudice and Change Agent Self-Efficacy." *Journal of Sport Management* 29, no. 3 (2015): 229–44. https://doi.org/10.1123/jsm.2013-0251.

Welty Peachey, Jon, Allison Musser, Na Ri Shin, and Adam Cohen. "Interrogating the Motivations of Sport for Development and Peace Practitioners." *International Review for the Sociology of Sport* 53, no. 7 (2018): 767–87.

Index

ABC Triangle, 211
Adidas, 224
Allport, Gordon, 10–12, 83

Beer, Michael, 10–12, 15

Contact Hypothesis, 10–12
Coakley, Jay, 32
Coalter, Fred, 15, 25–27, 32, 84, 204
Commonwealth Secretariat, 185–87
Corporate Social Responsibility, 121
    communication with SDP, 124–26, 129–33;
    definition, 121
    examples in practice, 126–29
    strategic and social perspectives, 122–24
Coubertin, Pierre de, 5
Culture Shock, 49

data analytics, 166
    decision-making, 166–67;
    definition, 167
    Key Performance Indicators (KPIs), 162
    impact on decisions, 173
    individuals involved in, 171
    measurements, 172
    stages of, 169–71
design thinking, 238

designers, 202, 207
development, 39
diplomacy, 88–89

event leveraging, 144
    managing the process of, 150–52

FIFA, 2020
The First Tee, 218
Foucauldian bio-power, 33
frames of reference, 211

Giulianotti, Richard, 14, 84, 181–82, 186, 239
glocalization, 9
global corporate social engagement, 123
Gramscian hegemony, 33

Identity, 64
    ability and disability, 65
    familial status, 69
    gender, 67
    race and Ethnicity, 68
    religion, 69
    sexuality, 68
    socioeconomic status, 70
implementers, 202, 207
inclusive sport, 62

definition, 64
impact on communities, 63
impact on individuals, 62
in conflict resolution, 63
inspiration effect, 151
The International Olympic Committee, 6, 30, 95, 226
intersectionality, 64

Key Performance Indicators (KPIs), 162

Levermore, Roger, 15, 84, 159
Lyras, Alexis, 11–13, 231

Magic Bus, 192
Mandela, Nelson, 4, 5, 90, 95
mega-event syndrome, 143
mega sport event, 142
Millennium Development Goals, 7

NBA, 2020
NIKE, 223
Nohria, Nitin, 10–11, 15
NVSC Future Stars Program, 47

Ping Pong Diplomacy, 5, 92
Play Ball, 219
Postcolonial theory, 33
program evaluation, 159
  definition of, 161
  logic model, 160, 163
  purposes of, 162
  role of data analytics, 165
  strategic planning, 164
  systems evaluation and analytics, 163

Real Madrid, 222
Reductionist theory, 161

Schulenkorf, Nico, 15, 83, 217, 229, 237
second-tier events, 142
Skateistan, 41, 45, 225
social exclusion, 28
social inclusion, 28
sport, 3
  as an intervention, 27–28;
  diplomatic qualities, 89–92;
  entry to, 40–41;
  for social development, 28
  history of, 90
  in conflict resolution, 92
  the power of, 3–4
  relationship with crime and violence, 29
  the role of competition, 51
  the role of policy/politics in intervention, 31
sport analytics. *See* data analytics
sport and conflict resolution, 82
  assumptions and conceptualizations of, 202–205;
  definition, 84
  history, 83
  intersections with sports diplomacy, 95–97;
  theory into practice, 85–87
sport and economic development, 105
  effects of sport facilities, 107–109;
  impact of sport events, 112–114;
  processes when using, 114
  public assembly sport facilities, 109–12
sport development, 39
  dimensions, 55
  distinctiveness, 50
  goals of, 40
  implementation, 54
  key tasks of, 42–50;
  pathways, 40
  role of competition, 51–54;
sports diplomacy, 87, 93;
  conflict resolution and nonstate actors, 95–97;
  definition, 93
  history of, 93
  Sports Visitors Program, 15–16, 67, 113
  theory into practice, 94
sport events, 141
  impacts on sport participation, 144–50;
  leveraging, 149–53;
  research trends on impact of, 142–44
sport for development and peace, 5, 105
  a glocal perspective, 9
  a success story, 15
  actors, 202
  critical perspectives, 32–34;

current trends, 231–36
definition, 7–9, 25, 40
for-profit involvement, 217
future directions, 236–20
goals of, 205–207
government involvement in, 181–85, 187–95;
historical development, 5–7
implementation, 54, 191
role of the Commonwealth Secretariat, 185–87;
significance of exploring practice, 208–10;
theoretical foundations, 10
Sugden, John, 30, 83, 240

Theory E, 10
Theory O, 10
Theory of Change, 202, 212
third culture, 207

Under Armour, 127–29
UNESCO, 5, 184, 188
Unilever, 128–29
Universal Design, 71
  principles, 72
Universal Design for Learning, 73
  principles, 73–76

Welty Peachey, Jon, 11–13, 53, 217, 231–32, 237

About the Editors

Pamela Hudson Baker

Pamela Hudson Baker is an associate professor and director of the Division of Special Education and disAbility Research. She also serves in a dual appointment with the Office of the Provost focusing on the expansion of online undergraduate academic programs. In addition to numerous presentations and publications, Dr. Baker has served as an investigator on a variety of state and federal grants to support the responsible inclusion of individuals with disabilities across a variety of settings. Her projects have included initiatives focused on sport diplomacy, special education leadership, and teacher preparation with funding in excess of $14 million dollars.

Robert E. Baker

Robert E. Baker is a professor in the School of Sport Recreation and Tourism Management and the director of the Center for Sport Management at George Mason University. He is currently serving as the interim dean of the College of Education and Human Development. He has served as president of the North American Society for Sport Management, as a founding commissioner of the Commission on Sport Management Accreditation, and a founding board member of the World Association of Sport Management. Dr. Baker has received NASSM's Distinguished Sport Management Educator Award and NASPE's Outstanding Achievement in Sport Management Award. In addition to numerous books and peer-reviewed articles, Dr. Baker has served as the principal investigator on more than $7 million in grants supporting sport diplomacy projects.

About the Editors

Craig Esherick

Craig Esherick is an associate professor in the School of Sport Recreation and Tourism Management and associate director of the Center for Sport Management at George Mason University. He also serves as the academic program coordinator for the sport management program. He engaged in a cooperative agreement with the US Department of State via the Sports Visitors program for seven years. Before his move to academia, he was a basketball player and basketball coach at Georgetown University. Esherick also participated in the Summer Olympics in 1988 in Seoul, Korea, as an assistant coach for the US Men's Olympic basketball team.

About the Contributors

Soolmaz Abooali

Dr. Soolmaz Abooali is a professor, author, and practitioner working at the intersection of sport, diplomacy, and conflict resolution. In this capacity, she designs and implements sport-based programs for a diverse group of actors, such as government, non-governmental organizations, and philanthropic figures seeking to address social and political conflict through soft power methods. Dr. Abooali is also a world champion and 14-time US national champion in Traditional Karate.

Kathy Babiak

Dr. Kathy Babiak is currently an associate professor of Sport Management and director of the Michigan Center for Sport and Social Responsibility. Additionally, she was a co-founder of the Sport, Health and Activity Research and Policy (SHARP) Center for Women and Girls. Dr. Babiak completed her PhD in Leisure and Sport Management at the University of British Columbia, Vancouver, Canada. She has published numerous articles in such journals as the *Journal of Sport Management*, *Sport Management Review*, *Nonprofit and Voluntary Sector Quarterly*, and the *Journal of Business Ethics (JBE)*. She is associate editor for *European Sport Management Quarterly* and is on the editorial board of numerous journals in sport management. Dr. Babiak is a North American Society for Sport Management Research Fellow, and she has received more than $1 million in grant funding from organizations such as the Women's Sport Foundation and the Social Sciences and Humanities Research Council of Canada. Her main line of research focuses on sport and social impact. In this area, she explores how organizations devise social responsibility strategies to maximize the value and benefit to both organizations and to society.

About the Contributors

Laurence Chalip

Dr. Laurence Chalip is a professor in the School of Sport Recreation and Tourism Management at George Mason University, where he serves as Program Coordinator of Recreation Management. He earned his PhD in policy analysis from the University of Chicago. He has co-authored or co-edited three books, four monographs, more than a dozen book chapters, and over one hundred peer-reviewed articles. He was founding editor of *Sport Management Review* and also served as editor for *Journal of Sport Management*. He is an associate editor of the *Journal of Sport and Tourism* and North American editor of the *International Journal of Event and Festival Management*. He serves on the editorial boards of six other scholarly journals and consults widely to industry. In addition to being a Fellow of the Academy of Leisure Sciences, he was a founding board member of the Sport Management Association of Australia and New Zealand, from which he won the Distinguished Service Award, and is a Research Fellow of the North American Society for Sport Management, from which he won the Earle F. Zeigler Award.

Bill Gerrard

Dr. Bill Gerrard is a professor of Business and Sports Analytics at Leeds University. His principal research focus is sports analytics defined as the statistical analysis of performance data within an evidence-based coaching regimen in both individual and team sports to support decisions on talent identification, player recruitment, athletic development, training priorities, team selection, game tactics, and injury management. He has published numerous academic papers on player valuation, managerial efficiency, the sporting and financial performance of football clubs, and the relationship between wage costs and sporting performance. Bill has worked with a number of elite sports teams around the world. He has acted as technical analyst for Saracens and London Irish in the Aviva Premiership (rugby union) as well as providing statistical analysis to support the SkySports coverage of Super League (rugby league). He has also worked with Billy Beane, the general manager of the Oakland Athletics in major league baseball, whose application of sports analytics has been the subject of the Hollywood film and best-selling book *Moneyball*. Bill currently works as a data analyst with AZ Alkmaar in the Dutch Eredivisie (football). The practical application of Bill's research in sports analytics has been developed into an REF impact case study.

B. Christine Green

Dr. B. Christine Green is a professor of Sport Management in the School of Sport, Recreation and Tourism Management at George Mason University, director of the Sport Development Lab, and past president of the North American Society for Sport Management (NASSM). Her work examines the growth and development of sport programs and systems and their relationship to the development of individuals and communities. She is a Research Fellow of NASSM and has served as editor of *Sport Management Review* and as associate editor for *Journal of Sport Management* and *Sport and Tourism*. She is currently co-editing a book series on sport development. Her work has been published in top journals in sport, leisure, and tourism and has been funded in five countries. In addition, Dr. Green was awarded the Earle F. Zeigler Award from NASSM for her contributions to the sport management field.

Shinae Haidley

Shinae Haidley studied a bachelor of laws and bachelor of international relations at Bond University, Australia. During her studies she provided research assistance to the faculty of Society and Design for a body of work on sports diplomacy, and she completed her honours thesis on the treatment of transnational corporations under international law. Shinae is now a qualified lawyer working in global investment management and has contributed to the Asia Pacific business community through the publication of a new cross-cultural resource alongside members of the Australia Japan Business Co-operation Committee's Future Leaders Program.

Edward Horne

Edward Horne, PhD, is an assistant professor of Sport Administration at the University of New Mexico, having completed his PhD from the University of Illinois at Urbana-Champaign in 2019. His primary research interests focus on sport development systems and the key actors within sport systems, and he has published his research in various peer-reviewed journals. His professional memberships include the North American Society for Sport Management and the Applied Sport Management Association.

Scott R. Jedlicka

Dr. Scott R. Jedlicka is an assistant professor of Sport Management at Washington State University. His research explores issues of sport governance, especially at the intersection of transnational sport and international politics. Scott's intellectual goal in the study of sport governance is concerned with explaining processes of power, authority, and regulation in sport contexts and to develop and test theoretical models that identify and account for the relationships among determinants of sport governance outcomes. His current work is specifically concerned with understanding transnational sport governance as a form of global governance. This work emphasizes international political system structure, domestic regime type, and hegemonic discourses of sport as factors that account for the stability and (increasingly) the flaws of current governance approaches in transnational sport.

About the Contributors

Carrie LeCrom

Carrie LeCrom has served as the executive director of the Center for Sport Leadership (CSL) at Virginia Commonwealth University (VCU) since 2015, holding various roles within the CSL since joining the staff in 2003. She is passionate about the use of sport for social change and has secured more than $1.3 million in grant funding from sources such as the US Department of State and the National Collegiate Athletic Association. Some of the notable initiatives she has coordinated include exchanges between the United States and Ethiopia, China, and South Africa. She is currently overseeing a multiyear project in South-Central Asia, which involves socially focused exchange programs with young athletes from Kazakhstan, Sri Lanka, Nepal, and India. Dr. LeCrom's research interests lie in sport for development, global sport, and sport consumer behavior. She has published in the *Journal of Sport Management*, *Sport Management Review*, *Sport in Society*, *Journal of Sport for Development*, and *Sport Marketing Quarterly*, among others. She holds degrees from Lynchburg College (BA in Business Administration and Sport Management) and VCU (MS in Sport Leadership; PhD in Education). She competed on the women's soccer team at Lynchburg College where she was named First Team All-American and Academic All-American.

Stuart Murray

Stuart Murray is an associate professor in International Relations at Bond University, Australia, and a Global Fellow at the Academy of Sport (Edinburgh University). Widely considered as the founder of the Innovative School of Diplomatic Thought, Stuart has written and published more than fifty peer-reviewed articles, chapters, and edited books. Many of these are on cross and interdisciplinary research, translational impact, and enhancing the relationships between academic and government institutions and nonstate actors. He also serves as an associate editor on the journal *Diplomacy and Foreign Policy*. Stuart has advised the Australian Department of Foreign Affairs and Trade, the Department of Health and the Office for Sport, Football Federation Australia, the Australian Grand Prix Corporation, the Consular Corps (Melbourne), and many others. He is a founding member of Sports Diplomacy Foundation, the world's first NGO that brings government institutions and sports organizations together via mutually reciprocal projects. In 2018, he published *Sports Diplomacy: Origins, Theory and Practice*, the world's first research monograph that focuses on sport as a diplomatic tool. Most recently, he was funded to investigate eSports diplomacy. This is yet another new area of theory and practice, which describes the use of electronic games as a means to enhance mental and physical well-being and social inclusion outcomes for youth in Australia.

About the Contributors

Nico Schulenkorf

Nico Schulenkorf is associate professor of Sport Management at the University of Technology–Sydney. His research focuses on the social, cultural, and health-related outcomes of sport and event projects within and between disadvantaged communities. For several years, Nico has been involved in sport-for-development and health-promotion programs in countries such as Sri Lanka and Israel, as well as the Pacific islands. He has been working with local and international nongovernmental organizations, government agencies, sport associations, and ministries in developing capacities to implement, monitor, and evaluate development projects. Nico is co-founder and past editor of the *Journal of Sport for Development* and currently serves on the journal's advisory board. He is also an editorial board member of *Sport Management Review*, the *European Journal for Sport and Society*, and *Sport and Entertainment Review*. In the past, Nico also held the role of director of the Sport Management Association of Australia and New Zealand.

Morgan Strimel

Morgan Strimel is a PhD student in the Policy and Research-Intensive Special Educators doctoral training program at George Mason University where she also earned her MEd in Special Education in 2019. Prior to beginning her doctoral studies, she worked as an access consultant within Disability Services at George Mason University and as a learning strategist for their Mason Autism Support Initiative (MASI Program). Based on her time working in higher education, Morgan's current research is focused on improving access to postsecondary education settings for college students with disabilities. Specifically, she plans to study both bridging the research to policy to practice gaps regarding preparing special education stakeholders to help students transition to postsecondary life and policy-related barriers to access for students with disabilities at the college level.

Per G. Svensson

Dr. Per Svensson is an assistant professor in Sport Management within the School of Kinesiology at Louisiana State University. His research is primarily focused on organizations operating sport-based programs aimed at addressing social issues. Specifically, his work examines organizational capacity and innovation in sport for development and peace, and his secondary research interest is focused on examining organizational aspects of student-athlete community service programs. Dr. Svensson's research has been published in numerous academic journals including *Journal of Sport Management*; *Sport Management Review*; *Nonprofit and Voluntary Sector Quarterly*; *VOLUNTAS: International Journal of Voluntary and Nonprofit*

About the Contributors

Organizations; *Sport, Education and Society*; *International Journal of Sport Communication*; *Sport in Society*; *Journal of Sport for Development*; *Journal of Higher Education Outreach and Engagement*; *Journal of Intercollegiate Sport*; *Journal of Issues in Intercollegiate Sport*; and the *International Journal of Sport Management and Marketing*.

Marijke Taks

Dr. Marijke Taks joined the faculty of Health Sciences at the University of Ottawa in August 2016. Dr. Taks's area of expertise is in socioeconomic aspects of sport and leisure. Her grant-supported research focuses particularly on impacts, outcomes, and leveraging of small and medium sport events and their meaning for host communities. She also studies sport consumer behavior of various groups in society. Mass participation and the "Sport for All" philosophy guide her research. She has published her work in leading journals of sport management and related fields. Dr. Taks is past editor of the *European Sport Management Quarterly* (2009–2011); associate editor of the *Journal of Sport Management* and the *Journal of Global Sport Management*; editorial board member of the *European Sport Management Quarterly* and the *Journal of Sport Sponsorship and Marketing*; and guest reviewer for a wide variety of journals in the field of sport management, sport marketing, and sport tourism. Her research interests include the socioeconomic aspects of sport, leisure and sport events, sport consumer behavior, sport participation and development, and sport and employment.

Georgia Teare

Georgia Teare is a PhD student at the University of Ottawa, School of Human Kinetics. She completed both her BA (Recreation and Sport Business, Tourism Option), and her MA (Recreation and Leisure Studies) at the University of Waterloo. Her research focuses on leveraging youth passive consumption of sport for their active participation in physical activity. Before starting her doctoral studies, Georgia worked as the engagement coordinator in the Office of Human Rights, Equity and Inclusion at the University of Waterloo, where she facilitated numerous professional development opportunities for students, staff, and faculty. She quickly realized her passion for graduate student professional development and had the opportunity to continue to do work in this area through serving on the 2018–2019 North American Society for Sport Management student board.

Jon Welty Peachey

Jon Welty Peachey, Ph.D., is associate professor of sport management in the Department of Recreation, Sport and Tourism at the University of Illinois at Urbana-Champaign. His research examines how sport for development programs should be best designed, managed, and led to achieve individual- and community-based

About the Contributors

outcomes. He is a research fellow with the North American Society for Sport Management, serves as editor-in chief of the *Journal of Intercollegiate Sport*, and associate editor for the *Journal of Sport Management* and *Event Management* journal. Dr. Welty Peachey is a frequent invited speaker and consultant internationally on leadership and sport for development. He has published more than 90 scholarly articles and book chapters, edited several books on sport for development and leadership, and given more than 130 presentations at academic conferences around the word. Prior to his work in academia, Dr. Welty Peachey served as a senior administrator in the international sport for development field for over a decade.

www.ingramcontent.com/pod-product-compliance
Lightning Source LLC
Chambersburg PA
CBHW030119240426
43673CB00041B/1338